C Programmer's Guide to

Graphics

C Programmer's Guide to

Graphics

James McCord

SAMS

A Division of Prentice Hall Computer Publishing
11711 North College, Carmel, Indiana 46032 USA

International Standard Book Number: 0-672-22784-3
Library of Congress Catalog Number: 90-63416

Acquisitions and Development Editor: *Gregory Croy*
Technical Editor: *Derrel Blain*
Manuscript Editor: *Susan Pink, TechRight*
Production Editor: *Katherine Stuart Ewing*

Cover Artist: *Glenn Santner*
Illustrator: *T.R. Emrick*
Production Assistants: *Hilary Adams, Brad Chinn, Martin A. Coleman, Denny Hager, Betty Kish, Bob LaRoche, Howard Peirce, Cindy L. Phipps, JohnnaVanHoose, Joe Ramon, Louise Shinault, Lisa A. Wilson*
Indexer: *Hilary Adams*

Printed in the United States of America

Trademarks

All terms mentioned in this book that are known to be trademarks or service marks are listed below. In addition, terms suspected of being trademarks or service marks have been appropriately capitalized. SAMS cannot attest to the accuracy of this information. Use of a term in this book should not be regarded as affecting the validity of any trademark or service mark.

8086, 8088, 286, 386, and 80486 (when used to reference Intel microprocessors) are trademarks of Intel Corporation.
86-DOS is a registered trademark of Seattle Computer Products, Inc.
IBM, Personal Computer AT, PS/1, PS/2 Models 25, 30, 50, 60, (70), and 80 are trademarks of International Business Machines Corporation.
MS-DOS and Microsoft are registered trademarks of Microsoft Corporation.
PC PaintBrush IV is a trademark of ZSoft.
PCX Programmer's Toolkit, PCX Effects, and PCX Text are trademarks of Genus Microprogramming

Contents

Preface   **xvii**

Acknowledgements   **xix**

1   Computer Graphics with Microsoft C

1   Introduction to IBM PCs and Compatibles   3

Microprocessors   3

  8086 and 8088   4

  80286   4

  80386   4

  80486   5

Operating Systems   5

  MS-DOS   5

  OS/2   5

Video Subsystems   6

  CGA   6

  EGA   7

  MCGA   8

  VGA   8

Monitors   8

  Direct Drive Monochrome Monitors   8

  Composite Monochrome Monitors   9

  Composite Color Monitors   9

RGB Color Monitors 9
Variable-Frequency Monitors 9
Input Devices 9
Keyboard 10
Mouse 10
Trackball 10
Digitizer Tablet 11
Light Pen 13

2 Software Development and C **15**

Advantages of C 15
Power 15
Speed 16
Versatility 16
Code Structure 16
Preprocessor Directives 17
Declarations 18
Definitions 19
Expressions 19
Statements 20
Function 22
The Software Development Process 24

3 Graphics Techniques **29**

Coordinate Systems 30
The Physical Coordinate System 30
The View Coordinate System 31
The Window Coordinate System 32
Coordinate Conversions 32
The Graphics Cursor 33
Aspect Ratios 35
Points and Pixels 36
Lines 37
Line Patterns 41
Set 1 41
Set 2 46
Set 3 49
Rectangles and Squares 52
Polygons 55

Circles and Ellipses   56
Arcs   58
Complex Curves   60
   Curves Using the _arc Functions   60
   The Straight-Line Approximation
   Method   61
   The Bezier Curve   62
Area Fills   64
Fill Patterns   65
Halftoning and Shading   72
Pie Charts and Wedges   79
Color and Palette Selection   88
Viewports and Clipping Regions   91

4   Text and Graphics   **97**
Text Types   97
Text Cursor   98
Text in Graphics Mode   100
Use of Font Text in Graphics   101
Text Colors   103
Creating a Character Set   104
   Unfilled Characters   107
   Filled Characters   108
   Shaded Characters   111
   Multicolored Characters   113
   Shadowed Characters   116
Character Examples   117
Text Windows   144

5   Presentation Graphics   **147**
Initializing the Presentation Graphics Environment   147
Pie Chart   150
Bar Chart   153
Column Chart   159
Scatter Diagram   165
Line Chart   173
Customizing the Presentation Graphics Environment   181
   The Color Pool   181
   The Style Pool   182

The Pattern Pool   182
The Character Pool   182
The chartenv Structure   184
The titletype Structure   185
The axistype Structure   186
The windowtype Structure   187
The legendtype Structure   188

6   Animation   189

The Art of Animation   189
Full Screen Animation   190
Partial Screen Animation   201
Hidden Pages with Partial Screen
Animation   205
Advanced Concepts in Animation   209
   Placing Images on Multicolored Backgrounds   209
   Combining Action Arguments for
   Complex Images   211
   Optimizing the Speed of Animation   215

7   Two- and Three-Dimensional Drawing   217

The Two-Dimensional Coordinate System   217
Formulas for Two-Dimensional Rotation   217
   Rotating the Rectangle   221
   Rotating the Polygon   224
   Rotating the Ellipse   227
The Three-Dimensional Coordinate
System   230
Hidden Surface Removal for Three-Dimensional Drawing   240
Summary   241

2   Reference Guide

8   Video BIOS Services   245

Video Service 00H
   Set Video Mode   245
Video Service 01H
   Set Cursor Size   246
Video Service 02H

Set Cursor Position   247

Video Service 03H

Read Cursor Position   247

Video Service 04H

Read Light Pen Position   248

Video Service 05H

Set Active Display Page   249

Video Service 06H

Scroll Active Window Up   249

Video Service 07H

Scroll Active Window Down   250

Video Service 08H

Read Character and Attribute   250

Video Service 09H

Write Character and Attribute   251

Video Service 0AH

Write Character   251

Video Service 0BH

Set Color Palette   252

Video Service 0CH

Write Pixel   252

Video Service 0DH

Read Pixel   253

Video Service 0EH

Write TTY Character   253

Video Service 0FH

Get Current Video Mode   254

Video Service 10H, Subservice 00H

Set Palette Register (EGA and
VGA Only)   254

Video Service 10H, Subservice 01H

Set EGA or VGA Overscan Register   255

Video Service 10H, Subservice 02H

Set Palette and Overscan Registers (EGA and VGA Only)   255

Video Service 10H, Subservice 03H

Toggle Blinking or Intensity (EGA and VGA Only)   256

Video Service 10H, Subservice 07H

Read VGA Palette Register   256

Video Service 10H, Subservice 08H

Read Overscan Register (VGA Only)   257

Video Service 10H, Subservice 09H
Read VGA Palette and Overscan
Registers   257

Video Service 10H, Subservice 10H
Set Individual VGA Color Register   258

Video Service 10H, Subservice 12H
Set Block of Color Registers
(VGA Only)   258

Video Service 10H, Subservice 13H
Select Color Page (VGA Only)   259

Video Service 10H, Subservice 15H
Read Individual Color Register
(VGA Only)   259

Video Service 10H, Subservice 17H
Read Block of Color Registers
(VGA Only)   260

Video Service 10H, Subservice 1AH
Read Current Color Page Number (VGA Only)   260

Video Service 10H, Subservice 1BH
Sum Color Values to Gray Scale (VGA Only)   261

Video Service 11H, Subservice 00H
Load Font (EGA and VGA Only)   261

Video Service 11H, Subservice 01H
Load ROM 8-by-14 Character Set
(EGA and VGA Only)   262

Video Service 11H, Subservice 02H
Load ROM 8-by-8 Character Set
(EGA and VGA Only)   262

Video Service 11H, Subservice 03H
Set Block Specifier (EGA and VGA
Only)   263

Video Service 11H, Subservice 04H
Load ROM 8-by-16 Character Set
(EGA and VGA Only)   263

Video Service 11H, Subservice 10H
Load Font (EGA and VGA Only)   264

Video Service 11H, Subservice 11H
Load ROM 8-by-14 Character Set
(EGA and VGA Only)   264

Video Service 11H, Subservice 12H
Load ROM 8-by-8 Character Set
(EGA and VGA Only)   265

Video Service 11H, Subservice 14H
Load ROM 8-by-16 Character Set
(VGA Only)   265

Video Service 11H, Subservice 20H
Load Character Pointer (EGA and
VGA Only)   266

Video Service 11H, Subservice 21H
Load Character Pointer (EGA and
VGA Only)   266

Video Service 11H, Subservice 22H
Load Graphics ROM 8-by-14 Character
Set (EGA and VGA Only)   267

Video Service 11H, Subservice 23H
Load Graphics ROM 8-by-8 Character
Set (EGA and VGA Only)   267

Video Service 11H, Subservice 24H
Load Graphics ROM 8-by-16 Character
Set (EGA and VGA Only)   268

Video Service 11H, Subservice 30H
Return Character Generator Data
(EGA and VGA Only)   268

Video Service 12H, Subservice 10H
Get Video Information (EGA and
VGA Only)   269

Video Service 12H, Subservice 20H
Select Alternate Print Screen Routine
(EGA and VGA Only)   269

Video Service 12H, Subservice 30H
Set Scan Lines for Alphanumeric
Modes (VGA Only)   270

Video Service 12H, Subservice 31H
Default Palette Loading during Mode
Set (VGA Only)   270

Video Service 12H, Subservice 32H
Video Enable or Disable (VGA Only)   271

Video Service 12H, Subservice 33H
Sum to Gray Scale (VGA Only)   271

Video Service 12H, Subservice 34H
  Cursor Emulation (VGA Only)   272
Video Service 12H, Subservice 35H
  Display Switch (VGA Only)   272
Video Service 12H, Subservice 36H
  Video Screen On or Off (VGA Only)   273
Video Service 13H, Subservice 00H
  Write Character String (VGA Only)   273
Video Service 13H, Subservice 01H
  Write Character String (EGA and VGA Only)   274
Video Service 13H, Subservice 02H
  Write Character String (EGA and VGA Only)   275
Video Service 13H, Subservice 03H
  Write Character String (EGA and VGA Only)   275
Video Service 1AH
  Read or Write Display Combination
  Code (VGA Only)   276
Video Service 1BH
  Return Functionality and State Data
  (VGA Only)   276
Video Service 1CH
  Save/Restore Video State (VGA Only)   277

9   Microsoft C Graphics Functions   279

_arc   280
_arc_w   283
_arc_wxy   287
_clearscreen   290
_displaycursor   295
_ellipse   298
_ellipse_w   301
_ellipse_wxy   305
_floodfill   308
_floodfill_w   312
_getactivepage   314
_getarcinfo   317
_getbkcolor   320
_getcolor   324

_getcurrentposition   327

_getcurrentposition_w   332

_getfillmask   335

_getfontinfo   338

_getgtextextent   341

_getgtextvector   343

_getimage   347

_getimage_w   350

_getimage_wxy   353

_getlinestyle   356

_getphyscoord   360

_getpixel   363

_getpixel_w   366

_gettextcolor   369

_gettextcursor   372

_gettextposition   374

_gettextwindow   377

_getvideoconfig   380

_getviewcoord   385

_getviewcoord_w   389

_getviewcoord_wxy   392

_getvisualpage   395

_getwindowcoord   397

_getwritemode   401

_grstatus   405

_imagesize   410

_imagesize_w   413

_imagesize_wxy   416

_lineto   419

_lineto_w   424

_moveto   427

_moveto_w   431

_outgtext   434

_outmem   437

_outtext   439

_pg_analyzechart   442

_pg_analyzechartms   445

_pg_analyzepie   449

_pg_analyzescatter   452

_pg_analyzescatterms   455

_pg_chart   459

_pg_chartms   462

_pg_chartpie   466

_pg_chartscatter   468

_pg_chartscatterms   471

_pg_defaultchart   475

_pg_getchardef   478

_pg_getpalette   481

_pg_getstyleset   485

_pg_hlabelchart   488

_pg_initchart   490

_pg_resetpalette   493

_pg_resetstyleset   497

_pg_setchardef   500

_pg_setpalette   503

_pg_setstyleset   506

_pg_vlabelchart   508

_pie   512

_pie_w   515

_pie_wxy   518

_polygon   523

_polygon_w   525

_polygon_wxy   528

_putimage   532

_putimage_w   535

_rectangle   538

_rectangle_w   541

_rectangle_wxy   545

_registerfonts   549

_remapallpalette   551

_remappalette   555

_scrolltextwindow   558

_selectpalette   561

_setactivepage   565

_setbkcolor   568

_setcliprgn   572

_setcolor   576

_setfillmask   579

_setfont   582

_setgtextvector   586

_setlinestyle   589

_setpixel   593

_setpixel_w   595

_settextcolor   597

_settextcursor   600

_settextposition   602

_settextrows   606

_settextwindow   608

_setvideomode   610

_setvideomoderows   613

_setvieworg   616

_setviewport   620

_setvisualpage   624

_setwindow   626

_setwritemode   628

_unregisterfonts   631

_wrapon   633

Bibliography   637

Index   639

Preface

Graphics programming can be the most fun, yet challenging, area of computer programming. The graphics programmer must visualize, create, and develop graphics-based applications in specialized environments, and these applications must meet the constraints of speed, functionality, and portability. *C Programmer's Guide to Graphics* introduces the concepts and principles of graphics programming for IBM personal computers, and their compatibles, using version 6.0 of the Microsoft C Compiler and version 2.5 of the Microsoft QuickC Compiler.

This book provides all the information necessary to get up and running with graphics and Microsoft C. Part 1, "Computer Graphics with Microsoft C," contains seven chapters that discuss a variety of information ranging from video hardware to animation techniques. The following paragraphs briefly describe each chapter in Part 1.

- Chapter 1, "Introduction to IBM PCs and Compatibles," discusses the fundamentals of the IBM PC and its compatibles. The hardware devices described include microprocessors, operating systems, graphics cards, monitors, and input devices.

- Chapter 2, "Software Development and C," describes the advantages and code structure of the C language. In addition, a generic software development process is presented.

- Chapter 3, "Graphics Techniques," is dedicated to presenting the basic drawing capabilities of the Microsoft graphics library. The concepts of coordinate systems, drawing, area fills, and viewports are presented.

- Chapter 4, "Text and Graphics," presents the methods for combining text with graphics. Three methods are presented: using the standard character set, using the fonts provided with the Microsoft compiler, and creating a user-defined character set.

- Chapter 5, "Presentation Graphics," gives extensive descriptions of the features in the presentation graphics library. This chapter provides many examples that use the full range of features included in the presentation graphics library.

- Chapter 6, "Animation," presents the art of animation. The basics of animation and the use of hidden pages are described, along with many examples that demonstrate these techniques.

- Chapter 7, "Two- and Three-Dimensional Drawing," presents the concepts used to develop both two- and three-dimensional drawings, and provides examples that use the concepts discussed.

Part 2, "Reference Guide," contains two chapters that provide extensive documentation of the use of the Video BIOS Services and the Microsoft C graphics libraries.

- Chapter 8, "Video BIOS Services," describes the Video ROM BIOS Services. For each video service and subservice, the following is provided: inputs, outputs, and a description.

- Chapter 9, "Microsoft C Graphics Functions," is a detailed reference guide of the functions in the graphics and presentation graphics libraries. For each function, the following wide range of information is provided: syntax, function, files to include, compatibility, description, values returned, related functions, similar Turbo C++ functions, suggested code structure and use, and an example.

This book is designed to provide all the information needed to develop graphics-based programs. By using the techniques and information described, you can develop graphics programs of all types and levels of complexity.

Acknowledgments

I would like to thank the staff at SAMS for the opportunity to write this book. I would also like to thank my wife, Jill, son, Joshua, and daughter, Jamie, for making my life great. Special thanks to T.B.T.

I

Computer Graphics with Microsoft C

1

Introduction to IBM PCs and Compatibles

To accomplish effective graphics programming, it is important to understand the basics of computer hardware. The physical limitations of the host system (the system that will run the developed graphics software) will drive the requirements and limitations of the graphics software. The video adapter and monitor will determine the range of resolution and colors available for the application. Other hardware factors, such as the microprocessor, memory, and operating speeds, play an important role in setting requirements and specifications for the graphics product.

Microprocessors

The microprocessor is the heart of the computer system. Sometimes called the central processing unit (CPU), the microprocessor executes the program by performing a series of computations, data transfers, and numeric comparisons. All of the computer's basic operations are controlled by the CPU. Data of all types is sent to the CPU through the bus (pathways for signals). The buses connect the CPU to various input/output (I/O) ports. These I/O ports are used to connect the memory and support chips to the bus and, ultimately, the CPU.

All IBM PCs and PS/2 models (and compatibles) use a microprocessor from the Intel 8086 family. See table 1.1. The following sections describe the current microprocessors in the 8086 family.

Table 1.1. Microprocessors used by IBM PC, AT, PS/1, and PS/2.

Model	Microprocessor
IBM PC	8088
PC XT	8088
AT	80286
PS/1	80286
PS/2 25	8086
PS/2 30	8086
PS/2 50	80286
PS/2 60	80286
PS/2 80	80386

8086 and 8088

The 8086 microprocessor, used in the PS/2 Models 25 and 30, is a 16-bit microprocessor with a 16-bit data bus. Fourteen registers are used to transfer data, process data, and store data, memory addresses, status and control flags, and instruction pointers. The 8086 can access one megabyte of memory.

The 8088 microprocessor, used for the IBM PC, PCjr, and PC XT, is a 16-bit microprocessor with an 8-bit data bus. The major difference between the 8088 and the 8086 is that the 8088 has an 8-bit data bus, and the 8086 has a 16-bit data bus. In all other respects, the 8088 is identical to the 8086 for programming purposes.

80286

The 80286, used in the IBM AT and PS/2 Models 50 and 60, is compatible with the 8086 and the 8088. The most important feature added to the 80286 is its multitasking capability, which is the capability to perform several tasks at one time. The 80286 accomplishes this by switching its processing between two tasks. An example of multitasking is editing one document using a word processor while printing another document.

The 80286 microprocessor operates in two modes. The first, the *real mode*, forces the 80286 to behave and respond exactly like the 8086. The second, the *protected mode*, reserves a predetermined amount of memory for program execution; this memory is protected from use by any other program. Multitasking capabilities originate in protected mode. By using the protected mode, several programs can run concurrently without affecting one another.

80386

The 80386 microprocessor is used in the PS/2 Model 80 and in many IBM PC compatibles. The 80386 is a powerful 32-bit microprocessor that incorporates 32-bit registers. Although the 80386 microprocessor supports the 8086 functions and the 80286 protected memory mode, it offers more flexible memory management than either of these CPUs.

80486

The 80486 microprocessor is the newest release in the line of 80x86 CPUs. Several manufacturers have released IBM compatibles that use the 80486. Although these systems are presently the most expensive IBM compatibles on the market, they offer the latest technology. The 80486 is faster and more integrated than any other microprocessor in the 8086 family. It combines the capabilities of an enhanced 80386 microprocessor with an equally fast 80387 math coprocessor, a sophisticated cache controller, and 8K of supporting cache memory.

Operating Systems

Every computer has an operating system. The operating system is a set of machine language computer programs that manages the variety of functions, including peripheral operations, required of the system. The IBM series of personal computers has two operating systems, MS-DOS and OS/2.

MS-DOS

MS-DOS began as QDOS, an operating system for an S-100 bus-designed system that used an 8086 microprocessor. QDOS, which became 86-DOS, was developed by Seattle Computer Products and purchased by Microsoft in 1980. Microsoft was one of the software development teams chosen by IBM to develop the operating system for its new computer. The resulting product, MS-DOS, became the standard for the IBM PC and its compatibles. MS-DOS has been revised several times (the current version is 4.01) and continues to be the dominant operating system for personal computers.

OS/2

When IBM introduced its PS/2 models, a new operating system, OS/2, was on-board. OS/2 was similar in functionality to MS-DOS versions 3.2 and 3.3, but was designed to run on and take advantage of the newer microprocessors.

To support the newer microprocessors, OS/2 operates in two modes: real mode and protected mode. The real mode responds in a manner almost identical to MS-DOS, so almost all applications designed for MS-DOS are supported by OS/2. Multitasking, however, is not supported in real mode.

OS/2 also operates in protected mode. Although this mode appears to operate like MS-DOS, it is much more powerful and flexible. The major advantage of OS/2 is its support of multitasking in protected mode. In addition, OS/2 in protected mode does not limit the size of the application to 640K of RAM (the real mode has this limitation).

Although MS-DOS is presently the dominant operating system, the features and capabilities of OS/2 make it appealing for future development. Unfortunately for graphics programming, most graphic features provided by Microsoft are not supported by OS/2.

Video Subsystems

The *video hardware subsystem* produces the screen images for the computer system. All IBM series of personal computers and their compatibles, except PS/2 models, require an adapter card (it is built into the PS/2). For compatibles, this card is usually included in the system configuration. The adapter card is a special video circuit board that is plugged into one of the system's expansion slots.

The adapter board, or video circuitry, contains a block of dedicated memory that holds the display information. The video subsystem transforms the display information into signals that drive the video display. The video subsystems designed for the PCs were the Monochrome Display Adapter (MDA), the Color Graphics Adapter (CGA), and the Enhanced Graphics Adapter (EGA). The Multi Color Graphics Array (MCGA) and the Video Graphics Array (VGA) were developed for the PS/2 series. A VGA adapter was also made for the PC series.

CGA

The Color Graphics Adapter (CGA) is at the lowest end of IBM compatible graphics adapters. The CGA is still common for home computers, but the EGA and VGA are the standard for business computers. Most applications software, however, is compatible with the CGA. The CGA, as well as all of the video subsystems, can operate in either of two modes. The first mode supports text, and the second supports graphics.

The graphics mode has several screen resolution options; the options supported by the CGA monitor are the _HRESBW high-resolution mode and the _MRES4COLOR and _MRESNOCOLOR medium-resolution modes. In the _HRESBW mode, only 2 colors are available: the foreground and background colors. The background color can be changed with the _setbkcolor function. On the positive side, the _HRESBW mode has a higher resolution (640 pixels wide by 200 pixels high) than the medium-resolution modes.

The _MRES4COLOR and _MRESNOCOLOR modes have a resolution of 320 pixels wide by 200 pixels high. The _MRES4COLOR mode is for use with color monitors and displays 4 colors. The first color, the background color, is selectable from the predefined sixteen-color palette. The other 3 colors are defined in a look-up table. The desired palette is selected with the _selectpalette function. Table 1.2 lists the available palettes in _MRES4COLOR mode.

Table 1.2 Palettes in _MRES4COLOR mode.

Palette Number	Color 0	Color 1	Color 2	Color 3
0	Selectable	Green	Red	Brown
1	Selectable	Cyan	Magenta	Light gray
2	Selectable	Light green	Light red	Yellow
3	Selectable	Light cyan	Light magenta	White

The _MRESNOCOLOR mode is designed for use with monochrome monitors, but can be used with color monitors. When used with a monochrome monitor, shades of gray are displayed. When used with a color monitor, the palettes listed in table 1.3 are available.

Table 1.3   CGA palettes in _MRESNOCOLOR mode.

Palette Number	Color 0	Color 1	Color 2	Color 3
0	Selectable	Blue	Red	Light gray
1	Selectable	Light blue	Light red	White

EGA

The Enhanced Graphics Adapter (EGA) supports all the graphics and text modes of the CGA. In _MRESNOCOLOR mode, however, the color palettes differ between the CGA and the EGA. See table 1.4.

Table 1.4   EGA palettes in _MRESNOCOLOR mode.

Palette Number	Color 0	Color 1	Color 2	Color 3
0	Selectable	Green	Red	Light gray
1	Selectable	Light green	Light red	Yellow
2	Selectable	Light cyan	Light red	Yellow

In addition to supporting the CGA graphics modes, four additional graphics modes were added: _MRES16COLOR, _HRES16COLOR, _ERESNOCOLOR, and _ERESCOLOR. In _ERESNOCOLOR, only 2 colors are available (the foreground and the background), but the resolution is 640 by 350. In _ERESCOLOR mode, the 16 colors shown in table 1.5 are available with a screen resolution of 640 by 350. In _MRES16COLOR mode, the 16 colors in table 1.5 are available, but the screen resolution is limited to 320 by 200. Similarly, in _HRES16COLOR mode, all colors in table 1.5 are available, but the screen resolution is limited to 640 by 200.

Table 1.5   Default palette for 16-color modes.

Pixel value	Color
0	Black
1	Blue
2	Green
3	Cyan
4	Red
5	Magenta
6	Brown

(continued)

7

Table 1.5 *(continued)*

Pixel value	Color
7	White
8	Dark gray
9	Light blue
10	Light green
11	Light cyan
12	Light red
13	Light magenta
14	Yellow
15	Bright white

MCGA

The Multi Color Graphics Array (MCGA) is found in the 8086-based models of the IBM PS/2 computers. The MCGA is an extension of the CGA and supports all CGA modes. In addition, the MCGA supports a 640-by-480 2-color mode (_VRES2COLOR) and a 320-by-200 256-color mode (_MRES256COLOR). The _MRES256COLOR mode can support varying shades of the 16 colors in table 1.5, with a resolution of 320 by 200.

VGA

The Video Graphics Array (VGA) is the current standard for IBM personal computers. The VGA is the video subsystem for the 80286-based and 80386-based IBM PS/2 series and is available in adapter form for the IBM personal computer series and compatibles. The VGA supports all CGA, MCGA, and EGA modes. In addition, a 640-by-480 16-color mode is supported. This additional mode, the _VRES16COLOR mode, is available only on the VGA.

Monitors

For each type of video subsystem, there is at least one compatible monitor. The monitor is just as important as the display adapter when selecting a hardware configuration. The five basic types of monitors are discussed in the following sections.

Direct Drive Monochrome Monitors

Direct drive monochrome monitors are used with the Monochrome Display Adapter (MDA) and the Enhanced Graphics Adapter (EGA). These monitors provide only 2 colors: the foreground and background colors.

Composite Monochrome Monitors

Composite monochrome monitors are used with the composite video output of the Color Graphics Adapter (CGA). These monitors provide 1-color displays and cannot be used with any adapter other than the CGA.

Composite Color Monitors

The composite color monitors use the composite video signal of the Color Graphics Adapter (CGA) to produce color text and graphics. The resolution of CGA output with composite color monitors is often poor. Simple graphics and text, however, are readable.

RGB Color Monitors

The red-green-blue (RGB) color monitor is used with the video signal of the CGA. The RGB monitor produces better results than the composite color monitor because separate red, blue, and green signals are processed. High-resolution color graphics and text can be displayed with this monitor.

Variable-Frequency Monitors

Because different video subsystems may produce different signals, some monitors cannot be used with certain adapters. For this reason, variable-frequency monitors that can be used with several video subsystems were created. Although these monitors cost more, they are often more practical because they allow the user to upgrade to newer technologies without having to buy a new monitor.

Input Devices

Graphics programming can be tedious and time consuming. The use of input devices other than the keyboard offers relief from the boredom of the manual input of points, but this relief has a price. To use alternate input devices, device drivers and user interfaces must be created. Commercial packages for the graphics programmer range from a simple device driver that outputs to a data file a series of coordinates to a complete paintbrush program. For most uses, these packages are never exactly what is needed. For example, to obtain coordinate points with the Microsoft graphics library, usually the programmer draws the image on graph paper, then reads and inputs the coordinates from the graph paper. Although this method is simple and straightforward, it is not very efficient.

The following sections introduce the capabilities of alternate input devices. These devices can gather data in many ways.

Keyboard

The keyboard, which is the primary input device, is very flexible and accepts input through any of its alphanumeric, cursor control, or function keys. The keyboard is a one-dimensional input device. The order, or sequence, of the input is important in one-dimensional devices. For text, the one-dimensional, sequential input of data is satisfactory. Effective graphics, however, requires two dimensions. Thus, the keyboard is not a good device for the input of graphics-oriented, or spatial, data.

Many features of the keyboard attempt to add a second dimension. The cursor control keys, as well as special function keys, are examples of this attempt at two-dimensional input by permitting both row and column manipulation.

Mouse

The mouse is probably the most commonly used alternate input device. For the most part, the mouse is used to simply manipulate the graphics or text cursor. This is accomplished through the monitoring of the internal sensors in the mouse. As the mouse is moved, positional (directional) information is input into the computer and used to position the on-screen cursor. The mouse has one, two, or three buttons, depending upon the manufacturer. These buttons provide additional, non-directional input.

The one-button mouse is the most simple mouse to use because there are no key sequences to remember. This simplistic approach, however, forces the user to input multiple clicks to make a menu selection. The two-button mouse offers more input options than the one-button mouse. The three-button mouse increases the number of possible button combinations to seven. The increased number of combinations might make the mouse more complicated to use.

The mouse is available in essentially two forms. The first is the mechanical mouse; the second is the optical mouse. See figure 1.1. A roller ball is used in the mechanical mouse. As the mouse is moved, the roller ball turns, which moves internal sensors in the mouse. These sensors translate the input into directional information that is used to move the cursor. The optical mouse uses two LEDs and two phototransistors to detect motion. One LED emits red light and the other produces infrared light. The optical mouse is used with a special pad that alters the light from the LEDs. The pad contains lines in two directions. When the mouse is moved in one direction, the red light is absorbed; in the other direction, the infrared light is absorbed. The color and number of light breaks determine the direction and distance of the mouse movement.

Trackball

The trackball is used primarily for the same functions as the mouse. The main difference is the configuration of the device, as shown in figure 1.2. With a mouse, you move the entire device. With a trackball, the body of the device remains in place while you use your palm to move the trackball.

The trackball was designed with limited desk space in mind. The mouse requires a good bit of space for use (several times the space of its physical dimensions), but the trackball requires only the space of its physical dimensions. Like the mouse, the trackball has buttons to permit additional, non-directional input.

Fig. 1.1. The mouse.

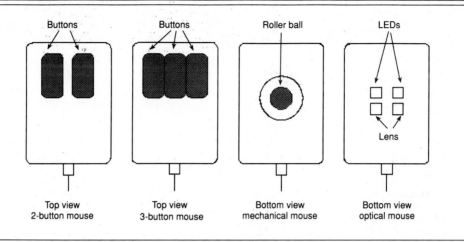

Top view
2-button mouse

Top view
3-button mouse

Bottom view
mechanical mouse

Bottom view
optical mouse

Fig. 1.2. Typical trackball.

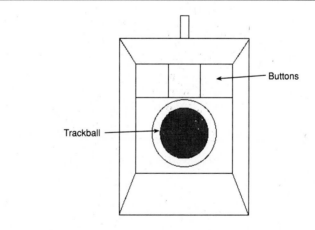

Digitizer Tablet

The digitizer tablet (see fig. 1.3), often called a graphics tablet, is useful for precision coordinate input. Most uses of the graphics tablet fall in the range of computer-aided design (CAD) and PC painting or drawing applications. The resolution of the graphics tablet is generally higher than that of a trackball or mouse, making it ideal for precision tracing, drawing, and design.

Fig. 1.3. Typical digitizing tablet.

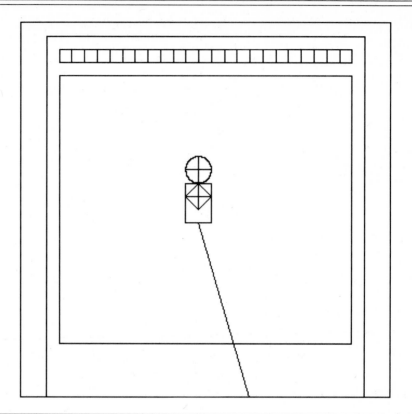

Most tablets are an electronic/magnetic type. The pointing device, a pen or a cursor, generates an electromagnetic field that is sensed by the screen-like wire grid embedded in the tablet (see fig. 1.4). Through the use of this grid and cursor combination, precise directional and coordinate information is determined. Other tablets use sound waves or resistive touch pads to provide information.

The pointing devices most typically used with graphics tablets are the pen, stylus, and cursor (see fig. 1.5). The pen and stylus are pen-like pointers used to provide input. The pen contains ink to provide feedback and is used for freehand drawing. The stylus contains no ink, only a blunt point, and is used for tracing existing drawings. The cursor is a hand-held device similar in appearance to a mouse, with the addition of a lens or reticle with wire crosshairs. The crosshairs are used to trace drawings, and the buttons provide non-directional input to the computer. Most cursors contain either four or sixteen buttons.

Fig. 1.4. Typical digitizing tablet using electromagnetic technology.

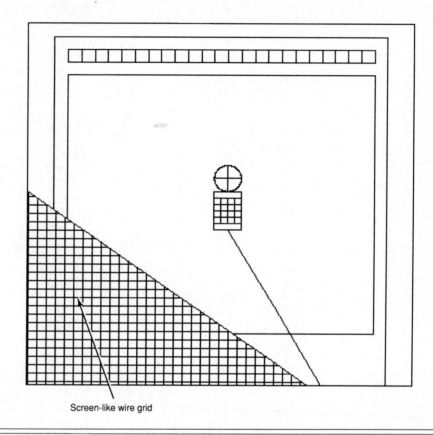

Screen-like wire grid

Light Pen

Light pens are useful as both a drawing and a point-and-shoot device. Figure 1.6 shows the basics of the light pen.

Light pens work by monitoring the interval between the time the electron beam used to illuminate the screen begins its refresh cycle and the time the location of the light pen is illuminated. The x and y screen coordinates are determined and passed to the computer through the graphics adapter.

Fig. 1.5. Input devices used with digitizing tablets.

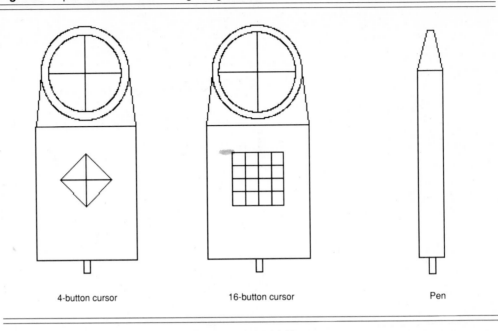

4-button cursor   16-button cursor   Pen

Fig. 1.6. Typical light pen.

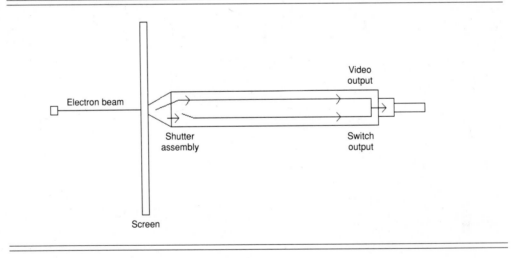

2

Software Development and C

The C language is compact, fast, and portable. This chapter introduces you to the power of the C language through proper structuring and development of code. C is a powerful language, but like any language, if the code is not structured effectively and the software is not developed properly, the result is inefficient, unreadable, and unmaintainable software code.

Advantages of C

The C language has become very popular over the past years. As described in the following paragraphs, the C language has three distinct advantages: power, speed, and versatility.

Power

A high-level language offers ease of use because each instruction closely resembles written text. The syntax of a low-level language is similar to the actual operations of the computer's registers. Source code written with a mid-level language still resembles the operation of the computer's registers, but it is easier to read than code written with a low-level language.

Because C has the characteristics of low-, mid-, and high-level languages, the programmer has the flexibility of optimizing the code relative to the application. For example, if speed is important, the low-level characteristics can be used more frequently. Similarly, if maintenance and rapid development are the most important issues, the high-level characteristics can be used.

Speed

The C language produces fast executable code. As mentioned, the flexible characteristics of the C language permit the programmer to optimize for speed by using specialized, low-level functions. Most high-level languages trade efficiency in executable code for ease in programming and maintainability; the low-level characteristics of the C language allow C code to run more quickly and efficiently. In addition, the C language's support of in-line assembly language makes speed optimization of time-critical functions possible.

Versatility

The C language has a wide range of functions and offers several methods for memory management. Memory management options in C, such as the use of pointers and structures, provide flexibility for a range of applications from database management to graphics to mathematically intensive applications. The range of functions provided by the standard C routines, when combined with the functions included in the Microsoft C libraries, provides the necessary flexibility for almost any type of programming application.

Code Structure

The structure of every C program is generally the same. As with other modular programming languages such as PASCAL and Ada, the operating system recognizes one function as the controlling function. For the C language, this controlling function is referred to as the `main()` function.

The `main()` function is the beginning and ending point of every C program. In general, processing begins at the start of this function and ends when the last line of code is executed. Other functions, often referred to as subroutines in other languages, are called from the main program. These functions, in turn, can then call other functions, and so on. After the execution of each called function has been completed, control is returned to the calling function. In this way, control is always returned to the `main()` function. Figure 2.1 illustrates the hierarchical relationship between the `main()` function and its supporting functions.

C is a modular language. This means that sections of code designed to do a specific task are usually removed from the `main()` function and placed in their own function. For example, suppose that it is necessary to perform a two-dimensional rotation on a pair of coordinates. Because this is a specific task that could be made in a generic fashion, a function that performs a two-dimensional rotation on a pair of passed parameters should be created.

There are many advantages to this type of design. First, a modular design eliminates code redundancy. It is easier and more efficient to call the function that performs a two-dimensional rotation than to add lines of code in the `main()` function every time this task is needed. Second, modular code is easier to read and understand. If the function name correctly describes its operation, interpreting the operation of the program is almost as simple as reading pseudo-code. Last, because modular code is easier to read and understand, it is easier to maintain. This point probably doesn't mean much to the beginning programmer. But to programmers who have had to work on someone

Fig. 2.1. The structure of C code.

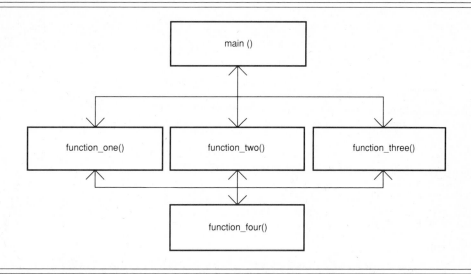

else's code, or even work on their own code after being away from it for some time, maintainability is a critical issue.

To understand the examples in this book, you do not need to be an expert in the C language. A solid understanding of the basic structure of C programs, however, is important. All C programs contain preprocessor directives, declarations, definitions, expressions, statements, and functions. These components of the C program structure are described in the following paragraphs.

Preprocessor Directives

A *preprocessor directive* is a command to the C preprocessor. One commonly used preprocessor directive is the `#include` directive. This directive allows external text files to be incorporated into a C program.

The `#include` directive instructs the preprocessor to substitute the contents of the specified file for the `#include` statement. When a C program is compiled, the preprocessor is invoked and the preprocessor modifies the source file prior to actual compilation.

```
#include <graph.h>
```

The `#include` statement is often used to include header files. The header files contain common variable and function declarations for the proper use of certain functions. For example, the graph.h header file must be included in order to use the graphics functions. Without the inclusion of the header file, the required definitions, declarations, and constants are not available for use.

The format of the `#include` directive determines the search path for the specified file. For example:

```
#include <graph.h>
```

In the preceding format, the computer searches for the graph.h file in the standard directories, not the working directory.

```
#include "graph.h"
```

In this format, the search for the graph.h file begins in the current directory, then moves to the standard directories, if necessary.

```
#include "c:\c600\graph.h"
```

In this format, the computer searches for the graph.h file in only the specified path.

Declarations

A *declaration* establishes the names and attributes of variables, functions, and types used in the program. The C language has the following set of standard data types for declaring variables and functions:

char
double
enum
float
int
long
long double
short
unsigned
unsigned char
unsigned long
unsigned short

The location of the declaration determines the visibility of a variable. (The *visibility* of a variable refers to its availabilty to the various functions in the program.) Global variables are declared prior to the m a i n ( ) function. Local variables are declared inside the function and, thus, are only visible inside the function.

A function declaration consists of a return type, the function name, and an argument-type list (if any). The function declaration is used to define the characteristics of the function; the contents of the function are not defined.

Definitions

A *definition* is used to assign the contents of a variable or function and allocate storage for the variable or function. A function definition consists of a function header and body. The function header contains the type of data returned by the function, the function name, and the list of formal parameters required by the function. The body of the function definition contains local declarations and a compound statement that describes the operation of the function.

Expressions

An *expression* is the combination of operators and operands that yields a single value. The operand is a constant or variable value that is manipulated in an expression. The operator defines the method by which the operands will interact. Table 2.1 lists the operators defined in the C language.

Table 2.1. *Operators for the C language.*

Operator	Name	Use	Meaning
		Arithmetic operators	
*	Multiplication	x*y	Multiply x and y
/	Division	x/y	Divide x by y
%	Modulo	x%y	Divide x remainder by y
+	Addition	x+y	Add x and y
-	Subtraction	x-y	Subtract y from x
++	Increment	x++	Increment x
——	Decrement	—x	Decrement x
-	Negation	-x	Negate x
		Relational and logical operators†	
>	Greater than	x>y	1 if x greater than y
>=	Greater than or equal to	x>=y	1 if x greater than or equal to y
<	Less than	x<y	1 if x less than y
<=	Less than or equal to	x<=y	1 if x less than or equal to y
==	Equal to	x==y	1 if x equals y
!=	Not equal to	x!=y	1 if x not equal to y
!	Logical NOT	!x	1 if x is 0
&&	Logical AND	x&&y	0 if either x or y is 0
||	Logical OR	x||y	0 if both x and y are 0
		Assignment operators	
=	Assignment	x=y	Set x to y value
?=	Compound assignment	x?=y	Same as x=x?y, where ? is one of the following: = - * / % << >> & ^ |

Table 2.1 *continues*

Table 2.1. cont. *Operators for the C language.*

Operator	Name	Use	Meaning
		Data access and size operators	
[ ]	Array element	x[0]	First element of x
.	Select member	y.x	Member x in structure y
-	Select member	p-x	Points to an address in memory
*	Indirection	*p	Contents of address p
&	Address of	&x	Address of x
sizeof	Size in bytes	sizeof(x)	Size of x in bytes
		Bitwise operators	
~	Bitwise complement	~x	Switches 1s and 0s
&	Bitwise AND	x&y	Bitwise AND of x and y
|	Bitwise OR	x|y	Bitwise OR of x and y
^	Bitwise exclusive OR	x^y	Exclusive OR of x and y
<<	Left shift	x<<2	Shift x left 2 bits
>>	Right shift	x>>2	Shift x right 2 bits
		Miscellaneous operators	
()	Function	malloc(x)	Call malloc function
(type)	Type cast	int(x)	Set x to type int
?:	Conditional	x1?x2:x3	If x is not 0, x2 is evaluated; else x3
,	Seqential evaluation	x++,y++	Increment x, then y

[†] 1 equals TRUE, and 0 equals FALSE.

Statements

Statements control the order of execution of a C program. A statement ends in a semicolon and contains keywords, expressions, and other statements. The following paragraphs briefly describe the C statements.

The assignment statement (=) assigns the value of the expression on the right to the variable on the left:

```
x = 500;
```

The break statement (**break;**) ends the innermost **do**, **for**, **switch**, or **while** statement:

```
while (c < 100)
{
     if (c == 55)
          break;
}
```

The continue statement (continue;) begins the next iteration of the innermost do, for, or while statement in which it appears, skipping the loop body:

```
while (c < 100)
{
     if (c == 55)
          continue;
}
```

The do-while loop executes a block of statements until the expression in the while statement fails:

```
do
{
     x = x + 1;
}  while (x < 1000);
```

The for loop evaluates the first of its three expressions once. The third expression is then evaluated after each pass through the loop until the second expression become false. For example:

```
for (x = 1; x < 100; x = x+10)
{
     y = y + x;
}
```

The goto statement transfers program control to the statement defined by the label:

```
     if (x == 100)
          goto X;
     x == x - 1;
X:     x == x + 1;
```

The if statement executes the following statements (enclosed in brackets) or the next statement (if no brackets) if the expression is true; otherwise, the second expression is executed. For example:

```
if (x == 0)
     y = 10;
else
     y = 0;
```

The NULL statement is used to indicate that nothing will happen:

```
if (x == 10)
    ;                        /*  do nothing   */
```

The **return** statement stops the execution of the current function and returns control to the calling function. A single value can be returned.

```
if (x == 10)
        return (y);
```

The **switch** statement evaluates an expression and attempts to match it to a set of **case** statements. If there is no match, the default statement is executed. For example:

```
switch (x)
{
        case BUY:   buy ();
                    break;
        case SELL:  sell ();
                    break;
        default:    do_nothing ();
                    break;
}
```

The **while** loop executes a statement or block of statements as long as the expression evaluates to a nonzero value:

```
while (x > 100)
{
        y = y + x;
}
```

Function

A *function* is a set of declarations, definitions, expressions, and statements that performs a specific job. The following code structure illustrates the use of preprocessor directives, declarations, definitions, expressions, statements, and functions.

```
#include <stdio.h>    /* preprocessor directives */
#include <graph.h>    /* include header files */

#define TRUE 1        /* define a constant */
```

```
short radius;          /* declare global variables */
short diameter_main;

int calc_diameter (int);   /* function prototype */


main ()
{                              /* begin main function */

   int x,y;                    /* declare local variables */

   _setvideomode (_ERESCOLOR);  /* call a function */
                 .
                 .
                 .
   radius = 10;
   diameter_main = calc_diameter(radius);
   getch ();
   _setvideomode (_DEFAULTMODE);
}                         /*  end main function   */


calc_diameter (radius)  /* function head */
{
   int diameter;          /* declare local variable */

   diameter = 2 * radius;

   return (diameter);  /* return value */
}                        /*  end diameter   */
```

Preprocessor directives are the first lines of any C program. They are commands to the C preprocessor, which is invoked before compiling the program. In the preceding structure, the #define and #include statements are the preprocessor directives.

The first two lines of this code structure are the #include commands, which permit the programmer to include certain files. To invoke a graphics call, such as the _lineto function, the graphics.h header file must be included. Although it is not always necessary to include the stdio.h header file, it is a good practice to include this file because it provides many functions that are necessary for most graphics programs. Sometimes other header files are needed to successfully use a particular graphics function. See chapter 9, "Graphics Functions," to determine which header files should be included for any of the graphics functions.

The next statements, prior to the main() function, are often the declaration statements. A declaration, as mentioned, establishes the name and attributes of variables, functions, and types used in the program. Global variables are declared outside the main() function and are visible to all functions.

The `main()` function is next. Local variables are declared inside the `main()` function, and are visible only inside the function. Next, the video mode is set using the `_setvideomode` function. The `_setvideomode` function is necessary for all output except text output (the computer system is internally set to a default text mode when booted).

Most of the example programs do not include functions other than the `()main` function and are not structured as efficiently as possible. This was done primarily to keep the example programs short and easy to understand.

Most example programs include at least one `getch();` function call. This function halts execution until a key is pressed, and is used commonly as a delay. The last thing to do before exiting the `main()` function when using a graphics mode is to use the `_setvideomode (_DEFAULTMODE);` call. This call returns the screen mode to the mode in use prior to the execution of the `main()` function.

This code structure is followed throughout the book and should provide a simple, yet effective, programming methodology for the interpretation of the programming examples.

The Software Development Process

In a product life-cycle approach to software development, three basic types of activities must be performed: the pre-development, development, and post-development phases. The intent of software development under a product life-cycle approach is to develop a software product that meets its intended purpose and is easily maintained and expanded as requirements for the product change. This section identifies the primary phases of development for a software product.

In the first phase, pre-development, activities are largely management oriented; the programmer is involved only as a consultant. During this phase, the product is defined and a market is identified. See figure 2.2. With careful analysis, the pre-development activities will result in a sound product idea and a functional description.

The software development phase is performed next. During this phase, the software product is developed according to the product definition created during the pre-development activities. The steps in figure 2.3 define a typical process of software development.

The first step in software development is the requirements phase. During this phase, you refine the product definition developed during the pre-development activities. This refinement is generally a consensus between management, the developers (programmers), and the users. The objectives of the software product are discussed and tradeoffs in the design are made. It is during this phase that formal, binding requirements are set for the software product. For this reason, it is important to involve all interested parties in this phase.

After the requirements phase has been completed, the specifications phase begins. During this phase, you define the tasks that must be performed. The specifications phase is actually a refinement of the previous phase and is sometimes combined with it. The intent of this phase is to simplify the design phase by developing a more precise, understandable description of the requirements document. The result of this phase is a set of specifications for measuring the performance of the developed software.

During the design phase, you develop the software specifications into a software architecture that represents the physical implementation of the software product. The software architecture can be thought of as a blueprint to be followed during the implementation phase. Two primary activities

Fig. 2.2. Pre-development phase.

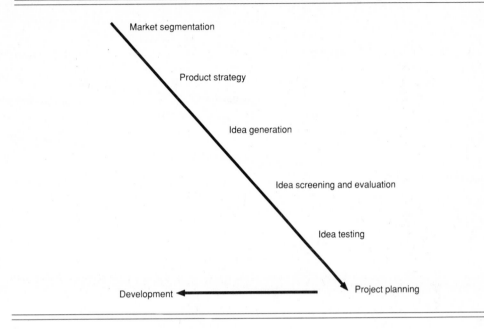

Market segmentation

Product strategy

Idea generation

Idea screening and evaluation

Idea testing

Development ◀————— Project planning

Fig. 2.3. Software development phase.

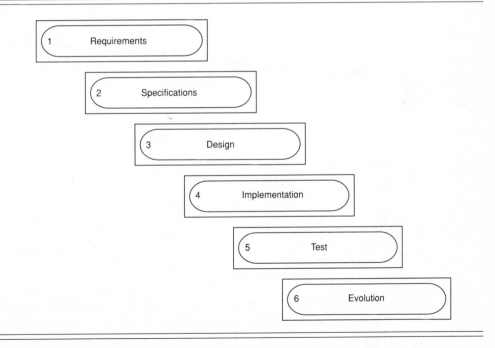

1   Requirements

2   Specifications

3   Design

4   Implementation

5   Test

6   Evolution

are performed during the design phase: external and internal design. External design is the definition of the externally observable characteristics of the software product. Internal design defines the details of the internal processing and structure of the software product.

In the implementation phase, you create the product structures, data structures, algorithms, and interfaces developed in the design phase. If the previous steps in the pre-development phase have been performed properly, this is a straightforward process. More often, however, the implementation phase is chaotic and difficult to track—even very effective requirements analysis, specifications, and design cannot predict all of the problems and technical difficulties in a major software development project. Design errors lead to incorrect assumptions by the programmer. In addition, the intricacies of various hardware configurations are often beyond the expertise and foresight of the design team. Through careful design, however, problems can be kept to a manageable level.

The testing phase follows the implementation phase. In this phase, you locate and isolate physical and logical errors in the product. Both formal and informal testing are conducted. Informal testing, which occurs during both the implementation and testing phases, is usually performed by the programmer and done on a modular basis. When the programmer completes a particular function, he or she then informally tests it to assure that it functions as intended. Formal testing begins as each function is completed. This testing attempts to identify exactly what the function is doing. Once all functions are tested individually, the functions are tested as a unit. Test results are then compared against the specifications.

The evolution phase is often called operations and maintenance. This phase follows the product throughout the rest of its functional life. Product changes such as enhancements are necessary to increase the short life of today's computer software products. There are three basic types of evolution in software products. These are perfective maintenance, adaptive maintenance, and corrective maintenance. Perfective maintenance is product enhancement. Suggestions or requests by the user or designer may identify the need for perfective maintenance. Adaptive maintenance is the planned modification of the product. These planned modifications usually are enhancements that were not considered feasible for the original product. Corrective maintenance refers to the modification of the product due to deficiencies or errors in the product after its release.

The evolution phase marks the end of the actual development process. The product in now ready to enter the post-development phase. See figure 2.4.

During the post-development phase, activities are performed to facilitate the release of the product into the market. These activities, however, are not performed in isolation and may begin during the development process. The key objective of these activities is to successfully launch the product into the target market. Like the pre-development phase, this phase is management oriented and the programmer has very little involvement.

Fig. 2.4. Post-development phase.

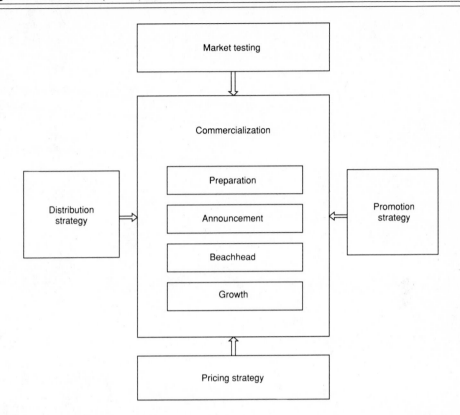

3

Graphics Techniques

This chapter introduces the basic graphics capabilities provided by the Microsoft graphics libraries. The functions provided by these graphics libraries can be divided into four broad categories: text (discussed in Chapter 4), presentation graphics (discussed in Chapter 5), animation (discussed in Chapter 6), and drawing (the subject of this chapter).

This chapter describes a variety of graphics techniques. The following Microsoft graphics functions are addressed in this chapter:

```
_ellipse                      _pie_w
_ellipse_w                    _pie_wxy
_ellipse_wxy                  _polygon
_floodfill                    _polygon_w
_floodfill_w                  _polygon_wxy
_getcurrentposition           _rectangle
_getcurrentposition_w         _rectangle_w
_getphyscoord                 _rectangle_wxy
_getpixel                     _selectpalette
_getpixel_w                   _setcliprgn
_getviewcoord                 _setcolor
_getviewcoord_w               _setfillmask
_getwindowcoord               _setlinestyle
_lineto                       _setpixel
_lineto_w                     _setpixel_w
_moveto                       _setvieworg
_moveto_w                     _setviewport
_pie
```

Coordinate Systems

While in graphics mode, the Microsoft graphics functions recognize three coordinate systems: the physical, view, and window coordinate systems.

The Physical Coordinate System

The physical coordinate system is determined by the hardware and display configuration of the system. This coordinate system has its origin in the upper left corner of the screen, as shown in figure 3.1. The positive x-axis extends to the right, and the positive y-axis extends toward the bottom of the screen. The maximum x value is determined by the number of pixels in the horizontal direction on the screen. Similarly, the maximum y value is determined by the number of pixels in the vertical direction. In _ERESCOLOR mode, 640 by 350 pixels are available; therefore, the x-axis extends from 0 to 639 and the y-axis extends from 0 to 349.

Fig. 3.1. The physical coordinate system.

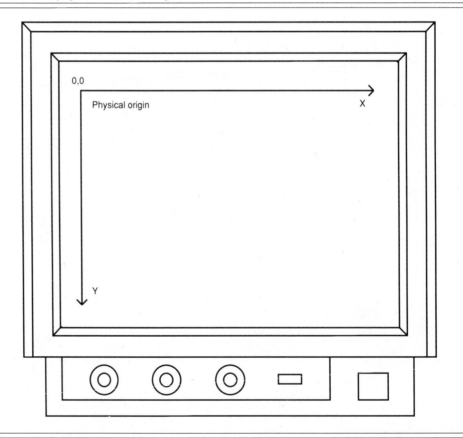

The View Coordinate System

The view coordinate system, by default, shares the same location and coordinate values as the physical coordinate system. The view coordinate system can be moved, however, by placing the view origin anywhere on the screen, as shown in figure 3.2. The x-axis, as well as the y-axis, extends in the same manner as the physical coordinate system.

Fig. 3.2. The view coordinate system.

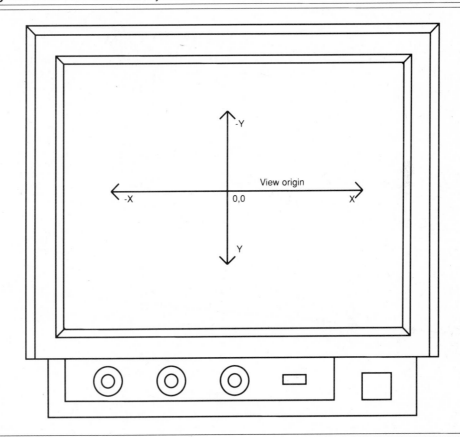

You use the _setvieworg function to place the view origin of the view coordinate system at a physical coordinate location. The x and y arguments identify the physical coordinates of the new view origin. The following syntax describes the proper use of the _setvieworg function.

```
struct xycoord _far _setvieworg (short x, short y);
short x, y;                Physical coordinates for view origin
```

31

Note: In version 5.1 of the Microsoft C optimizing compiler, the _setvieworg function was called the _setlogorg function, and the view coordinate system was called the logical coordinate system.

The Window Coordinate System

The window coordinate system is used only with the current viewport. You set the dimensions of the viewport with the _setwindow function. The syntax for the _setwindow function is as follows:

```
short _far _setwindow (short invertflag, double x1,
             double y1, double x2, double y2);
short invertflag;       Determines direction of y-axis
double x1, y1;          Upper left corner of window
double x2, y2;          Lower right corner of window
```

The window dimensions can be set to any values from 1 to 10,000. The most common dimensions are from -100.0 to 100.0 for both the x-axis and the y-axis. (This places the origin, 0.0, 0.0, at the center of the viewport.) The invertflag argument determines the direction of the y-axis. If the invertflag is set to TRUE (1), the y-axis increases from the screen bottom to the screen top. If set to FALSE (0), the y-axis increases from the screen top to the screen bottom. (This is the way the physical and view coordinate systems extend.)

The window coordinate system, as mentioned in the previous paragraphs, sets the dimensions of the current viewport. If no viewport has been set with the _setviewport function, the window coordinate system is applied to the entire screen, because the default viewport is the entire screen. For example, if no viewport has been set with the _setviewport function and the window dimensions are set to -100.0 to 100.0 in both the x and y directions with the invertflag set to FALSE, the upper left corner of the screen corresponds to window coordinates -100.0, -100.0 and the lower right corner of the screen corresponds to window coordinates 100.0, 100.0.

Coordinate Conversions

The Microsoft graphics library also provides several functions that convert a coordinate pair (x and y values) between the coordinate systems. You can find the physical coordinates of any view coordinate pair with the _getphyscoord function; its syntax is

```
struct xycoord _far _getphyscoord (short x, short y);
short x, y;             View coordinates to convert
```

You can find the view coordinates of any physical point with the _getviewcoord function; the syntax is

```
struct xycoord _far _getviewcoord (short x, short y);
short x, y;             Physical coordinates to convert
```

You can determine the view coordinates of any window coordinate pair with either the `_getviewcoord_w` or `_getviewcoord_wxy` function. The only difference in these functions is the way that the point to be converted is described. The syntax for each function is

```
struct xycoord _far _getviewcoord_w (double x1, double y1);
double x1, y1;                    Window coordinates to convert

struct xycoord _far _getviewcoord_wxy (struct _wxycoord
                          far *xy1);

struct _wxycoord far *xy1;    Window pair to convert
```

The window coordinates of specified view coordinates are returned with the `_getwindowcoord` function. The syntax for the `_getwindowcoord` function is

```
struct _wxycoord far _getwindowcoord (short x, short y);
short x, y;                Physical coordinates to convert
```

Chapter 9 provides additional information on the `_setvieworg`, `_setwindow`, `_getphyscoord`, `_getviewcoord`, `getviewcoord_w`, `getviewcoord_wxy`, and `_getwindowcoord` functions.

The Graphics Cursor

The Microsoft graphics library routines maintain, internally, a point from which several of the drawing routines originate. This point is called the *graphics cursor*. The graphics cursor is moved to the specified coordinates by the `_moveto` functions: `_moveto` and `_moveto_w`.

The `_moveto` function is used with the view coordinate system. Its syntax is

```
struct xycoord _far _moveto (short x, short y);
short x, y;                New view coordinate position
```

The `_moveto_w` function is used with the window coordinate system. Its syntax is
```
struct _wxycoord _far _moveto_w (double x, double y);

double x, y;                New window coordinate position
```

The `_moveto` functions place the graphics cursor at the location of the x and y arguments, as described in figure 3.3. No drawing takes place as the cursor is moved.

Fig. 3.3. The graphics cursor.

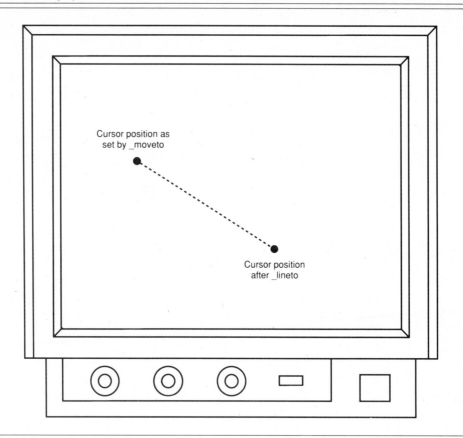

The _lineto functions, like the _moveto functions, alter the position of the graphics cursor. As the cursor is moved, a straight line is drawn from the previous location of the graphics cursor to the location specified by the x and y arguments. The new location of the graphics cursor is the end of the line, the point defined by x and y. The _lineto function is used with the view coordinate system; the _lineto_w function is used with the window coordinate system. The syntax for each function follows:

```
short _far _lineto (short x, short y);
short x, y;              End point in view coordinates

short _far _lineto_w (double x, double y);
short x, y;              End point in window coordinates
```

The Microsoft graphics library offers two functions that return the coordinates of the graphics cursor. The `_getcurrentposition` function returns the view coordinates of the current graphics cursor position. The `_getcurrentposition_w` function returns the window coordinates of the current graphics cursor position. The syntax for each function follows:

```
struct xycoord _far _getcurrentposition (void);

struct _wxycoord _far _getcurrentposition_w (void);
```

Chapter 9 provides additional information on the `_moveto`, `_moveto_w`, `_lineto`, `_lineto_w`, `_getcurrentposition`, and `_getcurrentposition_w` functions.

Aspect Ratios

The easiest and most common method for producing simple geometric shapes on the screen is to first draw the desired shape on graph paper, then mark all corner points, then mark all pertinent points on the figure, and finally transfer those points into coordinates for use in a program. Graph paper that uses a square coordinate system (the x and y dimensions are equal) is the most commonly used type of paper for drawing. The problem with this method, however, is that in most video modes, pixels (which are the smallest physical element of the screen) are not square; therefore, when the program is run, the image is distorted. To create the desired effects, the aspect ratio of the monitor must be considered.

The *aspect ratio* of the monitor is the ratio of the number of pixels along a vertical line on a screen compared to the number of pixels along a horizontal line of the same length. For the desired image to appear undistorted on the screen, the vertical (y) dimensions are multiplied by the aspect ratio. The image will then appear on the screen as it is drawn on the paper.

Use the following formula to determine the aspect ratio of the monitor:

```
aspect ratio = (width of the screen/height of the screen) *
               (number of y pixels/number of x pixels)
```

The `width` and `height` of the screen refer to the physical dimensions of the usable screen. These dimensions can be found in the monitor's technical manual or simply by measuring the screen. The number of pixels on the x-axis and the y-axis depends on the video mode in use. For example, in `_ERESCOLOR` mode, 640 pixels are on the x-axis and 350 pixels are on the y-axis. This information can be found in both this book (see Chapter 9, in the section on the `_setvideomode` function) and the Microsoft C Technical manuals or by using the `_getvideoconfig` function. Chapter 9 describes the use of the `_getvideoconfig` function, including the extraction of the number of pixels on both the x-axis and the y-axis.

The information in table 3.1 will help you determine the aspect ratios for particular video modes. The ratio of the width of the screen to the height of the screen for these calculations is assumed to be 10 inches to 7 inches, or 1.429. Most monitors will have approximately the same ratio. You may want to check your screen dimensions, however, before using the aspect ratios in table 3.1.

Table 3.1 *Aspect ratios.*

Mode	Ratio of X-Y dimensions	Aspect ratio
_MRES4COLOR	200/320=.625	.893
_MRESNOCOLOR	200/320=.625	.893
_HRESBW	200/640=.313	.447
_MRES16COLOR	200/320=.625	.893
_HRES16COLOR	200/640=.313	.447
_ERESNOCOLOR	350/640=.547	.782
_ERESCOLOR	350/640=.547	.782
_VRES2COLOR	480/640=.75	1.072
_VRES16COLOR	480/640=.75	1.072
_MRES256COLOR	200/320=.625	.893
_HERCMONO	348/720=.483	.690

*Based on a monitor that is 10 inches high by 7 inches wide, or 1.429.

Points and Pixels

The smallest portion of a screen is known as a *pixel*. The pixel size of a screen depends on the graphics mode in use. For most video modes, the pixels are not square because of the varying x and y screen coordinates for each mode. The size of the pixel is related to the resolution of the screen—the bigger the pixel, the lower the resolution. The relationship between the x and y lengths of each pixel relative to the mode in use is discussed in this chapter in the preceding section, "Aspect Ratios."

Each pixel on the screen can be set to only one color. The choice of available colors is limited by the video mode and palette in use. The colors and palettes available for each video graphics mode are described in Chapter 1, "Introduction to IBM PCs and Compatibles." The `_setcolor` function is used to select the current color.

The Microsoft graphics library includes two functions that set a pixel to the current color: the `_setpixel` and `_setpixel_w` functions. The `_setpixel` function is used with the view coordinate system, and the `_setpixel_w` function is used with the window coordinate system. The syntax for each function follows:

```
short _far _setpixel (short x, short y);
short x, y;        Pixel (view coordinates) to set

short _far _setpixel_w (double x, double y);
double x, y;       Pixel (window coordinates) to set
```

The x and y arguments identify the coordinates of the pixel that will be set to the current color.

Because the pixel is the smallest portion of the screen, setting a point on the screen is the same as setting a pixel to a particular color. Therefore, the `_setpixel` functions are most useful when there is a need to set a point on the screen.

The Microsoft graphics library has two functions that retrieve the pixel value (color) of a specified pixel: the `_getpixel` and `_getpixel_w` functions. The syntax for each function follows:

```
short _far _getpixel (short x, short y);
short x, y;            Pixel (view coordinates) position

short _far _getpixel_w (double x, double y);
double x, y;            Pixel (window coordinates) position
```

The `_getpixel` functions are useful when you need to determine the status of a pixel before setting it to the current color.

Chapter 9 provides additional information on the `_setpixel`, `_setpixel_w`, `_getpixel`, `_getpixel_w`, and `_setcolor` functions.

Lines

The line is one of the most basic features in any graphics package. The capability to draw straight lines is necessary for almost any graphics application. The line can be used to connect two points, approximate curves, create boxes, or draw very complex images.

The `_lineto` and `_lineto_w` functions, provided by the Microsoft graphics library, provide the capability to draw straight lines. See figure 3.4. The lines created by these functions do not have to be vertical or horizontal; these straight lines can be produced at any angle and almost any length. The `_lineto` function is used with the view coordinate system; the `_lineto_w` function is used with the window coordinate system.

The lines generated by the `_lineto` and `_lineto_w` functions begin at the current location of the graphics cursor and extend to the coordinates defined by the x and y arguments. Although the line may begin or extend beyond the physical coordinates of the screen, the line will be clipped at the edge of the screen. The screen borders act as a clipping region. (A *clipping region* is a rectangular area of the screen that physically limits all subsequent graphics output.) Any function that produces output outside this region will be cut off at the region's borders. If a viewport or clipping region has been defined, the lines will be clipped at the edge of the current viewport or clipping region. (See the "Viewports and Clipping Regions" section in this chapter.)

The color of the generated line is selected with the `_setcolor` function. The color of the line is limited to the available colors in the current palette. The availability of palettes depends on the graphics video mode in use. For example, in `_ERESCOLOR` mode, sixteen colors are available in the default palette. Chapter 1 describes in detail the availability and use of modes, colors, and palettes.

Both the `_lineto` and `_lineto_w` functions use a solid line pattern for drawing unless another line pattern is set with the `_setlinestyle` function. 16 bits are used to describe the line pattern used by Microsoft's graphics routines. A 1 bit in the line pattern indicates that the corresponding pixel will be set to the current color. The default pattern sets all pixels identified as part of the line to the current color. Thus, the default line pattern is

```
1111111111111111
```

in binary (FFFF in hexadecimal). A 0 bit in the line pattern indicates that the corresponding pixel will remain unchanged. Therefore, a line pattern of

0000000000000000

in binary (0000 in hexadecimal) will result in no change in any pixel along the line. The "Line Patterns" section discusses the derivation of various line patterns and the use of the _setlinestyle function; this section also provides numerous line patterns for use in graphics applications.

Fig. 3.4. Uses of the _lineto function.

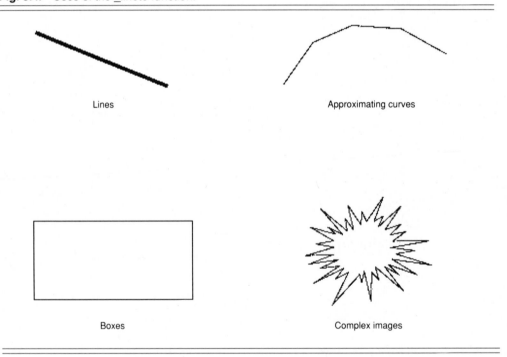

Lines

Approximating curves

Boxes

Complex images

The _lineto and _lineto_w functions are most commonly used with the _moveto and _moveto_w functions, respectively, to create various images. The _moveto and _moveto_w functions are frequently used to identify the starting point of the line. However, it is not always necessary to use the _moveto functions. When a line is drawn with the _lineto or _lineto_w function, the graphics cursor position is set to the position of the end of the line (the point specified by the x and y arguments). Therefore, if the beginning of one line is at the end of the last line drawn (provided no subsequent graphics call which alters the position of the graphics cursor is made), there is no need to use the _moveto or _moveto_w function.

When images created by the _lineto or _lineto_w function will be filled later with the _floodfill or _floodfill_w function, it is important to remember several things when creating the border of the area to be filled. First, a solid line pattern (the default) must be used. If the border has a break in it, such as a dashed line created by a non-solid line pattern, the outside areas will also be filled. This is true also if the border is drawn using more than one color. This happens because the _floodfill and _floodfill_w algorithm fills an area beginning at the point specified by the x and y arguments and extending in all directions until the border color is reached. Because only one border color can be specified, only one border color can be used. The syntax for the _floodfill and _floodfill_w functions follows:

```
short _far _floodfill (short x, short y, short bordercolor);
short x, y;                 Starting point (view coordinates)
short bordercolor;          Border color of fill area

short _far floodfill_w (double x, double y,
                        short bordercolor);
double x, y;                Starting point (window coordinates)
short bordercolor;          Border color of fill area
```

The following example demonstrates the use of the _lineto function in cooperation with the _moveto and _floodfill functions. This program is designed to draw an octagon with a border in one color and filled with another color. The first step is to draw an octagon of the desired size on graph paper. It is important to remember that regular graph paper, which uses a square grid pattern, will most likely produce irregularly shaped objects when translated to screen coordinates. This is due to the fact that pixels, except in some VGA modes, are not square. The aspect ratio of the pixels should be considered. Despite this limitation, the octagon was drawn on regular engineering graph paper for simplicity. The next step is to label the coordinates of the graph paper, choose the starting points and ending points for each line, and select a starting point for the _floodfill function. Figure 3.5 demonstrates many of these steps.

After these steps have been completed, it is easy to create the program that will generate this figure. A starting point at the upper left point of the octagon is selected with the _moveto function. The octagon is then drawn using eight calls to the _lineto function. Because the starting point of each line (except for the first) was the ending point of the previous line, it was not necessary to use the _moveto function prior to each line being drawn. There was no need to set a line pattern because the default (a solid line) was desired for this example. The _floodfill function is used as the last step to fill the octagon. It is important to ensure that the starting point of the fill is inside the border of the octagon. An error will occur if the starting fill point is on the border of the octagon. The code in Listing 3.1 was used for this example. Similar results can be accomplished with the _moveto_w, _lineto_w, and _floodfill_w functions.

Fig. 3.5. Octagon demonstration of the _lineto function.

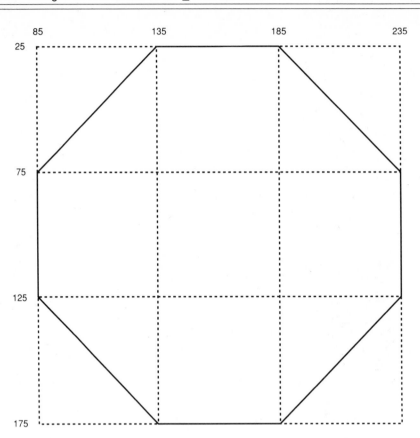

Listing 3.1. Octagon example.

```
#include <stdio.h>
#include <graph.h>

void main ()
{
    /* Initialization */
_setvideomode (_MRES4COLOR);
_setbkcolor (_BLUE);
_rectangle (_GBORDER,0,0,319,199);
```

```
        /* Draw and fill octagon */
_moveto (135,25);
_lineto (185,25);
_lineto (235,75);
_lineto (235,125);
_lineto (185,175);
_lineto (135,175);
_lineto (85,125);
_lineto (85,75);
_lineto (135,25);
_floodfill (135,75);

        /* Delay and exit */
getch ();
_setvideomode (_DEFAULTMODE);
}
```

Chapter 9 provides additional information on the _lineto, _lineto_w, _moveto, _moveto_w, _floodfill, _floodfill_w, _setcolor, and _setlinestyle functions.

Line Patterns

The following sets of line patterns provide many patterns and derivations that can be included in any Microsoft C graphics application.

Set 1

The following fifteen line patterns can be used to create various types of dashed lines. This set of patterns uses only one dash per line segment, where a line segment is defined as the 16-bit line pattern. The length of the dash is only one bit in the first line pattern of this set. With each subsequent line pattern, however, the length of the dash increases by one bit until the dash covers all but the last bit of the segment (15 bits turned on). Figure 3.6 illustrates the various line patterns relative to each other. The remaining pages in this section describe the derivation of the pattern designator for each line pattern.

The line pattern in figure 3.7 creates a dashed line. Only the first of every sixteen bits is turned on (set to 1). The pattern designator for this line pattern is 0x8000. This is determined by first drawing the desired pattern (as shown in fig. 3.7), then converting this pattern to its hexadecimal equivalent:

Binary	Hexadecimal
1000	8
0000	0
0000	0
0000	0

Fig. 3.6. Line patterns for set 1.

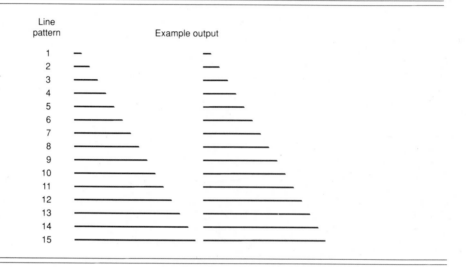

Fig. 3.7. Line pattern 0x8000.

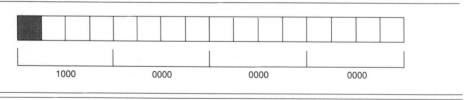

The line pattern in figure 3.8 creates a dashed line. The first two of every sixteen bits are turned on (set to 1). The pattern designator for this line pattern is 0xC000. This is determined by first drawing the desired pattern (as shown in fig. 3.8), then converting this pattern to its hexadecimal equivalent:

Binary	Hexadecimal
1100	C
0000	0
0000	0
0000	0

Fig. 3.8. Line pattern 0xC000.

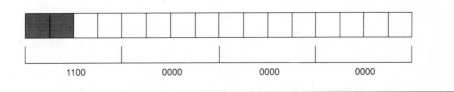

The line patterns shown in figures 3.9 through 3.21 are derived in the same way as those shown in figures 3.6 and 3.7. The line pattern model and pattern designator are provided for each pattern example.

Fig. 3.9. Line pattern 0xE000.

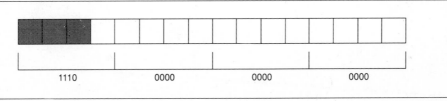

Fig. 3.10. Line pattern 0xF000.

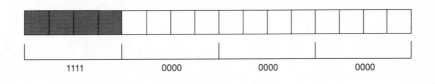

Fig. 3.11. Line pattern 0xF800.

Fig. 3.12. Line pattern 0xFC00.

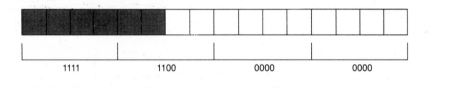

Fig. 3.13. Line pattern 0xFE00.

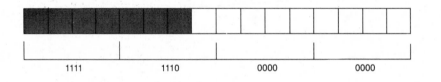

Fig. 3.14. Line pattern 0xFF00.

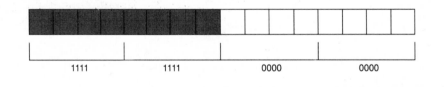

Fig. 3.15. Line pattern 0xFF80.

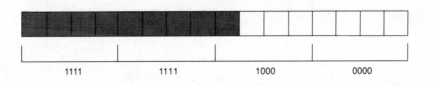

1111   1111   1000   0000

Fig. 3.16. Line pattern 0xFFC0.

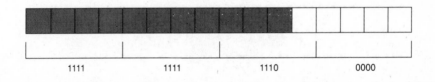

1111   1111   1100   0000

Fig. 3.17. Line pattern 0xFFE0.

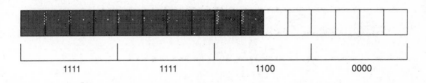

1111   1111   1110   0000

Fig. 3.18. Line pattern 0xFFF0.

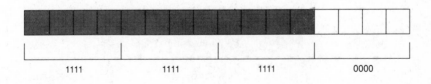

1111   1111   1111   0000

Fig. 3.19. Line pattern 0xFFF8.

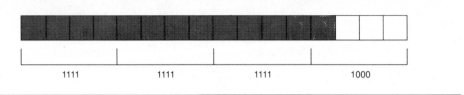

| 1111 | 1111 | 1111 | 1000 |

Fig. 3.20. Line pattern 0xFFFC.

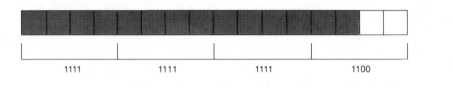

| 1111 | 1111 | 1111 | 1100 |

Fig. 3.21. Line pattern 0xFFFE.

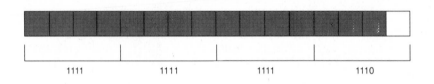

| 1111 | 1111 | 1111 | 1110 |

Set 2

The following seven line patterns can be used to create various types of dashed lines. This set of line patterns uses two dashes per line segment, where a line segment is defined as the 16-bit line pattern. The first pattern uses only one bit per dash for both dashes in the line segment. With each subsequent line pattern, the length of the dash is increased by one bit until the dash covers all but the last bit of its half of the line segment (7 bits turned on per half-line segment). Figure 3.22 illustrates the various line patterns relative to each other. The remaining pages in this section describe the derivation of the pattern designator for each line pattern.

The line pattern in figure 3.23 creates a line with two dashes per line segment. The first bit of every eight bits is turned on (set to 1). The pattern designator for this line pattern is 0x8080. This is determined by first drawing the desired pattern (as shown in fig. 3.23), then converting this pattern to its hexadecimal equivalent:

Binary	Hexadecimal
1000	8
0000	0
1000	8
0000	0

Fig. 3.22. Line patterns for set 2.

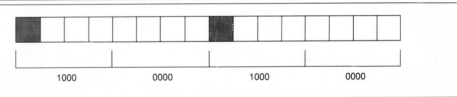

Fig. 3.23. Line pattern 0x8080.

The line pattern in figure 3.24 creates a line with two dashes per line segment. The first two bits of every eight bits are turned on (set to 1). The pattern designator for this line pattern is 0xC0C0. This is determined by first drawing the desired pattern (as shown in fig. 3.24), then converting this pattern to its hexadecimal equivalent:

Binary	Hexadecimal
1100	C
0000	0
1100	C
0000	0

Fig. 3.24. Line pattern 0xC0C0.

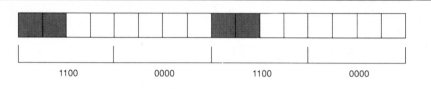

| | 1100 | | 0000 | | 1100 | | 0000 |

The line pattern in figure 3.25 creates a line with two dashes per line segment. The first three bits of every eight bits are turned on (set to 1). The pattern designator for this line pattern is 0xE0E0. This is determined by first drawing the desired pattern (as shown in fig. 3.25), then converting this pattern to its hexadecimal equivalent:

Binary	Hexadecimal
1110	E
0000	0
1110	E
0000	0

Fig. 3.25. Line pattern 0xE0E0.

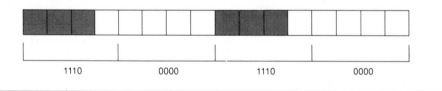

| | 1110 | | 0000 | | 1110 | | 0000 |

The line patterns shown in figures 3.26 through 3.29 are derived in the same way as those shown in figures 3.24 and 3.25. The line pattern model and pattern designator are provided for each example.

Fig. 3.26. Line pattern 0xF0F0.

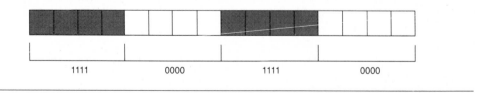

| | 1111 | | 0000 | | 1111 | | 0000 |

Fig. 3.27.   Line pattern 0xF8F8.

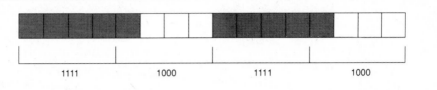

1111   1000   1111   1000

Fig. 3.28.   Line pattern 0xFCFC.

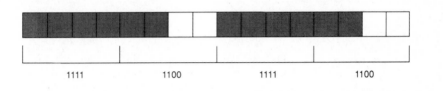

1111   1100   1111   1100

Fig. 3.29.   Line pattern 0xFEFE.

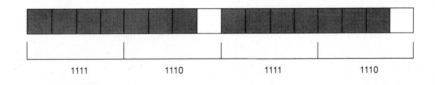

1111   1110   1111   1110

Set 3

The following eight line patterns can be used to create various effects including dashed, dashed-dotted, and solid lines. These patterns offer a variety of pattern types that can be used extensively in any application. As in the previous two sections, 16 bits are used to define a line pattern. The last pattern is the default line pattern, and is provided so that the line pattern can easily be restored to the default—a solid line. Figure 3.30 illustrates the various line patterns relative to each other. The remaining pages in this section describe the derivation of the pattern designator for each line pattern.

Fig. 3.30. Line patterns for set 3.

```
            Line
          pattern                    Example output
             1      —     —     —       —     —     —     —     —
             2      —    —    —    —    —    —    —    —
             3      ——    ——    ——    ——    ——    ——    ——    ——
             4      — —  — —  — —  — —  — —  — —  — —  — —
             5      ——  —  ——  —  ——  —  ——  —  ——  —
             6      ——   —  ——   —  ——   —  ——   —
             7      ———   —  ———   —  ———   —  ———
             8      ————————————————————————————————————
```

The line pattern in figure 3.31 creates a line with four dashes per line segment. The first bit of every four bits is turned on (set to 1). The pattern designator for this line pattern is 0x8888. This is determined by first drawing the desired pattern (as shown in fig. 3.31), then converting this pattern to its hexadecimal equivalent:

Binary	Hexadecimal
1000	8
1000	8
1000	8
1000	8

Fig. 3.31. Line pattern 0x8888.

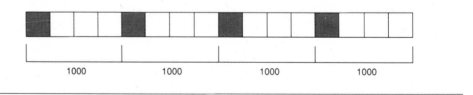

```
      1000        1000        1000        1000
```

The line pattern in figure 3.32 creates a line with four dashes per line segment. The first two bits of every four bits are turned on (set to 1). The pattern designator for this line pattern is 0xCCCC. This is determined by first drawing the desired pattern (as shown in fig. 3.32), then converting this pattern to its hexadecimal equivalent:

Binary	Hexadecimal
1100	C
1100	C
1100	C
1100	C

Fig. 3.32. Line pattern 0xCCCC.

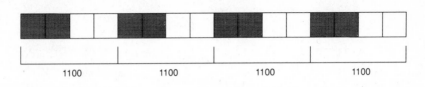

1100   1100   1100   1100

The line patterns in figures 3.33 through 3.38 are derived in the same way as those shown in figures 3.30 and 3.31. The line pattern model and pattern designator are provided for each pattern example.

Fig. 3.33. Line pattern 0xEEEE.

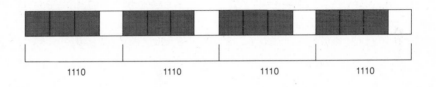

1110   1110   1110   1110

Fig. 3.34. Line pattern 0xAAAA.

1010   1010   1010   1010

Fig. 3.35. Line pattern 0xE4E4.

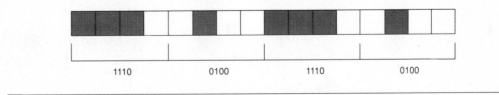

1110   0100   1110   0100

Fig. 3.36. Line pattern 0xF6F6.

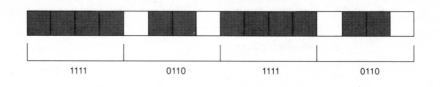

| 1111 | 0110 | 1111 | 0110 |

Fig. 3.37. Line pattern 0xFF18.

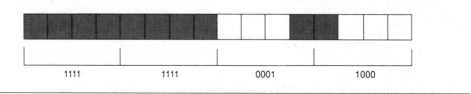

| 1111 | 1111 | 0001 | 1000 |

Fig. 3.38. Line pattern 0xFFFF.

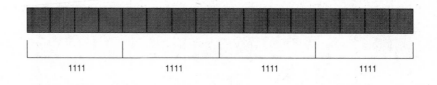

| 1111 | 1111 | 1111 | 1111 |

Rectangles and Squares

Microsoft provides the capability to create rectangles with the _rectangle, _rectangle_w, and _rectangle_wxy functions. The syntax for each of these functions follows:

```
short _far _rectangle (short fillflag, short x1, short y1,
                  short x2, short y2);
short fillflag;     Fill flag
short x1, y1;       Upper left corner (view coordinates)
short x2, y2;       Lower right corner (view coordinates)

short _far _rectangle_w (short fillflag, double x1,
                  double y1, double x2, double y2);
short fillflag;        Fill flag
double x1, y1;      Upper left corner (window coordinates)
double x2, y2;      Lower right corner (window coordinates)
```

```
short _far _rectangle_wxy (short fillflag, struct _wxycoord
                          _far *xy1, struct _wxycoord_far *xy2);
short fillflag;              Fill flag
struct _wxycoord_far *xy1;   Upper left corner (window)
struct _wxycoord_far *xy2;   Lower right corner (window)
```

The x1 and y1 arguments or the xy1 coordinate pair identify the coordinates of the upper left corner of the rectangle. The x2 and y2 arguments or the xy2 coordinate pair identify the coordinates of the lower right corner of the rectangle (see figure 3.39). The _rectangle function uses the view coordinate system; the _rectangle_w and _rectangle_wxy fuctions use the window coordinate system.

Fig. 3.39. The _rectangle function.

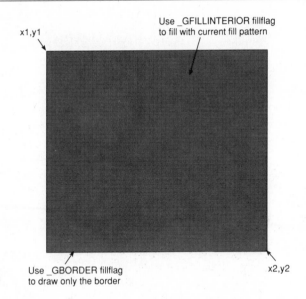

x1,y1

Use _GFILLINTERIOR fillflag
to fill with current fill pattern

Use _GBORDER fillflag
to draw only the border

x2,y2

The fillflag argument is used to specify the method by which the rectangle will be drawn. Use the _GFILLINTERIOR constant for the fillflag argument to fill the rectangle. Use the _GBORDER constant for the fillflag argument to draw only the border of the rectangle.

When you use the _GFILLINTERIOR fillflag, a filled rectangle is created using the current color and fill pattern. To select the current color, use the _setcolor function. The fill color is limited to the available colors in the current palette. The availability of palettes depends on the graphics video mode in use. For example, in _ERESCOLOR mode, sixteen colors are available in the default palette. Chapter 1 describes in detail the availability and use of modes, colors, and palettes.

The fill pattern used by the _rectangle function is a solid fill pattern by default. This means that every pixel within the rectangular area to be filled will be set to the current color. You can select and define other fill patterns with the _setfillmask function. This function defines the 64-bit fill pattern used by the _rectangle function. The "Fill Patterns" section later in this chapter describes in detail the use and derivation of fill patterns.

When you use the _GBORDER fillflag argument, only the border of the rectangle is drawn. The current color is used and the same limitations on color apply as described in the previous paragraphs. The border of the rectangle is drawn with a solid line by default. You can use a dashed line for the border, however, by redefining the current line style with the _setlinestyle function. The 16-bit line pattern used by the Microsoft graphics routines is defined with the _setlinestyle function. A 1 bit in this 16-bit pattern sets the corresponding border pixel to the current color. A 0 bit indicates that the corresponding border pixel remains unchanged. For example, a pattern of

1111111111111111

in binary (FFFF in hexadecimal) creates a solid line pattern. A line pattern of

0000000000000000

in binary (0000 in hexadecimal) draws no border. The "Line Patterns" section describes the derivation of various line patterns and the use of the _setlinestyle function. This section also provides numerous line patterns that you can easily include and use in graphics applications.

The _rectangle functions will generate only horizontal and vertical lines. This does not create a problem for most applications. For applications in which two- or three-dimensional rotations take place, however, the _rectangle function is unsatisfactory. As the corner points are shifted, the shape of the rectangle will change but the box will not rotate as desired (see figure 3.40). For this reason, it is important to consider the application before using the _rectangle functions. An alternate method for creating rectangles is with the _moveto, _lineto, and _floodfill functions. The combination of these functions will create all the same effects as the _rectangle function, including filled rectangles. When a rectangle is described with the combination of these functions, two- and three-dimensional rotation is supported. Chapter 7, "Two- and Three-Dimensional Drawing" describes this method in more detail.

Fig. 3.40. Rectangle rotations.

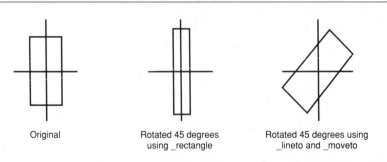

Original   Rotated 45 degrees   Rotated 45 degrees using
                     using _rectangle   _lineto and _moveto

Squares can also be generated with the _rectangle functions. When using the _rectangle functions to create a square, it is important to realize that just because the x distance between x1 and x2 is equal to the y distance between y1 and y2, the result will not always be a square because pixels are not square, except in some VGA modes. Thus, it it important to take into account the aspect ratio of the pixel when determining the corners of the square. After the corners have been identified, the features of the _rectangle functions can be used to draw and fill the square with the current line style, fill pattern, and color.

When using the _rectangle functions, the rectangle does not have to be filled using the _GFILLINTERIOR argument. You can use the _floodfill functions at any time to fill the rectangle with the current color and fill pattern. To avoid filling outside areas, however, a solid line pattern must be used to draw the rectangle's border.

Chapter 9 provides additional information on the _rectangle, _rectangle_w, _rectangle_wxy, _setcolor, _floodfill, _floodfill_w, _setlinestyle, and _setfillmask functions.

Polygons

The _polygon, _polygon_w, and _polygon_wxy functions are used to create multi-sided figures. The syntax for each of these functions follows:

```
short _far _polygon (short fillflag, struct xycoord _far
        *points, short numpoints);
short fillflag;              Fill flag
struct xycoord _far *points; Array of points (view)
short numpoints;             Number of points

short _far _polygon_w (short fillflag, double _far *points,
        short numpoints);
short fillflag;              Fill flag
double _far *points;         Array of points (window)
short numpoints;             Number of points

short _far _polygon_wxy (short fillflag, struct _wxycoord
        _far *points, short numpoints);
short fillflag;              Fill flag
struct _wxycoord _far *points; Array of points (window)
short numpoints;             Number of points
```

The numpoints argument is used to describe the number of points in the polygon. The actual points are described, in sequential order, with the points argument. The _polygon function uses the view coordinate system; the _polygon_w and _polygon_wxy functions use the window coordinate system.

The fillflag argument is used to specify the method for drawing the polygon. The same constants that are used for the rectangle functions are used for the polygon functions. The _GBORDER constant is used to create an outline of the polygon in the current color. The _GFILLINTERIOR constant is used to create a filled polygon in the current color and fill pattern.

The _polygon functions support two- and three-dimensional rotations. Because all points that define the figure are described, simple algorithms can be used to move the points in two- and three-dimensional space. Chapter 7, "Two- and Three-Dimensional Drawing," describes this method in more detail.

The _polygon functions create a closed figure. Therefore, as long as a solid line is used for the border, the figure can be filled at any time with the _floodfill functions.

Chapter 9 provides additional information on the _polygon, _polygon_w, _polygon_wxy, and _floodfill functions.

Circles and Ellipses

The _ellipse, _ellipse_w, and _ellipse_wxy functions can be used to create circles and ellipses. The syntax for each of these functions follows:

```
short _far _ellipse (short fillflag, short x1, short y1,
                   short x2, short y2);
short fillflag;    Fill flag
short x1, y1;      Upper left corner (view coordinates)
short x2, y2;      Lower right corner (view coordinates)

short _far _ellipse_w (short fillflag, double x1,
           double y1, double x2, double y2);
short fillflag;    Fill flag
double x1, y1;     Upper left corner (window coordinates)
double x2, y2;     Lower right corner (window coordinates)

short _far _ellipse_wxy (short fillflag, struct _wxycoord
             _far *xy1, struct _wxycoord _far *xy2);
short fillflag;            Fill flag
struct _wxycoord _far *xy1;   Upper left corner (window)
struct _wxycoord _far *xy2;   Lower right corner (window)
```

The x1 and y1 arguments or the xy1 coordinate pair identify the coordinates of the upper left corner of the rectangle that binds the ellipse. The x2 and y2 arguments or the xy2 coordinate pair identify the coordinates of the lower right corner of the binding rectangle. The binding rectangle is not drawn; it is used only for calculation. See figure 3.41. The _ellipse function uses the view coordinate system; the _ellipse_w and _ellipse_wxy functions use the window coordinate system.

Fig. 3.41. The _ellipse function.

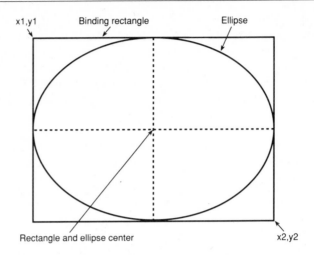

x1,y1   Binding rectangle   Ellipse

Rectangle and ellipse center   x2,y2

The f i l l f l a g argument is used to determine the method by which the _ e l l i p s e will be drawn. The _G F I L L I N T E R I O R f i l l f l a g argument fills the ellipse; the _G B O R D E R f i l l f l a g argument draws the ellipse using only a border.

When you use _G F I L L I N T E R I O R f i l l f l a g, the ellipse is filled with the current color and fill pattern. You can select the current color by using the _s e t c o l o r function. The current color is limited to the colors available in the current palette. The availability of palettes depends on the video mode is use. Chapter 1 describes in detail the availability and use of modes, colors, and palettes.

The ellipse is filled with a solid fill pattern by default when you use the _G F I L L I N T E R I O R f i l l f l a g argument. That is, every pixel in the ellipse is set to the current color. You can create and use other fill patterns with the _s e t f i l l m a s k function, which defines the 64-bit fill pattern.

When you use the _G B O R D E R f i l l f l a g argument, only the border of the ellipse is drawn. The current color is used and the same limitations on color apply as described in previous paragraphs. The ellipse border is drawn with a solid pattern only.

As mentioned, the ellipse to be drawn is defined by the binding rectangle described by its upper left and lower right corners. This creates the same problem as described in the "Rectangles and Squares" section in this chapter. Because the binding rectangle can be described with only horizontal and vertical lines, the midlines of the ellipse are in the vertical and horizontal directions. This is not satisfactory for two- or three-dimensional rotations. For this reason, it is important to consider the application before using the _e l l i p s e function. The same effects can be achieved using alternate methods or algorithms that permit two- and three-dimensional rotation of ellipses. Chapter 7, "Two- and Three-Dimensional Drawing," describes the methods for rotating ellipses and circles.

You can generate circles using the _ellipse functions. The most difficult part of generating the circle is calculating the binding rectangle or, in this case, square. For most graphics modes, a binding square is not the result when the distances between the x1 and x2 arguments and the y1 and y2 arguments are equal. For this reason, it is important to take into account the aspect ratio of the pixel when you determine the corners of the binding square. After you identify the corners of the binding square, you can use the options of the _ellipse function to draw and fill the circle with the current line style, fill pattern, and color.

The circle or ellipse generated by the _ellipse function does not have to be filled with the _GFILLINTERIOR argument. You can use the _floodfill function at any time to fill the circle or ellipse with the current color and fill pattern.

Chapter 9 provides additional information on the _ellipse, _ellipse_w, _ellipse_wxy, _setfillmask, _floodfill, _floodfill_w, and _setcolor functions.

Arcs

The _arc, _arc_w, and _arc_wxy functions are used to generate an arc, or a portion of an ellipse. These functions provide the curve-drawing capabilities needed for creating even the most basic shapes and figures. The syntax for each of the _arc functions follows:

```
short _far _arc (short x1, short y1, short x2, short y2,
                 short x3, short y3, short x4, short y4);
short x1, y1;        Upper left corner (view coordinates)
short x2, y2;        Lower right corner (view coordinates)
short x3, y3;        Start vector endpoint (view coordinates)
short x4, y4;        End vector endpoint (view coordinates

short _far _arc_w (double x1, double y1, double x2,
    double y2, double x3, double y3, double x4, double y4);
double x1, y1;       Upper left corner (window)
double x2, y2;       Lower right corner (window)
double x3, y3;       Start vector endpoint (window)
double x4, y4;       End vector endpoint (window)

short _far _arc_wxy (struct _wxycoord _far *xy1,
                     struct _wxycoord _far *xy2,
                     struct _wxycoord _far *xy3,
                     struct _wxycoord _far *xy4);
struct _wxycoord _far *xy1;  Upper left corner (window)
struct _wxycoord _far *xy2;  Lower right corner (window)
struct _wxycoord _far *xy3;  Start vector endpoint (window)
struct _wxycoord _far *xy4;  End vector endpoint (window)
```

The x1 and y1 arguments or the xy1 coordinate pair define the upper left corner of the rectangle that binds the ellipse from which the arc will be derived. The x2 and y2 arguments or the xy2 coordinate pair define the lower right corner of the binding rectangle. The x3 and y3 arguments or the xy3 coordinate pair, and the x4 and y4 arguments or the xy4 coordinate pair determine the points on the ellipse where the arc will begin and end, respectively. The arc will begin at the point where it intersects the vector which begins at the center of the ellipse and extends to the point x3, y3 (or xy3). The arc is then drawn in a counter-clockwise direction until it intersects the vector which begins at the center of the ellipse and extends to the point x4, y4 (or xy4).

Figure 3.42 illustrates the use of the _arc functions. The _arc function uses the view coordinate system; the _arc_w and _arc_wxy functions use the window coordinate system.

Fig. 3.42. The _arc function.

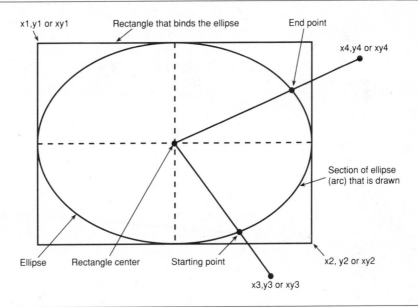

The arc is drawn in the current color, which can be set by the _setcolor function. The current color is limited to the available colors in the current palette. The availability of palettes depends on the graphics mode in use. Chapter 1 describes in detail the availability and use of modes, colors, and palettes.

The _arc functions are useful for creating both simple and complex curves. Simple curves can be drawn easily with minimum planning. Complex curves consisting of separate arcs joined together, however, require a great deal of planning. For all but the most critical complex curves, it is often easier to use other methods, such as those described in the next section, "Complex Curves." Due to the limitations discussed in the "Rectangles and Squares" and "Ellipses and Circles" sections in this chapter, the _arc function is impractical for applications that require two- or three-dimensional rotations.

Chapter 9 provides additional information on the _setcolor, _arc, _arc_w, and _arc_wxy functions.

Complex Curves

The Microsoft graphics library does not provide an easy way to create complex curves. The _arc functions are the only curve-drawing functions provided. This section describes several methods for creating complex curves. The first method discussed is the careful use of the _arc functions.

Curves Using the _arc Functions

Microsoft's _arc functions provide an easy way to create a simple curve. Creating complex curves, however, requires careful planning and often involves trial and error.

A complex curve can be thought of as a series of simple curves. Because the _arc functions allow the programmer to specify any size of ellipse and produce only a portion of it, it is possible to create very complex curves. But the planning required to do this makes the creation of complex curves with the _arc functions often impractical.

One of the easiest complex curves to create is a sinusoidal wave. See figure 3.43. The first step in creating the waveform is to draw the desired complex curve on graph paper, remembering that the use of square graph paper may result in some distortion of the displayed image due to pixel size variations.

Fig. 3.43.   Sinusoidal wave created with the _arc function.

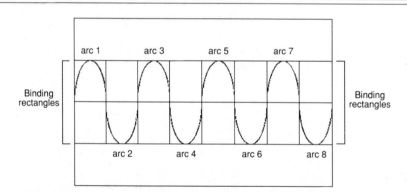

The next step is to identify logical sections of the curve to recreate using the _arc functions. Looking at figure 3.43, it is obvious that arcs which represent one-half of an ellipse will recreate the waveform quite nicely. After the arcs have been identified, the binding rectangles, start vectors, and stop vectors must be defined. Next, the information is inserted into the appropriate _arc functions and the functions are executed. Listing 3.2 creates a sinusoidal wave as previously described.

Listing 3.2. Sinusiodal wave example.

```
#include <stdio.h>
#include <graph.h>

void main ()
{

_setvideomode (_MRES4COLOR);
_setbkcolor (_RED);
_rectangle (_GBORDER,0,0,319,199);


_moveto (0,100);
_lineto (319,100);

_arc (0,50,40,150,40,100,0,100);
_arc (40,50,80,150,40,100,80,100);
_arc (80,50,120,150,120,100,80,100);
_arc (120,50,160,150,120,100,160,100);
_arc (160,50,200,150,200,100,160,100);
_arc (200,50,240,150,200,100,240,100);
_arc (240,50,280,150,280,100,240,100);
_arc (280,50,320,150,280,100,320,100);

getch ();

_setvideomode (_DEFAULTMODE);
}
```

The _getarcinfo function is useful when creating complex curves using the _arc functions. This function retrieves the start and end points, as well as a fill point, for the most recently drawn arc. This information is vital when trying to link two arcs.

The Straight-Line Approximation Method

The easiest way to create a curve is to simply connect a series of short lines that approximate the shape of the curve. The straight-line approximation method produces good results with small curves that require the entry of only a few points. This method, however, requires a lot a patience and time. Figure 3.44 shows the method for making a straight-line approximation. The length of the line should be kept as short as possible to provide the best results.

Fig. 3.44. Straight-line approximation.

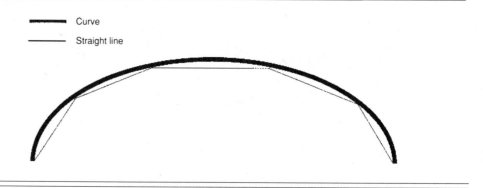

The Bezier Curve

The Bezier curve was developed by the French mathematician Pierre Bezier for the design of automobiles. This curve is generally defined by four points: the two end points and two control points. The curve begins at one end point, ends at the other end point, and uses the two control points to determine the curvature of the line.

Figure 3.45 illustrates, in geometric terms, the principle behind the Bezier curve. The first step is to draw the end points and control points. Then three lines are drawn to connect the control points and to connect the control points with the end points. From these lines, two more lines are drawn to connect the midpoints of the lines. Next, from the four inner line segments, more lines are drawn to connect the midpoints of the line segments. This process, if repeated, gives the basic shape of the expected curve.

Fig. 3.45. Geometric derivation of the Bezier curve.

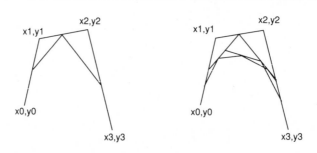

The mathematics of the Bezier curve are not trivial. But you need to know only how to use the equations, not how to derive them. The Bezier curve uses parametric cubic equations, which contain variables raised to the third power. These equations are described in the following equation, where t represents a variable that ranges from 0 to 1:

$$x(t) = a_x t^3 + b_x t^2 + c_x t + d_x$$

$$y(t) = a_y t^3 + b_y t^2 + c_y t + d_y$$

The x0 and y0 parameters define the intial point of the curve. The x1 and y1 parameters define the first control point, and x2 and y2 define the second control point. The ending point of the curve is defined by x3 and y3. In this equation, a, b, c, and d are constants.

Several assumptions are made in the mathematical representation of the Bezier curve. The first is that the curve passes through the point x0, y0 when $t = 0$. The second assumption is that the curve passes through the point x3, y3 when $t = 1$. The other assumptions deal with the slope of the lines at the initial and ending points. The assumptions made to derive the Bezier curve are summarized in the following list:

1. When $t = 0$: $x(0) = x0$
   $y(0) = y0$

2. When $t = 1$: $x(1) = x3$
   $y(1) = y3$

3. Initial slope: $x'(0) = 3(x1 - x0)$
   $y'(0) = 3(y1 - y0)$

4. Ending slope: $x'(1) = 3(x3 - x2)$
   $y'(1) = 3(y3 - y2)$

The final form of the Bezier curve formulas follows:

$$x(t) = (1 - t)^3 x0 + 3t(1 - t)^2 x1 + 3t^2(1 - t)x2 + t^3 x3$$

$$y(t) = (1 - t)^3 y0 + 3t(1 - t)^2 y1 + 3t^2(1 - t)y2 + t^3 y3$$

You can easily incorporate these formulas into a function that creates a curve. The resolution of the curve can be adjusted by the variable t. As t gets bigger (remember that t must be between 0 and 1), the curve becomes less smooth. Similarly, as t gets smaller, the curve becomes smoother but requires more time for calculation and execution. The following code demonstrates the implementation of the Bezier curve using four points.

```
void bezier (int x0, int y0, int x1, int y1, int x2, int y2,
    int x3, int y3)
{
```

```
float x, y;
int x_temp, y_temp;
float i, t;
t=.01; /* corresponds to 100 line segments in the curve */

_moveto (x0,y0);

i = 0.0;

do {
   x = (((1-i)*(1-i)*(1-i))*x0)+(3*i*((1-i)*(1-i))*x1)+
       (3*(i*i)*(1-i)*x2)+((i*i*i)*x3);
   y = (((1-i)*(1-i)*(1-i))*y0)+(3*i*((1-i)*(1-i))*y1)+
       (3*(i*i)*(1-i)*y2)+((i*i*i)*y3);
   x_temp = (int)x;
   y_temp = (int)y;
   _lineto (x_temp,y_temp);
   i = i + t;
   } while (i <= 1.0);
 }
```

Area Fills

To create many complex images, you must be able to fill an area with a particular color. This capability is provided in the Microsoft graphics library by the _floodfill and _floodfill_w functions. The syntax for each of these functions follows:

```
short _far _floodfill (short x, short y, short bordercolor);
short x,y;              Staring point (view coordinates)
short bordercolor;      Border color of fill area

short _far _floodfill_w (double x, double y,
                         short bordercolor);
double x, y;            Starting point (window coordinates)
short bordercolor;      Border color of fill area
```

The _floodfill and _floodfill_w functions fill any bound area with the current color and fill pattern. The x and y arguments define the seed, or beginning point, for the fill algorithm. The bordercolor argument identifies the border color of the area to be filled. The fill algorithm internal to the Microsoft graphics library uses the seed point as the initial point to fill. The algorithm then begins filling the area by moving in all directions until the border color is encountered. It is important to remember that only one border color can be specified. For this reason, the area to be filled must be totally surrounded by the border color. If lines are used to surround the area to be filled, these lines must be solid. Figure 3.46 illustrates an area fill.

Fig. 3.46. Area fill.

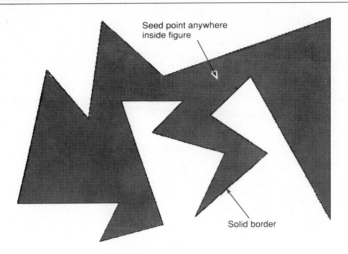

Seed point anywhere
inside figure

Solid border

The _floodfill functions will fill any shape. The fill algorithm is very efficient and fast. To use the _floodfill functions without error, the seed point (the pixel identified by the x and y arguments) must be within the area to be filled. Errors will occur if the seed point is placed on the border color or outside the current clipping region.

The _floodfill functions use the current color. The current color is selected with the _setcolor function. The current color, and thus the fill color, is limited to the available colors in the current palette. The availability of palettes depends on the graphics video mode in use. Chapter 1 describes in detail the availability and use of modes, colors, and palettes.

The fill pattern used by the _floodfill functions is a solid fill by default. A solid fill pattern sets every pixel in the area to be filled to the current color. You can select and define other fill patterns with the _setfillmask function, which defines the 64-bit fill pattern. The following section on fill patterns describes the use and derivation of fill patterns in detail.

Chapter 9 provides additional information on the _floodfill, _floodfill_w, _setcolor, and _setfillmask functions.

Fill Patterns

The following pages describe thirteen fill patterns that can be used to create intricate background and area shading and filling. These fill patterns are described, and the derivations of their pattern designators are discussed. The pattern designator is described in the form

```
\x--\x--\x--\x--\x--\x--\x--\x--
```

Figure 3.47 shows a generic fill pattern, an area 8 bits by 8 bits. Each row is evaluated and converted from binary to hexadecimal to obtain the fill pattern for that row. Then the rows are combined to determine the fill pattern.

Fig. 3.47. Fill pattern evaluation.

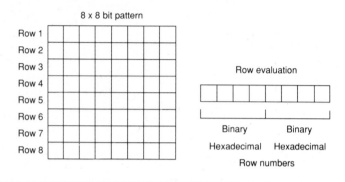

The fill pattern in figure 3.48 is a 0% fill pattern; no filling will be done with this pattern. The pattern designator is

$$\backslash x00\backslash x00\backslash x00\backslash x00\backslash x00\backslash x00\backslash x00\backslash x00$$

This is determined by converting each row to its binary equivalent, then converting this binary code to hexadecimal:

Row	Binary	Hexadecimal
1	0000 0000	00
2	0000 0000	00
3	0000 0000	00
4	0000 0000	00
5	0000 0000	00
6	0000 0000	00
7	0000 0000	00
8	0000 0000	00

The fill pattern in figure 3.49 indicates that 3% of the area to be filled will be set to the current color. The pattern designator is

$$\backslash x00\backslash x20\backslash x00\backslash x00\backslash x00\backslash x02\backslash x00\backslash x00$$

This is determined by converting each row to its binary equivalent, then converting this binary code to hexadecimal:

Row	Binary	Hexadecimal
1	0000 0000	00
2	0010 0000	20
3	0000 0000	00
4	0000 0000	00
5	0000 0000	00
6	0000 0010	02
7	0000 0000	00
8	0000 0000	00

Fig. 3.48. 0% fill pattern: \x00\x20\x00\x00\x00\x02\x00\x00.

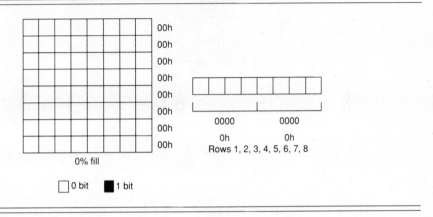

Fig. 3.49. 3% fill pattern: \x00\x20\x00\x00\x00\x02\x00\x00.

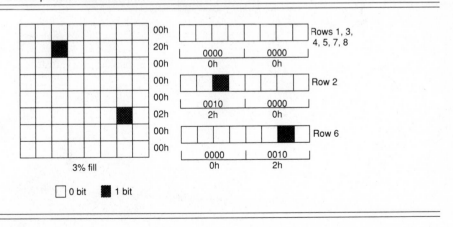

The fill patterns shown in figures 3.50 through 3.60 are derived in the same manner as those in figures 3.48 and 3.49. The fill pattern and pattern designator are provided for each.

Fig. 3.50. 6% fill pattern: \x20\x00\x02\x00\x80\x00\x08\x00.

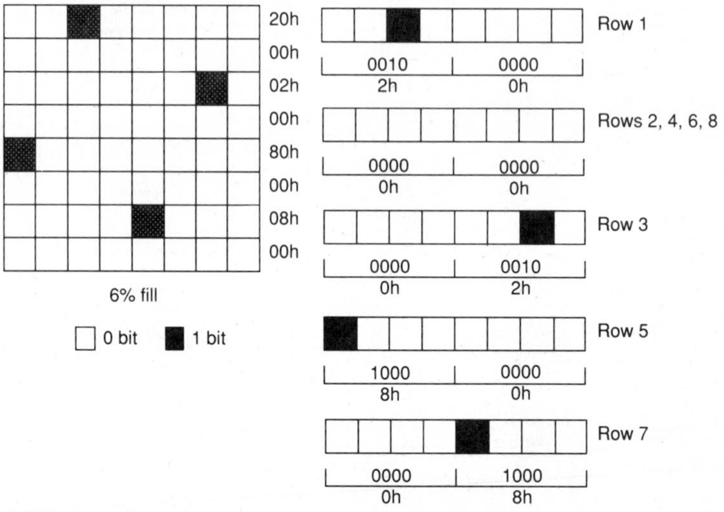

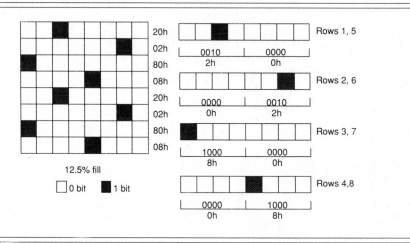

Fig. 3.51. 12.5% fill pattern: \x20\x02\x80\x08\x20\x02\x80\x08.

Fig. 3.52.   25% fill pattern: \x44\x11\x44\x11\x44\x11\x44\x11.

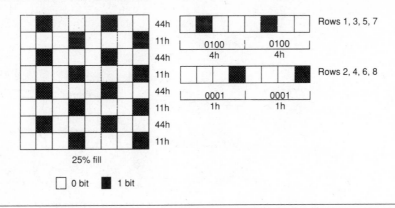

Fig. 3.53.   37.5% fill pattern: \xAA\x44\xAA\x11\xAA\x44\xAA\x11.

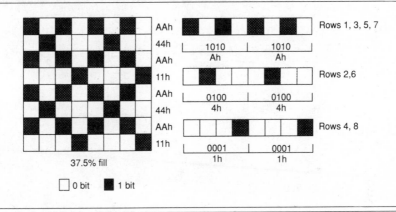

Fig. 3.54.   50% fill pattern: \x55\xAA\x55\xAA\x55\xAA\x55\xAA.

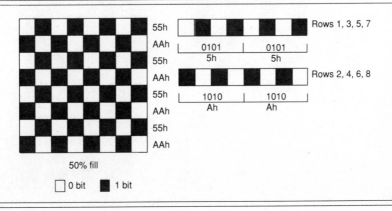

Fig. 3.55. 62.5% fill pattern: \x55\xBB\x55\xEE\x55\xBB\x55\xEE.

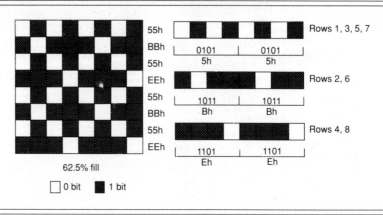

62.5% fill

□ 0 bit ■ 1 bit

Fig. 3.56. 75% fill pattern: \xBB\xEE\xBB\xEE\xBB\xEE\xBB\xEE.

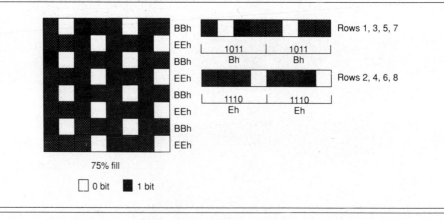

75% fill

□ 0 bit ■ 1 bit

Fig. 3.57. 87.5% fill pattern: \xDF\xFD\x7F\xF7\xDF\xFD\x7F\xF7.

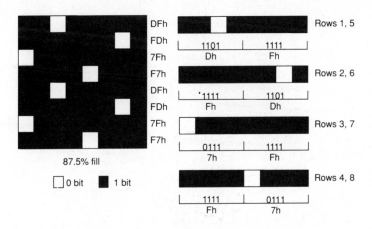

Fig. 3.58. 94% fill pattern: \xDF\xFF\xFD\xFF\x7F\xFF\xF7\xFF.

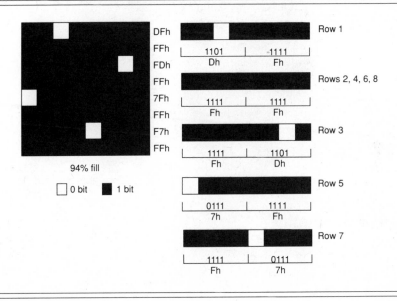

Fig. 3.59. 97% fill pattern: \xFF\xDF\xFF\xFF\xFF\xFD\xFF\xFF.

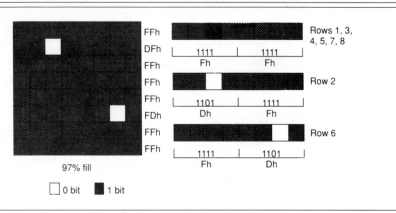

97% fill

□ 0 bit ■ 1 bit

Fig. 3.60. 100% fill pattern: \xFF\xFF\xFF\xFF\xFF\xFF\xFF\xFF.

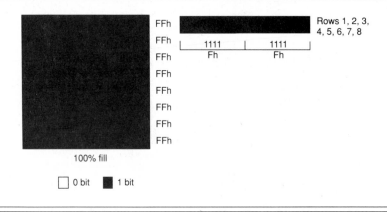

100% fill

□ 0 bit ■ 1 bit

Halftoning and Shading

Shading and halftoning effects are created by the partial filling of an area. (Halftoning is produced by varying the degree, or percentage, of the fill patttern.) For example, with the colors black and white, and the fill patterns provided in the previous section, thirteen shades of gray can be created, including the 0% and 100% fills. With shade and halftone, the programmer can make the most out of limited colors. This is especially important in black-and-white, two-color, and four-color modes.

Listing 3.3 demonstrates the use of the fill patterns provided in the preceding section while using only black (the background color) and white (the foreground color). The thirteen shades of gray are displayed in the first thirteen rectangles; for comparison, the fourteenth rectangle contains no shading. Figure 3.61 shows a printout of the screen produced by this example.

Listing 3.3. Shading and halftoning example.

```
#include <stdio.h>
#include <graph.h>

            /* Initialization of fill patterns */

unsigned char *(fillpattern [13])=

{"\x00\x00\x00\x00\x00\x00\x00\x00",      /*       0% fill     */
 "\x00\x20\x00\x00\x00\x02\x00\x00",      /*       3% fill     */
 "\x20\x00\x02\x00\x80\x00\x08\x00",      /*       6% fill     */
 "\x20\x02\x80\x08\x20\x02\x80\x08",      /*    12.5% fill     */
 "\x44\x11\x44\x11\x44\x11\x44\x11",      /*      25% fill     */
 "\xAA\x44\xAA\x11\xAA\x44\xAA\x11",      /*    37.5% fill     */
 "\x55\xAA\x55\xAA\x55\xAA\x55\xAA",      /*      50% fill     */
 "\x55\xBB\x55\xEE\x55\xBB\x55\xEE",      /*    62.5% fill     */
 "\xBB\xEE\xBB\xEE\xBB\xEE\xBB\xEE",      /*      75% fill     */
 "\xDF\xFF\x7F\xF7\xDF\xFD\x7F\xF7",      /*    87.5% fill     */
 "\xDF\xFF\xFD\xFF\x7F\xFF\xF7\xFF",      /*      94% fill     */
 "\xFF\xDF\xFF\xFF\xFF\xFD\xFF\xFF",      /*      97% fill     */
 "\xFF\xFF\xFF\xFF\xFF\xFF\xFF\xFF"};     /*     100% fill     */

void main ()
{
int color;
int x;

_setvideomode (_MRES4COLOR);
_rectangle (_GBORDER,0,0,319,199);
color = -1;

            /*   Draw 14 rectangles      */

for (x=5; x<276; x=x+45)
  {
  _rectangle (_GBORDER,x,20,x+40,90);
  _rectangle (_GBORDER,x,110,x+40,180);
  }

            /* Fill top rectangles       */

for (x=6; x<277; x=x+45)
  {
```

Listing 3.3. *continues*

Listing 3.3. cont.   Shading and halftoning example.

```
color = color + 1;
_setfillmask ((char far *)(fillpattern [color]));
_floodfill (x,21,3);
}

                    /* Fill bottom rectangles */

for (x=6; x<232; x=x+45)
   {
   color = color + 1;
   _setfillmask ((char far *)(fillpattern [color]));
   _floodfill (x,111,3);
   }

_settextposition (24,10);
_outtext ("Press a Key to Exit");

                    /*  Delay and reset  */

getch ();

_setvideomode (_DEFAULTMODE);

}
```

With shade and halftone, the programmer can also produce special effects, such as non-distinct horizons and airbrushing. By dividing a large area into smaller areas and filling the smaller areas with an increasing or a decreasing percentage of fill pattern, some incredible results can be obtained. Listing 3.4 demonstrates the use of the fill patterns provided in the preceding section to create a non-distinct horizon. Figure 3.62 is a printout of the screen produced by this listing.

Listing 3.4.   Horizon example.

```
#include <stdio.h>
#include <graph.h>
                /* Initialization of fill patterns */
unsigned char *(fillpattern [13])=
{"\x00\x00\x00\x00\x00\x00\x00\x00",    /*       0% fill    */
"\x00\x20\x00\x00\x00\x02\x00\x00",     /*       3% fill    */
"\x20\x00\x02\x00\x80\x00\x08\x00",     /*       6% fill    */
"\x20\x02\x80\x08\x20\x02\x80\x08",     /*      12.5% fill  */
```

Fig. 3.61. Example output from listing 3.3.

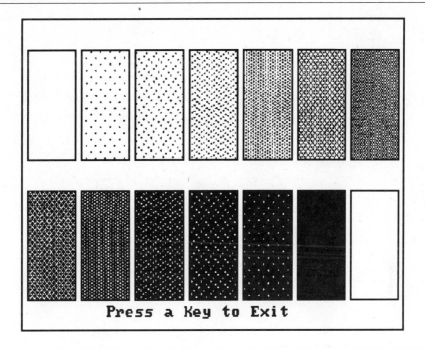

```
"\x44\x11\x44\x11\x44\x11\x44\x11",      /*      25% fill      */
"\xAA\x44\xAA\x11\xAA\x44\xAA\x11",      /*      37.5% fill    */
"\x55\xAA\x55\xAA\x55\xAA\x55\xAA",      /*      50% fill      */
"\x55\xBB\x55\xEE\x55\xBB\x55\xEE",      /*      62.5% fill    */
"\xBB\xEE\xBB\xEE\xBB\xEE\xBB\xEE",      /*      75% fill      */
"\xDF\xFF\x7F\xF7\xDF\xFD\x7F\xF7",      /*      87.5% fill    */
"\xDF\xFF\xFD\xFF\x7F\xFF\xF7\xFF",      /*      94% fill      */
"\xFF\xDF\xFF\xFF\xFF\xFD\xFF\xFF",      /*      97% fill      */
"\xFF\xFF\xFF\xFF\xFF\xFF\xFF\xFF"};     /*      100% fill     */
void main ()
{int color;
int y;
_setvideomode (_ERESCOLOR);
_rectangle (_GBORDER,0,0,639,349);
color = -1;
     /* Draw Horizon */
for (y=150; y<215; y=y+5)
  {
  color = color + 1;
```

Listing 3.4. *continues*

Listing 3.4. cont. Horizon example.

```
    _setfillmask ((char far *)(fillpattern [color]));
    _rectangle (_GFILLINTERIOR,1,y,638,y+10);
    }
      /* Draw filled bottom of screen and prompt */
_setfillmask ((char far *)(fillpattern [12]));
_rectangle (_GFILLINTERIOR,1,215,638,349);
_settextposition (24,30);
_outtext ("Press a Key to Exit");
getch ();
_setvideomode (_DEFAULTMODE);
}
```

Fig. 3.62. Example output from listing 3.4.

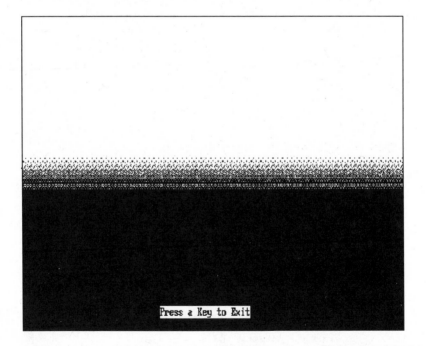

Airbrushed effects can lead to spectacular results. For example, listing 3.5 creates a series of overlaying rectangles, each filled with an increasing percentage of fill pattern. The result is a rectangle that appears to be airbrushed. Similar schemes can be used to create other airbrush effects. Figure 3.63 is a printout of the screen produced by this listing.

Listing 3.5. Airbrushing example.

```c
#include <stdio.h>
#include <graph.h>

/* Initialization of fill patterns */

unsigned char *(fillpattern [13])=

"\x00\x00\x00\x00\x00\x00\x00\x00",     /*        0% fill     */
"\x00\x20\x00\x00\x00\x02\x00\x00",     /*        3% fill     */
"\x20\x00\x02\x00\x80\x00\x08\x00",     /*        6% fill     */
"\x20\x02\x80\x08\x20\x02\x80\x08",     /*       12.5% fill   */
"\x44\x11\x44\x11\x44\x11\x44\x11",     /*       25% fill     */
"\xAA\x44\xAA\x11\xAA\x44\xAA\x11",     /*       37.5% fill   */
"\x55\xAA\x55\xAA\x55\xAA\x55\xAA",     /*       50% fill     */
"\x55\xBB\x55\xEE\x55\xBB\x55\xEE",     /*       62.5% fill   */
"\xBB\xEE\xBB\xEE\xBB\xEE\xBB\xEE",     /*       75% fill     */
"\xDF\xFF\x7F\xF7\xDF\xFD\x7F\xF7",     /*       87.5% fill   */
"\xDF\xFF\xFD\xFF\x7F\xFF\xF7\xFF",     /*       94% fill     */
"\xFF\xDF\xFF\xFF\xFF\xFD\xFF\xFF",     /*       97% fill     */
"\xFF\xFF\xFF\xFF\xFF\xFF\xFF\xFF"};    /*       100% fill    */

void main ()
{

int color;
int y1, y2, x1, x2;

_setvideomode (_ERESCOLOR);
_rectangle (_GBORDER,0,0,639,349);
x1 = 195;
x2 = 405;
y1 = 89;
y2 = 211;
color = 12;


/* Draw rectangles */

do
  {
  _setcolor (14);
  _setfillmask ((char far *)(fillpattern [color]));
```

Listing 3.5. *continues*

Listing 3.5. cont.   Airbrushing example.

```
        _rectangle (_GFILLINTERIOR,x1,y1,x2,y2);
        x1 = x1 - 5;
        x2 = x2 + 5;
        y1 = y1 - 3;
        y2 = y2 + 3;
        color = color - 1;
        }  while (color != -1);


    _settextposition (24,30);
    _outtext ("Press a Key to Exit");

    /*  Delay and reset  */

    getch ();
    _setvideomode (_DEFAULTMODE);

    }
```

Fig. 3.63.   Example output from listing 3.5.

Press a Key to Exit

Pie Charts and Wedges

With the _pie, _pie_w, and _pie_wxy functions, the programmer can easily create a pie-like wedge on the screen. The syntax for each function follows:

```
short _far _pie (short fillflag, short x1, short y1,
          short x2, short y2, short x3, short y3,
          short x4, short y4);
short fillflag;      Fill flag
short x1, y1;        Upper left corner (view)
short x2, y2;        Lower right corner (view)
short x3, y3;        Start vector endpoint (view)
short x4, y4;        End vector endpoint (view)


short _far _pie_w (short fillflag, double x1, double y1,
          double x2, double y2, double x3, double y3,
          double x4, double y4);
short fillflag;      Fill flag
double x1, y1;       Upper left corner (window)
double x2, y2;       Lower right corner (window)
double x3, y3;       Start vector endpoint (window)
double x4, y4;       End vector endpoint (window)


short _far _pie_wxy (short fillflag, struct _wxycoord _far
          *xy1, struct _wxycoord _far *xy2, struct
          _wxycoord _far *xy3, struct _wxycoord _far *xy4);
short fillflag;                  Fill flag
struct _wxycoord _far *xy1;      Upper left corner (window)
struct _wxycoord _far *xy2;      Lower right corner (window)
struct _wxycoord _far *xy3;      Start vector endpoint (window)
struct _wxycoord _far *xy4;      End vector endpoint (window)
```

When the _pie functions are called, the program draws a pie-like wedge of an ellipse that is bound by the rectangular region defined by x1-y1 (or xy1) and x2-y2 (or xy2). See figure 3.64 for information on how to use this function. The x1 and y1 arguments or the xy1 coordinate pair define the upper left corner of the binding rectangle. The x2 and y2 arguments or the xy2 coordinate pair define the lower right corner of the rectangle.

Fig. 3.64.   The _pie function.

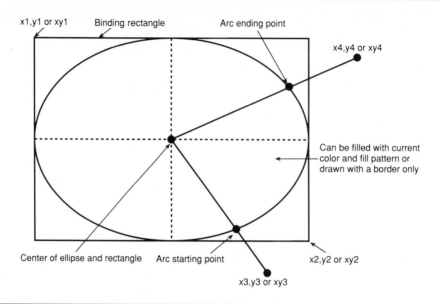

The _p i e functions define the rounded part of the wedge in a manner similar to the _a r c functions. The rounded part begins where the vector that starts at the center of the ellipse and extends to the point defined by the x 3 , y 3 arguments or the x y 3 coordinate pair intersects the ellipse. The rounded part (arc) is then drawn in a counter-clockwise direction and ends where the vector that starts at the center of the ellipse and extends to the point defined by the x 4 , y 4 arguments or the x y 4 coordinate pair intersects the ellipse. With the _p i e functions, unlike the _a r c functions, the vectors are drawn up to the point where the vector intersects the ellipse.

Another difference between the _p i e functions and the _a r c functions is that you can use fill patterns with the _p i e functions. The f i l l f l a g argument is used to determine if the wedge will be filled or not. The legal constants for the f i l l f l a g argument are _G B O R D E R and _G F I L L I N T E R I O R. The _G B O R D E R argument draws only the border of the wedge. The _G F I L L I N T E R I O R argument fills the wedge with the current color and fill pattern.

The current color is used for both the border and the fill color. The current color is limited to the available colors in the current palette. You can use the _s e t c o l o r function to select a color from the current palette. Chapter 1 describes the availability of palettes and colors relative to the video mode in use.

The _p i e functions are often used to create pie charts. (Chapter 5 describes the use of the presentation graphics package to create pie charts and other charts.) To create the pie chart, careful planning is required. The first step is to determine the varying percentages of the pie, which should total 100% (for example, 30%, 30%, and 40%). The next step is to determine the wedge sizes relative to the percentages used. Drawing it on graph paper and then entering the points manually is the easiest way, but it is not efficient. The best method is to divide the pie automatically with a generic function.

Listing 3.6 can be used to do this. This function accepts five inputs (more could be added if desired), then creates a pie chart of a predetermined size using various fill patterns. The most complex part of the function is the translation of a point to define the beginning and ending vectors. A simple two-dimensional translation algorithm is used, as described in Chapter 7, "Two- and Three-Dimensional Drawing." The angle argument is expressed in radians. Figure 3.65 shows a printout of the screen using this function.

Listing 3.6. Pie chart example.

```c
#include <stdio.h>
#include <graph.h>
#include <math.h>

                    /* Initialization of fill patterns */

unsigned char *(fillpattern [13])=

{"\x00\x00\x00\x00\x00\x00\x00\x00",     /*      0% fill    */
 "\x00\x20\x00\x00\x00\x02\x00\x00",     /*      3% fill    */
 "\x20\x00\x02\x00\x80\x00\x08\x00",     /*      6% fill    */
 "\x20\x02\x80\x08\x20\x02\x80\x08",     /*      12.5% fill */
 "\x44\x11\x44\x11\x44\x11\x44\x11",     /*      25% fill   */
 "\xAA\x44\xAA\x11\xAA\x44\xAA\x11",     /*      37.5% fill */
 "\x55\xAA\x55\xAA\x55\xAA\x55\xAA",     /*      50% fill   */
 "\x55\xBB\x55\xEE\x55\xBB\x55\xEE",     /*      62.5% fill */
 "\xBB\xEE\xBB\xEE\xBB\xEE\xBB\xEE",     /*      75% fill   */
 "\xDF\xFF\x7F\xF7\xDF\xFD\x7F\xF7",     /*      87.5% fill */
 "\xDF\xFF\xFD\xFF\x7F\xFF\xF7\xFF",     /*      94% fll     */
 "\xFF\xDF\xFF\xFF\xFF\xFD\xFF\xFF",     /*      97% fill   */
 "\xFF\xFF\xFF\xFF\xFF\xFF\xFF\xFF"};    /*      100% fill  */

void main ()
{

 /* Initialize screen and set logical origin
          to center of screen                      */

_setvideomode (_ERESCOLOR);
_setbkcolor (_BLUE);
_rectangle (_GBORDER,0,0,639,349);
_setlogorg (320,175);
```

Listing 3.6. *continues*

Listing 3.6. cont.   Pie chart example.

```
/* Call pie chart function--sum of percentages should
                               equal 100%                    */

pie_chart (.20,.10,.10,.30,.30);

_settextposition (24,32);
_outtext ("Press a Key to Exit");

                /*   Delay and reset   */

getch ();
_setvideomode (_DEFAULTMODE);


}

/* Pie chart function for drawing a five-wedge chart */


void pie_chart (double p1, double p2, double p3, double p4,
        double p5)

{
float x,y;
float oldx, oldy;
double angle;
int z1,z2;

x=0.0;
y=-150.0;
z1 = 0;
z2 = -150;

   /* Clear area where chart will be drawn */

_setcolor (0);
_rectangle (_GFILLINTERIOR,-170,-125,170,125);
_setcolor (15);

     /* The following statements draw the chart */
   /* The angle argument is in radians */
   /* The x parameter is multiplied by 1.33 to compensate
           for the aspect ratio */
```

```
oldx = x;
oldy = y;
angle = (p1*360.0*.017453);
x = (1.333 * ((oldx * cos (angle))+(oldy * sin (angle))));
y = ((oldy * cos (angle))-(oldx * sin (angle)));
_setfillmask ((char far *)(fillpattern [3]));
_pie (_GFILLINTERIOR,-170,-125,170,125,(int)oldx,(int)oldy,
     (int)x,(int)y);
_pie (_GBORDER,-170,-125,170,125,(int)oldx,(int)oldy,
     (int)x,(int)y);
oldx = x;
oldy = y;
angle = (p2*360*.017453);
x =   (1.333 * ((oldx * cos (angle))+(oldy * sin (angle))));
y =   ((oldy * cos (angle))-(oldx * sin (angle)));
_setfillmask ((char far *)(fillpattern [5]));
_pie (_GFILLINTERIOR,-170,-125,170,125,(int)oldx,(int)oldy,
     (int)x,(int)y);
_pie (_GBORDER,-170,-125,170,125,(int)oldx,(int)oldy,
     (int)x,(int)y);
oldx = x;
oldy = y;
angle = (p3*360*.017453);
x = (1.333 * ((oldx * cos (angle))+(oldy * sin (angle))));
y = ((oldy * cos (angle))-(oldx * sin (angle)));
_setfillmask ((char far *)(fillpattern [7]));
_pie (_GFILLINTERIOR,-170,-125,170,125,(int)oldx,(int)oldy,
     (int)x,(int)y);
_pie (_GBORDER,-170,-125,170,125,(int)oldx,(int)oldy,
     (int)x,(int)y);
oldx = x;
oldy = y;
angle = (p4*360*.017453);
x = (1.333 * ((oldx * cos (angle))+(oldy * sin (angle))));
y = ((oldy * cos (angle))-(oldx * sin (angle)));
_setfillmask ((char far *)(fillpattern [9]));
_pie (_GFILLINTERIOR,-170,-125,170,125,(int)oldx,(int)oldy,
     (int)x,(int)y);
_pie (_GBORDER,-170,-125,170,125,(int)oldx,(int)oldy,
     (int)x,(int)y);
oldx = x;
oldy = y;
_setfillmask ((char far *)(fillpattern [0]));
```

Listing 3.6. *continues*

Listing 3.6. cont. Pie chart example.

```
_pie (_GFILLINTERIOR,-170,-125,170,125,(int)oldx,(int)oldy,
    z1,z2);
_pie (_GBORDER,-170,-125,170,125,(int)oldx,(int)oldy,z1,z2);

}
```

Fig. 3.65. Example output from listing 3.6.

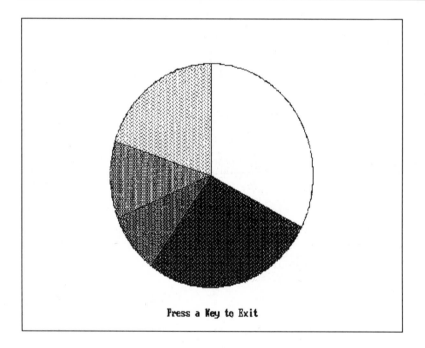

Press a Key to Exit

The _pie functions can be used also to create exploded pie charts. In an exploded pie chart, one or more of the pieces are removed slightly from the pie. A function similar to the previous one can be used for this purpose. Listing 3.7 creates a five-wedge pie with the fourth piece slightly removed. When creating a generic exploded pie chart function (the following one is not truly generic), it is important to remember to check the location of the wedge that will be exploded. The location of this wedge indicates which way to shift the binding rectangle. In the following example, the wedge is shifted to the right; therefore, the binding rectangle for that wedge is shifted to the right. Figure 3.66 is a printout of the screen produced by this function.

Listing 3.7. Exploded pie chart example.

```
#include <stdio.h>
#include <graph.h>
#include <math.h>

   /* Initialization of fill patterns */

unsigned char *(fillpattern [13])=

{"\x00\x00\x00\x00\x00\x00\x00\x00",    /*        0% fill    */
 "\x00\x20\x00\x00\x00\x02\x00\x00",    /*        3% fill    */
 "\x20\x00\x02\x00\x80\x00\x08\x00",    /*        6% fill    */
 "\x20\x02\x80\x08\x20\x02\x80\x08",    /*     12.5% fill    */
 "\x44\x11\x44\x11\x44\x11\x44\x11",    /*       25% fill    */
 "\xAA\x44\xAA\x11\xAA\x44\xAA\x11",    /*     37.5% fill    */
 "\x55\xAA\x55\xAA\x55\xAA\x55\xAA",    /*       50% fill    */
 "\x55\xBB\x55\xEE\x55\xBB\x55\xEE",    /*     62.5% fill    */
 "\xBB\xEE\xBB\xEE\xBB\xEE\xBB\xEE",    /*       75% fill    */
 "\xDF\xFF\x7F\xF7\xDF\xFD\x7F\xF7",    /*     87.5% fill    */
 "\xDF\xFF\xFD\xFF\x7F\xFF\xF7\xFF",    /*       94% fill    */
 "\xFF\xDF\xFF\xFF\xFF\xFD\xFF\xFF",    /*       97% fill    */
 "\xFF\xFF\xFF\xFF\xFF\xFF\xFF\xFF"};   /*      100% fill    */

void main ()
{

   /* Initialize screen and set logical origin
        to center of screen                      */

_setvideomode (_ERESCOLOR);
_setbkcolor (_BLUE);
_rectangle (_GBORDER,0,0,639,349);
_setlogorg (320,175);

   /* Call pie chart function--sum of percentages should
              equal 100%          */

pie_chart (.30,.20,.15,.20,.15);


_settextposition (24,32);
_outtext ("Press a Key to Exit");
```

Listing 3.7. *continues*

Listing 3.7. cont.   Exploded pie chart example.

```
                       /*   Delay and reset   */

getch ();

_setvideomode (_DEFAULTMODE);

}


 /* Pie chart function for drawing a five-wedge chart */
 /*   Fourth wedge is exploded */

void pie_chart (double p1, double p2, double p3, double p4,
     double p5)

{
float x,y;
float oldx, oldy;
double angle;
int z1,z2;


x=0.0;
y=-150.0;
z1 = 0;
z2 = -150;

        /* Clear area where chart will be drawn */

_setcolor (0);
_rectangle (_GFILLINTERIOR,-170,-125,170,125);
_setcolor (15);

     /* The following statements draw the chart */
  /* The angle argument is in radians */
  /* The x parameter is multiplied by 1.33 to compensate
     for the aspect ratio */

oldx = x;
oldy = y;
angle = (p1*360.0*.017453);
x = (1.333 * ((oldx * cos (angle))+(oldy * sin (angle))));
y = ((oldy * cos (angle))-(oldx * sin (angle)));
```

```
_setfillmask ((char far *)(fillpattern [3]));
_pie (_GFILLINTERIOR,-170,-125,170,125,(int)oldx,oldy,
     (int)x,(int)y);
_pie (_GBORDER,-170,-125,170,125,(int)oldx,(int)oldy,
     (int)x,(int)y);
oldx = x;
oldy = y;
angle = (p2*360*.017453);
x =  (1.333 * ((oldx * cos (angle))+(oldy * sin (angle))));
y =  ((oldy * cos (angle))-(oldx * sin (angle)));
_setfillmask ((char far *)(fillpattern [5]));
_pie (_GFILLINTERIOR,-170,-125,170,125,(int)oldx,(int)oldy,
     (int)x,(int)y);
_pie (_GBORDER,-170,-125,170,125,(int)oldx,(int)oldy,
     (int)x,(int)y);
oldx = x;
oldy = y;
angle = (p3*360*.017453);
x = (1.333 * ((oldx * cos (angle))+(oldy * sin (angle))));
y = ((oldy * cos (angle))-(oldx * sin (angle)));
_setfillmask ((char far *)(fillpattern [7]));
_pie (_GFILLINTERIOR,-170,-125,170,125,(int)oldx,(int)oldy,
     (int)x,(int)y);
_pie (_GBORDER,-170,-125,170,125,(int)oldx,(int)oldy,
     (int)x,(int)y);
oldx = x;
oldy = y;
angle = (p4*360*.017453);
x = (1.333 * ((oldx * cos (angle))+(oldy * sin (angle))));
y = ((oldy * cos (angle))-(oldx * sin (angle)));
_setfillmask ((char far *)(fillpattern [9]));
_setlogorg (360,175);
_pie (_GFILLINTERIOR,-170,-125,170,125,(int)oldx,(int)oldy,
     (int)x,(int)y);
_pie (_GBORDER,-170,-125,170,125,(int)oldx,(int)oldy,
     (int)x,(int)y);
oldx = x;
oldy = y;
_setfillmask ((char far *)(fillpattern [0]));
_setlogorg (320,175);
_pie (_GFILLINTERIOR,-170,-125,170,125,(int)oldx,(int)oldy,
     z1,z2);
_pie (_GBORDER,-170,-125,170,125,(int)oldx,(int)oldy,z1,z2);

}
```

Fig. 3.66. Example output from listing 3.7.

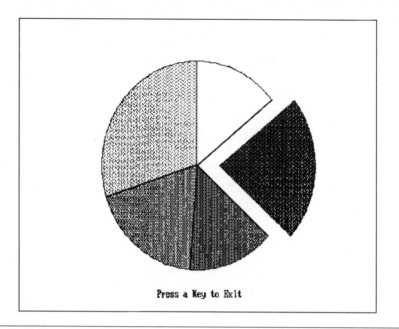

Press a Key to Exit

Chapter 9 describes the `_pie`, `_pie_w`, and `_pie_wxy` functions in detail.

Color and Palette Selection

The colors and palettes available when using the Microsoft graphics library depend on the video hardware and video mode in use. This section describes the colors and palettes available in the graphics modes.

In the CGA modes (`_MRES4COLOR` and `_MRESNOCOLOR`), the color palettes are preselected. The `_MRES4COLOR` mode provides four predefined palettes, each with four colors. Colors 1, 2, and 3 are defined, and color 0 (the background color) is selectable. Table 3.2 describes the `_MRES4COLOR` palettes and colors.

The color 0 can be set to any of the 16 colors in the default 16-color palette. The default for color 0 is black. You can use the `_setbkcolor` function to select the background color. The following syntax is used for the `_setbkcolor` function:

```
long far _setbkcolor (long color);

long color;                 Desired color
```

Table 3.2. *Palettes in _MRES4COLOR mode.*

	Pixel value			
Palette number	**Color 0**	**Color 1**	**Color 2**	**Color 3**
0	Selectable	Green	Red	Brown
1	Selectable	Cyan	Magenta	Light gray
2	Selectable	Light green	Light red	Yellow
3	Selectable	Light cyan	Light magenta	White

The **_MRESNOCOLOR** function can be used with color monitors and monochrome monitors that support shades of gray. Tables 3.3 and 3.4 show the available colors and palettes when using a color CGA or EGA monitor. Two palettes are available when you use the **_MRESNOCOLOR** mode with CGA graphics hardware. Four palettes are available when you use the **_MRESNOCOLOR** mode with EGA hardware.

Table 3.3. *CGA palettes in _MRESNOCOLOR mode.*

	Pixel value			
Palette number	**Color 0**	**Color 1**	**Color 2**	**Color 3**
0	Selectable	Blue	Red	Light grey
1	Selectable	Light blue	Light red	White

Table 3.4. *EGA palettes in _MRESNOCOLOR mode.*

	Pixel value			
Palette number	**Color 0**	**Color 1**	**Color 2**	**Color 3**
0	Selectable	Green	Red	Light gray
1	Selectable	Light green	Light red	Yellow
2	Selectable	Light cyan	Light red	Yellow
3	Selectable	Light green	Light red	Yellow

You use the **_selectpalette** function to select the proper palette when in the CGA modes. The syntax of the **_selectpalette** function follows:

```
short far _selectpalette (short palette_number);
short palette_number;          Desired palette
```

When in the EGA and VGA 16-color modes, the default palette is the same as in table 3.5. The colors, however, can be redefined with the `_remapallpalette` and `_remappalette` functions. The `_remapallpalette` function redefines the entire palette; the `_remappalette` function redefines only one color. The syntax for each function follows:

```
short_far _remapallpallete (long_far *color_array);
long_far *color_array;          Array of colors

Long_far _remappalette (short pixel_value, long color);
short pixel_value;              Pixel value
long color;                     Color
```

Table 3.5. *Default color palette for 16-color modes.*

Pixel value	Color
0	Black
1	Blue
2	Green
3	Cyan
4	Red
5	Magenta
6	Brown
7	White
8	Dark gray
9	Light blue
10	Light green
11	Light cyan
12	Light red
13	Light magenta
14	Yellow
15	Bright white

The `_setcolor` function is used in all graphics modes to select the current color from the current palette. The default color is always the highest numbered color in the palette. The syntax for the `_setcolor` function follows:

```
short far _setcolor (short color);
short color;                    Desired color
```

Chapter 9 provides more information on the `_setbkcolor`, `_selectpalette`, `_setcolor`, `_remapallpalette`, and `_remappalette` functions.

Viewports and Clipping Regions

A viewport is a rectangular region of the screen that all subsequent graphics output will be limited to. The output of any graphics call that draws outside the viewport's border will be clipped. The Microsoft graphics library provides the _setviewport function to create viewports. The _setviewport function has the following syntax:

```
void_far _setviewport (short x1, short y1, short x2,
               short y2);
short x1, y1;    Upper left corner (physical coordinates)
short x2, y2;    Lower right corner (physical coordinates)
```

The x1 and y1 arguments identify the upper left corner of the viewport; the x2 and y2 arguments identify the lower right corner of the viewport. The _setviewport function places the view origin at the upper left corner of the viewport (at x1,y1). The viewport is very similar to the clipping region, which is discussed next. The main difference is that the viewport alters the position of the view origin, but the clipping region does not. See figure 3.67.

Fig. 3.67. The _setviewport function.

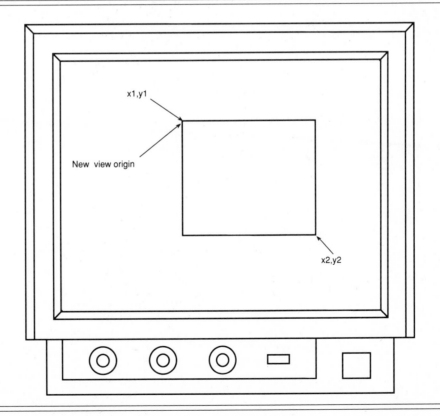

The viewport is useful for limiting output to a particular area of the screen while resetting the logical origin. Listing 3.8 demonstrates the effects of the _setviewport function. Figure 3.68 is a printout of the screen produced by this function.

Listing 3.8.   Viewport example.

```c
#include <stdio.h>
#include <graph.h>


void main ()
{

 /* Initialization */

_setvideomode (_ERESCOLOR);
_setbkcolor (_BLUE);
_rectangle (_GBORDER,0,0,639,349);

     /* Draw ellipse with logical origin 100,100 */

_setlogorg (100,100);
_ellipse (_GBORDER,-50,-50,50,50);

  /* Set viewport at 200,100 - 450,250 */
  /* Sets logical origin at 200,100 */

_setviewport (200,100,450,250);

   /* Outline viewport */

_rectangle (_GBORDER,0,0,250,150);

   /* Draw ellipse like above */
   /* Result is 1/4 ellipse */

_ellipse (_GBORDER,-50,-50,50,50);

    /* Delay and exit */

getch ();
_setvideomode (_DEFAULTMODE);
}
```

Fig. 3.68. Example output from listing 3.8.

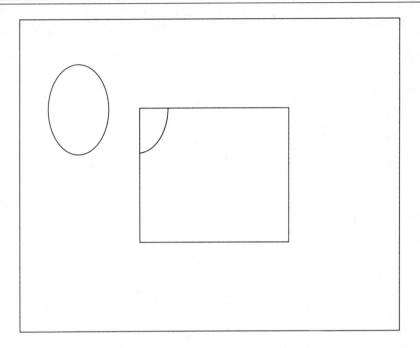

A clipping region is a rectangular section of the screen that graphics output is limited to. The output of any graphics call that draws outside this region is clipped at the border of the clipping region. The clipping region is like the viewport except that the view origin is not replaced. The Microsoft graphics library provides the `_setcliprgn` function for establishing a clipping region. The syntax for the `_setcliprgn` function follows:

```
void _far _setcliprgn (short x1, short y1, short x2,
          short y2);
short x1, y1;       Upper left corner (physical)
short x2, y2;       Lower right corner (physical)
```

Figure 3.69 will help you understand the proper use and function of a clipping region.

The clipping region is useful for restricting output to a specified area of the screen without resetting the location of the view origin. Listing 3.9 demonstrates the use of the `_setcliprgn` function. Figure 3.70 is a printout of the screen produced by this function.

Chapter 9 provides additional information on the `_setviewport` and `_setcliprgn` functions.

Fig. 3.69. The _setcliprgn function.

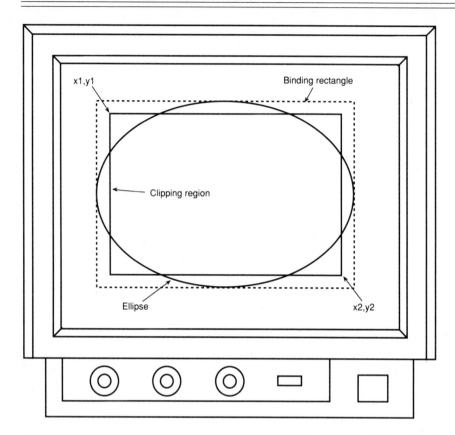

Listing 3.9. Clipping region example.

```
#include <stdio.h>
#include <graph.h>

void main ()
{
  /* Initialization */
_setvideomode (_ERESCOLOR);
_setbkcolor (_RED);
_rectangle (_GBORDER,0,0,639,349);
  /* Draw an unclipped ellipse */
```

```
      /* View origin is at the default (0,0) */
_ellipse (_GBORDER, 50,50,100,100);
   /* Create a clipping region at
          200,100 - 450,250          */
_setcliprgn (200,100,450,250);
   /* Place border on clipping region */
_rectangle (_GBORDER,200,100,450,250);
   /* Draw a clipped ellipse centered
        on the upper left corner
        of the region              */
_ellipse (_GBORDER,150,50,250,150);

   /* Delay and exit */
getch ();
_setvideomode (_DEFAULTMODE);
}
```

Fig. 3.70.   Example output from listing 3.9.

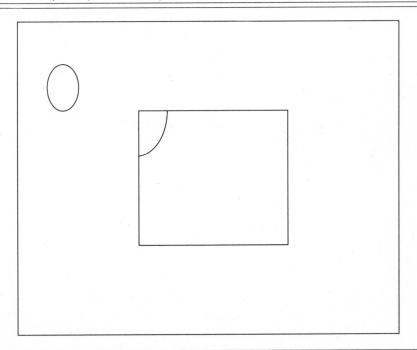

4

Text and Graphics

This chapter explains the use of text with graphics. The Microsoft graphics library provides several ways in which text can conveniently be used while in graphics modes. It is essential that the graphics programmer understand the behavior of text output with graphics; otherwise, the results are usually less than desirable. The following Microsoft graphics and text functions are explained in this chapter:

```
_gettextposition          _setcolor
_outgtext                  _setgtextvector
_outmem                    _settextcolor
_outtext                   _settextposition
_pg_hlabelchart            _settextwindow
_pg_vlabelchart            _setfont
_registerfonts             _wrapon
```

Text Types

Three types of text are used with graphics in the Microsoft environment: the standard character set provided in ROM BIOS (referred to as text) for use with both graphics and text modes, loadable fonts provided by Microsoft (referred to as font text) for use in only graphics modes, and raster fonts provided by Microsoft for use with the presentation graphics package. Raster fonts are for use only in graphics modes.

The standard character set uses the text cursor to mark the starting point of the text. (The text cursor is described in the next section.) The _outtext and _outmem functions display text with the standard character set. This character set is defined internally by the video mode in use.

Font text is provided for use in graphics modes. After the programmer selects a font, it is registered, set, and then displayed. (This procedure is described later in the chapter, in the "Use of Font Text in Graphics" section. Font text uses the current position of the graphics cursor as a starting point for output. The _outgtext function displays font text.

Raster fonts are used when operating in the presentation graphics environment. All text in the presentation graphics environment (including titles, subtitles, and so on) is displayed using raster fonts. The _pg_hlabelchart and _pg_vlabelchart functions display text using the raster fonts.

Text Cursor

The text cursor marks the starting position of subsequent text output using the standard character set, and is similar to the graphics cursor. The position of the text cursor, like the graphics cursor, is maintained internally by the graphics routines and can be controlled by the programmer. The main difference between these cursors is that the graphics cursor is based on the coordinate system, and the text cursor is based on the number of rows and columns of text available on the screen. For example, in _MRES4COLOR video mode, the coordinate system is 320 pixels wide by 200 pixels deep. This coordinate system is used only for graphical output. The default character size in this mode limits the screen to 40 characters per row and 25 characters per column. Therefore, the cursor position is set relative to this 40-by-25 grid. See figure 4.1. Note that the upper left corner is 1,1 (row 1, column 1). This differs from the graphics coordinate system, in which the upper left corner corresponds to 0,0 (x=0, y=0).

The programmer can control the position of the graphics cursor with the _settextposition function. The following syntax is used for this function:

```
struct rccoord _far _settextposition (short row, short column);
short row, column;                New position of cursor
```

The _settextposition function is extremely useful because the location of the text cursor marks the starting location of all subsequent text output initiated by such functions as _outtext, _outmem, and printf.

You can retrieve the current position of the graphics cursor with the _gettextposition function. The following syntax is used with this function:

```
struct rccoord _far _gettextposition(void);
```

The current row and column position of the text cursor is returned in the rccoord structure. The _gettextposition function is useful, for example, when a string of text must be placed relative to another string or when the text cursor must be set to its original position after text has been output.

Whenever text is output to the screen, the position of the text cursor is updated internally by the graphics routines. The position of the text cursor is generally set to the screen location next to the last character printed. For example, if the last character was written at row 20, column 10, the text cursor would be set to row 20, column 11. But when text extends past the right side of the screen,

Fig. 4.1. Text mode coordinates.

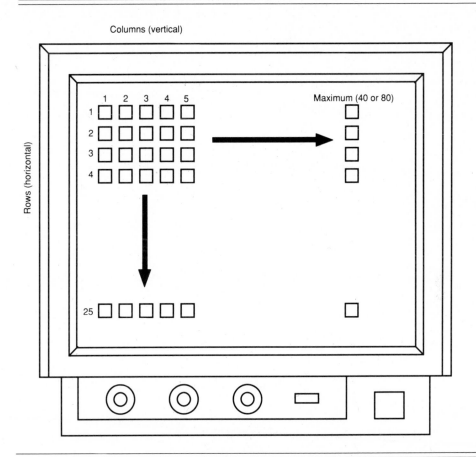

the cursor position can be updated in either of two ways. The first method, the default setting, moves the cursor position to the first column of the next row. The second method truncates the line to the last character position at the end of the current row. The programmer can use the _wrapon function to control the behavior of text when it reaches the right side of the screen. The syntax of the _wrapon function follows:

```
short _far _wrapon(short wrapflag);
short wrapflag;                Turn wrap feature on/off
```

The wrapflag argument is used to indicate the behavior of the text when it reaches the right edge of the screen. The _GWRAPON wrapflag argument turns the text wrapping feature on; text that extends past the right edge of the screen is positioned on the next row beginning at the first column. The _GWRAPOFF wrapflag argument truncates text to the farthest right position

99

of the current row. Each character that extends beyond the column limitation of the current row is written, in turn, on the last column of the current row.

Chapter 9 provides additional information on the use of the _settextposition, _gettextposition, and _wrapon functions.

Text in Graphics Mode

Text, using the standard character set, can be output to the screen in graphics modes with the _outtext and _outmem functions. These functions have limited capabilities but, fortunately, can produce both formatted (when used with the sprintf function) and unformatted text output in graphics modes. The _outtext and _outmem functions use the following syntax:

```
void _far _outtext (unsigned char _far *buffer);
unsigned char _far *buffer;    Text to display

void _far _outmem(unsigned char _far *buffer, short length);
unsigned char _far *buffer;    Text to display
short length;                  Number of characters to display
```

The _outtext function displays a null-terminated C string beginning at the current text position. The current text color is used (see the "Text Colors" section for additional information). After the text is output to the screen, the position of the text cursor is updated, as described in the "Text Cursor" section.

The _outmem function is used like the _outtext function but it has a length argument. The length argument is used to specify the number of characters in the character string to output. For example, if the character string is 80 characters long, a length argument of 40 would result in the display of the first half of the character string.

The _outtext and _outmem functions display only unformatted text. The following call demonstrates the ease by which unformatted text can be placed on the screen:

```
_outtext ("This line demonstrates unformatted text");
```

This line of text would be placed, as is, on the screen beginning at the current position of the text cursor. The capability to print only unformatted text is often inadequate for many applications. Fortunately, you can output formatted text with the _outtext and _outmem functions by first preparing an output buffer with the sprintf function, then using the _outtext or _outmem function to display the contents of the buffer.

Listing 4.1 illustrates the method by which a formatted text buffer prepared by the sprintf function can be output with the _outtext function.

Listing 4.1. · Formatted text in graphics modes.

```
#include <stdio.h>
#include <graph.h>

void main ()
{
char buffer [40];
int ch;

_setvideomode (_MRES4COLOR);
_settextposition (5,10);
_outtext ("Press Any Key");
ch = getch ();

sprintf (buffer, "ASCII Value of Key: %d", ch);
_settextposition (10,10);
_outtext (buffer);

_settextposition (20,10);
_outtext ("Press Any Key to Exit");
getch ();
_setvideomode (_DEFAULTMODE);
}
```

Chapter 9 provides additional information on the **_outtext** and **_outmem** functions.

Use of Font Text in Graphics

Microsoft provides several fonts for displaying text while in graphics mode. These fonts are shown in table 4.1.

Table 4.1. *Font files.*

File name	Typeface	Size in pixels	Mapping	Spacing
COURB.FON	Courier	10 x 8, 12 x 9, 15 x 12	Bit	Fixed
HELVB.FON	Helvetica	10 x 5, 12 x 7, 15 x 8, 18 x 9, 22 x 12, 28 x 16	Bit	Proportional
MODERN.FON	Modern	Scaled	Vector	Proportional
ROMAN.FON	Roman	Scaled		
SCRIPT.FON	Script	Scaled	Vector	Proportional
TMSRB.FON	Times Roman	10 x 5, 12 x 6, 15 x 8, 16 x 9 20 x 12, 26 x 16	Bit	Proportional

To use the font text, the font must be registered and set as follows:

1. Register the fonts to be used.

2. Set the current font.

3. Display the font text.

In step 1, registering the fonts, you use the _registerfonts function to read the specified font files (.FON) and load the font information into memory. The specified font files (.FON) are read and the font information loaded into memory when the _registerfonts function is called. The following syntax is used with the _registerfonts function:

```
short _far _registerfonts (unsigned char _far *path);
unsigned char _far *path;    Path to find .FON files
```

In step 2, you use the _setfont function to select one of the registered fonts. The font will be made current, that is, used for all subsequent font text output. The following syntax is used with the _setfont function:

```
short _far _setfont (unsigned char _far *options);
unsigned char _far *options;  Characteristics of font
```

For step 3, displaying the font text, you first use the _moveto function to mark the starting position of the font text. The position identified by the _moveto function is the top left corner of the first character in the string. Next, you use the _outgtext function to display the font text. The font text is drawn using the current color and text vector orientation. The possible values for the text vector orientation, as set by the _setgtextvector function, are shown in table 4.2.

Table 4.2. *Vector orientation.*

Values of x,y	Orientation
1,0	Horizontal text (default)
0,1	Rotated 90 degrees counterclockwise
-1,0	Rotated 180 degrees counterclockwise
0,-1	Rotated 270 degrees counterclockwise

The following syntax is used with the _outgtext function:

```
void _far _outgtext (unsigned char _far *text);
unsigned char _far *text;        Text to display
```

The _outgtext function, like the _outtext and _outmem functions, displays only unformatted text. You can use the sprintf function, however, to format a text buffer prior to displaying it.

Chapter 9 provides additional information on the _outgtext, _registerfonts, _setfont, and _setgtextvector functions.

Text Colors

When text is output using the standard character set, the current text color is used. The colors listed in table 4.3 are available in text mode. In graphics mode, however, the colors are limited to those in the current palette.

Table 4.3. *Predefined text colors.*

Pixel value for normal text	Pixel value for blinking text	Text color
0	16	Black
1	17	Blue
2	18	Green
3	19	Cyan
4	20	Red
5	21	Magenta
6	22	Brown
7	23	White
8	24	Dark gray
9	25	Light blue
10	26	Light green
11	27	Light cyan
12	28	Light red
13	29	Light magenta
14	30	Yellow
15	31	Bright white

You use the _settextcolor function to designate the text color. The following syntax is used with this function:

```
short _far _settextcolor (short color);
short color;                    Desired text color
```

As mentioned, the text color in graphics mode is limited to the colors available in the current palette. When using font text, the current color is used as the text color. Therefore, the _setcolor function is used to select the color of font text.

The color of the raster font output, as used with the presentation graphics package, is controlled by the palette used for the chart environment. Therefore, you use the _pg_getpalette and _pg_setpalette functions to retrieve and set the palette, and thus the text color, of the presentation graphics environment.

Chapter 9 provides additional information on the _settextcolor, _setcolor, _pg_setpalette, and _pg_getpalette, functions.

Creating a Character Set

The standard character sets provided by the ROM Video Services, combined with the fonts provided by Microsoft, are sufficient for most simple text input and output. For advanced graphics text output (such as title screens), however, it is often necessary to create a character set. If only a few characters will be printed, it may not be worth the effort to create a whole set of characters. But if you plan to do a lot of graphics programming, creating a character set that is flexible enough for multicolor text, scaled text, and shadowed text will save you a lot of time in the long run. This section describes how the character set in the upcoming "Character Examples" section was derived. This character set is simple in design and therefore very flexible.

The first step in developing a character set is to determine the use of the character set. For small-sized text, characters defined by single lines are sufficient. For large text output (such as the character set in this chapter), a skeleton (outlined) character is necessary.

After you define the use of the character set, you must determine the minimum character size. The character set in this chapter is designed for an EGA monitor (it will work on any monitor, but the size was designed with the EGA aspect ratio in mind) and a minimum character size of 15-by-15 pixels.

Next, you define the character type. The character set in this chapter is not based on any commercial fonts; it was created using 45 degree angles and vertical and horizontal lines. Many arts and crafts stores or business supply stores carry rub-on letters that you can use as models of the character set. Note that characters sets with curves are harder to create than simpler straight-line characters.

The next step is to transfer the selected character set onto a grid of the minimum character size. For the character set in this chapter, the minimum character size is 15 by 15.

Finally, you write code to create the characters. The best way to do this is to divide each character into simple curves and lines that can be described in relation to the upper left corner of the grid. For example, using a minimum character size of 15 x 15, the lower right corner of the grid is described by x + 14, y + 14. By carefully describing the character, it is possible to create a character set that can be scaled to any size. One way to describe a character is shown in figure 4.2 and the following code.

```
void c (void)
{    _moveto (x+fraction[2],y);
     _lineto (x+fraction[12],y);
     _lineto (x+fraction[14],y+fraction[2]);
     _lineto (x+fraction[14],y+fraction[5]);
     _lineto (x+fraction[11],y+fraction[5]);
     _lineto (x+fraction[11],y+fraction[4]);
     _lineto (x+fraction[10],y+fraction[3]);
     _lineto (x+fraction[4],y+fraction[3]);
     _lineto (x+fraction[3],y+fraction[4]);
     _lineto (x+fraction[3],y+fraction[10]);
     _lineto (x+fraction[4],y+fraction[11]);
     _lineto (x+fraction[10],y+fraction[11]);
```

```
    _lineto (x+fraction[11],y+fraction[10]);
    _lineto (x+fraction[11],y+fraction[9]);
    _lineto (x+fraction[14],y+fraction[9]);
    _lineto (x+fraction[14],y+fraction[12]);
    _lineto (x+fraction[12],y+fraction[14]);
    _lineto (x+fraction[2],y+fraction[14]);
    _lineto (x,y+fraction[12]);
    _lineto (x,y+fraction[2]);
    _lineto (x+fraction[2],y);
}
```

Fig. 4.2. Model character.

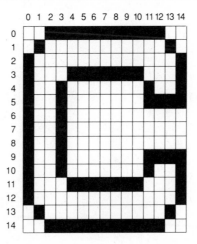

This code is made scalable by the method in which the character is defined. The beginning and ending points of each line are described in relation to a fraction of the overall size of the grid. The following f o r loop (in listing 4.2) defines the components of an array called f r a c t i o n, which contains all the possible starting and stopping x and y values on the grid. The s c a l e argument identifies the size of the grid (15 indicates a 15 x 15 grid, 100 would indicate a 100 x 100 grid, and so on). The f a c t o r argument is similar to a counter for the fifteen arguments in the array. In a minimum-sized character, with scale = 15, the fifteen components in the array would be 0, 1, 2, 3, 4, 5, 6, 7, 8, 9, 10, 11, 12, 13, and 14. Therefore, the call:

```
    _lineto (x, y+fraction[14]);
```

would draw a line from x to y + (14 • scale)/15. By describing the character in this manner, any size text is possible (down to the minimum size).

Listing 4.2. Outlined character example.

```c
#include <graph.h>
#include <stdio.h>
#include <stdlib.h>
#include <math.h>
int x,y;
div_t result;
int fraction [15];
int scale;
int factor;
int i;

void main ()
{


_setvideomode (_ERESCOLOR);
_setbkcolor (_BLUE);
_rectangle (_GBORDER,0,0,639,349);

scale = 15;
factor = 0;
x = 20;
y = 20;

for (i=0; i<15; i=i+1)
      {
      result = div ((factor*scale),15);
      fraction [i] = result.quot;
      factor = factor + 1;
      }

c ();

getch ();
_setvideomode (_DEFAULTMODE);
}
```

The f o r loop in listing 4.2 needs to be implemented only once in the program, assuming that the scale of the text remains the same. If the scale is changed, the array must be redefined and the for loop must be reexecuted. There is no need to change the character's code when the scale changes.

Unfilled Characters

If the characters have been created in a manner similar to that described in the preceding section, it is easy to generate unfilled characters. By using the for loop presented in the preceding section, setting a scaling factor, and identifying the upper left corner of the rectangular region in which the character will be drawn (the x and y variables), an outlined, unfilled character of virtually any size can be drawn anywhere on the screen. Listing 4.3 demonstrates the method by which an *A* can be placed on the screen with a scale of 105 (105-by-105 pixels). You can use the _setcolor function prior to calling the a ( ) ; function to specify the color of the character. Figure 4.3 shows the output from listing 4.3.

Listing 4.3.   Unfilled character example.

```
#include <graph.h>
#include <stdio.h>
#include <stdlib.h>
#include <math.h>

int x,y;
div_t result;
int fraction [15];
int scale;
int factor;
int i;

void main ()
{
scale = 105;
x=270;
y=125;
factor = 0;

_setvideomode (_ERESCOLOR);
_setbkcolor (_BLUE);
_rectangle (_GBORDER,0,0,639,349);

for (i=0; i<15; i=i+1)
        {
        result = div ((factor*scale),15);
        fraction [i] = result.quot;
```

Listing 4.3 *continues*

107

Listing 4.3. cont.   Unfilled character example.

```
            factor = factor + 1;
            }
    _setcolor (15);
    a ();
    getch();
    _setvideomode (_DEFAULTMODE);
    }
    void a (void)
    {

        _moveto (x+fraction[2],y);
        _lineto (x+fraction[12],y);
        _lineto (x+fraction[14],y+fraction[2]);
        _lineto (x+fraction[14],y+fraction[14]);
        _lineto (x+fraction[11],y+fraction[14]);
        _lineto (x+fraction[11],y+fraction[9]);
        _lineto (x+fraction[3],y+fraction[9]);
        _lineto (x+fraction[3],y+fraction[14]);
        _lineto (x,y+fraction[14]);
        _lineto (x,y+fraction[2]);
        _lineto (x+fraction[2],y);
        _moveto (x+fraction[4],y+fraction[3]);
        _lineto (x+fraction[10],y+fraction[3]);
        _lineto (x+fraction[11],y+fraction[4]);
        _lineto (x+fraction[11],y+fraction[6]);
        _lineto (x+fraction[3],y+fraction[6]);
        _lineto (x+fraction[3],y+fraction[4]);
        _lineto (x+fraction[4],y+fraction[3]);
    }
```

Filled Characters

Creating filled characters is a simple extension of creating unfilled characters, but you must add a call to the _floodfill function. The _floodfill function requires a starting point and the color of the character's border. The starting point should be defined in relation to the dimensions of the character's overall size, just like the character's border was defined. The border color, in this example, is entered manually but could easily be made a global or local parameter. Listing 4.4 creates a character that is 105-by-105 pixels in size and filled with the same color as the border. Figure 4.4 shows the output of the program.

Fig. 4.3. Example output from listing 4.3.

Listing 4.4. Filled character example.

```
#include <graph.h>
#include <stdio.h>
#include <stdlib.h>
#include <math.h>

int x,y;
div_t result;
int fraction [15];
int scale;
int factor;
int i;

void main ()
{
scale = 105;
x=270;
```

Listing 4.4 *continues*

Listing 4.4. cont. Filled character example.

```
y=125;
factor = 0;

_setvideomode (_ERESCOLOR);
_setbkcolor (_BLUE);
_rectangle (_GBORDER,0,0,639,349);

for (i=0; i<15; i=i+1)
{
result = div ((factor*scale),15);
fraction [i] = result.quot;
factor = factor + 1;
}
_setcolor (15);
a ();
_floodfill (x+fraction[3],y+fraction[1],15);
getch ();
_setvideomode (_DEFAULTMODE);
}
void a (void)
{
_moveto (x+fraction[2],y);
_lineto (x+fraction[12],y);
_lineto (x+fraction[14],y+fraction[2]);
_lineto (x+fraction[14],y+fraction[14]);
_lineto (x+fraction[11],y+fraction[14]);
_lineto (x+fraction[11],y+fraction[9]);
_lineto (x+fraction[3],y+fraction[9]);
_lineto (x+fraction[3],y+fraction[14]);
_lineto (x,y+fraction[14]);
_lineto (x,y+fraction[2]);
_lineto (x+fraction[2],y);
_moveto (x+fraction[4],y+fraction[3]);
_lineto (x+fraction[10],y+fraction[3]);
_lineto (x+fraction[11],y+fraction[4]);
_lineto (x+fraction[11],y+fraction[6]);
_lineto (x+fraction[3],y+fraction[6]);
_lineto (x+fraction[3],y+fraction[4]);
_lineto (x+fraction[4],y+fraction[3]);
 }
```

Fig. 4.4. Example output from listing 4.4.

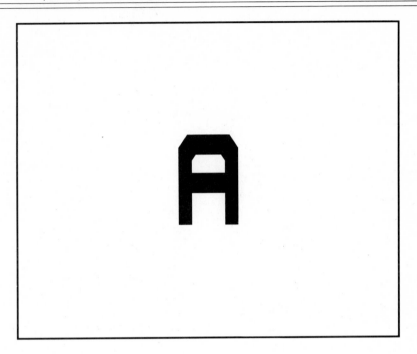

Shaded Characters

One effect that you can easily add to the previous capabilities is shading the inside of the character. The previous method used a solid fill pattern to create a filled character. A more flexible method, shown in listing 4.5, is to specify a fill pattern. The "Fill Patterns" section in Chapter 3 provides several fill patterns that you can use. Figure 4.5 uses the `_setfillmask` function to specify a 37.5% fill pattern.

Listing 4.5. Shaded character example.

```
#include <graph.h>
#include <stdio.h>
#include <stdlib.h>
#include <math.h>

int x,y;
div_t result;
int fraction [15];
```

Listing 4.5 *continues*

Listing 4.5. cont. Shaded character example.

```
int scale;
int factor;
int i;

void main ()
{


scale = 105;
x=270;
y=125;
factor = 0;

_setvideomode (_ERESCOLOR);
_setbkcolor (_BLUE);
_rectangle (_GBORDER,0,0,639,349);
for (i=0; i<15; i=i+1)
     {
     result = div ((factor*scale),15);
     fraction [i] = result.quot;
     factor = factor + 1;
     }
a ();
_setfillmask ("\xAA\x44\xAA\x11\xAA\x44\xAA\x11");
_floodfill (x+fraction[3],y+fraction[1],15);
getch();
_setvideomode (_DEFAULTMODE);
}
void a (void)
{

_moveto (x+fraction[2],y);
_lineto (x+fraction[12],y);
_lineto (x+fraction[14],y+fraction[2]);
_lineto (x+fraction[14],y+fraction[14]);
_lineto (x+fraction[11],y+fraction[14]);
_lineto (x+fraction[11],y+fraction[9]);
_lineto (x+fraction[3],y+fraction[9]);
_lineto (x+fraction[3],y+fraction[14]);
_lineto (x,y+fraction[14]);
_lineto (x,y+fraction[2]);
_lineto (x+fraction[2],y);
_moveto (x+fraction[4],y+fraction[3]);
```

```
_lineto (x+fraction[10],y+fraction[3]);
_lineto (x+fraction[11],y+fraction[4]);
_lineto (x+fraction[11],y+fraction[6]);
_lineto (x+fraction[3],y+fraction[6]);
_lineto (x+fraction[3],y+fraction[4]);
_lineto (x+fraction[4],y+fraction[3]);

    }
```

Fig. 4.5. Example output from listing 4.5.

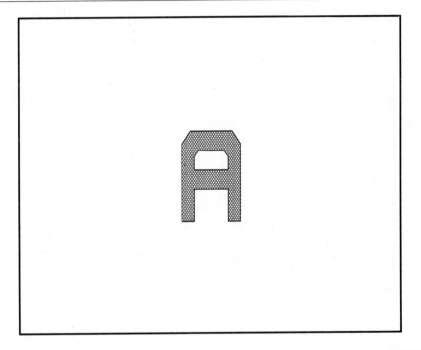

Multicolored Characters

The previous effects of shading and filling the character can be made more spectacular by adding variations of border and fill colors. The combination of border and fill colors adds to the overall visual effects of the text. Creating multicolored characters is a simple task; an extra call to the `_setcolor` function provides this capability. Listing 4.6 demonstrates how to generate a multicolored character. The output of this listing is shown in figure 4.6.

Listing 4.6.   Multicolored character example.

```
#include <graph.h>
#include <stdio.h>
#include <stdlib.h>
#include <math.h>

int x,y;
div_t result;
int fraction [15];
int scale;
int factor;
int i;

void main ()
{
scale = 105;
x=270;
y=125;
factor = 0;

_setvideomode (_ERESCOLOR);
_setbkcolor (_BLUE);
_rectangle (_GBORDER,0,0,639,349);

for (i=0; i<15; i=i+1)
     {
     result = div ((factor*scale),15);
     fraction [i] = result.quot;
     factor = factor + 1;
     }

_setcolor (15);
a ();
_setcolor (4);
_floodfill (x+fraction[3],y+fraction[1],15);

getch();
_setvideomode (_DEFAULTMODE);
}

void a (void)
{
     _moveto (x+fraction[2],y);
```

```
    _lineto (x+fraction[12],y);
    _lineto (x+fraction[14],y+fraction[2]);
    _lineto (x+fraction[14],y+fraction[14]);
    _lineto (x+fraction[11],y+fraction[14]);
    _lineto (x+fraction[11],y+fraction[9]);
    _lineto (x+fraction[3],y+fraction[9]);
    _lineto (x+fraction[3],y+fraction[14]);
    _lineto (x,y+fraction[14]);
    _lineto (x,y+fraction[2]);
    _lineto (x+fraction[2],y);
    _moveto (x+fraction[4],y+fraction[3]);
    _lineto (x+fraction[10],y+fraction[3]);
    _lineto (x+fraction[11],y+fraction[4]);
    _lineto (x+fraction[11],y+fraction[6]);
    _lineto (x+fraction[3],y+fraction[6]);
    _lineto (x+fraction[3],y+fraction[4]);
    _lineto (x+fraction[4],y+fraction[3]);
}
```

Fig. 4.6. Example output from listing 4.6.

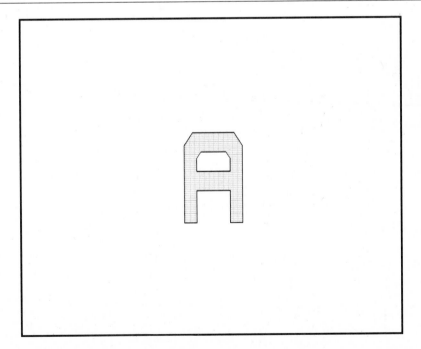

Shadowed Characters

Another effect that you can use with filled characters is to shadow the character. The best effects come from a dark-colored, solid-filled shadow character with a light-colored, solid-filled top character. Other combinations of colors and fill patterns are available, but with non-solid fill patterns, especially on the top character, the multicolored background (due to background and shadow letter colors) shows through. Best results are obtained with solid fills. Listing 4.7 demonstrates the shadowing effect. The output of this listing is shown in figure 4.7.

Listing 4.7.   Shadowed character example.

```
#include <graph.h>
#include <stdio.h>
#include <stdlib.h>
#include <math.h>

int x,y;
div_t result;
int fraction [15];
int scale;
int factor;
int i;

void main ()
{
scale = 105;
factor = 0;

_setvideomode (_ERESCOLOR);
_setbkcolor (_BLUE);
_rectangle (_GBORDER,0,0,639,349);
for (i=0; i<15; i=i+1)
     {
     result = div ((factor*scale),15);
     fraction [i] = result.quot;
     factor = factor + 1;
     }

     /* Create shadow */

x=280;
y=130;
_setcolor (15);
a();
```

```
_floodfill (x+fraction[3],y+fraction[1],15);

    /* Create top character */
x=270;
y=125;

_setcolor (4);
a ();
_floodfill (x+fraction[3],y+fraction[1],4);
getch();
_setvideomode (_DEFAULTMODE);
}

void a  (void)
{      _moveto (x+fraction[2],y);
       _lineto (x+fraction[12],y);
       _lineto (x+fraction[14],y+fraction[2]);
       _lineto (x+fraction[14],y+fraction[14]);
       _lineto (x+fraction[11],y+fraction[14]);
       _lineto (x+fraction[11],y+fraction[9]);
       _lineto (x+fraction[3],y+fraction[9]);
       _lineto (x+fraction[3],y+fraction[14]);
       _lineto (x,y+fraction[14]);
       _lineto (x,y+fraction[2]);
       _lineto (x+fraction[2],y);
       _moveto (x+fraction[4],y+fraction[3]);
       _lineto (x+fraction[10],y+fraction[3]);
       _lineto (x+fraction[11],y+fraction[4]);
       _lineto (x+fraction[11],y+fraction[6]);
       _lineto (x+fraction[3],y+fraction[6]);
       _lineto (x+fraction[3],y+fraction[4]);
       _lineto (x+fraction[4],y+fraction[3]);
   }
```

Character Examples

This section contains the functions for all uppercase letters. Each listing is accompanied by a figure showing the model character used to develop the function. By following the techniques described in the previous section, you can use these characters in a variety of ways. These characters can be used in any application, and should give you an idea of the power of creating a scalable character set.

117

Fig. 4.7. Example output from listing 4.7.

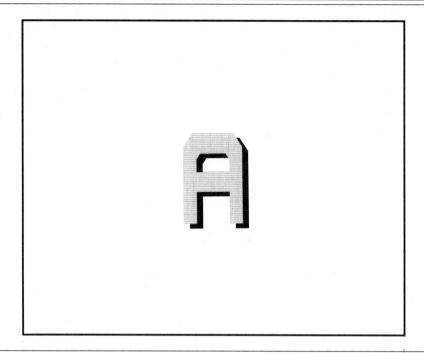

Listing 4.8. Function for A model.

```
void a  (void)
{
    _moveto (x+fraction[2],y);
    _lineto (x+fraction[12],y);
    _lineto (x+fraction[14],y+fraction[2]);
    _lineto (x+fraction[14],y+fraction[14]);
    _lineto (x+fraction[11],y+fraction[14]);
    _lineto (x+fraction[11],y+fraction[9]);
    _lineto (x+fraction[3],y+fraction[9]);
    _lineto (x+fraction[3],y+fraction[14]);
    _lineto (x,y+fraction[14]);
    _lineto (x,y+fraction[2]);
    _lineto (x+fraction[2],y);
    _moveto (x+fraction[4],y+fraction[3]);
    _lineto (x+fraction[10],y+fraction[3]);
    _lineto (x+fraction[11],y+fraction[4]);
    _lineto (x+fraction[11],y+fraction[6]);
```

```
    _lineto (x+fraction[3],y+fraction[6]);
    _lineto (x+fraction[3],y+fraction[4]);
    _lineto (x+fraction[4],y+fraction[3]);
}
```

Fig. 4.8. Character model for A.

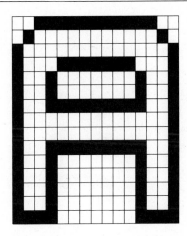

Listing 4.9. Function for B model.

```
void b (void)
{
    _moveto (x,y);
    _lineto (x+fraction[12],y);
    _lineto (x+fraction[14],y+fraction[2]);
    _lineto (x+fraction[14],y+fraction[5]);
    _lineto (x+fraction[12],y+fraction[7]);
    _lineto (x+fraction[14],y+fraction[9]);
    _lineto (x+fraction[14],y+fraction[12]);
    _lineto (x+fraction[12],y+fraction[14]);
    _lineto (x,y+fraction[14]);
    _lineto (x,y);
    _moveto (x+fraction[3],y+fraction[3]);
    _lineto (x+fraction[9],y+fraction[3]);
    _lineto (x+fraction[10],y+fraction[4]);
```

Listing 4.9 *continues*

119

Listing 4.9. cont.   Function for B model.

```
        _lineto (x+fraction[10],y+fraction[5]);
        _lineto (x+fraction[9],y+fraction[6]);
        _lineto (x+fraction[3],y+fraction[6]);
        _lineto (x+fraction[3],y+fraction[3]);
        _moveto (x+fraction[3],y+fraction[8]);
        _lineto (x+fraction[9],y+fraction[8]);
        _lineto (x+fraction[10],y+fraction[9]);
        _lineto (x+fraction[10],y+fraction[10]);
        _lineto (x+fraction[9],y+fraction[11]);
        _lineto (x+fraction[3],y+fraction[11]);
        _lineto (x+fraction[3],y+fraction[8]);
    }
```

Fig. 4.9.   Character model for B.

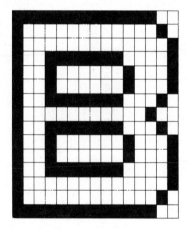

Listing 4.10.   Function for C model.

```
void c (void)
{
    _moveto (x+fraction[2],y);
    _lineto (x+fraction[12],y);
    _lineto (x+fraction[14],y+fraction[2]);
    _lineto (x+fraction[14],y+fraction[5]);
    _lineto (x+fraction[11],y+fraction[5]);
```

```
_lineto (x+fraction[11],y+fraction[4]);
_lineto (x+fraction[10],y+fraction[3]);
_lineto (x+fraction[4],y+fraction[3]);
_lineto (x+fraction[3],y+fraction[4]);
_lineto (x+fraction[3],y+fraction[10]);
_lineto (x+fraction[4],y+fraction[11]);
_lineto (x+fraction[10],y+fraction[11]);
_lineto (x+fraction[11],y+fraction[10]);
_lineto (x+fraction[11],y+fraction[9]);
_lineto (x+fraction[14],y+fraction[9]);
_lineto (x+fraction[14],y+fraction[12]);
_lineto (x+fraction[12],y+fraction[14]);
_lineto (x+fraction[2],y+fraction[14]);
_lineto (x,y+fraction[12]);
_lineto (x,y+fraction[2]);
_lineto (x+fraction[2],y);
}
```

Fig. 4.10. Character model for C.

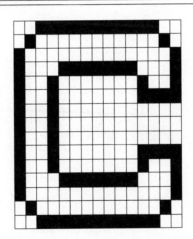

Listing 4.11. Function for D model.

```
void d (void)
{
    _moveto (x,y);
    _lineto (x+fraction[12],y);
    _lineto (x+fraction[14],y+fraction[2]);
    _lineto (x+fraction[14],y+fraction[12]);
    _lineto (x+fraction[12],y+fraction[14]);
    _lineto (x,y+fraction[14]);
    _lineto (x,y);
    _moveto (x+fraction[3],y+fraction[3]);
    _lineto (x+fraction[10],y+fraction[3]);
    _lineto (x+fraction[11],y+fraction[4]);
    _lineto (x+fraction[11],y+fraction[10]);
    _lineto (x+fraction[10],y+fraction[11]);
    _lineto (x+fraction[3],y+fraction[11]);
    _lineto (x+fraction[3],y+fraction[3]);

}
```

Fig. 4.11. Character model for D.

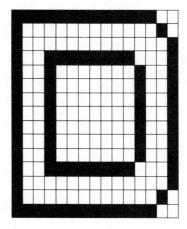

Listing 4.12. Function for E model.

```
void e (void)
{
```

```
        _moveto (x+fraction[2],y);
        _lineto (x+fraction[13],y);
        _lineto (x+fraction[14],y+fraction[1]);
        _lineto (x+fraction[14],y+fraction[2]);
        _lineto (x+fraction[13],y+fraction[3]);
        _lineto (x+fraction[4],y+fraction[3]);
        _lineto (x+fraction[3],y+fraction[4]);
        _lineto (x+fraction[3],y+fraction[5]);
        _lineto (x+fraction[4],y+fraction[6]);
        _lineto (x+fraction[9],y+fraction[6]);
        _lineto (x+fraction[9],y+fraction[8]);
        _lineto (x+fraction[4],y+fraction[8]);
        _lineto (x+fraction[3],y+fraction[9]);
        _lineto (x+fraction[3],y+fraction[10]);
        _lineto (x+fraction[4],y+fraction[11]);
        _lineto (x+fraction[13],y+fraction[11]);
        _lineto (x+fraction[14],y+fraction[12]);
        _lineto (x+fraction[14],y+fraction[13]);
        _lineto (x+fraction[13],y+fraction[14]);
        _lineto (x+fraction[2],y+fraction[14]);
        _lineto (x,y+fraction[12]);
        _lineto (x,y+fraction[2]);
        _lineto (x+fraction[2],y);
    }
```

Fig. 4.12. Character model for E.

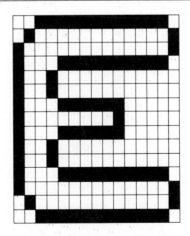

Listing 4.13. Function for F model.

```
void f (void)
{
    _moveto (x+fraction[2],y);
    _lineto (x+fraction[13],y);
    _lineto (x+fraction[14],y+fraction[1]);
    _lineto (x+fraction[14],y+fraction[2]);
    _lineto (x+fraction[13],y+fraction[3]);
    _lineto (x+fraction[4],y+fraction[3]);
    _lineto (x+fraction[3],y+fraction[4]);
    _lineto (x+fraction[3],y+fraction[6]);
    _lineto (x+fraction[9],y+fraction[6]);
    _lineto (x+fraction[9],y+fraction[8]);
    _lineto (x+fraction[3],y+fraction[8]);
    _lineto (x+fraction[3],y+fraction[14]);
    _lineto (x,y+fraction[14]);
    _lineto (x,y+fraction[2]);
    _lineto (x+fraction[2],y);
}
```

Fig. 4.13. Character model for F.

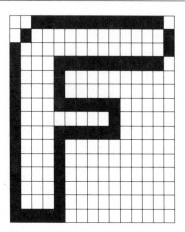

Listing 4.14. Function for G model.

```
void g (void)
{
    _moveto (x+fraction[2],y);
    _lineto (x+fraction[12],y);
    _lineto (x+fraction[14],y+fraction[2]);
    _lineto (x+fraction[14],y+fraction[4]);
    _lineto (x+fraction[11],y+fraction[4]);
    _lineto (x+fraction[11],y+fraction[3]);
    _lineto (x+fraction[4],y+fraction[3]);
    _lineto (x+fraction[3],y+fraction[4]);
    _lineto (x+fraction[3],y+fraction[10]);
    _lineto (x+fraction[4],y+fraction[11]);
    _lineto (x+fraction[11],y+fraction[11]);
    _lineto (x+fraction[11],y+fraction[9]);
    _lineto (x+fraction[7],y+fraction[9]);
    _lineto (x+fraction[7],y+fraction[7]);
    _lineto (x+fraction[13],y+fraction[7]);
    _lineto (x+fraction[14],y+fraction[8]);
    _lineto (x+fraction[14],y+fraction[12]);
    _lineto (x+fraction[12],y+fraction[14]);
    _lineto (x+fraction[2],y+fraction[14]);
    _lineto (x,y+fraction[12]);
    _lineto (x,y+fraction[2]);
    _lineto (x+fraction[2],y);
}
```

Fig. 4.14. Character model for G.

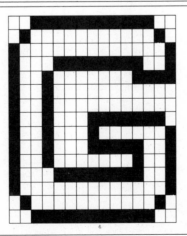

Listing 4.15. Function for H model.

```
void h (void)
{
    _moveto (x,y);
    _lineto (x+fraction[3],y);
    _lineto (x+fraction[3],y+fraction[6]);
    _lineto (x+fraction[11],y+fraction[6]);
    _lineto (x+fraction[11],y);
    _lineto (x+fraction[14],y);
    _lineto (x+fraction[14],y+fraction[14]);
    _lineto (x+fraction[11],y+fraction[14]);
    _lineto (x+fraction[11],y+fraction[8]);
    _lineto (x+fraction[3],y+fraction[8]);
    _lineto (x+fraction[3],y+fraction[14]);
    _lineto (x,y+fraction[14]);
    _lineto (x,y);
}
```

Fig. 4.15. Character model for H.

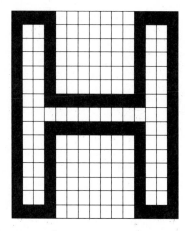

Listing 4.16. Function for I model.

```
void i (void)
{
    _moveto (x,y);
    _lineto (x+fraction[14],y);
    _lineto (x+fraction[14],y+fraction[3]);
    _lineto (x+fraction[9],y+fraction[3]);
    _lineto (x+fraction[9],y+fraction[11]);
    _lineto (x+fraction[14],y+fraction[11]);
    _lineto (x+fraction[14],y+fraction[14]);
    _lineto (x,y+fraction[14]);
    _lineto (x,y+fraction[11]);
    _lineto (x+fraction[5],y+fraction[11]);
    _lineto (x+fraction[5],y+fraction[3]);
    _lineto (x,y+fraction[3]);
    _lineto (x,y);
}
```

Fig. 4.16. Character model for I.

Listing 4.17. Function for J model.

```
void j (void)
{
    _moveto (x+fraction[10],y);
    _lineto (x+fraction[14],y);
    _lineto (x+fraction[14],y+fraction[12]);
    _lineto (x+fraction[12],y+fraction[14]);
    _lineto (x+fraction[2],y+fraction[14]);
    _lineto (x,y+fraction[12]);
    _lineto (x,y+fraction[9]);
    _lineto (x+fraction[3],y+fraction[9]);
    _lineto (x+fraction[3],y+fraction[10]);
    _lineto (x+fraction[4],y+fraction[11]);
    _lineto (x+fraction[9],y+fraction[11]);
    _lineto (x+fraction[10],y+fraction[10]);
    _lineto (x+fraction[10],y);
}
```

Fig. 4.17. Character model for J.

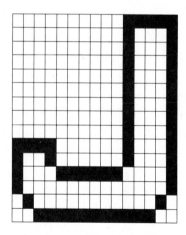

Listing 4.18. Function for K model.

```
void k (void)
{
    _moveto (x,y);
    _lineto (x+fraction[3],y);
    _lineto (x+fraction[3],y+fraction[5]);
    _lineto (x+fraction[6],y+fraction[5]);
    _lineto (x+fraction[11],y);
    _lineto (x+fraction[14],y);
    _lineto (x+fraction[14],y+fraction[1]);
    _lineto (x+fraction[8],y+fraction[7]);
    _lineto (x+fraction[14],y+fraction[13]);
    _lineto (x+fraction[14],y+fraction[14]);
    _lineto (x+fraction[11],y+fraction[14]);
    _lineto (x+fraction[6],y+fraction[9]);
    _lineto (x+fraction[3],y+fraction[9]);
    _lineto (x+fraction[3],y+fraction[14]);
    _lineto (x,y+fraction[14]);
    _lineto (x,y);
}
```

Fig. 4.18. Character model for K.

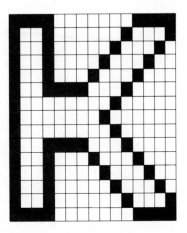

Listing 4.19. Function for L model.

```
void l (void)
{
    _moveto (x,y);
    _lineto (x+fraction[4],y);
    _lineto (x+fraction[4],y+fraction[11]);
    _lineto (x+fraction[14],y+fraction[11]);
    _lineto (x+fraction[14],y+fraction[14]);
    _lineto (x,y+fraction[14]);
    _lineto (x,y);
}
```

Fig. 4.19. Character model for L.

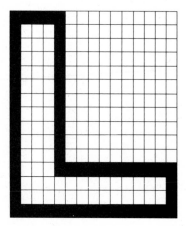

Listing 4.20. Function for M model.

```
void m (void)
{
    _moveto (x,y);
    _lineto (x+fraction[3],y);
    _lineto (x+fraction[7],y+fraction[4]);
    _lineto (x+fraction[11],y);
    _lineto (x+fraction[14],y);
    _lineto (x+fraction[14],y+fraction[14]);
    _lineto (x+fraction[11],y+fraction[14]);
```

```
        _lineto (x+fraction[11],y+fraction[5]);
        _lineto (x+fraction[7],y+fraction[9]);
        _lineto (x+fraction[3],y+fraction[5]);
        _lineto (x+fraction[3],y+fraction[14]);
        _lineto (x,y+fraction[14]);
        _lineto (x,y);
    }
```

Fig. 4.20. Character model for M.

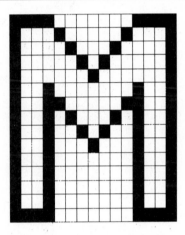

Listing 4.21. Function for N model.

```
void n (void)
{
    _moveto (x,y);
    _lineto (x+fraction[3],y);
    _lineto (x+fraction[11],y+fraction[8]);
    _lineto (x+fraction[11],y);
    _lineto (x+fraction[14],y);
    _lineto (x+fraction[14],y+fraction[14]);
    _lineto (x+fraction[12],y+fraction[14]);
    _lineto (x+fraction[3],y+fraction[5]);
    _lineto (x+fraction[3],y+fraction[14]);
    _lineto (x,y+fraction[14]);
    _lineto (x,y);
}
```

Fig. 4.21. Character model for N.

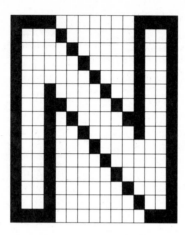

Listing 4.22. Function for O model.

```
void o (void)
{
    _moveto (x+fraction[2],y);
    _lineto (x+fraction[12],y);
    _lineto (x+fraction[14],y+fraction[2]);
    _lineto (x+fraction[14],y+fraction[12]);
    _lineto (x+fraction[12],y+fraction[14]);
    _lineto (x+fraction[2],y+fraction[14]);
    _lineto (x,y+fraction[12]);
    _lineto (x,y+fraction[2]);
    _lineto (x+fraction[2],y);
    _moveto (x+fraction[4],y+fraction[3]);
    _lineto (x+fraction[10],y+fraction[3]);
    _lineto (x+fraction[11],y+fraction[4]);
    _lineto (x+fraction[11],y+fraction[10]);
    _lineto (x+fraction[10],y+fraction[11]);
    _lineto (x+fraction[4],y+fraction[11]);
    _lineto (x+fraction[3],y+fraction[10]);
    _lineto (x+fraction[3],y+fraction[4]);
    _lineto (x+fraction[4],y+fraction[3]);
}
```

Fig. 4.22. Character model for O.

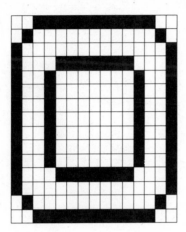

Listing 4.23. Function for P model.

```
void p (void)
{
    _moveto (x,y);
    _lineto (x+fraction[12],y);
    _lineto (x+fraction[14],y+fraction[2]);
    _lineto (x+fraction[14],y+fraction[6]);
    _lineto (x+fraction[12],y+fraction[8]);
    _lineto (x+fraction[4],y+fraction[8]);
    _lineto (x+fraction[4],y+fraction[14]);
    _lineto (x,y+fraction[14]);
    _lineto (x,y);
    _moveto (x+fraction[4],y+fraction[3]);
    _lineto (x+fraction[10],y+fraction[3]);
    _lineto (x+fraction[10],y+fraction[5]);
    _lineto (x+fraction[4],y+fraction[5]);
    _lineto (x+fraction[4],y+fraction[3]);
}
```

Fig. 4.23.   Character model for P.

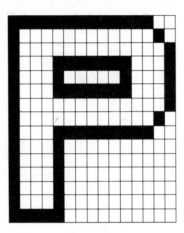

Listing 4.24.   Function for Q model.

```
void q (void)
{
    _moveto (x+fraction[2],y);
    _lineto (x+fraction[12],y);
    _lineto (x+fraction[14],y+fraction[2]);
    _lineto (x+fraction[14],y+fraction[11]);
    _lineto (x+fraction[13],y+fraction[12]);
    _lineto (x+fraction[14],y+fraction[13]);
    _lineto (x+fraction[13],y+fraction[14]);
    _lineto (x+fraction[12],y+fraction[13]);
    _lineto (x+fraction[11],y+fraction[14]);
    _lineto (x+fraction[2],y+fraction[14]);
    _lineto (x,y+fraction[12]);
    _lineto (x,y+fraction[2]);
    _lineto (x+fraction[2],y);
    _moveto (x+fraction[4],y+fraction[3]);
    _lineto (x+fraction[10],y+fraction[3]);
    _lineto (x+fraction[11],y+fraction[4]);
    _lineto (x+fraction[11],y+fraction[10]);
    _lineto (x+fraction[9],y+fraction[8]);
    _lineto (x+fraction[8],y+fraction[9]);
    _lineto (x+fraction[10],y+fraction[11]);
    _lineto (x+fraction[4],y+fraction[11]);
```

```
    _lineto (x+fraction[3],y+fraction[10]);
    _lineto (x+fraction[3],y+fraction[4]);
    _lineto (x+fraction[4],y+fraction[3]);
}
```

Fig. 4.24. Character model for Q.

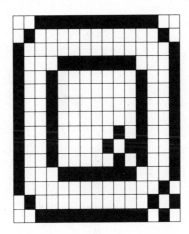

Listing 4.25. Function for R model.

```
void r (void)
{
    _moveto (x,y);
    _lineto (x+fraction[12],y);
    _lineto (x+fraction[14],y+fraction[2]);
    _lineto (x+fraction[14],y+fraction[6]);
    _lineto (x+fraction[12],y+fraction[8]);
    _lineto (x+fraction[9],y+fraction[8]);
    _lineto (x+fraction[14],y+fraction[13]);
    _lineto (x+fraction[14],y+fraction[14]);
    _lineto (x+fraction[10],y+fraction[14]);
    _lineto (x+fraction[4],y+fraction[8]);
    _lineto (x+fraction[4],y+fraction[14]);
    _lineto (x,y+fraction[14]);
    _lineto (x,y);
```

Listing 4.25 *continues*

Listing 4.25. cont. Function for R model.

```
    _moveto (x+fraction[4],y+fraction[3]);
    _lineto (x+fraction[10],y+fraction[3]);
    _lineto (x+fraction[10],y+fraction[5]);
    _lineto (x+fraction[4],y+fraction[5]);
    _lineto (x+fraction[4],y+fraction[3]);
}
```

Fig. 4.25. Character model for R.

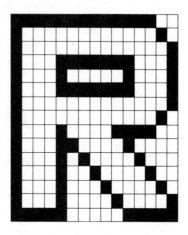

Listing 4.26. Function for S model.

```
void s (void)
{
    _moveto (x+fraction[2],y);
    _lineto (x+fraction[12],y);
    _lineto (x+fraction[14],y+fraction[2]);
    _lineto (x+fraction[14],y+fraction[4]);
    _lineto (x+fraction[11],y+fraction[4]);
    _lineto (x+fraction[11],y+fraction[3]);
    _lineto (x+fraction[4],y+fraction[3]);
    _lineto (x+fraction[3],y+fraction[4]);
    _lineto (x+fraction[3],y+fraction[5]);
    _lineto (x+fraction[4],y+fraction[6]);
    _lineto (x+fraction[13],y+fraction[6]);
```

```
        _lineto (x+fraction[14],y+fraction[7]);
        _lineto (x+fraction[14],y+fraction[12]);
        _lineto (x+fraction[12],y+fraction[14]);
        _lineto (x+fraction[2],y+fraction[14]);
        _lineto (x,y+fraction[12]);
        _lineto (x,y+fraction[10]);
        _lineto (x+fraction[3],y+fraction[10]);
        _lineto (x+fraction[3],y+fraction[11]);
        _lineto (x+fraction[10],y+fraction[11]);
        _lineto (x+fraction[11],y+fraction[10]);
        _lineto (x+fraction[11],y+fraction[9]);
        _lineto (x+fraction[10],y+fraction[8]);
        _lineto (x+fraction[2],y+fraction[8]);
        _lineto (x,y+fraction[6]);
        _lineto (x,y+fraction[2]);
        _lineto (x+fraction[2],y);
    }
```

Fig. 4.26. Character model for S.

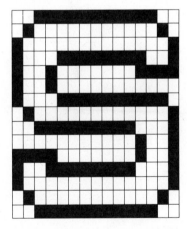

Listing 4.27. Function for T model.

```
void t (void)
{
    _moveto (x,y);
```

Listing 4.27 *continues*

Listing 4.27. cont.   Function for T model.

```
        _lineto (x+fraction[14],y);
        _lineto (x+fraction[14],y+fraction[3]);
        _lineto (x+fraction[9],y+fraction[3]);
        _lineto (x+fraction[9],y+fraction[14]);
        _lineto (x+fraction[5],y+fraction[14]);
        _lineto (x+fraction[5],y+fraction[3]);
        _lineto (x,y+fraction[3]);
        _lineto (x,y);
   }
```

Fig. 4.27.   Character model for T.

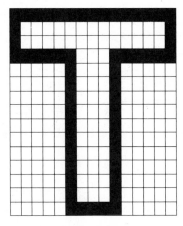

Listing 4.28.   Function for U model.

```
   void u (void)
   {
        _moveto (x,y);
        _lineto (x+fraction[3],y);
        _lineto (x+fraction[3],y+fraction[10]);
        _lineto (x+fraction[4],y+fraction[11]);
        _lineto (x+fraction[10],y+fraction[11]);
        _lineto (x+fraction[11],y+fraction[10]);
        _lineto (x+fraction[11],y);
        _lineto (x+fraction[14],y);
```

```
        _lineto (x+fraction[14],y+fraction[12]);
        _lineto (x+fraction[12],y+fraction[14]);
        _lineto (x+fraction[2],y+fraction[14]);
        _lineto (x,y+fraction[12]);
        _lineto (x,y);
    }
```

Fig. 4.28. Character model for U.

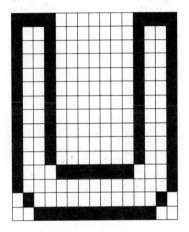

Listing 4.29. Function for V model.

```
    void v (void)
    {
        _moveto (x,y);
        _lineto (x+fraction[3],y);
        _lineto (x+fraction[3],y+fraction[5]);
        _lineto (x+fraction[7],y+fraction[9]);
        _lineto (x+fraction[11],y+fraction[5]);
        _lineto (x+fraction[11],y);
        _lineto (x+fraction[14],y);
        _lineto (x+fraction[14],y+fraction[7]);
        _lineto (x+fraction[7],y+fraction[14]);
        _lineto (x,y+fraction[7]);
        _lineto (x,y);
    }
```

Fig. 4.29. Character model for V.

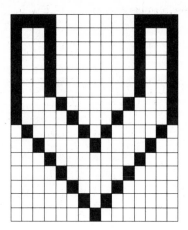

Listing 4.30. Function for W model.

```
void w (void)
{
    _moveto (x,y);
    _lineto (x+fraction[3],y);
    _lineto (x+fraction[3],y+fraction[9]);
    _lineto (x+fraction[7],y+fraction[5]);
    _lineto (x+fraction[11],y+fraction[9]);
    _lineto (x+fraction[11],y);
    _lineto (x+fraction[14],y);
    _lineto (x+fraction[14],y+fraction[14]);
    _lineto (x+fraction[11],y+fraction[14]);
    _lineto (x+fraction[7],y+fraction[10]);
    _lineto (x+fraction[3],y+fraction[14]);
    _lineto (x,y+fraction[14]);
    _lineto (x,y);
}
```

Fig. 4.30. Character model for W.

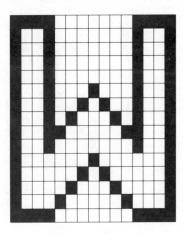

Listing 4.31. Function for X model.

```
void x (void)
{
    _moveto (x,y);
    _lineto (x+fraction[3],y);
    _lineto (x+fraction[7],y+fraction[4]);
    _lineto (x+fraction[11],y);
    _lineto (x+fraction[14],y);
    _lineto (x+fraction[14],y+fraction[2]);
    _lineto (x+fraction[9],y+fraction[7]);
    _lineto (x+fraction[14],y+fraction[12]);
    _lineto (x+fraction[14],y+fraction[14]);
    _lineto (x+fraction[11],y+fraction[14]);
    _lineto (x+fraction[7],y+fraction[10]);
    _lineto (x+fraction[3],y+fraction[14]);
    _lineto (x,y+fraction[14]);
    _lineto (x,y+fraction[12]);
    _lineto (x+fraction[5],y+fraction[7]);
    _lineto (x,y+fraction[2]);
    _lineto (x,y);
}
```

Fig. 4.31. Character model for X.

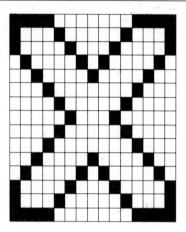

Listing 4.32. Function for Y model.

```
void y (void)
{
    _moveto (x,y);
    _lineto (x+fraction[3],y);
    _lineto (x+fraction[7],y+fraction[4]);
    _lineto (x+fraction[11],y);
    _lineto (x+fraction[14],y);
    _lineto (x+fraction[14],y+fraction[2]);
    _lineto (x+fraction[9],y+fraction[7]);
    _lineto (x+fraction[9],y+fraction[14]);
    _lineto (x+fraction[5],y+fraction[14]);
    _lineto (x+fraction[5],y+fraction[7]);
    _lineto (x,y+fraction[2]);
    _lineto (x,y);
}
```

Fig. 4.32. Character model for Y.

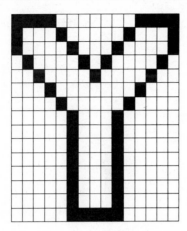

Listing 4.33. Function for Z model.

```
void z (void)
{
    _moveto (x,y);
    _lineto (x+fraction[14],y);
    _lineto (x+fraction[14],y+fraction[2]);
    _lineto (x+fraction[5],y+fraction[11]);
    _lineto (x+fraction[14],y+fraction[11]);
    _lineto (x+fraction[14],y+fraction[14]);
    _lineto (x,y+fraction[14]);
    _lineto (x,y+fraction[12]);
    _lineto (x+fraction[9],y+fraction[3]);
    _lineto (x,y+fraction[3]);
    _lineto (x,y);
}
```

Fig. 4.33. Character model for Z.

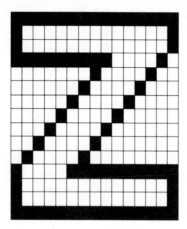

Text Windows

The graphics library provides the `_settextwindow` function for creating a text window on the screen. See figure 4.34. A text window is an area of the screen in which text output is restricted.

The following syntax is used with the `_settextwindow` function:

```
void _far _settextwindow(short r1, short c1, short r2,
                         short c2);
short r1,c1;           Upper left corner of window
short r2,c2;           Lower right corner of window
```

The text window is specified by the row and column coordinates `r1`, `c1` and `r2`, `c2`. The `r1` and `c1` arguments specify the upper left corner of the window; the `r2` and `c2` arguments define the lower right corner of the window. All subsequent text cursor positioning is defined relative to the upper left corner of the text window. When the text window is full, it scrolls up; therefore, the top line of text is no longer in view.

Chapter 9 provides additional information on the use of the `_settextwindow` function.

Fig. 4.34. The _settextwindow function.

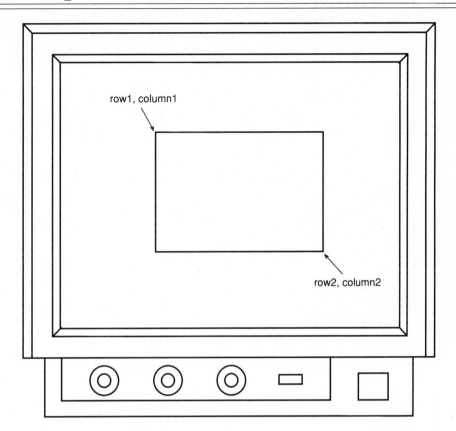

5

Presentation Graphics

The presentation graphics library contains 22 functions that are used to generate presentation graphics. Presentation graphics are charts and graphs used to display data. The presentation graphics functions are preceded by `_pg`, and are for use only inside the presentation graphics environment. Graphics functions not preceded by `_pg` should not be used inside the presentation graphics environment. Although the more primitive graphics functions, such as `_pie` and `_lineto`, can be used to generate presentation graphics, the presentation graphics environment produces graphs and charts more easily. A list of all presentation graphics functions follows:

`_pg_analyzechart`	`_pg_getchardef`
`_pg_analyzechartms`	`_pg_getpalette`
`_pg_analyzepie`	`_pg_getstyleset`
`_pg_analyzescatter`	`_pg_hlabelchart`
`_pg_analyzescatterms`	`_pg_initchart`
`_pg_chart`	`_pg_resetpalette`
`_pg_chartms`	`_pg_resetstyleset`
`_pg_chartpie`	`_pg_setchardef`
`_pg_chartscatter`	`_pg_setpalette`
`_pg_chartscatterms`	`_pg_setstyleset`
`_pg_defaultchart`	`_pg_vlabelchart`

Initializing the Presentation Graphics Environment

The first step to creating a presentation graphics display is to initialize the presentation graphics environment. Only functions with the `_pg` prefix are used with the chart, or presentation graphics, environment. Low-level graphics functions, those without a `_pg` prefix, should not be used with the presentation graphics environment.

The `_pg_initchart` function is used to initialize the presentation graphics environment. The syntax for the `_pg_initchart` function follows:

```
short _far _pg_initchart (void);
```

This function is used to initialize the color and style pools, reset the style set, build default palette modes, and register the character font used for the presentation graphics environment. (Some of these terms may be new to you; they are explained later in this chapter in "Customizing the Presentation Graphics Environment.") The `_pg_initchart` function is also the first step in creating presentation graphics; it must be called whenever you use the presentation graphics environment to display presentation graphics.

The next step is to set the default chart type using the `_pg_defaultchart` function. The `_pg_defaultchart` function initializes all the required variables in the presentation graphics environment for the specified chart type. The syntax for the `_pg_defaultchart` function follows:

```
short _far _pg_defaultchart (chartenv _far *env,
          short charttype, short chartstyle);
chartenv _far *env;        Environment structure
short charttype;           Chart type constant
short chartstyle;          Chart characteristics
```

After these steps have been completed, the chart can be analyzed, customized, and drawn. Table 5.1 lists the chart type and chart styles for the line, bar, column, scatter, and pie charts. To illustrate the structure of a typical chart program, listing 5.1 is provided.

Table 5.1. Presentation graphics chart types and styles.

Constant	Type	Meaning
	Bar chart types	
_PG_BARCHART	_PG_PLAINBARS	Side-by-side-bars
	_PG_STACKEDBARS	Stacked bars
	Column chart types	
_PG_COLUMNCHART	_PG_PLAINBARS	Side-by-side-bars
	_PG_STACKEDBARS	Stacked bars
	Line chart types	
_PG_LINECHART	_PG_POINTANDLINE	Points with lines
	_PG_POINTONLY	Points only
	Pie chart types	
_PG_PIE_CHART	_PG_PERCENT	With percentages
	_PG_NOPERCENT	Without percentages

Constant	Type	Meaning
Scatter diagram types		
_PG_SCATTERCHART	_PG_POINTANDLINE	Points with lines
	_PG_POINTONLY	Points only

Listing 5.1. Presentation graphics chart example.

```
#include <stdio.h>
#include <graph.h>
#include <pgchart.h>
#include <string.h>

#define TRUE 1
#define FALSE 0

    /* Define chart data */

float _far values[# of values] = {4.0, ..., 3.0};

char _far *categories[# of values] = {"One", ..., "Max"};

char _far *series[# of series] = {"Series One", ...,
                                  "Series Max"};

void main ()
{
chartenv env;
_setvideomode ( mode );

    /* Initialize presentation graphics environment */

_pg_initchart();
_pg_defaultchart (&env, chart type, chart specs);

    /* Define titles */

strcpy (env.maintitle.title,"Main Title");
strcpy (env.xaxis.axistitle.title, "X Title");
strcpy (env.yaxis.axistitle.title, "Y Title");
```

Listing 5.1. *continues*

Listing 5.1. cont.   Presentation graphics chart example.

```
          /* Customize chart if desired */

env.xaxis.autoscale = TRUE;
env.yaxis.autoscale = TRUE;

     /* Draw chart */

_pg_chartms (&env, categories, values, # of series,
                # of values, row dim, series);

     /* Delay and exit */

getch ();
_setvideomode (_DEFAULTMODE);
}
```

Pie Chart

The pie chart is used to display data in the shape of a pie. The pie chart created by the Microsoft _pg_chartpie function can support only one series of data. This series of data can be displayed either with or without the corresponding percentages.

Another option for displaying the pie chart is the use of exploded pieces of the pie chart. (In an exploded pie chart, one or more of the pieces of the pie are slightly removed from the pie.) The following examples explode one piece of the pie chart. The explode array is used in these examples to specify which pieces, if any, will be exploded. In both examples, the third piece of the pie is exploded. Inside the explode array, a 0 means that the piece is not exploded, and a 1 means that the piece is exploded.

Listing 5.2 demonstrates the use of the pie chart to display a single series of data with percentages for each piece of the pie. The third piece is exploded. Figure 5.1 is a printout of the screen produced by this program.

Listing 5.2.   Pie chart with percentages.

```
#include <stdio.h>
#include <graph.h>
#include <pgchart.h>
#include <string.h>
```

```
                /* Data initialization */

float _far values[10] = {12.0,16.0,22.0,8.0,10.0,
                         13.0,20.0,14.0,9.0,19.0};

char _far *categories[10] = {"1","2","3","4","5",
                             "6","7","8","9","10"};

short _far explode[10] = {0,0,1,0,0,0,0,0,0,0};

void main ()
{
chartenv env;
_setvideomode (_ERESCOLOR);


            /* Environment initialization */

_pg_initchart();
_pg_defaultchart (&env, _PG_PIECHART, _PG_PERCENT);


            /* Titles */

strcpy (env.maintitle.title,"Employee Salary as
        Percentage of Total Salary");


            /* Draw chart */

_pg_chartpie (&env, categories, values, explode, 10);


            /* Delay and exit */

getch ();
_setvideomode (_DEFAULTMODE);
}
```

Fig. 5.1. Example output from listing 5.2.

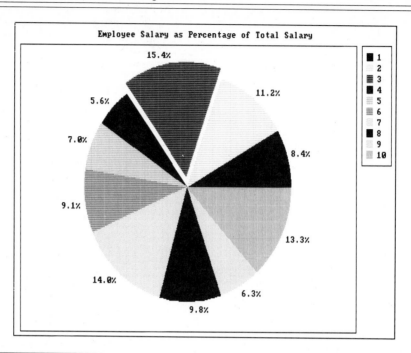

Listing 5.3 demonstrates the use of the pie chart for displaying a single series of data without percentages for each piece. This example is almost identical to the previous example but does not display the percentages. Figure 5.2 is an example of the screen produced with this program.

Listing 5.3. Pie chart without percentanges.

```
#include <stdio.h>
#include <graph.h>
#include <pgchart.h>
#include <string.h>

          /* Data initialization */

float _far values[10] = {12.0,16.0,22.0,8.0,10.0,
                         13.0,20.0,14.0,9.0,19.0};

char _far *categories[10] = {"1","2","3","4","5",
                            "6","7","8","9","10"};
```

```
chartenv env;
_setvideomode (_ERESCOLOR);

        /* Environment initialization */

_pg_initchart();
_pg_defaultchart (&env, _PG_PIECHART, _PG_NOPERCENT);

        /* Title */

strcpy (env.maintitle.title,"Employee Salary as
        Percentage of Total Salary");

        /* Draw chart */

_pg_chartpie (&env, categories, values, explode, 10);

        /* Delay and exit */

getch ();
_setvideomode (_DEFAULTMODE);
}
```

Bar Chart

The bar chart displays a single or multiple series of data using horizontal bars. The `_pg_chart` function is used to display the bar chart with a single series of data. The `_pg_chartms` function is used to display a multiple series of data.

The bar chart has two display options. The first option displays the data using plain bars. In a single-series chart, each bar is displayed singularly. In a multiseries chart, the bars for each series are presented in side-by-side fashion.

The second option is to use stacked bars. For single-series bar charts, the stacked bar option displays the same chart as the plain bar option. For multiseries bar charts, however, the bars are stacked to display the multiple series.

Listing 5.4 demonstrates the use of a single-series bar chart with the `_PG_PLAINBARS` option. Figure 5.3 is an example of the screen produced with this program. If you use the single-series bar chart with the `_PG_STACKEDBARS` option, the result is the same as with the `_PG_PLAINBARS` option because there is no second series to stack. Therefore, the output is the same as in Figure 5.3.

Fig. 5.2. Example output from listing 5.3.

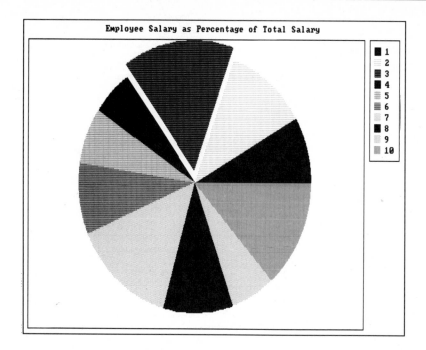

Listing 5.4. Single-series bar chart with plain bars.

```
#include <stdio.h>
#include <graph.h>
#include <pgchart.h>
#include <string.h>

        /* Data initialization */

float _far values[10] = {17.0,18.0,23.0,17.0,29.0,
                    24.0,19.0,21.0,20.0,28.0};

char _far *categories[10] = {"1","2","3","4","5",
                    "6","7","8","9","10"};

void main ()
{
chartenv env;
_setvideomode (_ERESCOLOR);
```

```
            /* Chart initialization */

_pg_initchart();
_pg_defaultchart (&env, _PG_BARCHART, _PG_PLAINBARS);

            /* Titles */

strcpy (env.maintitle.title,"Employee Age");
strcpy (env.xaxis.axistitle.title, "Age in Years");
strcpy (env.yaxis.axistitle.title, "Employee Number");

            /* Draw chart */

_pg_chart (&env, categories, values, 10);

            /* Delay and exit */

getch ();
_setvideomode (_DEFAULTMODE);
}
```

Listing 5.5 demonstrates the use of a multiseries bar chart with the **_PG_PLAINBARS** option. The two series of data are placed in a side-by-side fashion, as shown in figure 5.4.

Listing 5.5. Multiseries bar chart with plain bars.

```
#include <stdio.h>
#include <graph.h>
#include <pgchart.h>
#include <string.h>

#define TRUE 1
#define FALSE 0

            /* Data initialization */

float _far values[20] = {4.0,4.0,3.0,4.0,4.0,
                         4.0,3.0,4.0,4.0,4.0,
                         1.0,4.0,0.0,2.0,6.0,
                         2.0,0.0,3.0,1.0,1.0};
```

Listing 5.5. *continues*

155

Fig. 5.3. Example output from listing 5.4.

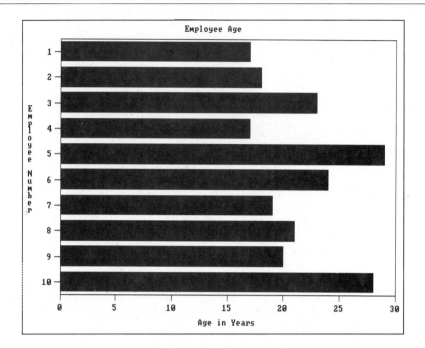

Listing 5.5. cont. Multiseries bar chart with plain bars.

```
char _far *categories[10] = {"1","2","3","4","5",
                             "6","7","8","9","10"};

char _far *series[2] = {"Years High School",
                        "Years College"};

void main ()
{
chartenv env;
_setvideomode (_ERESCOLOR);

        /* Environment initialization */

_pg_initchart();
_pg_defaultchart (&env, _PG_BARCHART, _PG_PLAINBARS);

        /* Titles */
```

```
strcpy (env.maintitle.title,"Employee Education");
strcpy (env.xaxis.axistitle.title, "Years");
strcpy (env.yaxis.axistitle.title, "Employee Number");

env.xaxis.autoscale = TRUE;
env.yaxis.autoscale = TRUE;

        /* Draw chart */

_pg_chartms (&env, categories, values, 2, 10, 10, se-
ries);

        /* Delay and exit */

getch ();
_setvideomode (_DEFAULTMODE);
}
```

Fig. 5.4.   Example output from listing 5.5.

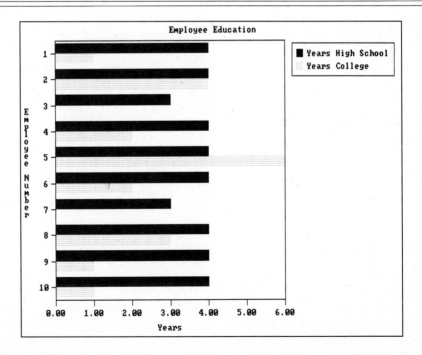

Listing 5.6 is almost identical to the previous example but uses the _PG_STACKEDBARS option rather than the _PG_PLAINBARS option. In the resulting display, shown in figure 5.5, the bars are stacked on top of each other. (Compare figure 5.5 with the side-by-side representation in figure 5.4.)

Listing 5.6. Multiseries bar chart with stacked bars.

```
#include <stdio.h>
#include <graph.h>
#include <pgchart.h>
#include <string.h>

#define TRUE 1
#define FALSE 0

        /* Data initialization */

float _far values[20] = {4.0,4.0,3.0,4.0,4.0,
                         4.0,3.0,4.0,4.0,4.0,
                         1.0,4.0,0.0,2.0,6.0,
                         2.0,0.0,3.0,1.0,1.0};

char _far *categories[10] = {"1","2","3","4","5",
                             "6","7","8","9","10"};

char _far *series[2] = {"Years High School",
                        "Years College"};

void main ()
{
chartenv env;
_setvideomode (_ERESCOLOR);

        /* Environment initialization */

_pg_initchart();
_pg_defaultchart (&env, _PG_BARCHART, _PG_STACKEDBARS);

        /* Titles */

strcpy (env.maintitle.title,"Employee Education");
strcpy (env.xaxis.axistitle.title, "Years");
strcpy (env.yaxis.axistitle.title, "Employee Number");
```

```
env.xaxis.autoscale = TRUE;
env.yaxis.autoscale = TRUE;

        /* Draw chart */

_pg_chartms (&env, categories, values, 2, 10, 10, series);

        /* Delay and exit */

getch ();
_setvideomode (_DEFAULTMODE);
}
```

Fig. 5.5. Example output from listing 5.6

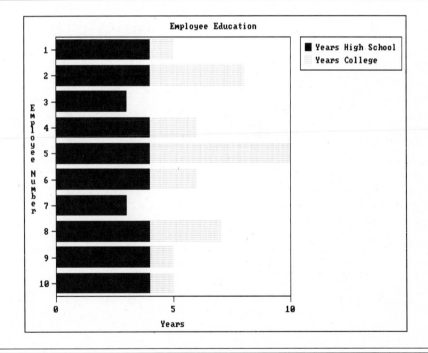

Column Chart

The column chart is very similar to the bar chart. The main difference is that the column chart produces vertical bars to represent the data, and the bar chart produces horizontal bars. Like the bar chart, the column chart can be used to display a single or multiple series of data. The _pg_chart function is used to display a single-series column chart. The _pg_chartms function is used to display a multiseries column chart.

The two options used for the bar chart are also used with the column chart. The plain bar option displays multiseries data in a side-by-side fashion. The stacked bar option stacks multiple series of data.

Listing 5.7 demonstrates the use of a single-series column chart with the _PG_PLAINBARS option. The resulting display is shown in Figure 5.6. If you use the single-series column chart with the _PG_STACKEDBARS option, the result is the same as with the _PG_PLAINBARS option because there is no second series to stack. Therefore, the output is the same as in Figure 5.6.

Listing 5.7. Single-series column chart with plain bars.

```
#include <stdio.h>
#include <graph.h>
#include <pgchart.h>
#include <string.h>

            /* Data initialization */

float _far values[10] = {17.0,18.0,23.0,17.0,29.0,
                         24.0,19.0,21.0,20.0,28.0};

char _far *categories[10] = {"1","2","3","4","5",
                            "6","7","8","9","10"};

void main ()
{
chartenv env;
_setvideomode (_ERESCOLOR);

            /* Initialize environment */

_pg_initchart();
_pg_defaultchart (&env, _PG_COLUMNCHART, _PG_PLAINBARS);

            /* Titles */

strcpy (env.maintitle.title,"Employee Age");
strcpy (env.yaxis.axistitle.title, "Age in Years");
strcpy (env.xaxis.axistitle.title, "Employee Number");

            /* Draw chart */
```

```
_pg_chart (&env, categories, values, 10);

        /* Delay and exit */

getch ();
_setvideomode (_DEFAULTMODE);
}
```

Fig. 5.6. Example output from listing 5.7.

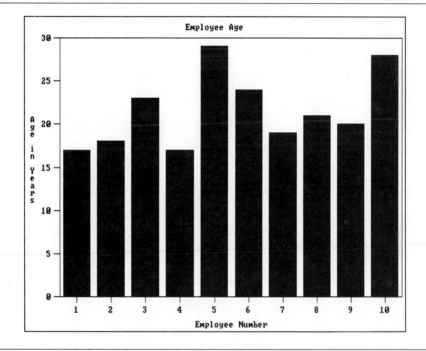

Listing 5.8 demonstrates the use of the **_PG_PLAINBARS** option when displaying a multiseries column chart. The multiple series are displayed in a side-by-side fashion, as shown in figure 5.7.

Listing 5.8. Multiseries column chart with plain bars.

```
#include <stdio.h>
#include <graph.h>
#include <pgchart.h>
#include <string.h>

#define TRUE 1
#define FALSE 0

        /* Data initialization */

float _far values[20] = {4.0,4.0,3.0,4.0,4.0,
                         4.0,3.0,4.0,4.0,4.0,
                         1.0,4.0,0.0,2.0,6.0,
                         2.0,0.0,3.0,1.0,1.0};

char _far *categories[10] = {"1","2","3","4","5",
                             "6","7","8","9","10"};

char _far *series[2] = {"Years High School",
                        "Years College"};

void main ()
{
chartenv env;
_setvideomode (_ERESCOLOR);

        /* Environment initialization */

_pg_initchart();
_pg_defaultchart (&env, _PG_COLUMNCHART, _PG_PLAINBARS);

        /* Titles */

strcpy (env.maintitle.title,"Employee Education");
strcpy (env.yaxis.axistitle.title, "Years");
strcpy (env.xaxis.axistitle.title, "Employee Number");

env.xaxis.autoscale = TRUE;
env.yaxis.autoscale = TRUE;

        /* Draw chart */
```

```
_pg_chartms (&env, categories, values, 2, 10, 10, series);

        /* Delay and exit */

getch ();
_setvideomode (_DEFAULTMODE);
}
```

Fig. 5.7. Example output from listing 5.8.

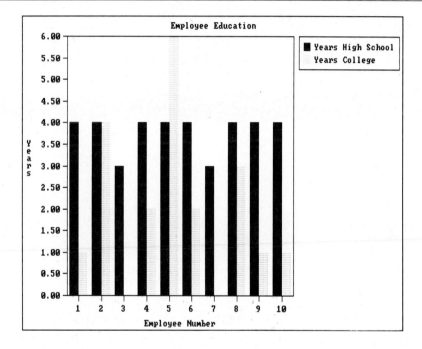

Listing 5.9 is almost identical to the previous example but uses the **_PG_STACKEDBARS** option rather than the **_PG_PLAINBARS** option. The multiple series of data is stacked, as shown in figure 5.8, instead of placed side-by-side, as in the previous example.

Listing 5.9. Multiseries column chart with stacked bars.

```c
#include <stdio.h>
#include <graph.h>
#include <pgchart.h>
#include <string.h>

#define TRUE 1
#define FALSE 0

        /* Date initialization */

float _far values[20] = {4.0,4.0,3.0,4.0,4.0,
                         4.0,3.0,4.0,4.0,4.0,
                         1.0,4.0,0.0,2.0,6.0,
                         2.0,0.0,3.0,1.0,1.0};

char _far *categories[10] = {"1","2","3","4","5",
                             "6","7","8","9","10"};

char _far *series[2] = {"Years High School",
                        "Years College"};

void main ()
{
chartenv env;
_setvideomode (_ERESCOLOR);

        /* Environment initialization */

_pg_initchart();
_pg_defaultchart (&env, _PG_COLUMNCHART, _PG_STACKEDBARS);

        /* Titles */

strcpy (env.maintitle.title,"Employee Education");
strcpy (env.yaxis.axistitle.title, "Years");
strcpy (env.xaxis.axistitle.title, "Employee Number");

env.xaxis.autoscale = TRUE;
env.yaxis.autoscale = TRUE;

        /* Draw chart */
```

```
_pg_chartms (&env, categories, values, 2, 10, 10, series);

        /* Delay and exit */

getch ();
_setvideomode (_DEFAULTMODE);
}
```

Fig. 5.8. Example output from listing 5.9.

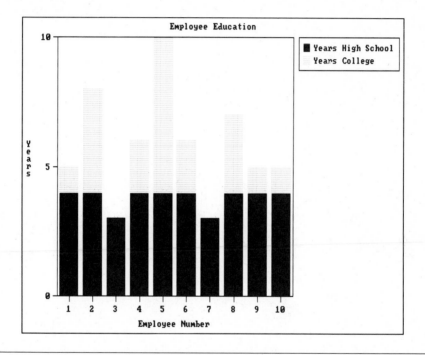

Scatter Diagram

The scatter diagram is used to display the relationship between data points expressed using two values (that is, an x and a y value). The scatter diagram can display single or multiple series of data. The _pg_chartscatter function is used to display a single-series scatter diagram. The _pg_chartscatterms function is used to display a multiseries scatter diagram.

The scatter diagram can be drawn using one of two options. The first option displays only the points. The second option displays the points and a line connecting the points.

Listing 5.10 demonstrates the use of the single-series scatter diagram with the _PG_POINTONLY option. Only points are displayed, as shown in figure 5.9.

Listing 5.10.   Single-series scatter diagram: points only.

```
#include <stdio.h>
#include <graph.h>
#include <pgchart.h>
#include <string.h>

#define TRUE 1
#define FALSE 0

          /* Data initialization */

float _far yvalues[10] = {17.0,18.0,23.0,17.0,29.0,
                          24.0,19.0,21.0,20.0,28.0};

float _far xvalues[10] = {1.0,2.0,3.0,4.0,5.0,
                          6.0,7.0,8.0,9.0,10.0};

void main ()
{
chartenv env;
_setvideomode (_ERESCOLOR);

          /* Environment initialization */

_pg_initchart();
_pg_defaultchart (&env, _PG_SCATTERCHART, _PG_POINTONLY);

          /* Titles */

strcpy (env.maintitle.title,"Employee Age");
strcpy (env.yaxis.axistitle.title, "Age in Years");
strcpy (env.xaxis.axistitle.title, "Employee Number");

env.xaxis.autoscale = TRUE;
env.yaxis.autoscale = TRUE;

          /* Draw chart */

_pg_chartscatter (&env, xvalues, yvalues, 10);
```

```
              /* Delay and exit */

getch ();
_setvideomode (_DEFAULTMODE);
}
```

Fig. 5.9.   Example output from listing 5.10.

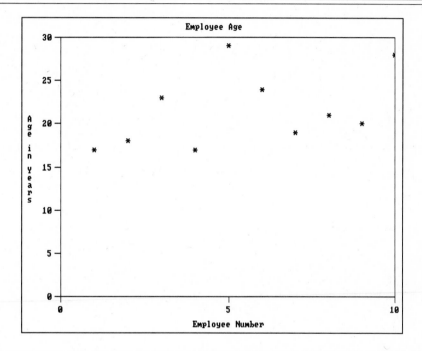

Listing 5.11 is almost the same as the previous example but uses the `_PG_POINTANDLINE` option rather than the `_PG_POINTONLY` option. All points are plotted and then connected with a line, as shown in figure 5.10.

Listing 5.11. Single-series scatter diagram: points and lines.

```c
#include <stdio.h>
#include <graph.h>
#include <pgchart.h>
#include <string.h>

#define TRUE 1
#define FALSE 0

          /* Data initialization */

float _far yvalues[10] = {17.0,18.0,23.0,17.0,29.0,
                          24.0,19.0,21.0,20.0,28.0};

float _far xvalues[10] = {1.0,2.0,3.0,4.0,5.0,
                          6.0,7.0,8.0,9.0,10.0};

void main ()
{
chartenv env;
_setvideomode (_ERESCOLOR);

          /* Environment initialization */

_pg_initchart();
_pg_defaultchart (&env, _PG_SCATTERCHART, _PG_POINTANDLINE);

          /* Titles */

strcpy (env.maintitle.title,"Employee Age");
strcpy (env.yaxis.axistitle.title, "Age in Years");
strcpy (env.xaxis.axistitle.title, "Employee Number");

env.xaxis.autoscale = TRUE;
env.yaxis.autoscale = TRUE;

          /* Draw chart */

_pg_chartscatter (&env, xvalues, yvalues, 10);

          /* Delay and exit */
```

```
getch ();
_setvideomode (_DEFAULTMODE);
}
```

Fig. 5.10. Example output from listing 5.11.

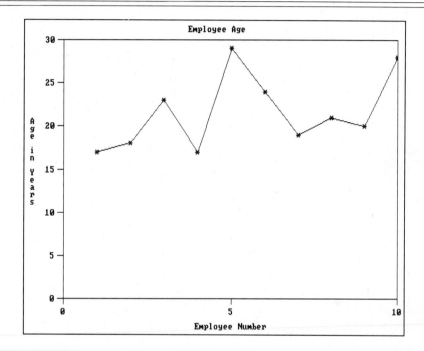

Listing 5.12 displays a multiple series of data in a scatter diagram. This example uses the _PG_POINTONLY option. Therefore, only the data points are displayed, as shown in figure 5.11.

Listing 5.12. Multiseries scatter diagram: points only.

```
#include <stdio.h>
#include <graph.h>
#include <pgchart.h>
#include <string.h>

#define TRUE 1
#define FALSE 0
```

Listing 5.12. *continues*

Listing 5.12. cont.   Multiseries scatter diagram: points only.

```
                    /* Data initialization */

float _far yvalues[20] = {17.0,18.0,23.0,17.0,29.0,
                          24.0,19.0,21.0,20.0,28.0,
                          11.0,12.0,15.0,11.0,13.0,
                          12.0,12.0,13.0,12.0,18.0};

float _far xvalues[20] = {1.0,2.0,3.0,4.0,5.0,
                          6.0,7.0,8.0,9.0,10.0,
                          1.0,2.0,3.0,4.0,5.0,
                          6.0,7.0,8.0,9.0,10.0};

char _far *series[2] = {"Age","Yrs Education"};


void main ()
{
chartenv env;
_setvideomode (_ERESCOLOR);

        /* Environment initialization */

_pg_initchart();
_pg_defaultchart (&env, _PG_SCATTERCHART, _PG_POINTONLY);

        /* Titles */

strcpy (env.maintitle.title,"Employee Age and Education");
strcpy (env.yaxis.axistitle.title, "Age and Education in
                 Years");
strcpy (env.xaxis.axistitle.title, "Employee Number");

env.xaxis.autoscale = TRUE;
env.yaxis.autoscale = TRUE;

        /* Draw chart */

_pg_chartscatterms (&env, xvalues, yvalues,
                 2, 10, 10, series);

        /* Delay and exit */
```

```
getch ();
_setvideomode (_DEFAULTMODE);
}
```

Fig. 5.11. Example output from listing 5.12.

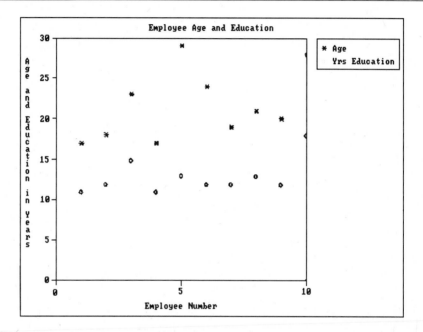

Listing 5.13 displays a multiple series of data in a scatter diagram, using the `_PG_POINTANDLINE` option. The resulting display is shown in figure 5.12. This example is similar to the previous example output, except this one connects the points.

Listing 5.13. Multiseries scatter diagram: points and lines.

```
#include <stdio.h>
#include <graph.h>
#include <pgchart.h>
#include <string.h>

#define TRUE 1
#define FALSE 0
```

Listing 5.13. *continues*

171

Listing 5.13. cont. Multiseries scatter diagram: points and lines.

```
                /* Data initialization */

float _far yvalues[20] = {17.0,18.0,23.0,17.0,29.0,
                          24.0,19.0,21.0,20.0,28.0,
                          11.0,12.0,15.0,11.0,13.0,
                          12.0,12.0,13.0,12.0,18.0};

float _far xvalues[20] = {1.0,2.0,3.0,4.0,5.0,
                          6.0,7.0,8.0,9.0,10.0,
                          1.0,2.0,3.0,4.0,5.0,
                          6.0,7.0,8.0,9.0,10.0};

char _far *series[2] = {"Age","Yrs Education"};


void main ()
{
chartenv env;
_setvideomode (_ERESCOLOR);

        /* Environment initialization */

_pg_initchart();
_pg_defaultchart (&env, _PG_SCATTERCHART, _PG_POINTANDLINE);

        /* Titles */

strcpy (env.maintitle.title,"Employee Age and Education");
strcpy (env.yaxis.axistitle.title, "Age and Education in
                    Years");
strcpy (env.xaxis.axistitle.title, "Employee Number");

env.xaxis.autoscale = TRUE;
env.yaxis.autoscale = TRUE;

        /* Draw chart */

_pg_chartscatterms (&env, xvalues, yvalues,
                2, 10, 10, series);
```

```
                    /* Delay and exit */

getch ();
_setvideomode (_DEFAULTMODE);
}
```

Fig. 5.12. Example output from listing 5.13.

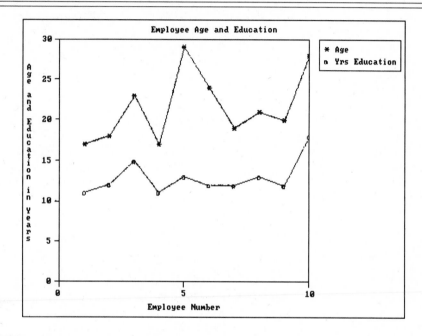

Line Chart

The line chart is a combination of the column chart and the scatter diagram. The code structure is almost identical to the column chart, but the display looks like a scatter diagram. The line chart can display both single and multiple series. The **_pg_chart** function is used to display a single-series line chart. The **_pg_chartms** function is used to display a multiseries line chart.

The line chart has two options. The first option displays only the points. The second option displays the points and draws the lines.

Listing 5.14 displays a single series of data using the **_PG_POINTONLY** option. Only the data points are displayed, as shown in figure 5.13.

Listing 5.14.   Single-series line chart: points only.

```
#include <stdio.h>
#include <graph.h>
#include <pgchart.h>
#include <string.h>

        /* Data initialization */

float _far values[10] =
     {17.0,18.0,23.0,17.0,29.0,24.0,19.0,21.0,20.0,28.0};

char _far *categories[10] =
     {"1","2","3","4","5","6","7","8","9","10"};

void main ()
{
chartenv env;
_setvideomode (_ERESCOLOR);

        /* Environment initialization */

_pg_initchart();
_pg_defaultchart (&env, _PG_LINECHART, _PG_POINTONLY);

        /* Titles */

strcpy (env.maintitle.title,"Employee Age");
strcpy (env.yaxis.axistitle.title, "Age in Years");
strcpy (env.xaxis.axistitle.title, "Employee Number");

        /* Draw chart */

_pg_chart (&env, categories, values, 10);

        /* Delay and exit */

getch ();
_setvideomode (_DEFAULTMODE);
}
```

Fig. 5.13. Example output from listing 5.14.

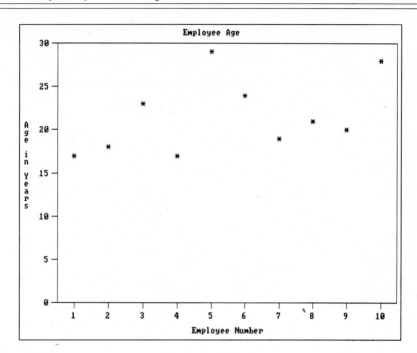

Listing 5.15 displays a single series of data using the **_PG_POINTANDLINE** option. The data points are connected by lines, as shown in figure 5.14.

Listing 5.15. Single-series line chart: points and lines.

```
#include <stdio.h>
#include <graph.h>
#include <pgchart.h>
#include <string.h>

        /* Data initialization */

float _far values[10] =
    {17.0,18.0,23.0,17.0,29.0,24.0,19.0,21.0,20.0,28.0};

char _far *categories[10] =
    {"1","2","3","4","5","6","7","8","9","10"};
void main ()
```

Listing 5.15. *continues*

175

Listing 5.15. cont.   Single-series line chart: points and lines.

```
{
chartenv env;
_setvideomode (_ERESCOLOR);

        /* Environment initialization */

_pg_initchart();
_pg_defaultchart (&env, _PG_LINECHART, _PG_POINTANDLINE);

        /* Titles */

strcpy (env.maintitle.title,"Employee Age");
strcpy (env.yaxis.axistitle.title, "Age in Years");
strcpy (env.xaxis.axistitle.title, "Employee Number");

        /* Draw chart */

_pg_chart (&env, categories, values, 10);

        /* Delay and exit */

getch ();
_setvideomode (_DEFAULTMODE);
}
```

Listing 5.16 demonstrates the use of the **_PG_POINTONLY** option to display a multiseries line chart. Only the data points are displayed, as shown in figure 5.15.

Listing 5.16.   Multiseries line chart: points only.

```
#include <stdio.h>
#include <graph.h>
#include <pgchart.h>
#include <string.h>

#define TRUE 1
#define FALSE 0

        /* Data initialization */
```

Fig. 5.14. Example output from listing 5.15.

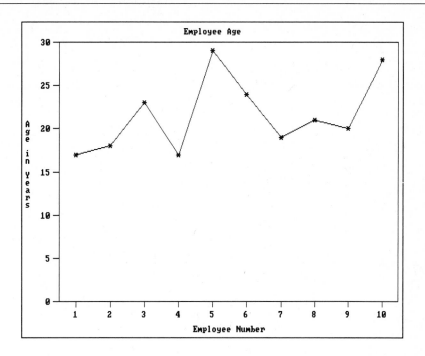

```
float _far values[20] = {4.0,4.0,3.0,4.0,4.0,
                         4.0,3.0,4.0,4.0,4.0,
                         1.0,4.0,0.0,2.0,6.0,
                         2.0,0.0,3.0,1.0,1.0};

char _far *categories[10] =
     {"1","2","3","4","5","6","7","8","9","10"};

char _far *series[2] = {"Years High School",
                        "Years College"};

void main ()
{
chartenv env;
_setvideomode (_ERESCOLOR);

        /* Environment initialization */
```

Listing 5.16. *continues*

177

Listing 5.16. cont.   Multiseries line chart: points only.

```
        _pg_initchart();
        _pg_defaultchart (&env, _PG_LINECHART, _PG_POINTONLY);

                /* Titles */

        strcpy (env.maintitle.title,"Employee Education");
        strcpy (env.yaxis.axistitle.title, "Years");
        strcpy (env.xaxis.axistitle.title, "Employee Number");

        env.xaxis.autoscale = TRUE;
        env.yaxis.autoscale = TRUE;

                /* Draw chart */

        _pg_chartms (&env, categories, values, 2, 10, 10, series);

                /* Delay and exit */

        getch ();
        _setvideomode (_DEFAULTMODE);
        }
```

Listing 5.17 demonstrates the use of the **_PG_POINTANDLINE** option to display a multiseries line chart. The data points are connected by lines, as shown in figure 5.16.

Listing 5.17.   Multiseries line chart: points and lines.

```
#include <stdio.h>
#include <graph.h>
#include <pgchart.h>
#include <string.h>

#define TRUE 1
#define FALSE 0

        /* Data initialization */

float _far values[20] = {4.0,4.0,3.0,4.0,4.0,
                         4.0,3.0,4.0,4.0,4.0,
                         1.0,4.0,0.0,2.0,6.0,
                         2.0,0.0,3.0,1.0,1.0};
```

Fig. 5.15. Example output from listing 5.16.

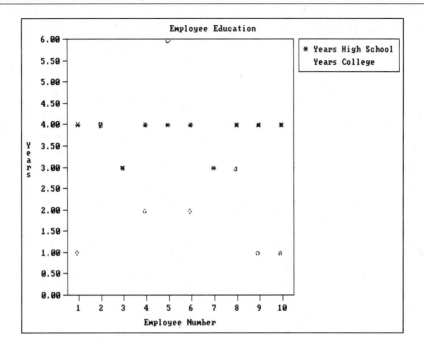

```c
char _far *categories[10] =
        {"1","2","3","4","5","6","7","8","9","10"};

char _far *series[2] = {"Years High School",
                        "Years College"};

void main ()
{
chartenv env;
_setvideomode (_ERESCOLOR);

        /* Environment initialization */

_pg_initchart();
_pg_defaultchart (&env, _PG_LINECHART, _PG_POINTANDLINE);

        /* Titles */
```

Listing 5.17. *continues*

Listing 5.17. cont.   Multiseries line chart: points and lines.

```
strcpy (env.maintitle.title,"Employee Education");
strcpy (env.yaxis.axistitle.title, "Years");
strcpy (env.xaxis.axistitle.title, "Employee Number");

env.xaxis.autoscale = TRUE;
env.yaxis.autoscale = TRUE;

        /* Draw chart */

_pg_chartms (&env, categories, values, 2, 10, 10, series);

        /* Delay and exit */

getch ();
_setvideomode (_DEFAULTMODE);
}
```

Fig. 5.16.   Example output from listing 5.17.

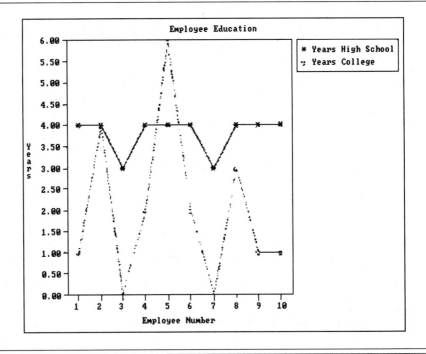

Customizing the Presentation Graphics Environment

Most of the previous examples used the default settings for the presentation graphics environment. When presenting graphics, default settings are a good place to start, but you can also customize colors, fill patterns, line styles, titles, legends, and so on. By using the flexibility of chart customization, an almost endless combination of charts can be displayed. The remainder of this chapter provides information on the customizing parameters of the presentation graphics environment.

The presentation graphics environment uses a unique palette for every series in a chart display. This palette contains information on the color, line style, fill pattern, and point character used for the series. This palette is not the same palette used for the low-level functions and should not be confused with it. The following palette structure is defined in pgchart.h.

```
                /* Bitmap for fill pattern */

typedef unsigned char fillmap [8];

                /* Palette structure */

typedef struct
{
        unsigned short color;
        unsigned short style;
        fillmap fill;
        char plotchar;
} paletteentry;

                /* Palette definition */

typedef paletteentry palettetype[_PG_PALETTELEN];
```

Note: Each of the following pools correspond to a structure member in the `paletteentry` structure.

The Color Pool

All chart colors are organized in a color pool that holds the valid color values for the current graphics mode. These colors are used to draw the chart. The first element of the color pool is 0, the background color. The second element is the highest color number of the available colors given the current video mode. The remainder of the palette consists of this same sequence beginning at number 1. Table 5.2 illustrates this procedure by showing the first 16 colors of a color pool using the default 16 colors available with EGA and VGA.

Table 5.2. *Color pool for EGA and VGA presentation graphics.*

Pool number	Color number	Color
0	0	Black
1	15	Bright white
2	1	Blue
3	2	Green
4	3	Cyan
5	4	Red
6	5	Magenta
7	6	Brown
8	7	White
9	8	Dark gray
10	9	Light blue
11	10	Light green
12	11	Light cyan
13	12	Light red
14	13	Light magenta
15	14	Yellow

The Style Pool

The style pool is used with the color pool to give the presentation graphics environment many different appearances. The entries of the style pool define the style of the lines used in the presentation graphics environment.

The style member of a palette structure is used to define the style of the line that connects points in a line chart or scatter diagram. When you generate a multiseries chart and the number of series exceeds the number of foreground colors, different line styles can make the different series appear unique.

The Pattern Pool

The pattern pool contains a series of fill patterns used to fill column, bar, and pie charts. Each fill pattern is an 8-by-8 bit pattern. Chapter 3, "Graphics Techniques," describes how to derive a fill pattern. The fill array member of the palette describes the fill pattern used by that palette.

The Character Pool

The plotchar member of the palette structure is an index number from the ASCII character pool. This member is used as a plot point for line graphs and scatter diagrams.

Listing 5.18 demonstrates the method by which the color pool, the style pool, the pattern pool, and the character pool can be altered.

Listing 5.18. Custom presentation graphics chart.

```c
#include <graph.h>
#include <stdio.h>
#include <string.h>
#include <pgchart.h>
#include <memory.h>

        /* Data initialization */

float _far values [# of values] = {1.0, ..., 10.0);

char _far *categories [# of categories] = {"1",...,"10"};

char _far *series [# of series] = {"One", ..., "Two"};

fillmap fill1 = {0x..,0x..,0x..,0x..,0x..,0x..,0x..,0x..};
fillmap fill2 = {0x..,0x..,0x..,0x..,0x..,0x..,0x..,0x..};

styleset styles;
palettetype pal;

void main ()
{
chartenv env;
_setvideomode ( mode );

_pg_initchart ();

        /* Modify styleset */

_pg_getstyleset (styles);
styles[0] = 0x....;
styles[1] = 0x....;
_pg_setstyleset (styles);

_pg_defaultchart (&env, chart type, chart specs);

        /* Modify palette */

_pg_getpalette (pal);
pal[1].plotchar = 30;       /* Change the plot character */
memcpy (pal[1].fill, fill1, 8);  /* Set new fill mask */
```

Listing 5.18. *continues*

183

Listing 5.18. cont.   Custom presentation graphics chart.

```
pal[1].color = 2;          /* Set new color */
pal[1].style = 0x...;      /* Set palette line style */
_pg_setpalette (pal);
         .
         .
         .

_pg_chartms (&env, categories, values, # series, # values,
             # categories, series);
         .
         .
         .

getch ();
_setvideomode (_DEFAULTMODE);
}
```

The chartenv Structure

The chartenv structure is used to define the presentation graphics environment. The chartenv structure follows:

```
typedef struct
{
      short charttype;
      short chartstyle;
      windowtype chartwindow;
      windowtype datawindow;
      titletype maintitle;
      titletype subtitle;
      axistype xaxis;
      axistype yaxis;
      legendtype legend;
} chartenv;
```

The values for the data in the chartenv structure are initialized when you call the _pg_defaultchart function. Following is a brief description of each member of the chartenv structure.

charttype   The charttype member is used to determine the type of chart to display. The following constants should be used to define this member: _PG_BARCHART, _PG_COLUMNCHART, _PG_LINECHART, _PG_PIECHART, and _PG_SCATTERCHART.

chartstyle   The chartstyle member is used to determine the style of the chart. There are two chart styles for every chart type. For the pie chart, the styles are _PG_PERCENT and **_PG_NOPERCENT**. For column charts, the styles are **_PG_PLAINBARS** and **_PG_STACKEDBARS**. For bar charts, the styles are **_PG_PLAINBARS** and **_PG_STACKEDBARS**. For line charts, the styles are **_PG_POINTONLY** and **_PG_POINTANDLINE**. For scatter diagrams, the styles are **_PG_POINTONLY** and **_PG_POINTANDLINE**.

chartwindow   The **chartwindow** member is a structure of type **windowtype** that defines the appearance of the chart window. (The **windowtype** structure is defined later in this chapter in "The windowtype Structure.")

datawindow   The **datawindow** member is a structure of type **windowtype** that defines the appearance of the data window. (The **windowtype** structure is defined later in this chapter in "The windowtype Structure.")

legend   The **legend** member is a structure of type **legendtype** that defines the appearance of the legend window. (The **legendtype** structure is defined later in this chapter in "The legendtype Structure.")

maintitle   The **maintitle** member is a structure of type **titletype** that defines the appearance of the main title of the chart. (The **titletype** structure is defined later in this chapter in "The titletype Structure.")

subtitle   The **subtitle** member is a structure of type **titletype** that defines the appearance of the chart's subtitle. (The **titletype** structure is defined later in this chapter in "The titletype Structure.")

xaxis   The **xaxis** member is a structure of type **axistype** which defines the appearance of the x axis. (The **axistype** structure is defined later in this chapter in "The axistype Structure.")

yaxis   The **yaxis** member is a structure of type **axistype** that defines the appearance of the y axis. (The **axistype** structure is defined later in this chapter in "The axistype Structure.")

The titletype Structure

The **titletype** structure is used to define the text, color, and placement of chart titles. The **titletype** structure is defined as follows:

```
typedef struct
{
    char title[_PG_TITLELEN];
    short titlecolor;
    short justify;
} titletype;
```

Following is a brief description of the members of the **titletype** structure.

title[_PG_TITLELEN]   The **title[_PG_TITLELEN]** member is a character array that contains the title.

titlecolor   The **titlecolor** member is an integer between 1 and **_PG_PALETTELEN** and is used to specify the color of the title. The default title color is 1.

justify   The **justify** member is an integer that determines the location of the text title. The following constants are defined for use: **_PG_LEFT** places text justified on the left side of the screen, **_PG_RIGHT** places text justified on the right side of the screen, and **_PG_CENTER** centers text on the screen.

The axistype Structure

The **axistype** structure is used to define the color, scale, grid style, and tick marks for the axes. The **axistype** structure is defined as follows:

```
typedef struct
{
        short grid;
        short gridstyle;
        titletype axistitle;
        short axiscolor;
        short labeled;
        short rangetype;
        float logbase;
        short autoscale;
        float scalemin;
        float scalemax;
        float scalefactor;
        titletype scaletitle;
        float ticinterval;
        short ticformat;
        short ticdecimals;
} axistype;
```

Following is a brief description of the members of the **axistype** structure.

grid   The **grid** member is a boolean value used to determine whether or not the grid lines are drawn for the associated axis. If TRUE, the grid is drawn. If FALSE, no grid is drawn.

gridstyle   The **gridstyle** member is an integer value between 1 and **_PG_PALETTELEN** that specifies the grid's line style.

axistitle   The **axistitle** member is a structure of type **titletype** that describes the title of the associated axis.

axiscolor   The **axiscolor** member is an integer value between 1 and **_PG_PALETTELEN** that specifies the color for the axis and its corresponding grid lines.

labeled   The **labeled** member is a boolean value that determines whether tick marks and labels are drawn on the axis. If TRUE, tick marks and titles are drawn.

rangetype   The **rangetype** member is an integer that determines if the scale of the axis is linear or logarithmic. This value applies only to values in the data. The possible constants are **_PG_LINEARAXIS** and **_PGLOGAXIS**.

logbase   This member determines the base of the log scale when the **rangetype** is logarithmic. The default value is 10.

autoscale   The `autoscale` variable is a boolean value. If TRUE, the `scalefactor`, `scalemax`, `scalemin`, `scaletitle`, `ticdecimals`, `ticformat`, and `ticinterval` are set automatically. If FALSE, these must be entered manually.

scalemin   The `scalemin` member represents the lowest value on the axix.

scalemax   The `scalemax` member represents the highest value on the axis.

scalefactor   The `scalefactor` member defines the scale by which the axis is divided. This is 1 for small numbers, but division by 100, 1000, and so on is also possible. This member is set automatically when `autoscale` is TRUE.

scaletitle   The `scaletitle` member is a structure of type `titletype`. When `autoscale` is TRUE, any scaling factor is written to `scaletitle`. If FALSE, the scaling factor must be set manually.

ticinterval   The `ticinterval` member sets the distance between the tick marks on the axis.

ticformat   The `ticformat` member sets the format of the label for each tick mark. The `_PG_EXPFORMAT` constant sets exponential format. The `_PG_DECFORMAT` constants sets decimal format.

ticdecimals   The `ticdecimals` member sets the number of digits to display after the decimal. The maximum value is 9.

The windowtype Structure

The `windowtype` structure contains the sizes, locations, and color codes for the chart, data, and legend windows. The `windowtype` structure is defined as follows:

```
typedef struct
{
        short x1;
        short y1;
        short x2;
        short y2;
        short border;
        short background;
        short borderstyle;
        short bordercolor;
}  windowtype;
```

Following is a brief description of the members of the `windowtype` structure.

x1   The `x1` member describes the x coordinate of the upper left corner of the window.

y1   The `y1` member describes the y coordinate of the upper left corner of the window.

x2   The `x2` member describes the x coordinate of the lower right corner of the window.

y2   The `y2` member describes the y coordinate of the lower right corner of the window.

border   The `border` member is a boolean variable that specifies whether a border is drawn around the window. If TRUE, a border is drawn. If FALSE, no border is drawn.

background   The `background` member is an integer between 1 and `_PG_PALETTELEN` that determines the background color. The default is 1.

borderstyle   The `borderstyle` member is an integer value between 1 and `_PG_PALETTELEN` that determines the line style of the window border. The default is 1.

bordercolor   The `bordercolor` member is an integer value between 1 and `_PG_PALETTELEN` that determines the color of the window's border. The default is 1.

The legendtype Structure

The `legendtype` structure contains size, location, and color information for the chart legend. The `legendtype` structure is defined as follows:

```
typedef struct
{
     short legend;
     short place;
     short textcolor;
     short autosize;
     windowtype legendwindow;
} legendtype;
```

Following is a brief description of the members of the `legendtype` structure.

legend   The `legend` member is a boolean variable used to specify whether a legend will appear on the screen. If TRUE, a legend is drawn. If FALSE, no legend is drawn. This value is used only for multiseries charts.

place   The `place` member is an integer value that specifies the location of the legend. The `_PG_RIGHT` constant places the legend at the right of the data window. The `_PG_BOTTOM` constant places the legend at the bottom of the data window. The `_PG_OVERLAY` constant places the legend within the data window.

textcolor   The `textcolor` member is an integer between 1 and `_PG_PALETTELEN` that sets the color of the text displayed within the legend window.

autosize   The `autosize` function is a boolean variable used to determine whether the size of the legend will be calculated automatically. If TRUE, the size is calculated automatically. If FALSE, the legend window must be described in the `legendwindow` structure.

legendwindow   The legendwindow member is a structure of type windowtype. This member is used to describe the coordinates, colors, and border for the legend.

6

Animation

Animation is the art of making a series of distinct images appear to have life or motion. For computer graphics, animation is often associated with computer video games. The art of animation is both challenging and exciting for the computer graphics programmer. This chapter introduces the basic animation concepts behind advanced computer graphics. By combining the techniques introduced in this chapter with the concepts discussed in the other chapters, you can produce sophisticated computer graphics packages and programs.

The Art of Animation

The key to successful animation is the artwork. If you are like the average computer programmer, however, you lack the skills to create intricate sketchings. Fortunately, this is usually not a problem because you can obtain images from many sources, such as magazines and clip-art libraries. You only need to find the image, trace it onto a sheet of properly sized graph paper (keep in mind that the aspect ratio of the target screen must be considered), and transfer the image into coordinates that the computer can work with and display. This is the trace-draw-transfer method.

The trace-draw-transfer method can be time consuming and lengthy. For small programming projects, this process is sufficient; big projects, however, may require alternate methods. The examples in this chapter follow the trace-draw-transfer method. All applicable copyright laws should be considered when using this method.

One alternate method of creating complex screens and images for use in animation is a screen capture program. Many paintbrush programs (including PC PaintBrush IV by ZSoft) create screen images that can be saved as files in the .PCX file format. Then, using programs such as PCX Programmer's Toolkit, PCX Effects, and PCX Text (all by Genus Microprogramming), the .PCX images can be manipulated and included in a Microsoft C application. These programs also include a variety of functions that add to the overall graphics progamming flexibility of Microsoft C.

You can create and edit the image much more quickly by using a paintbrush program that allows on-screen editing of the image than with the trace-draw-transfer method. In addition, most paintbrush programs permit the use of alternate input devices such as mice, trackballs, and digitizer tablets that greatly help the creation and editing process.

No matter what method you use to create the image, it is important that the programmer creates an image that serves the desired purpose or produces the desired effect.

Full Screen Animation

The two basic types of animation are full screen animation and partial screen animation. With full screen animation, the entire screen is used to create animation. With partial screen animation, only parts of the screen are used to create animation.

To successfully accomplish full screen animation with the Microsoft C functions, the video adapter must be either EGA or VGA, and have sufficient memory to support multiple pages of graphics output. The `_getvideoconfig` function can be used to retrieve the number of graphics pages available in video memory.

Assuming that the video adapter has sufficient memory, the `_setactivepage` and `_setvisualpage` functions can be used to alternate video pages in memory to simulate animation. The syntax for each follows:

```
short _far _setactivepage (short page);
short page;                Page number

short _far _setvisualpage (short page);
short page;                Page number
```

The *visual page* is the page in video memory that is currently being displayed on the screen. The *active page* is the page in video memory where all graphics output is currently being sent. These pages do not have to be the same. The default setting for both is page 0.

The following example should help you understand the method for alternating pages. Let's assume that two pages of video graphics memory are available, page 0 and page 1. Upon entering the graphics mode, both the visual page and active page are 0. Therefore, we have the following:

Active page = 0   Visual page = 0

We want to create a screen to accomplish the desired animation. It is a good idea to draw on a non-visual screen when developing an application so that the end-user doesn't see the lines or objects being drawn. Therefore, the active page would be set to 1 with the `_setactivepage (1);` call. We now have the following:

Active page = 1   Visual page = 0

At present, nothing is being displayed. When the first screen has been completed, that screen should be made visual, and the active screen should be made the non-visual page. The _setvisualpage (1); and_setactivepage (0); calls will do this. We now have the following:

Active page = 0   Visual page = 1

When the non-visual screen has been completed, the screens (0 and 1) can be alternated to produce the animation effects. The _setvisualpage and _setactivepage functions would be used again to accomplish this. The following would continue until interrupted:

Active page = 1   Visual page = 0
Active page = 0   Visual page = 1
Active page = 1   Visual page = 0
.   .
.   .
.   .

The following example demonstrates the use of the _setvisualpage and _setactivepage functions for full screen animation. In this example, viewers should get the impression that they are traveling down a hallway. The first image is the view you would see looking down the hallway, as shown in figure 6.1. The second image, shown in figure 6.2, is a slight modification of the first. By altering the blocks on the floor and wall, the image appears to be one-half block closer. When we alternate these image screens, the viewer has the impression of traveling down a hallway or corridor.

Fig. 6.1. Scene one.

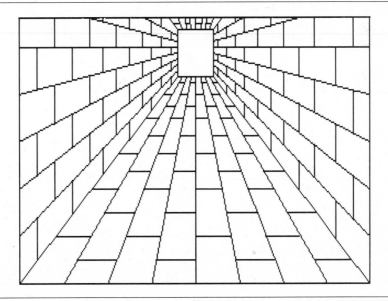

Fig. 6.2. Scene two.

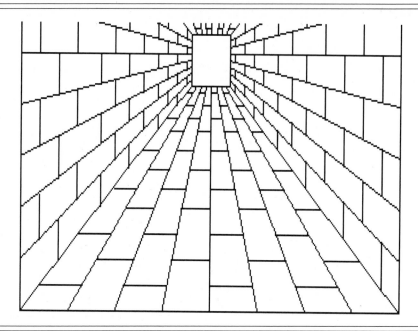

As this simple example illustrates, it is important to be able to conceptualize how objects should appear when modified. In addition, the images must be modified in such a way that they appear to maintain motion when repeated.

Listing 6.1 generates the hallway example. Like most examples in this book, the code is written so that it is easy to understand. This code can be easily optimized for efficiency. It may be necessary to alter this program for high-speed systems. By modifying the f o r loop that calls the p a u s e ( ) function, you can control the speed with which the pages alternate.

Listing 6.1. Hallway animation example.

```
#include <stdio.h>
#include <graph.h>

void main ()
{
int page, x;
page = 1;

_setvideomode (_MRES16COLOR);
_clearscreen (_GCLEARSCREEN);
```

```
                 /* Draw first screen */

_setvisualpage (0);
_setactivepage (1);
_setcolor (15);
_drawline1 ();

                 /* Draw second screen */

_setvisualpage (1);
_setactivepage (0);
_setcolor (15);
_drawline2 ();

                 /* Flip images until a key is pressed */

do
        {
     _setvisualpage (0);

     for (x=1; x<5; x=x+1)
          _pause ();

     _setvisualpage (1);

     for (x=1; x<5; x=x+1)
          _pause ();

        }  while (!kbhit ());

                 /* Reset and exit */

_setvideomode (_DEFAULTMODE);
}

                 /* Pause function */

_pause ()
{
int loop;
loop = 0;

do
   {
```

Listing 6.1 *continues*

Listing 6.1. cont.   Hallway animation example.

```
            loop = loop + 1;

    }   while (loop != 10000);
}


            /* Code for drawing first hallway scene */

void _drawline1 (void)
{
_rectangle (_GBORDER,144,40,176,8);
_rectangle (_GBORDER,0,0,319,180);

_moveto (144,40);    _lineto (0,180);
_moveto (148,40);    _lineto (40,180);
_moveto (152,40);    _lineto (80,180);
_moveto (156,40);    _lineto (120,180);
_moveto (160,40);    _lineto (160,180);
_moveto (164,40);    _lineto (200,180);
_moveto (168,40);    _lineto (240,180);
_moveto (172,40);    _lineto (280,180);
_moveto (176,40);    _lineto (319,180);
_moveto (176,36);    _lineto (319,148);
_moveto (176,32);    _lineto (319,116);
_moveto (176,28);    _lineto (319,84);
_moveto (176,24);    _lineto (319,52);
_moveto (176,20);    _lineto (319,20);
_moveto (176,16);    _lineto (256,0);
_moveto (176,12);    _lineto (204,0);
_moveto (176,8);     _lineto (184,0);
_moveto (172,8);     _lineto (176,0);
_moveto (168,8);     _lineto (170,0);
_moveto (164,8);     _lineto (166,0);
_moveto (160,8);     _lineto (160,0);
_moveto (156,8);     _lineto (154,0);
_moveto (152,8);     _lineto (150,0);
_moveto (148,8);     _lineto (144,0);
_moveto (144,8);     _lineto (136,0);
_moveto (144,12);    _lineto (114,0);
_moveto (144,16);    _lineto (64,0);
_moveto (144,20);    _lineto (0,20);
_moveto (144,24);    _lineto (0,52);
_moveto (144,28);    _lineto (0,84);
_moveto (144,32);    _lineto (0,116);
```

```
_moveto (144,36);     _lineto (0,148);
_moveto (16,164);     _lineto (52,164);
_moveto (88,164);     _lineto (124,164);
_moveto (160,164);    _lineto (196,164);
_moveto (232,164);    _lineto (268,164);
_moveto (65,148);     _lineto (97,148);
_moveto (128,148);    _lineto (160,148);
_moveto (192,148);    _lineto (224,148);
_moveto (256,148);    _lineto (286,148);
_moveto (49,132);     _lineto (76,132);
_moveto (105,132);    _lineto (132,132);
_moveto (160,132);    _lineto (187,132);
_moveto (215,132);    _lineto (243,132);
_moveto (90,116);     _lineto (113,116);
_moveto (136,116);    _lineto (160,116);
_moveto (184,116);    _lineto (207,116);
_moveto (232,116);    _lineto (253,116);
_moveto (80,104);     _lineto (99,104);
_moveto (119,104);    _lineto (140,104);
_moveto (160,104);    _lineto (180,104);
_moveto (202,104);    _lineto (222,104);
_moveto (109,92);     _lineto (125,92);
_moveto (143,92);     _lineto (160,92);
_moveto (177,92);     _lineto (195,92);
_moveto (213,92);     _lineto (229,92);
_moveto (104,80);     _lineto (117,80);
_moveto (132,80);     _lineto (145,80);
_moveto (160,80);     _lineto (174,80);
_moveto (188,80);     _lineto (203,80);
_moveto (126,68);     _lineto (138,68);
_moveto (149,68);     _lineto (160,68);
_moveto (172,68);     _lineto (183,68);
_moveto (194,68);     _lineto (204,68);
_moveto (124,60);     _lineto (132,60);
_moveto (141,60);     _lineto (151,60);
_moveto (160,60);     _lineto (168,60);
_moveto (178,60);     _lineto (187,60);
_moveto (140,52);     _lineto (146,52);
_moveto (153,52);     _lineto (160,52);
_moveto (167,52);     _lineto (174,52);
_moveto (181,52);     _lineto (188,52);
_moveto (141,44);     _lineto (145,44);
_moveto (150,44);     _lineto (155,44);
_moveto (161,44);     _lineto (165,44);
```

Listing 6.1 *continues*

Listing 6.1. cont. Hallway animation example.

```
_moveto (170,44);     _lineto (175,44);
_moveto (16,136);     _lineto (16,108);
_moveto (16,78);      _lineto (16,49);
_moveto (16,20);      _lineto (16,0);
_moveto (32,20);      _lineto (32,46);
_moveto (32,72);      _lineto (32,98);
_moveto (32,124);     _lineto (32,149);
_moveto (48,111);     _lineto (48,88);
_moveto (48,65);      _lineto (48,43);
_moveto (48,20);      _lineto (48,0);
_moveto (68,20);      _lineto (68,39);
_moveto (68,58);      _lineto (68,76);
_moveto (68,96);      _lineto (68,115);
_moveto (80,86);      _lineto (80,70);
_moveto (80,53);      _lineto (80,37);
_moveto (80,20);      _lineto (80,4);
_moveto (92,0);       _lineto (92,6);
_moveto (92,20);      _lineto (92,34);
_moveto (92,48);      _lineto (92,62);
_moveto (92,77);      _lineto (92,91);
_moveto (104,67);     _lineto (104,56);
_moveto (104,44);     _lineto (104,32);
_moveto (104,20);     _lineto (104,8);
_moveto (116,1);      _lineto (116,11);
_moveto (116,20);     _lineto (116,29);
_moveto (116,39);     _lineto (116,48);
_moveto (116,59);     _lineto (116,67);
_moveto (124,52);     _lineto (124,44);
_moveto (124,36);     _lineto (124,28);
_moveto (124,20);     _lineto (124,12);
_moveto (124,4);      _lineto (124,0);
_moveto (132,7);      _lineto (132,14);
_moveto (132,20);     _lineto (132,26);
_moveto (132,33);     _lineto (132,39);
_moveto (132,45);     _lineto (132,52);
_moveto (140,39);     _lineto (140,35);
_moveto (140,30);     _lineto (140,25);
_moveto (140,20);     _lineto (140,15);
_moveto (140,5);      _lineto (140,11);
_moveto (146,4);      _lineto (150,4);
_moveto (155,4);      _lineto (160,4);
_moveto (165,4);      _lineto (169,4);
_moveto (174,4);      _lineto (180,4);
_moveto (180,10);     _lineto (180,15);
```

```
   _moveto (180,20);    _lineto (180,25);
   _moveto (180,30);    _lineto (180,34);
   _moveto (180,39);    _lineto (180,44);
   _moveto (188,45);    _lineto (188,39);
   _moveto (188,33);    _lineto (188,26);
   _moveto (188,20);    _lineto (188,14);
   _moveto (188,7);     _lineto (188,0);
   _moveto (196,4);     _lineto (196,12);
   _moveto (196,20);    _lineto (196,28);
   _moveto (196,36);    _lineto (196,43);
   _moveto (196,52);    _lineto (196,59);
   _moveto (204,10);    _lineto (204,20);
   _moveto (204,30);    _lineto (204,39);
   _moveto (204,49);    _lineto (204,58);
   _moveto (216,8);     _lineto (216,0);
   _moveto (216,20);    _lineto (216,32);
   _moveto (216,44);    _lineto (216,55);
   _moveto (216,67);    _lineto (216,79);
   _moveto (228,76);    _lineto (228,62);
   _moveto (228,34);    _lineto (228,48);
   _moveto (228,20);    _lineto (228,5);
   _moveto (240,0);     _lineto (240,3);
   _moveto (240,20);    _lineto (240,36);
   _moveto (240,53);    _lineto (240,69);
   _moveto (240,103);   _lineto (240,86);
   _moveto (256,98);    _lineto (256,79);
   _moveto (256,59);    _lineto (256,40);
   _moveto (256,20);    _lineto (256,0);
   _moveto (272,20);    _lineto (272,42);
   _moveto (272,65);    _lineto (272,88);
   _moveto (272,111);   _lineto (272,133);
   _moveto (288,123);   _lineto (288,98);
   _moveto (288,72);    _lineto (288,46);
   _moveto (288,20);    _lineto (288,0);
   _moveto (304,20);    _lineto (304,49);
   _moveto (304,78);    _lineto (304,107);
   _moveto (304,136);   _lineto (304,165);
}


void _drawline2 (void)
{
_rectangle (_GBORDER,144,40,176,8);
_rectangle (_GBORDER,0,0,319,180);
```

Listing 6.1 *continues*

Listing 6.1. cont. Hallway animation example.

```
_moveto (0,180);        _lineto (144,40);
_moveto (148,40);       _lineto (40,180);
_moveto (152,40);       _lineto (80,180);
_moveto (156,40);       _lineto (120,180);
_moveto (160,40);       _lineto (160,180);
_moveto (164,40);       _lineto (200,180);
_moveto (168,40);       _lineto (240,180);
_moveto (172,40);       _lineto (280,180);
_moveto (176,40);       _lineto (319,180);
_moveto (176,36);       _lineto (319,148);
_moveto (176,32);       _lineto (319,116);
_moveto (176,28);       _lineto (319,84);
_moveto (176,24);       _lineto (319,52);
_moveto (176,20);       _lineto (319,20);
_moveto (176,16);       _lineto (256,0);
_moveto (176,12);       _lineto (204,0);
_moveto (176,8);        _lineto (184,0);
_moveto (172,8);        _lineto (176,0);
_moveto (168,8);        _lineto (170,0);
_moveto (164,8);        _lineto (166,0);
_moveto (160,8);        _lineto (160,0);
_moveto (156,8);        _lineto (154,0);
_moveto (152,8);        _lineto (150,0);
_moveto (148,8);        _lineto (144,0);
_moveto (144,8);        _lineto (136,0);
_moveto (144,12);       _lineto (114,0);
_moveto (144,16);       _lineto (64,0);
_moveto (144,20);       _lineto (0,20);
_moveto (144,24);       _lineto (0,52);
_moveto (144,28);       _lineto (0,84);
_moveto (144,32);       _lineto (0,116);
_moveto (144,36);       _lineto (0,148);
_moveto (16,20);        _lineto (16,48);
_moveto (16,78);        _lineto (16,107);
_moveto (16,136);       _lineto (16,164);
_moveto (52,164);       _lineto (88,164);
_moveto (124,164);      _lineto (160,164);
_moveto (196,164);      _lineto (232,164);
_moveto (268,164);      _lineto (302,164);
_moveto (304,136);      _lineto (304,108);
_moveto (304,79);       _lineto (304,49);
_moveto (304,20);       _lineto (304,0);
_moveto (288,20);       _lineto (288,46);
```

```
_moveto (288,72);    _lineto (288,97);
_moveto (288,124);   _lineto (288,149);
_moveto (254,148);   _lineto (223,148);
_moveto (192,148);   _lineto (160,148);
_moveto (128,148);   _lineto (97,148);
_moveto (64,148);    _lineto (33,148);
_moveto (32,123);    _lineto (32,97);
_moveto (32,72);     _lineto (32,46);
_moveto (32,20);     _lineto (32,0);
_moveto (48,20);     _lineto (48,42);
_moveto (48,65);     _lineto (48,88);
_moveto (48,110);    _lineto (48,132);
_moveto (77,132);    _lineto (104,132);
_moveto (132,132);   _lineto (160,132);
_moveto (188,132);   _lineto (215,132);
_moveto (243,132);   _lineto (269,132);
_moveto (268,108);   _lineto (268,86);
_moveto (268,64);    _lineto (268,42);
_moveto (268,20);    _lineto (268,0);
_moveto (254,20);    _lineto (254,40);
_moveto (254,58);    _lineto (254,78);
_moveto (254,98);    _lineto (254,116);
_moveto (230,116);   _lineto (207,116);
_moveto (184,116);   _lineto (160,116);
_moveto (136,116);   _lineto (113,116);
_moveto (89,116);    _lineto (66,116);
_moveto (64,97);     _lineto (64,79);
_moveto (64,59);     _lineto (64,40);
_moveto (64,20);     _lineto (64,0);
_moveto (76,0);      _lineto (76,3);
_moveto (76,20);     _lineto (76,37);
_moveto (76,54);     _lineto (76,72);
_moveto (76,88);     _lineto (76,105);
_moveto (99,104);    _lineto (119,104);
_moveto (140,104);   _lineto (160,104);
_moveto (180,104);   _lineto (201,104);
_moveto (221,104);   _lineto (240,104);
_moveto (240,86);    _lineto (240,70);
_moveto (240,53);    _lineto (240,37);
_moveto (240,20);    _lineto (240,4);
_moveto (228,0);     _lineto (228,6);
_moveto (228,20);    _lineto (228,34);
_moveto (228,48);    _lineto (228,62);
_moveto (228,77);    _lineto (228,90);
```

Listing 6.1 *continues*

Listing 6.1. cont.   Hallway animation example.

```
_moveto (212,92);      _lineto (195,92);
_moveto (177,92);      _lineto (160,92);
_moveto (142,92);      _lineto (126,92);
_moveto (108,92);      _lineto (90,92);
_moveto (88,79);       _lineto (88,65);
_moveto (88,49);       _lineto (88,35);
_moveto (88,20);       _lineto (88,5);
_moveto (100,0);       _lineto (100,8);
_moveto (100,20);      _lineto (100,32);
_moveto (100,45);      _lineto (100,58);
_moveto (100,70);      _lineto (100,82);
_moveto (118,80);      _lineto (132,80);
_moveto (146,80);      _lineto (160,80);
_moveto (175,80);      _lineto (188,80);
_moveto (204,80);      _lineto (216,80);
_moveto (216,68);      _lineto (216,56);
_moveto (216,44);      _lineto (216,32);
_moveto (216,20);      _lineto (216,8);
_moveto (204,0);       _lineto (204,10);
_moveto (204,20);      _lineto (204,30);
_moveto (204,40);      _lineto (204,48);
_moveto (204,58);      _lineto (204,67);
_moveto (193,68);      _lineto (182,68);
_moveto (171,68);      _lineto (160,68);
_moveto (148,68);      _lineto (137,68);
_moveto (126,68);      _lineto (115,68);
_moveto (112,60);      _lineto (112,50);
_moveto (112,40);      _lineto (112,30);
_moveto (112,20);      _lineto (112,10);
_moveto (120,2);       _lineto (120,12);
_moveto (120,20);      _lineto (120,28);
_moveto (120,38);      _lineto (120,46);
_moveto (120,54);      _lineto (120,62);
_moveto (133,60);      _lineto (141,60);
_moveto (151,60);      _lineto (160,60);
_moveto (169,60);      _lineto (178,60);
_moveto (187,60);      _lineto (196,60);
_moveto (196,52);      _lineto (196,44);
_moveto (196,36);      _lineto (196,28);
_moveto (196,20);      _lineto (196,12);
_moveto (196,3);       _lineto (196,0);
_moveto (188,6);       _lineto (188,14);
_moveto (188,20);      _lineto (188,27);
```

```
_moveto (188,33);      _lineto (188,40);
_moveto (188,46);      _lineto (188,52);
_moveto (181,52);      _lineto (174,52);
_moveto (166,52);      _lineto (160,52);
_moveto (152,52);      _lineto (146,52);
_moveto (132,52);      _lineto (138,52);
_moveto (129,47);      _lineto (129,41);
_moveto (129,34);      _lineto (129,27);
_moveto (129,20);      _lineto (129,13);
_moveto (129,6);       _lineto (129,0);
_moveto (138,10);      _lineto (138,15);
_moveto (138,20);      _lineto (138,25);
_moveto (138,30);      _lineto (138,36);
_moveto (138,40);      _lineto (138,45);
_moveto (145,44);      _lineto (150,44);
_moveto (155,44);      _lineto (160,44);
_moveto (165,44);      _lineto (170,44);
_moveto (175,44);      _lineto (180,44);
_moveto (180,40);      _lineto (180,34);
_moveto (180,29);      _lineto (180,25);
_moveto (180,20);      _lineto (180,15);
_moveto (180,10);      _lineto (180,5);
_moveto (174,4);       _lineto (170,4);
_moveto (160,4);       _lineto (166,4);
_moveto (155,4);       _lineto (151,4);
_moveto (140,4);       _lineto (145,4);
}
```

Partial Screen Animation

In partial screen animation, only a small portion of the screen is used to create the animation. The portion of the screen used for animation is usually saved in memory and then moved about the screen. Another possibility is to store several images, then place them on top of each other to simulate motion.

The Microsoft graphics library includes two series of functions for use with partial screen animation: the _getimage and _putimage functions. The syntax for each member of these series follows:

```
void _far _getimage (short x1, short y1, short x2, short y2,
                   char _huge *image);
short x1, y1;              Upper left corner of image
```

```
    short x2, y2;                Lower right corner of image
    char _huge *image;           Image buffer


    void _far _getimage_w (double x1, double y1, double x2,
                           double y2, char _huge *image);
    double x1, y1;               Upper left corner of image
    double x2, y2;               Lower right corner of image
    char _huge *image;           Image buffer


    void _far _getimage_wxy (struct _wxycoord _far *xy1,
                             struct _wxycoord _far *xy2,
                             char _huge *image);
    struct _wxycoord _far *xy1;   Upper left corner of image
    struct _wxycoord _far *xy2;   Lower right corner of image
    char _huge *image;            Image buffer


    void _far _putimage (short x, short y, char _huge *image,
                         short action);
    double x, y;                 Upper left corner of placed image
    char _huge *image;           Image buffer
    short action;                Method to place image buffer


    void _far _putimage_w (double x, double y, char _huge
                           *image, short action);
    short x, y;                  Upper left corner of placed image
    char _huge *image;           Image buffer
    short action;                Method to place image buffer
```

The _getimage functions store a rectangular image in a buffer. The upper left and lower right corners of the rectangular image are identified and passed to the function. Then the specified rectangular region is stored in the buffer identified in the image argument. The _getimage function is used with the view coordinate system; the _getimage_w and _getimage_wxy functions are used with the window coordinate system.

The _putimage functions place onto the screen (hidden or visual) an image stored by the _getimage functions. You specify the image, the location of the upper left corner of the image, and how the image will interact with its background. For example, the _GXOR action performs an exclusive OR on each pixel and the background. This is a frequently performed action because doing an exclusive OR twice will return the background to its original position. The image, however, is often distorted, as will be discussed later in this chapter in "Placing Images on Multicolored Backgrounds."

Table 6.1 lists the five action arguments for use with the _putimage functions. The _putimage function is used with the view coordinate system, and the _putimage_w function is used with the window coordinate system.

Table 6.1 *Action arguments for the _putimage functions.*

Constant	Purpose
_GAND	The displayed pixels are the logical AND of the existing pixel values and the transferred pixel values.
_GOR	The displayed pixels are the logical OR of the existing pixel values and the transferred pixel values.
_GPRESET	The image is the negative of the stored image; each pixel is inverted before it is placed on the screen.
_GPSET	The image is placed on the screen exactly as it was stored.
_GXOR	The displayed pixels are the exclusive OR of the existing pixel values and the transferred pixel values.

Listing 6.2 demonstrates the _getimage and _putimage functions. This example uses the view coordinate system but the window coordinate system could have been used just as easily. In this example, a circular image, or ball, bounces around the screen. The _GXOR action argument is used for the animation. This example is simplistic—only one page is used. (You could make this example more realistic by using hidden pages with partial screens, which is demonstrated in the next example.) In addition, the _GXOR function works well only with plain backgrounds. When using multicolored backgrounds, the background will tend to bleed through, obscuring the image. For simple animation, however, the _GXOR argument works well. Other methods are discussed later in the chapter in "Placing Images on Multicolored Backgrounds."

Listing 6.2. Animation with _GXOR.

```
#include <graph.h>
#include <stdio.h>
#include <malloc.h>

void main ()
{
char _huge *ball;
short x1,y1;
short oldx, oldy;
short x_dir, y_dir;
x_dir = -5;
y_dir = +5;

_setvideomode (_ERESCOLOR);
```

Listing 6.2 *continues*

Listing 6.2. cont.   Animation with _GXOR.

```
_rectangle (_GBORDER,0,0,639,349);

_ellipse (_GFILLINTERIOR,310,168,330,182);

ball=(char far *)malloc((unsigned int)
                    _imagesize(310,168,330,182));
_getimage (310,168,330,182,ball);

x1 = 310;
y1 = 168;

do
{
oldx = x1;
oldy = y1;
x1 = x1 + x_dir;
y1 = y1 + y_dir;

if (x1 < 0)
{
     x1 = x1 + 5;
     x_dir = 5;
}

if (x1 > 619)
{
     x1 = x1 - 5;
     x_dir = -5;
}

if (y1 > 329)
{
     y1 = y1 - 5;
     y_dir = -5;
}

if (y1 < 0)
{
     y1 = y1 + 5;
     y_dir = 5;
}
```

```
_putimage (oldx,oldy,ball,_GXOR);
_putimage (x1,y1,ball,_GXOR);

} while ( !kbhit() );

_setvideomode (_DEFAULTMODE);
}
```

Hidden Pages with Partial Screen Animation

In the previous example, one image was moved over the screen to produce motion. The output was far from optimal—the image appeared to flicker as it moved. (This is a characteristic of single page animation.) The best way to overcome this is to use multiple pages of graphics to store several images, each slightly different from the other, then move the object on a hidden page. Listing 6.3 is an example of this type of animation. We use the same basic code structure as before, but track two screens and ball locations. This example uses the pause() function to control the speed of the animation. For fast machines, you may have to slow the animation by modifying the for loop that calls the pause() function.

Listing 6.3. Spinning ball example.

```
#include <graph.h>
#include <stdio.h>
#include <malloc.h>

void main ()
{
char _huge *ball1;
char _huge *ball2;
char _huge *ball3;
char _huge *ball4;
char _huge *ball5;
char _huge *ball6;
int i;

_setvideomode (_ERESCOLOR);
_rectangle (_GBORDER,0,0,639,349);

        /* Draw and save ball one */
```

Listing 6.3 *continues*

Listing 6.3. cont.   Spinning ball example.

```
_setcolor (15);
_ellipse (_GBORDER,30,145,110,205);
_ellipse (_GBORDER,55,145,85,205);
_setcolor(1);
_floodfill (32,175,15);
_setcolor (4);
_floodfill (70,175,15);
_setcolor (2);
_floodfill (108,175,15);
ball1=(char far *)malloc((unsigned int)
                        _imagesize(30,145,110,205));
_getimage (30,145,110,205,ball1);

        /* Draw and save ball two */

_setcolor (15);
_ellipse (_GBORDER,130,145,210,205);
_ellipse (_GBORDER,155,145,185,205);
_setcolor(14);
_floodfill (132,175,15);
_setcolor (1);
_floodfill (170,175,15);
_setcolor (4);
_floodfill (208,175,15);
ball2=(char far *)malloc((unsigned int)
                        _imagesize(130,145,210,205));
_getimage (130,145,210,205,ball2);

        /* Draw and save ball three */

_setcolor (15);
_ellipse (_GBORDER,230,145,310,205);
_ellipse (_GBORDER,255,145,285,205);
_setcolor(3);
_floodfill (232,175,15);
_setcolor (14);
_floodfill (270,175,15);
_setcolor (1);
_floodfill (308,175,15);
ball3=(char far *)malloc((unsigned int)
                        _imagesize(230,145,310,205));
_getimage (230,145,310,205,ball3);
```

```
          /* Draw and save ball four */

_setcolor (15);
_ellipse (_GBORDER,330,145,410,205);
_ellipse (_GBORDER,355,145,385,205);
_setcolor(15);
_floodfill (332,175,15);
_setcolor (3);
_floodfill (370,175,15);
_setcolor (14);
_floodfill (408,175,15);
ball4=(char far *)malloc((unsigned int)
            _imagesize(330,145,410,205));
_getimage (330,145,410,205,ball4);

          /* Draw and save ball five */

_setcolor (15);
_ellipse (_GBORDER,430,145,510,205);
_ellipse (_GBORDER,455,145,485,205);
_setcolor(2);
_floodfill (432,175,15);
_setcolor (15);
_floodfill (470,175,15);
_setcolor (3);
_floodfill (508,175,15);
ball5=(char far *)malloc((unsigned int)
            _imagesize(430,145,510,205));
_getimage (430,145,510,205,ball5);

          /* Draw and save ball six */

_setcolor (15);
_ellipse (_GBORDER,530,145,610,205);
_ellipse (_GBORDER,555,145,585,205);
_setcolor(4);
_floodfill (532,175,15);
_setcolor (2);
_floodfill (570,175,15);
_setcolor (15);
_floodfill (608,175,15);
ball6=(char far *)malloc((unsigned int)
            _imagesize(530,145,610,205));
```

Listing 6.3 *continues*

Listing 6.3. cont.   Spinning ball example.

```
_getimage (530,145,610,205,ball6);

_settextposition (23,5);
_outtext ("Press Any Key To Continue");
getch ();
_clearscreen (_GCLEARSCREEN);
_rectangle (_GBORDER,0,0,639,349);
_setactivepage (1);
_clearscreen (_GCLEARSCREEN);
_rectangle (_GBORDER,0,0,639,349);

do
{
_setactivepage (1);
_putimage (280,145,ball1,_GPSET);
_setvisualpage (1);
for (i=1; i<5; i = i+1)
     {
     pause ();
     }
_setactivepage (0);
_putimage (280,145,ball2,_GPSET);
_setvisualpage (0);
for (i=1; i<5; i = i+1)
     {
     pause ();
     }
_setactivepage (1);
_putimage (280,145,ball3,_GPSET);
_setvisualpage (1);
for (i=1; i<5; i = i+1)
     {
     pause ();
     }
_setactivepage (0);
_putimage (280,145,ball4,_GPSET);
_setvisualpage (0);
for (i=1; i<5; i=i+1)
     {
     pause ();
     }
_setactivepage (1);
_putimage (280,145,ball5,_GPSET);
```

```
_setvisualpage (1);
for (i=1; i<5; i= i+1)
        {
        pause ();
        }
_setactivepage (0);
_putimage (280,145,ball6,_GPSET);
_setvisualpage (0);
} while ( !kbhit() );

_setvideomode (_DEFAULTMODE);
}

pause ()
{
int x;
x = 0;

do
        {
            x = x + 1;
        } while (x != 10000);

}
```

The methods presented for partial and full screen animation in the previous examples can be used in combination to generate almost any graphics application. These basic techniques are the foundation for most personal computer graphics applications.

Advanced Concepts in Animation

To make the most out of animation, it is important to understand a few of its more complex concepts. When you combine these concepts with techniques previously introduced, you greatly enhance the flexibility and results of your graphics programs.

Placing Images on Multicolored Backgrounds

The _putimage functions are the primary means of animation. Therefore, it is important to fully understand these functions and their corresponding arguments. For this reason, listing 6.4 is provided. In this example, an image is created, stored, and placed on a multicolored background using each of the five action constants described in table 6.1.

Listing 6.4. Using the _putimage function.

```c
#include <graph.h>
#include <stdio.h>
#include <malloc.h>

void main ()
{
char _huge *image;
int x, y;
int color;
color = 1;

_setvideomode (_ERESCOLOR);
_setbkcolor (_BLUE);

        /* Create multicolored lines */

for (x = 0; x<639; x=x+10)
{
    _setcolor (color);
    _moveto (x,0);
    _lineto (x,349);
    color = color + 1;
    if (color > 15)
        color = 1;
}

for (y = 0; y<349; y=y+10)
{
    _setcolor (color);
    _moveto (0,y);
    _lineto (639,y);
    color = color + 1;
    if (color > 15)
        color = 1;
}

_rectangle (_GBORDER,0,0,639,349);

        /* Create and store image using hidden page */

_setactivepage (1);
```

```
_clearscreen (_GCLEARSCREEN);
_setcolor (4);
_ellipse (_GFILLINTERIOR,30,30,80,80);
image=(char far *)malloc((unsigned int)
                _imagesize(30,30,80,80));
_getimage (30,30,80,80,image);

        /* Place image on screen using 5 action arguments */

_setactivepage (0);

_putimage (155,10,image,_GXOR);
_putimage (225,80,image,_GAND);
_putimage (295,150,image,_GOR);
_putimage (365,220,image,_GPSET);
_putimage (435,290,image,_GPRESET);

_settextposition (24,5);
_outtext ("_GXOR, _GAND, _GOR, _GPSET, _GPRESET Arguments");

        /* Delay and exit */

getch ();
_setvideomode (_DEFAULTMODE);
}
```

From this example, it is apparent that none of these action arguments provides a good means of placing an image on a multicolored background. Fortunately, there is a way to successfully place complex images onto complex backgrounds.

Combining Action Arguments for Complex Images

As the previous example demonstrated, no single action argument effectively places a complex (non-rectangular) image on a multicolored background. You can use a combination of action arguments, however, to place an image cleanly on the multicolored background. A preparatory image is placed on the screen with the _GOR action argument, then the complex image is placed on the screen with the _GAND argument. The result is an undistorted image that allows the background around the image to show, even if the image is irregularly shaped. You cannot restore the background when you use the _GOR and _GAND combination; therefore, save the background, if necessary, prior to using this combination.

Listing 6.5 demonstrates the use of the _GOR and _GAND combination. When a key is pressed, the program clears the screen, draws a multicolored background, then places the preparatory and display images on the screen with the _GOR and _GAND arguments, respectively. The preparatory image consists of a white ellipse on a black background. When the preparatory image is placed on the screen, each white pixel in the image turns any colored background pixel white. The complex image is created as follows: pixels placed over the white preparatory image are transferred "as is" (they retain their appearance); pixels that aren't placed on the preparatory image allow the background color to show through unchanged. Therefore, even with the _GOR and _GAND combination, the background must be displayed very carefully. The final image is shown in figure 6.3.

Listing 6.5. Example of the _GOR and _GAND combination.

```
#include <graph.h>
#include <stdio.h>
#include <malloc.h>

void main ()
{
char _huge *prepimage;
char _huge *image;
int x, y;

_setvideomode (_ERESCOLOR);
_rectangle (_GBORDER,0,0,639,349);

        /* Draw white preparatory image */

_setcolor (15);
_ellipse (_GFILLINTERIOR,210,100,310,200);

        /* Draw complex image */

_setcolor (4);
_rectangle (_GFILLINTERIOR,330,100,430,200);
_setcolor (2);
_rectangle (_GFILLINTERIOR,350,120,410,180);
_setcolor (14);
_rectangle (_GFILLINTERIOR,370,140,390,160);

        /* Save preparatory image */

prepimage=(char far *)malloc((unsigned int)_imagesize
        (210,100,310,200));
```

```
_getimage (210,100,310,200,prepimage);

        /* Save complex image */

image = (char far *)malloc((unsigned int) _imagesize
        (330,100,430,200));
_getimage (330,100,430,200,image);

        /* Delay */

_settextposition (23,5);
_outtext ("Press Any Key To Demonstrate _GOR/_GAND
        Combination");
getch ();

        /* Create multicolored background */

_clearscreen (_GCLEARSCREEN);
_setcolor (4);

        /* Draw vertical lines */

for (x = 0; x<639; x=x+10)
    {
    _moveto (x,0);
    _lineto (x,349);
    }

        /* Draw horizontal lines */

for (y = 0; y<349; y=y+10)
    {
    _moveto (0,y);
    _lineto (639,y);
    }

_setcolor (15);
_rectangle (_GBORDER,0,0,639,349);

        /* Place preparatory and complex images */

_putimage (270,125,prepimage,_GOR);
_putimage (270,125,image,_GAND);
```

Listing 6.4 *continues*

Listing 6.4. cont.   Example of the _GOR and _GAND combination.

```
                    /* Delay and exit */

_settextposition (23,5);
_outtext ("Complex Image Successfully Placed");
_settextposition (24,5);
_outtext ("Press Any Key To Continue");

getch ();
_setvideomode (_DEFAULTMODE);
}
```

Fig. 6.3.   Example output from listing 6.5.

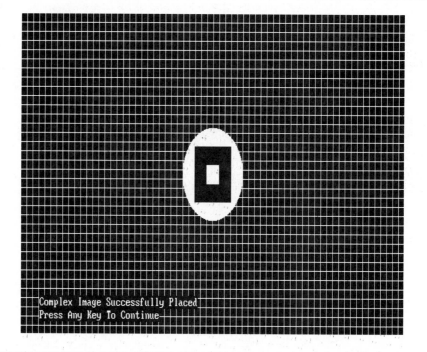

Optimizing the Speed of Animation

To achieve good results with animation, the program must have adequate speed. The programmer can affect the speed of animation by properly designing the application.

The first method for animation optimization is to create several screens in memory and flip through them. Unfortunately, this is seldom a viable alternative because only a limited number of pages can be created and manipulated in video RAM. Some applications use assembly routines to save screens in computer memory—even with this, the computer's total memory (video and computer) can be used up quickly. Therefore, other solutions must be considered.

The only other method is to use a combination of techniques introduced in this chapter. You should keep in mind certain rules of thumb, however. The first is that images manipulated with the `_getimage` and `_putimage` functions should be kept as small as possible. The smaller the image, the faster it is transferred. Second, you should consider the method by which the images are placed. For example, when using the `_GOR` and `_GAND` combination for animation, the background immediately behind the image must be saved, then the preparatory and complex images placed, then the background restored. This is a total of four placements for every animation iteration. Using the `_GPRESET` argument could save one iteration; using the `_GXOR` argument could save two iterations. The speed and complexity of the animation depends, of course, on the intended application. Last, it is often more efficient to move several small images than one large image.

Planning and implementation are necessary for effective graphics animation programming. By carefully considering the application, you can select the best combination of techniques to make the optimal trade-off between speed and graphics detail.

7

Two- and Three-Dimensional Drawing

Advanced drawing packages, such as computer-aided design (CAD) packages, can usually operate with either two- or three-dimensional images. This chapter introduces the basic concepts and mathematical formulas behind two- and three-dimensional drawing.

The Two-Dimensional Coordinate System

The drawing techniques discussed in the previous chapters were all based on the two-dimensional coordinate system. The two-dimensional coordinate system consists of two axes: the x-axis extends horizontally, and the y-axis extends vertically. By labeling the axes in the manner shown in figure 7.1, the two-dimensional coordinate system corresponds to the screen coordinates described by the Microsoft C graphics library.

The most obvious thing to note on the way that this coordinate system is labeled is that the positive y-axis extends downward. This may cause some initial problems with engineers who are unfamiliar with this convention. By labeling the coordinate system in this way, however, you can transfer sketchings, drawings, and so on to the screen without transforming coordinates.

Formulas for Two-Dimensional Rotation

In a two-dimensional setting, it is easy to rotate a coordinate pair (defined by an x and y value) about a point. The key to two-dimensional rotation, however, is that the rotation must be about the origin of the coordinate system. Initially, this seems like a severe limitation when using Microsoft C because the upper left corner of the screen is the physical origin of the screen's two-dimensional coordinate system.

Fig. 7.1. Two-dimensional coordinate system.

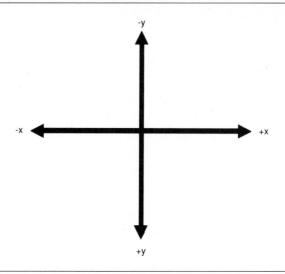

Fortunately, the Microsoft graphics environment supports three coordinate systems, which overlay each other. These coordinate systems are the physical, view, and window coordinate systems, as discussed in Chapter 3. By moving the origin of the view or window coordinate system to the point from which rotation will occur, you can rotate any coordinate pair (on or off the screen) about any physical point on the screen. The view or window origin must remain in the physical coordinates of the screen. Figure 7.2 illustrates the relationship between the physical and view coordinate systems.

In a two-dimensional coordinate system, rotation of coordinate pairs can be accomplished in either a clockwise or counterclockwise direction. Simple trigonometric algorithms perform these coordinate pair rotations. The formulas for two-dimensional rotation follow:

x = (x' * cos(angle)) + (y' * sin(angle))
y = (y' * cos(angle)) – (x' * sin(angle))

where x' and y' are the values of x and y prior to transformation. Note: the *angle* argument must be expressed as type double and in radians. A positive angle rotates in a counterclockwise direction; a negative angle rotates in a clockwise direction.

When describing the amount of rotation desired, an *angle* argument is used in the equations just shown. For example, if you want a 45-degree clockwise rotation, you would use an *angle* parameter of – 45 degrees. You would use an *angle* parameter of 45 degrees for counterclockwise rotation. The trigonometric functions provided by Microsoft (s i n, c o s, and so on) require the *angle* argument to be in radians. Because it is easier and more natural to think in degrees, a simple conversion can be used to convert degrees to radians. The relationships between radians and degrees are shown in figure 7.3.

Fig. 7.2. Physical and view coordinate systems.

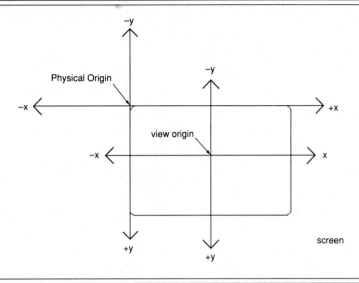

Fig. 7.3. Degree and radian relationships.

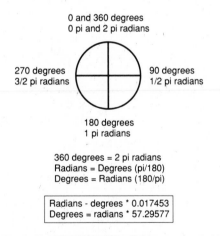

0 and 360 degrees
0 pi and 2 pi radians

270 degrees
3/2 pi radians

90 degrees
1/2 pi radians

180 degrees
1 pi radians

360 degrees = 2 pi radians
Radians = Degrees (pi/180)
Degrees = Radians (180/pi)

Radians - degrees * 0.017453
Degrees = radians * 57.29577

Listing 7.1 demonstrates the simple rotation of a point about the center of the screen. A point must first be identified by its x and y coordinates and placed on the screen. In this case, the initial point is 100,0 with respect to the view origin at the center of the screen. The program is designed to rotate this point, in 10 degree increments, about the view origin. Figure 7.4 shows the screen output of this rotation demonstration.

Listing 7.1. Two-dimensional rotation example.

```
#include <stdio.h>
#include <graph.h>
#include <math.h>

void main ()
{

      /* Initialization */
float x,y;
float oldx, oldy;
double angle;
int rotation;

x = 100.0;
y = 0.0;
rotation = 0;

_setvideomode (_ERESCOLOR);
_rectangle (_GBORDER,0,0,639,349);
_setvieworg (320,175);
_setpixel (x,y);
angle = 10.0 * .017453;

      /* Loops until the point is rotated 360 degrees */
do {
    oldx = x;
    oldy = y;
    x = (oldx * cos (angle))+(oldy * sin (angle));
    y = (oldy * cos (angle))-(oldx * sin (angle));
    _setpixel (x, .75 * y);
    rotation = rotation + 10;
    } while (rotation < 360);

      /* Delay and exit */
_settextposition (24,32);
_outtext ("Press a Key to Exit");

getch ();
_setvideomode (_DEFAULTMODE);
}
```

Fig. 7.4. Example output from listing 7.1.

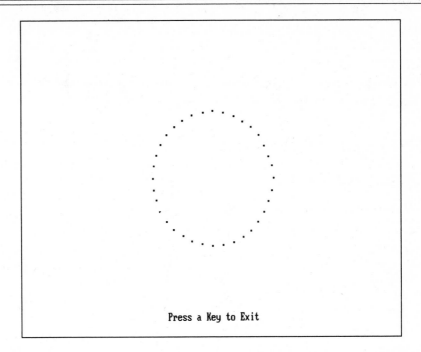

Press a Key to Exit

Several issues must be considered when doing this seemingly simple example. The first issue is that an aspect ratio must be used to make a circular, as opposed to an elliptical, pattern. For the video mode used in this example (_ERESCOLOR), multiplying the rotated y coordinate by .75 works well. The use of .75 is due to the pixel size of the mode in use. (Chapter 3 explains aspect ratios in more detail.) The second issue is the proper use of variable types. When using the trigonometric functions, the *angle* argument must be expressed as type double and in radians. If this is not done properly, the rotational results will be unpredictable.

Rotating the Rectangle

The formulas provided for two-dimensional rotation in the previous section are good for only one purpose: to rotate a coordinate pair through a given angle. Although these formulas do an excellent job with coordinate pairs, they fall short when attempting to rotate objects.

When using the Microsoft _rectangle functions, a rectangle is described through the identification of its upper left and lower right corners. Because the rectangle is described by two-coordinate pairs, rotating those coordinate pairs and, thus, rotating the rectangle would seem, on the surface, to be an easy task. Unfortunately, this is not the case.

The method by which the rectangle is drawn—using two coordinate pairs—presents a problem for rotation. When the two coordinate pairs are passed to the _rectangle function, four line segments are created. These four line segments are described as follows:

Line 1: high y, low x to high y, high x
Line 2: low y, low x to low y, high x
Line 3: low y, high x to high y, high x
Line 4: low y, low x to high y, low x

Given two corner points, the _rectangle functions calculate the other two corner points. Although this function is easy to use, it is not a good way to describe a rectangle that must be rotated due to the limitations in the way the other two corner points are evaluated. By looking at the preceding equations, you can see that only vertical and horizontal lines are generated using this method. Therefore, rotating the two corner points does no good. Figure 7.5 illustrates this point by showing what a square rotated through 45 degrees looks like. The result is a vertical rectangle if rotated counterclockwise, and a horizontal rectangle if rotated clockwise. Obviously, this is not the desired output.

Fig. 7.5.   Rectangle rotation when using the _rectangle functions.

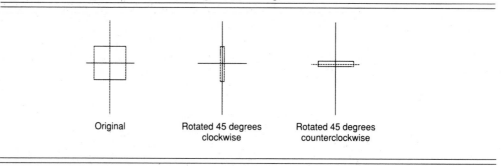

Original	Rotated 45 degrees clockwise	Rotated 45 degrees counterclockwise

Fortunately, there is an easy solution to this problem. By creating a rectangle with four line segments, and defining all four corner points, you can easily rotate the rectangle about any point. Listing 7.2 demonstrates this method. Initially, a rectangle is described by four coordinate pairs. Then these coordinate pairs are rotated in a counterclockwise fashion through 360 degrees, in 20-degree increments. The resulting output is shown in figure 7.6.

Listing 7.2.   Two-dimensional rectangle rotation example.

```
#include <stdio.h>
#include <graph.h>
#include <math.h>

void main ()
{
float x1,y1;
float x2,y2;
float x3,y3;
float x4,y4;
float oldx1,oldy1;
float oldx2,oldy2;
float oldx3,oldy3;
float oldx4,oldy4;
double angle;
int rotation;

x1 = -100.0;
y1 = -50.0;
x2 = 100.0;
y2 = -50.0;
x3 = 100.0;
y3 = 50.0;
x4 = -100.0;
y4 = 50.0;
angle = 20.0 * .017453;
rotation = 0;

_setvideomode (_ERESCOLOR);
_rectangle (_GBORDER,0,0,639,349);
_setvieworg (320,175);
_moveto ((int)x1, (int)y1);
_lineto ((int)x2, (int)y2);
_lineto ((int)x3, (int)y3);
_lineto ((int)x4, (int)y4);
_lineto ((int)x1, (int)y1);
_setpixel (0,0);

do {
        oldx1 = x1;
        oldy1 = y1;
```

Listing 7.2   *continues*

Listing 7.2. cont.   Two-dimensional rectangle rotation example.

```
x1 = (oldx1 * cos (angle))+(oldy1 * sin (angle));
y1 = (oldy1 * cos (angle))-(oldx1 * sin (angle));
oldx2 = x2;
oldy2 = y2;
x2 = (oldx2 * cos (angle))+(oldy2 * sin (angle));
y2 = (oldy2 * cos (angle))-(oldx2 * sin (angle));
oldx3 = x3;
oldy3 = y3;
x3 = (oldx3 * cos (angle))+(oldy3 * sin (angle));
y3 = (oldy3 * cos (angle))-(oldx3 * sin (angle));
oldx4 = x4;
oldy4 = y4;
x4 = (oldx4 * cos (angle))+(oldy4 * sin (angle));
y4 = (oldy4 * cos (angle))-(oldx4 * sin (angle));

_moveto ((int)x1, (int)y1);
_lineto ((int)x2, (int)y2);
_lineto ((int)x3, (int)y3);
_lineto ((int)x4, (int)y4);
_lineto ((int)x1, (int)y1);

rotation = rotation + 20;
} while (rotation < 360);

_settextposition (24,32);
_outtext ("Press a Key to Exit");

getch ();
_setvideomode (_DEFAULTMODE);
}
```

Rotating the Polygon

Two-dimensional rotation formulas work well with Microsoft's _polygon functions. The _rectangle functions require an alternate drawing method because two of the rectangle's corners are interpreted by the function. This type of problem is not present in the _polygon functions, however, because the polygon is defined by a set of points that fully describe the object.

Listing 7.3 demonstrates the use of the rotation algorithms for the rotation of a polygon. In this example, a triangle is created using the _polygon function. Then this triangle is rotated in 90-degree increments. Each coordinate pair that describes a point in the polygon (in this case the triangle) is passed through the rotation algorithms. The window coordinate system is used in this example. The output of this example is shown in figure 7.7.

Fig. 7.6. Example output from listing 7.2.

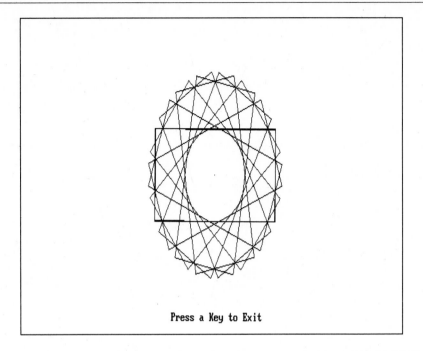

Press a Key to Exit

Listing 7.3. Two-dimensional polygon rotation example.

```
#include <stdio.h>
#include <graph.h>
#include <math.h>

void main ()
{
        /* Initialization */

struct _wxycoord points[3];
double angle;
double ang;
int holdx;
int holdy;

_setvideomode (_ERESCOLOR);
_rectangle (_GBORDER,0,0,639,349);
```

Listing 7.3 *continues*

Listing 7.3. cont. Two-dimensional polygon rotation example.

```
            /* Open window */
_setviewport (0,0,639,349);
_setwindow (0,-100.0,-100.0,100.0,100.0);

            /* Define points for polygon */
points[0].wx = 0.0;
points[0].wy = 0.0;
points[1].wx = 25.0;
points[1].wy = 50.0;
points[2].wx = -25.0;
points[2].wy = 50.0;

            /* Rotate 360 degrees, in 90-degree increments */
for (angle = 0.0; angle < 360.0; angle = angle + 90.0)
{
     ang = angle * .017453;
     holdx = points[0].wx;
     holdy = points[0].wy;
     points[0].wx = (holdx * cos (ang))+(holdy * sin (ang));
     points[0].wy = (holdy * cos (ang))-(holdx * sin (ang));

     holdx = points[1].wx;
     holdy = points[1].wy;
     points[1].wx = (holdx * cos (ang))+(holdy * sin (ang));
     points[1].wy = (holdy * cos (ang))-(holdx * sin (ang));

     holdx = points[2].wx;
     holdy = points[2].wy;
     points[2].wx = (holdx * cos (ang))+(holdy * sin (ang));
     points[2].wy = (holdy * cos (ang))-(holdx * sin (ang));

     _polygon_wxy (_GBORDER,points,3);
}


            /* Delay and exit */
_settextposition (24,5);
_outtext ("Press Any Key To Exit");

getch ();
_setvideomode (_DEFAULTMODE);
    }
```

Fig. 7.7. Example output from listing 7.3.

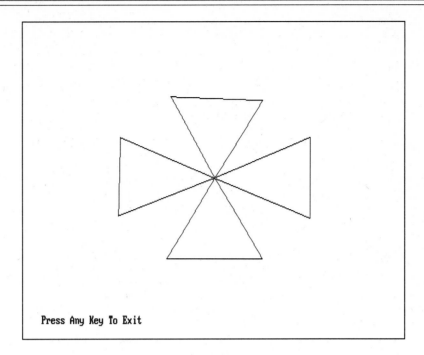

Press Any Key To Exit

Rotating the Ellipse

The _ellipse functions provided by Microsoft share the same problems as the _rectangle functions. Because each point that describes the object is not defined, the function interprets, or calculates, the points of the object. For the _ellipse functions, the ellipse is defined using a rectangular binding region. Only two of the four corners are described, so the translation of these corner points to accomplish rotation of the ellipse is futile. Therefore, an alternate drawing method for creating the rotated ellipse must be found.

Listing 7.4 offers an effective, but slow, implementation of ellipse rotation. The rotation function in this listing is based on a function in *Graphics Programming in C* by Roger T. Stevens. This function is far from optimal but provides one method by which you can define the ellipse to accomplish two-dimensional rotation. The listing demonstrates the use of the _rotate_ellipse function. Figure 7.8 shows the output of listing 7.4.

Listing 7.4. Two-dimensional ellipse rotation example.

```c
#include <graph.h>
#include <stdio.h>
#include <math.h>

void main ()
{
_setvideomode (_ERESCOLOR);
_rectangle (_GBORDER,0,0,639,349);
_setvieworg (320,175);

_rotate_ellipse (0,0,75,0.0);
_rotate_ellipse (0,0,75,45.0);
_rotate_ellipse (0,0,75,90.0);
_rotate_ellipse (0,0,75,135.0);

_settextposition (23,5);
_outtext ("Press Any Key To Exit");
getch ();
_setvideomode (_DEFAULTMODE);
}

_rotate_ellipse (int x, int y, int radius, double angle)
{
float aspect;
float aspect_square;
int column, row;
int i;
int x1, y1;
long one_square, two_square;
long two_one_square, two_two_square;
long four_one_square, four_two_square;
long d;
double sin_angle, cos_angle;


aspect = 0.50;
angle = (360.0 - angle) * .01754329;

sin_angle = sin (angle);
cos_angle = cos (angle);

aspect_square = aspect * aspect;
```

```
two_square = radius * radius;
one_square = two_square/aspect_square;

row = radius;
column = 0;

two_one_square = one_square << 1;
four_one_square = one_square << 2;
four_two_square = two_square << 2;
two_two_square = two_square << 1;

d = two_one_square * ((row - 1) * (row )) + one_square +
        two_two_square * (1 - one_square);

while (one_square * (row ) > two_square * (column))
{
    x1 = x + column * cos_angle - row * sin_angle;
    y1 = y + column * sin_angle + row * cos_angle;
    _setpixel (x1, y1);

    x1 = x + column * cos_angle + row * sin_angle;
    y1 = y + column * sin_angle - row * cos_angle;
    _setpixel (x1, y1);

    x1 = x - column * cos_angle - row * sin_angle;
        y1 = y - column * sin_angle + row * cos_angle;
    _setpixel (x1, y1);

    x1 = x - column * cos_angle + row * sin_angle;
        y1 = y - column * sin_angle - row * cos_angle;
    _setpixel (x1, y1);

    if (d >= 0)
    {
        row--;
        d -= four_one_square*(row);
    }
    d += two_two_square * (3 + (column << 1));
    column ++;
}

d = two_two_square * (column + 1) * column + two_one_square*
  (row * (row - 2) + 1) + (1 - two_one_square) * two_square;
```

Listing 7.4   *continues*

Listing 7.4. cont. Two-dimensional ellipse rotation example.

```
while ((row) + 1)
{
     x1 = x + column * cos_angle - row * sin_angle;
     y1 = y + column * sin_angle + row * cos_angle;
     _setpixel (x1, y1);

     x1 = x + column * cos_angle + row * sin_angle;
     y1 = y + column * sin_angle - row * cos_angle;
     _setpixel (x1, y1);

     x1 = x - column * cos_angle - row * sin_angle;
     y1 = y - column * sin_angle + row * cos_angle;
     _setpixel (x1, y1);

     x1 = x - column * cos_angle + row * sin_angle;
     y1 = y - column * sin_angle - row * cos_angle;
     _setpixel (x1, y1);

     if (d <= 0)
     {
          column++;
          d += four_two_square * column;
     }
     row--;
     d += two_one_square * (3 - (row << 1));
     }
radius++;
}
```

Listing 7.4 uses the view coordinate system. In addition, the method used to describe the ellipse is different than the method used with Microsoft's _ellipse functions. The ellipse in this example is described according to its center point (x,y), its radius, and its aspect ratio. The aspect ratio for this function (and this function only) is described as the ratio between the width of the ellipse relative to its length. An aspect ratio of .50, for this example, indicates that the ellipse is half as wide as it is long.

The Three-Dimensional Coordinate System

The three-dimensional coordinate system is similar to the two-dimensional coordinate system, but adds a third dimension. So far, we have discussed flat, or two-dimensional, drawings exclusively. The remainder of this chapter focuses on drawing three-dimensional objects, or objects with depth.

Fig. 7.8. Example ouput from listing 7.4.

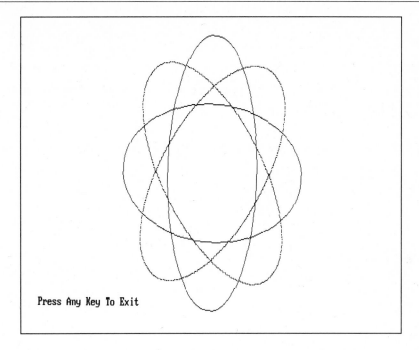

Press Any Key To Exit

The three-dimensional coordinate system, like the two-dimensional coordinate system, has a horizontal x-axis and a vertical y-axis. The difference in these coordinate systems, however, lies in the addition of a z-axis, which adds depth. The three-dimensional coordinate system is shown in figure 7.9.

The problem with the three-dimensional coordinate system, when used with computer graphics, is that the three dimensions must be placed on the screen, which is a flat, or two-dimensional, surface. Fortunately, three primary sets of algorithms do exactly that. These algorithm sets describe rotation about the x, y, and z axes.

Rotation about the x-axis:

$x = x'$

$y = (\sin(angle) * z') + (\cos(angle) * y')$

$z = (\cos(angle) * z') - (\sin(angle) * y')$

Rotation about the y-axis:

$x = (\cos(angle) * x') - (\sin(angle) * z')$

$y = y'$

$z = (\sin(angle) * x') + (\cos(angle) * z')$

Fig. 7.9. Three-dimensional coordinate system.

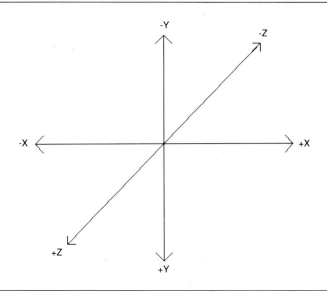

Rotation about the z axis:

$$x = (\cos(angle) * x') + (\sin(angle) * y')$$
$$y = (\cos(angle) * y') - (\sin(angle) * x')$$
$$z = z'$$

By using these three sets of algorithms in combination, you can rotate a three-dimensional object in literally any direction.

Listing 7.5 demonstrates the use of these algorithms for the rotation of two rectangles. Initially, the first rectangle overlays the other. The rectangles are the same size; one initially exists in the positive z plane, and the other initially exists in the negative z plane. With the Num Lock key on, the cursor keys manipulate, or rotate, the figures about the x (4 and 6 keys) and the y (8 and 2 keys) axes. The listing is written so that you can easily understand the operation of the program and its algorithms; the code is not written to be efficient.

Listing 7.5. Three-dimensional rotation example.

```
#include <graph.h>
#include <stdio.h>
#include <math.h>

void main ()
{
```

```
              /* Variable initialization */

double angle;
int x1, y1, z1;
int x2, y2, z2;
int x3, y3, z3;
int x4, y4, z4;
int x5, y5, z5;
int x6, y6, z6;
int x7, y7, z7;
int x8, y8, z8; int ch;
int oldx, oldy, oldz;


_setvideomode (_ERESCOLOR);
_setvieworg (320,175);

         /* Define corners for rectangle one */

x1 = 100;  y1 = 100;  z1 = -100;
x2 = 100;  y2 = -100; z2 = -100;
x3 = -100; y3 = -100; z3 = -100;
x4 = -100; y4 = 100;  z4 = -100;

         /* Define corners for rectangle two */

x5 = 100;  y5 = 100;  z5 = 100;
x6 = 100;  y6 = -100; z6 = 100;
x7 = -100; y7 = -100; z7 = 100;
x8 = -100; y8 = 100;  z8 = 100;

         /* Draw rectangle one */

_setcolor (1);
_moveto (x1,y1);
_lineto (x2,y2);
_lineto (x3,y3);
_lineto (x4,y4);
_lineto (x1,y1);

         /* Draw rectangle two */
```

Listing 7.5 *continues*

233

Listing 7.5. cont. Three-dimensional rotation example.

```
_setcolor (4);
_moveto (x5,y5);
_lineto (x6,y6);
_lineto (x7,y7);
_lineto (x8,y8);
_lineto (x5,y5);

            /* Perform rotation of rectangles */

do
{
     ch = getch ();

            /* If 4, rotate clockwise about y-axis */

     if (ch == '4')
     {
          angle = (-10.0) * .017453;
          oldx = x1;
          oldy = y1;
          oldz = z1;
          x1 = (cos(angle) * oldx) - (sin(angle) * oldz);
          y1 = y1;
          z1 = (sin(angle) * oldx) + (cos(angle) * oldz);

          oldx = x2;
          oldy = y2;
          oldz = z2;
          x2 = (cos(angle) * oldx) - (sin(angle) * oldz);
          y2 = y2;
          z2 = (sin(angle) * oldx) + (cos(angle) * oldz);

          oldx = x3;
          oldy = y3;
          oldz = z3;
          x3 = (cos(angle) * oldx) - (sin(angle) * oldz);
          y3 = y3;
          z3 = (sin(angle) * oldx) + (cos(angle) * oldz);

          oldx = x4;
          oldy = y4;
          oldz = z4;
          x4 = (cos(angle) * oldx) - (sin(angle) * oldz);
          y4 = y4;
```

```
z4 = (sin(angle) * oldx) + (cos(angle) * oldz);

oldx = x5;
oldy = y5;
oldz = z5;
x5 = (cos(angle) * oldx) - (sin(angle) * oldz);
y5 = y5;
z5 = (sin(angle) * oldx) + (cos(angle) * oldz);

oldx = x6;
oldy = y6;
oldz = z6;
x6 = (cos(angle) * oldx) - (sin(angle) * oldz);
y6 = y6;
z6 = (sin(angle) * oldx) + (cos(angle) * oldz);

oldx = x7;
oldy = y7;
oldz = z7;
x7 = (cos(angle) * oldx) - (sin(angle) * oldz);
y7 = y7;
z7 = (sin(angle) * oldx) + (cos(angle) * oldz);

oldx = x8;
oldy = y8;
oldz = z8;
x8 = (cos(angle) * oldx) - (sin(angle) * oldz);
y8 = y8;
z8 = (sin(angle) * oldx) + (cos(angle) * oldz);
}

    /* If 6, rotate counterclockwise about y-axis */

if (ch == '6')
{
    angle = 10.0 * .017453;
    oldx = x1;
    oldy = y1;
    oldz = z1;
    x1 = (cos(angle) * oldx) - (sin(angle) * oldz);
    y1 = y1;
    z1 = (sin(angle) * oldx) + (cos(angle) * oldz);
```

Listing 7.5 *continues*

Computer Graphics with Microsoft C

Listing 7.5. cont.   Three-dimensional rotation example.

```
            oldx = x2;
            oldy = y2;
            oldz = z2;
            x2 = (cos(angle) * oldx) - (sin(angle) * oldz);
            y2 = y2;
            z2 = (sin(angle) * oldx) + (cos(angle) * oldz);

            oldx = x3;
            oldy = y3;
            oldz = z3;
            x3 = (cos(angle) * oldx) - (sin(angle) * oldz);
            y3 = y3;
            z3 = (sin(angle) * oldx) + (cos(angle) * oldz);

            oldx = x4;
            oldy = y4;
            oldz = z4;
            x4 = (cos(angle) * oldx) - (sin(angle) * oldz);
            y4 = y4;
            z4 = (sin(angle) * oldx) + (cos(angle) * oldz);

            oldx = x5;
            oldy = y5;
            oldz = z5;
            x5 = (cos(angle) * oldx) - (sin(angle) * oldz);
            y5 = y5;
            z5 = (sin(angle) * oldx) + (cos(angle) * oldz);

            oldx = x6;
            oldy = y6;
            oldz = z6;
            x6 = (cos(angle) * oldx) - (sin(angle) * oldz);
            y6 = y6;
            z6 = (sin(angle) * oldx) + (cos(angle) * oldz);

            oldx = x7;
            oldy = y7;
            oldz = z7;
            x7 = (cos(angle) * oldx) - (sin(angle) * oldz);
            y7 = y7;
            z7 = (sin(angle) * oldx) + (cos(angle) * oldz);

            oldx = x8;
```

```
            oldy = y8;
            oldz = z8;
            x8 = (cos(angle) * oldx) - (sin(angle) * oldz);
            y8 = y8;
            z8 = (sin(angle) * oldx) + (cos(angle) * oldz);
    }


            /* If 8, rotate clockwise about x-axis */

    if (ch == '8')
    {
            angle = (-10.0) * .017453;
            oldx = x1;
            oldy = y1;
            oldz = z1;
            x1 = x1;
            y1 = (sin(angle) * oldz) + (cos(angle) * oldy);
            z1 = (cos(angle) * oldz) - (sin(angle) * oldy);

            oldx = x2;
            oldy = y2;
            oldz = z2;
            x2 = x2;
            y2 = (sin(angle) * oldz) + (cos(angle) * oldy);
            z2 = (cos(angle) * oldz) - (sin(angle) * oldy);

            oldx = x3;
            oldy = y3;
            oldz = z3;
            x3 = x3;
            y3 = (sin(angle) * oldz) + (cos(angle) * oldy);
            z3 = (cos(angle) * oldz) - (sin(angle) * oldy);

            oldx = x4;
            oldy = y4;
            oldz = z4;
            x4 = x4;
            y4 = (sin(angle) * oldz) + (cos(angle) * oldy);
            z4 = (cos(angle) * oldz) - (sin(angle) * oldy);

            oldx = x5;
            oldy = y5;
            oldz = z5;
```

Listing 7.5 *continues*

Listing 7.5. cont. Three-dimensional rotation example.

```
    x5 = x5;
    y5 = (sin(angle) * oldz) + (cos(angle) * oldy);
    z5 = (cos(angle) * oldz) - (sin(angle) * oldy);

    oldx = x6;
    oldy = y6;
    oldz = z6;
    x6 = x6;
    y6 = (sin(angle) * oldz) + (cos(angle) * oldy);
    z6 = (cos(angle) * oldz) - (sin(angle) * oldy);

    oldx = x7;
    oldy = y7;
    oldz = z7;
    x7 = x7;
    y7 = (sin(angle) * oldz) + (cos(angle) * oldy);
    z7 = (cos(angle) * oldz) - (sin(angle) * oldy);

    oldx = x8;
    oldy = y8;
    oldz = z8;
    x8 = x8;
    y8 = (sin(angle) * oldz) + (cos(angle) * oldy);
    z8 = (cos(angle) * oldz) - (sin(angle) * oldy);
}

    /* If 2, rotate counterclockwise about x-axis */

if (ch == '2')
{
    angle = 10.0 * .017453;
    oldx = x1;
    oldy = y1;
    oldz = z1;
    x1 = x1;
    y1 = (sin(angle) * oldz) + (cos(angle) * oldy);
    z1 = (cos(angle) * oldz) - (sin(angle) * oldy);

    oldx = x2;
    oldy = y2;
    oldz = z2;
    x2 = x2;
```

```
y2 = (sin(angle) * oldz) + (cos(angle) * oldy);
z2 = (cos(angle) * oldz) - (sin(angle) * oldy);

oldx = x3;
oldy = y3;
oldz = z3;
x3 = x3;
y3 = (sin(angle) * oldz) + (cos(angle) * oldy);
z3 = (cos(angle) * oldz) - (sin(angle) * oldy);

oldx = x4;
oldy = y4;
oldz = z4;
x4 = x4;
y4 = (sin(angle) * oldz) + (cos(angle) * oldy);
z4 = (cos(angle) * oldz) - (sin(angle) * oldy);

oldx = x5;
oldy = y5;
oldz = z5;
x5 = x5;
y5 = (sin(angle) * oldz) + (cos(angle) * oldy);
z5 = (cos(angle) * oldz) - (sin(angle) * oldy);

oldx = x6;
oldy = y6;
oldz = z6;
x6 = x6;
y6 = (sin(angle) * oldz) + (cos(angle) * oldy);
z6 = (cos(angle) * oldz) - (sin(angle) * oldy);

oldx = x7;
oldy = y7;
oldz = z7;
x7 = x7;
y7 = (sin(angle) * oldz) + (cos(angle) * oldy);
z7 = (cos(angle) * oldz) - (sin(angle) * oldy);

oldx = x8;
oldy = y8;
oldz = z8;
x8 = x8;
y8 = (sin(angle) * oldz) + (cos(angle) * oldy);
```

Listing 7.5 *continues*

Listing 7.5. cont.   Three-dimensional rotation example.

```
z8 = (cos(angle) * oldz) - (sin(angle) * oldy);
    }

        /* Clear screen and draw new rectangles */

    _clearscreen (_GCLEARSCREEN);
    _setcolor (1);
    _moveto ((int) x1, (int) y1);
    _lineto ((int) x2, (int) y2);
    _lineto ((int) x3, (int) y3);
    _lineto ((int) x4, (int) y4);
    _lineto ((int) x1, (int) y1);

    _setcolor (4);
    _moveto ((int) x5, (int) y5);
    _lineto ((int) x6, (int) y6);
    _lineto ((int) x7, (int) y7);
    _lineto ((int) x8, (int) y8);
    _lineto ((int) x5, (int) y5);

        /* Exit when Esc key is pressed */

} while (ch != 27);

_setvideomode (_DEFAULTMODE);
}
```

Hidden Surface Removal for Three-Dimensional Drawing

Three-dimensional drawing can become very complex. Most three-dimensional models are created with a series of planes that represent the shell of the object. If the planes are filled, the plane is considered non-transparent. Similarly, if the plane is not filled, it is considered transparent.

When rotating or moving three-dimensional objects, it is often necessary to remove parts of objects, or even entire objects, to provide realistic representations of the environment. The method by which these objects are altered is called *hidden surface removal*. The most common types of hidden surface removal are discussed in this section.

The two basic types of hidden surface removal are object-space methods and image-space methods. Three-dimensional information is used with object-space methods to decide which surfaces should be hidden and which surfaces should overlay others. Image-space methods use two-dimensional information to determine the hidden surfaces.

The most common method of hidden surface removal for personal computers is probably the plane equation method, which is an object-space method. In general terms, the plane equation method determines if a point is in front of, on, or behind a specified plane. By testing each point against the viewing position, which is always (0,0,0), the visible and hidden planes are determined.

The equation of a plane is

$$Ax + By + Cz + D$$

where x, y, and z define a point on the surface of the plane. The A, B, C, and D values are constants and are derived as follows when three points on the plane are specified (x1,y1,z1 and x2,y2,z2 and x3,y3,z3).

$$A = y1(z2-z3) + y2(z3-z1) + y3(z1-z2)$$
$$B = z1(x2-x3) + z2(x3-x1) + z3(x1-x2)$$
$$C = x1(y2-y3) + x2(y3-y1) + x3(y1-y2)$$
$$D = -x1(y2z3-y3z2) - x2(y3z1-y1z3) - x3(y1z2-y2z1)$$

These constants are then placed into the plane equation, and the equation is evaluated for each point using this new plane equation. If the equation evaluates to a positive value, the point is hidden. If the equation evaluates to zero, the point is on the plane. If the equation evaluates to a negative value, the point is visible.

When using the plane equation method, it is important that the points used to derive the equations are plotted in a counterclockwise direction and can be viewed as part of a convex polyhedron. A convex polyhedron is a figure that has many faces and is curved outward, such as a cube.

Summary

The techniques described in Part 1, Chapters 1 through 7, provide the basics for graphics programming with Microsoft C. By studying the discussions and examples in these chapters, you should be able to create a variety of graphics-based software applications, from simple two-dimensional figures to complex three-dimensional windowing systems. Part 2 provides reference information on the video BIOS services and the Microsoft C graphics libraries.

II

Reference Guide

8

Video BIOS Services

This chapter introduces alternate methods of accomplishing many of the functions provided by the Microsoft Graphics Libraries using the read-only memory (ROM) basic input /output system (BIOS). ROM BIOS provides services that permit low-level control over the hardware. In this chapter, the ROM BIOS video services are discussed. The intent of this chapter is to provide useful information on the capabilities of the ROM BIOS video services. Fortunately, there is not much need to use these services because the graphics libraries provided by Microsoft are so extensive and, in general, faster than these services.

Video Service 00H

Set Video Mode

Input:

AH   00H
AL   Video mode

Output:

None

Description:

Video service 00H is used to set the video configuration to one of the video modes in table 8.1. The desired video mode is specified in the AL register. When the new video mode is set, the screen is cleared.

Table 8.1.   *Video modes.*

Mode	Screen Type	Resolution	Colors	Supported By
00H	Text	40x25	16	CGA, EGA, MCGA, VGA
01H	Text	40x25	16	CGA, EGA, MCGA, VGA
02H	Text	80x25	16	CGA, EGA, MCGA, VGA
03H	Text	80x25	16	CGA, EGA, MCGA, VGA
04H	Graphics	320x200	4	CGA, EGA, MCGA, VGA
05H	Graphics	320x200	4	CGA, EGA, MCGA, VGA
06H	Graphics	640x200	2	CGA, EGA, MCGA, VGA
07H	Text	80x25	Mono	EGA, VGA
0DH	Graphics	320x200	16	EGA, VGA
0EH	Graphics	640x200	16	EGA, VGA
0FH	Graphics	640x350	Mono	EGA, VGA
10H	Graphics	640x350	16	EGA, VGA
11H	Graphics	640x480	2	MCGA, VGA
12H	Graphics	640x480	16	VGA
13H	Graphics	320x200	256	MCGA, VGA

Video Service 01H

Set Cursor Size

Input:

AH	01H
CH	Starting scan line for cursor
CL	Ending scan line for cursor

Output:

None

Description:

Video Service 01H is for use only with text modes. The cursor, which is a line, or set of lines, blinks at the current character display position. This service defines the number of lines displayed. In CGA modes, 8 scan lines (numbered 0-7) are used for the cursor; in EGA modes, 14 lines (numbered 0-13) are used. The MCGA and VGA adapters have a cursor height of 16 lines (numbered 0-15). The default settings are as follows:

CGA
> CH = 6
> CL = 7

EGA
> CH = 11
> CL = 12

MCGA and VGA
> CH = 13
> CL = 14

Video Service 02H

Set Cursor Position

Input:

AH	02H
BH	Page number of cursor
DH	Row number for cursor position
DL	Column number for cursor position

Output:

None

Description:

Video Service 02H is used to set the cursor position to the specified row and column position. This service can be used in both text and graphics modes; the cursor, however, is displayed in only text modes. The upper left corner of the screen is the origin of the row, column coordinate system and has a value of 0,0. For text and graphics modes that support multiple pages, the page number must be specified to ensure that the correct cursor position is altered.

Video Service 03H

Read Cursor Position

Input:

AH	03H
BH	Page number

Output:

CH	Starting line for cursor
CL	Ending line for cursor
DH	Row number
DL	Column number

Description:

Video Service 03H is used to retrieve the cursor size and position of the specified page. The page number is specified in BH. The starting scan line of the cursor is returned in CH; the ending scan line of the cursor is returned in CL. The row position is returned in DH; the column position is returned in DL.

Video Service 04H

Read Light Pen Position

Input:

AH	04H

Output:

AH	0 = Not triggered
	1 = Triggered
BX	Vertical pixel column number
CX	Horizontal pixel line number
DH	Character row number
DL	Character column number

Description:

Video Service 04H is used to report the status of the light pen for the CGA or EGA. If the light pen has not been triggered, AH equals 0. If triggered, AH equals 1 and the trigger position is returned. The character column and pixel row are initially determined by the hardware; the character row and pixel column are then determined. Then all these values are returned. The pixel column number is returned in BX. The horizontal pixel line number is returned in CH for modes 04H, 05H, and 06H or returned in CX for all other EGA modes. The character row number is returned in DH; the character column number is returned in DL.

Video Service 05H

Set Active Display Page

Input:

AH	05H
AL	Active page number

Output:

None

Description:

Video Service 05H is used to set the active display page number for text and graphics modes. The desired page number is specified in AL. For most text modes, page numbers range from 0-7. For EGA and VGA with sufficient video memory, multiple pages of graphics can be supported. Page 0 is the default for all text and graphics modes.

Video Service 06H

Scroll Active Window Up

Input:

AH	06H
AL	Number of lines to scroll
BH	Attribute for blank lines
CH	Upper left row number
CL	Upper left column number
DH	Lower right row number
DL	Lower right column number

Output:

None

Description:

Video Service 06H is used to create and scroll a text window. The upper left corner of the text window is defined in CH and CL. CH defines the upper left row number; CL defines the upper left column number. The lower right corner of the text window is defined in DH and DL. DH defines the lower right row; DL defines the lower right column number. AL defines the number of lines to scroll up. If AL equals 00H, the text window is blanked. When the window is scrolled, the bottom line is blanked as defined by the display attribute in BH.

Video Service 07H

Scroll Active Window Down

Input:

AH	07H
AL	Number of lines to scroll
BH	Attribute for blank lines
CH	Upper left row number
CL	Upper left column number
DH	Lower right row number
DL	Lower right column number

Output:

None

Description:

Video Service 07H is used to create and scroll a text window. The upper left corner of the text window is defined in CH and CL. CH defines the upper left row number; CL defines the upper left column number. The lower right corner of the text window is defined in DH and DL. DH defines the lower right row number; DL defines the lower right column number. AL defines the number of lines to scroll down. If AL equals 00H, the text window is blanked. When the window is scrolled down, the top line of the window is blanked as defined by the display attribute in BH.

Video Service 08H

Read Character and Attribute

Input:

AH	08H
BH	Active page number

Output:

AH	Character attribute
AL	ASCII character retrieved

Description:

Video Service 08H is used to read the character at the current cursor location in either text or video mode. In graphics mode, the retrieved character is compared with the character-generation table used with graphics modes. In text mode, the ASCII character code is retrieved. The attributes of the character are returned in AH; the ASCII code of the character is returned in AL. In graphics mode, the contents of AH are meaningless.

Video Service 09H

Write Character and Attribute

Input:

AH	09H
AL	ASCII character to write
BL	Attribute of character to write
BH	Active page number
CX	Number of times to repeat character and attribute

Output:

None

Description:

Video Service 09H writes a character to the screen at the current cursor position. The ASCII character of the code to write is specified in AL. For text modes, the character's attributes are specified in BL. For graphics modes, BL specifies the foreground color. The specified character can be repeated. CX defines the number of times the character and attribute pair will be written.

Video Service 0AH

Write Character

Input:

AH	0AH
AL	ASCII character to write
BL	Attribute of character to write
BH	Active page number
CX	Number of times to repeat character and attribute

Output:

None

Description:

Video Service 0AH is used to write a character to the screen. In text modes, BL is not used because the character attributes cannot be altered with this service. In graphics mode, BL defines the foreground color. For both text and graphics modes, AL specifies the ASCII character to write and CX indicates the number of times to write the character.

Video Service 0BH

Set Color Palette

Input:

AH	0BH
BH	Color number
BL	Color value

Output:

None

Description:

Video Service 0BH is used to set the palette or the background, or border, color. When BH is set to 00H, you can set the border color in CGA text modes or the background color in CGA graphics modes. BL specifies the color. When BH is 01H, one of two 4-color palettes used in the 320-by-200 4-color mode can be selected. If BL is 1, the cyan-magenta-white palette is selected. If BL is 0, the red-green-brown palette is selected.

Video Service 0CH

Write Pixel

Input:

AH	0CH
AL	Pixel color
BH	Display page
CX	Column number of pixel
DX	Row number of pixel

Output:

None

Description:

Video Service 0CH is used to write a pixel on the screen at the specified location in a specified color. The AL register is used to specify the color and write mode of the pixel. The desired location of the pixel is defined in CX and DX. CX defines the column position of the pixel; DX defines the row position.

Video Service 0DH

Read Pixel

Input:

AH	0DH
BH	Display page
CX	Column number of pixel
DX	Row number of pixel

Output:

AL	Pixel color value

Description:

Video Service 0DH is used to read the color of a pixel at a specified location. BH specifies the display page number. The position to read is defined by CX and DX. CX defines the column number of the pixel; DX defines the row number.

Video Service 0EH

Write TTY Character

Input:

AH	0EH
AL	ASCII character to write
BH	Active display page
BL	Foreground color (graphics mode only)

Output:

None

Description:

Video Service 0EH is used to write a character at the current position in teletype (TTY) mode. BL specifies the foreground color and works in only graphics modes. AL specifies the ASCII character to display. In teletype mode, ASCII characters 07H, 08H, 0AH, and 0DH are not written to the screen. Instead they are interpreted in the following manner:

07H	Beep from computer speaker
08H	Backspace one position
0AH	Do one line feed
0DH	Do one carriage return

Video Service 0FH

Get Current Video Mode

Input:

AH	0FH

Output:

AH	Number of characters per line
AL	Current display
BH	Active page number

Description:

Video Subservice 0FH is used to retrieve the current video mode, the screen width in characters, and the active display page number. The video display mode is returned in AL. The screen width, in characters, is returned in AH. The active page number is returned in BH.

Video Service 10H, Subservice 00H

Set Palette Register (EGA and VGA Only)

Input:

AH	10H
AL	00H
BH	Color to be loaded
BL	Palette number

Output:

None

Description:

Video Service 10H, Subservice 00H is used to set the color for a specified palette register. The palette register number is described in BL. BH contains the color to be loaded.

Video Service 10H, Subservice 01H

Set EGA and VGA Overscan Register

Input:

AH	10H
AL	01H
BH	Color code for overscan

Output:

None

Description:

Video Service 10H, Subservice 01H is used to set the border color (often called the overscan border) for the EGA or VGA. The color code is passed in BH.

Video Service 10H, Subservice 02H

Set Palette and Overscan Registers (EGA and VGA Only)

Input:

AH	10H
AL	02H
ES:DX	Pointer to 17-byte array of palette and overscan colors

Output:

None

Description:

Video Service 10H, Subservice 02H is used to set all 16 palette registers plus the overscan, or border, register. Before this subservice is called, the 17 values must be placed into a 17-byte table. The segment and offset (address) of the table is specified in ES and DX.

Video Service 10H, Subservice 03H

Toggle Blinking or Intensity (EGA and VGA Only)

Input:

AH	10H
AL	03H
BL	0 = Toggle intensity
	1 = Toggle blinking

Output:

None

Description:

Video Service 10H, Subservice 03H is used to enable or disable the blinking and intensity bits. The default settings of these bits are low intensity with no blinking. When this subservice is called with BL equal to 0, the intensity is toggled (if high, it is set to low; if low, it is set to high). When this subservice is called with BL equal to 1, the blinking bit is toggled (if blinking, it is set to no blinking; if not blinking, it is set to blinking).

Video Service 10H, Subservice 07H

Read VGA Palette Register

Input:

AH	10H
AL	07H
BL	Palette register number to read

Output:

BH	Palette register color value

Description:

Video Service 10H, Subservice 07H, is used to read the color for a particular palette register. BL specifies the palette register to read. The color of the specified register is returned to BH.

Video Service 10H, Subservice 08H

Read Overscan Register (VGA Only)

Input:

AH   10H
AL   08H

Output:

BH   Overscan register color value

Description:

Video Service 10H, Subservice 08H is used to read the color of the overscan, or border, register. The retrieved color is returned in BH.

Video Service 10H, Subservice 09H

Read VGA Palette and Overscan Registers

Input:

AH   10H
AL   .   09H
ES:DX   Pointer to 17-byte array of palette and overscan values

Output:

Retrieved information returned to 17-byte array at ES:DX

Description:

Video Service 10H, Subservice 09H is used to read all VGA palette registers. These registers include the palette and overscan registers. The 17 bytes of register information are returned to the memory location pointed to by ES:DX.

Video Service 10H, Subservice 10H

Set Individual VGA Color Register

Input:

AH	10H
AL	10H
BX	Color register to set
CH	Intensity of green
CL	Intensity of blue
DH	Intensity of red

Output:

None

Description:

Video Service 10H, Subservice 10H is used to set an individual digital-to-analog convertor (DAC) register to a 6-bit value for red, green, and blue. This subservice should be called with 6-bit red, green, and blue values in registers DH, CH, and CL, respectively. BX specifies the register to set.

Video Service 10H, Subservice 12H

Set Block of Color Registers (VGA Only)

Input:

AH	10H
AL	12H
BX	Number of first color register
CX	Number of color registers to set
ES:DX	Pointer to array of colors

Output:

None

Description:

Video Service 10H, Subservice 12H is used to set a block of digital-to-analog convertor (DAC) registers to the specified colors. BX specifies the first register to set; CX indicates the number of registers to set. The table that contains the 3-byte red, green, and blue values for the registers is pointed to by ES and DX.

Video Service 10H, Subservice 13H

Select Color Page (VGA Only)

Input:

AH	10H
AL	13H
BL	0 = Select mode
	1 = Select page
BH	0 = Select 4 pages of 64-color registers if BL = 0
	1 = Select 16 pages of 16-color registers if BL = 0
	Color page number if BL = 1

Output:

None

Description:

Video Service 10H, Subservice 13H is used with the VGA to select the color page or the color page mode. If BL equals 0, the color page mode can be selected. When BL equals 0 and BH equals 0, 4 pages of 64 colors are selected. When BL equals 0 and BH equals 1, 16 pages of 16 colors are selected. When BL equals 1, BH specifies the color page number.

Video Service 10H, Subservice 15H

Read Individual Color Register (VGA Only)

Input:

AH	10H
AL	15H
BX	Number of color register to read

Output:

CH	Intensity of green
CL	Intensity of blue
DH	Intensity of red

Description:

Video Service 10H, Subservice 15H is used to read the color values from a color register for VGA only. BX specifies the number of the color register to read. The red, green, and blue values of the specified register are returned in DH, CH, and CL, respectively.

Video Service 10H, Subservice 17H

Read Block of Color Registers (VGA Only)

Input:

AH	10H
AL	17H
BX	Number of first register to read
CX	Number of registers
ES:DX	Pointer to array of color values

Output:

Colors returned to array pointed to by ES:DX

Description:

Video Service 10H, Subservice 17H is used to read a block of color registers. BX specifies the number of the first register to read. CX defines the number of registers to read. The block of red, green, and blue values is returned to the table pointed to by ES:DX.

Video Service 10H, Subservice 1AH

Read Current Color Page Number (VGA Only)

Input:

AH	10H
AL	1AH

Output:

BH	Current color page
BL	Paging mode

Description:

Video Service 10H, Subservice 1AH is used to read the current color page and color paging mode. The current color page is returned in BH. The current color paging mode is returned in BL.

Video Service 10H, Subservice 1BH

Sum Color Values to Gray Scale (VGA Only)

Input:

AH	10H
AL	1BH
BX	First color register to convert
CX	Number of color registers to convert

Output:

None

Description:

Video Service 10H, Subservice 1BH is used to convert the color values in a block of consecutive video digital-to-analog convertor (DAC) color registers to their corresponding shades of gray. BX specifies the first color register to convert. CX defines the number of registers to convert.

Video Service 11H, Subservice 00H

Load Font (EGA and VGA Only)

Input:

AH	11H
AL	00H
BL	Block to load
BH	Number of bytes per character
CX	Number of characters to load
DX	Character offset
ES:BP	Pointer to font buffer

Output:

None

Description:

Video Service 11H, Subservice 00H is used to load a user character font into the loadable character generator. BL identifies the block to load. BH defines the number of bytes per character. CX contains the number of characters. The ASCII code of the first character is specified in DX. The address of the block (segment and offset) is specified in ES:BP.

Video Service 11H, Subservice 01H

Load ROM 8-by-14 Character Set (EGA and VGA Only)

Input:

AH	11H
AL	01H
BL	Block to load

Output:

None

Description:

Video Service 11H, Subservice 01H is used to load the ROM 8-by-14 monochrome character set. The block to load is specified in BL.

Video Service 11H, Subservice 02H

Load ROM 8-by-8 Character Set (EGA and VGA Only)

Input:

AH	11H
AL	02H
BL	Block to load

Output:

None

Description:

Video Service 11H, Subservice 02H is used to load the ROM 8-by-8 double dot character set. The block to load is specified in BL.

Video Service 11H, Subservice 03H

Set Block Specifier (EGA and VGA Only)

Input:

AH	11H
AL	03H
BL	Value to load into the character map select register

Output:

None

Description:

Video Service 11H, Subservice 03H is used to select among text-mode character sets after they are loaded into character generator RAM. The EGA has four tables; the VGA has eight tables. The BL register is used to specify one or two of these tables, which will be used to display text-mode characters.

Video Service 11H, Subservice 04H

Load ROM 8-by-16 Character Set (EGA and VGA Only)

Input:

AH	11H
AL	04H
BL	Block number to load

Output:

None

Description:

Video Service 11H, Subservice 04H is used to load the ROM 8-by-16 character set. The block to load is specified in BL.

Video Service 11H, Subservice 10H

Load Font (EGA and VGA Only)

Input:

AH	11H
AL	10H
BH	Number of bytes per character
BL	Block to load
CX	Number of characters
DX	Character offset of memory block
ES:BP	Pointer to font buffer

Output:

None

Description:

Video Service 11H, Subservice 10H is used to load a user font. The address of the font to load is contained in ES:BP. The block to load is specified in BL. BH contains the number of bytes per character; CX specifies the number of characters to load.

Video Service 11H, Subservice 11H

Load ROM 8-by-14 Character Set (EGA and VGA Only)

Input:

AH	11H
AL	11H
BL	Block to load

Output:

None

Description:

Video Service 11H, Subservice 11H is used to load the ROM 8-by-14 character set. The block to load is specified in BL.

Video Service 11H, Subservice 12H

Load ROM 8-by-8 Character Set (EGA and VGA Only)

Input:

AH	11H
AL	12H
BL	BLock to load

Output:

None

Description:

Video Service 11H, Subservice 12H is used to load the ROM 8-by-8 character set. The block to load is specified in BL.

Video Service 11H, Subservice 14H

Load ROM 8-by-16 Character Set (VGA Only)

Input:

AH	11H
AL	14H
BL	Target block

Output:

None

Description:

Video Service 11H, Subservice 14H is used to load the ROM 8-by-16 character set. The block to load is specified in BL.

Video Service 11H, Subservice 20H

Load Character Pointer (EGA and VGA Only)

Input:

AH   11H
AL   20H
ES:BP   Pointer to font buffer

Output:

None

Description:

Video Service 11H, Subservice 20H is used to store a pointer to the table of graphics characters represented by ASCII codes 128 to 255. The pointer is specified in ES:BP.

Video Service 11H, Subservice 21H

Load Character Pointer (EGA and VGA Only)

Input:

AH   11H
AL   21H
BL   01H = 14 screen rows
          02H = 25 screen rows
          03H = 43 screen rows
CX   Number of bytes per character
DL   Number of character rows
ES:BP   Pointer to font buffer

Output:

None

Description:

Video Service 11H, Subservice 21H is used to store a pointer to the table of all graphics characters. DL specifies the number of character rows. The contents of CX specify the number of bytes per character.

Video Service 11H, Subservice 22H

Load Graphics ROM 8-by-14 Character Set (EGA and VGA Only)

Input:

AH	11H
AL	22H
BL	01H = 14 screen rows
	02H = 25 screen rows
	03H = 43 screen rows
DL	Number of character rows

Output:

None

Description:

Video Service 11H, Subservice 22H is used to load the ROM 8-by-14 character set for graphics mode. DL specifies the number of character rows.

Video Service 11H, Subservice 23H

Load Graphics ROM 8-by-8 Character Set (EGA and VGA Only)

Input:

AH	11H
AL	23H
BL	01H = 14 screen rows
	02H = 25 screen rows
	03H = 43 screen rows
DL	Number of character rows

Output:

None

Description:

Video Service 11H, Subservice 23H is used to load the ROM 8-by-8 character set for use in graphics mode. DL specifies the number of character rows.

Video Service 11H, Subservice 24H

Load Graphics ROM 8-by-16 Character Set (EGA and VGA Only)

Input:

AH	11H
AL	24H
BL	01H = 14 screen rows
	02H = 25 screen rows
	03H = 43 screen rows
DL	Number of character rows

Output:

None

Description:

Video Service 11H, Subservice 24H is used to load the ROM 8-by-16 character set. The contents of DL specify the number of character rows.

Video Service 11H, Subservice 30H

Return Character Generator Data (EGA and VGA Only)

Input:

AH	11H
AL	30H
BH	00H = INT 1FH pointer
	01H = INT 43H pointer
	02H = ROM 8-by-14 pointer
	03H = ROM 8-by-8 pointer
	04H = ROM 8-by-8 pointer
	05H = ROM 9-by-14 pointer
	06H = ROM 8-by-16 pointer
	07H = ROM 9-by-16 pointer

Output:

CX	Bytes per character
DL	Number of rows in EGA
	Number of rows minus 1 in VGA
ES:BP	Pointer

Description:

Video Service 11H, Subservice 30H is used to retrieve information on the ROM BIOS character generator. The contents of BH determine the address returned in ES:BP. The bytes per character are returned in CX. The number of rows is returned in DL.

Video Service 12H, Subservice 10H

Get Video Information (EGA and VGA Only)

Input:

AH	12H
BL	10H

Output:

BH	0 = Color mode
	1 = Monochrome mode
BL	Memory size
	00H = 64K
	01H = 128K
	02H = 192K
	03H = 256K
CH	Feature control bits
CL	Video switch setting

Description:

Video Service 12H, Subservice 10H is used to retrieve information on the EGA or VGA configuration. The contents of BL indicate whether the current video mode is color (00H) or monochrome (01H). The video RAM size is indicated in BL as described under "Output." CH indicates the status of the input from the feature connector. The contents of CL indicate the settings of the configuration switches.

Video Service 12H, Subservice 20H

Select Alternate Print Screen Routine (EGA and VGA Only)

Input:

AH	12H
BL	20H

Output:

None

Description:

Video Service 12H, Subservice 20H is used to change the print-screen routine from the motherboard ROM BIOS to the adapter ROM BIOS. The adapter ROM BIOS for EGA and VGA is capable of printing text mode screens in excess of 25 rows.

Video Service 12H, Subservice 30H

Set Scan Lines for Alphanumeric Modes (VGA Only)

Input:

AH	12H
BL	30H
AL	0 = 200 scan lines
	1 = 350 scan lines
	2 = 400 scan lines

Output:

AL	12 H = Valid call
	Anything else = Call was not valid

Description:

Video Service 12H, Subservice 30H is used to set the number of scan lines and the default character set for alphanumeric modes. The contents of AL indicate the number of scan lines to set.

Video Service 12H, Subservice 31H

Default Palette Loading during Mode Set (VGA Only)

Input:

AH	12H
BL	31H
AL	0 = Enable palette loading
	1 = Disable palette loading

Output:

AL   12H = Valid call
             Anything else = Call was not valid

Description:

Video Service 12H, Subservice 31H is used to enable or disable palette loading when a new VGA video mode is set. When AL is 0, default palette loading is enabled; when AL is 1, default palette loading is disabled.

Video Service 12H, Subservice 32H

Video Enable or Disable (VGA Only)

Input:

AH   12H
BL   32H
AL   0 = Enable video
            1 = Disable video

Output:

AL   12H = Valid call
            Anything else = Call was not valid

Description:

Video Service 12H, Subservice 32H is used to enable or disable the video input port and buffer address decode. The contents of AL enable (00H) or disable (01H) the buffer and port addressing.

Video Service 12H, Subservice 33H

Sum to Gray Scale (VGA Only)

Input:

AH   12H
BL   33H
AL   0 = Enable summing
            1 = Disable summing

Output:

AL   12H = Valid call

            Anything else = Call was not valid

Description:

Video Service 12H, Subservice 33H is used to enable or disable the gray-scale features of the VGA. When AL is 00H, gray-scaling is enabled; when AL is 01H, gray-scaling is disabled.

Video Service 12H, Subservice 34H

Cursor Emulation (VGA Only)

Input:

AH   12H

BL   34H

AL   0 = Enable cursor emulation

            1 = Disable cursor emulation

Output:

AL   12 = Valid call

            Anything else = Call was not valid

Description:

Video Service 12H, Subservice 34H is used to enable or disable the cursor emulation for VGA in text modes. When AL is 00H and the video mode or cursor size in altered, the cursor is emulated using CGA text-mode cursor sizing. When AL is 01H, the text-mode cursor emulation is disabled.

Video Service 12H, Subservice 35H

Display Switch (VGA Only)

Input:

AH   12

BL   35H

AL   0 = Switch off adapter

            1 = Switch on planar video

            2 = Switch off active video

            3 = Switch on inactive video

ES:DX   Pointer to 128-byte buffer

Output:

AL   12H = Valid call
                 Anything else = Call was not valid

Description:

Video Service 12H, Subservice 35H is used to select or deselect a video device. AL specifies the desired switching action. The options for AL are described under "Input."

Video Service 12H, Subservice 36H

Video Screen On or Off (VGA Only)

Input:

AH   12H
BL   36H
AL   0 = Enable video output
                 1 = Disable video output

Output:

AL   12H = Valid call
                 Anything else = Call was not valid

Description:

Video Service 12H, Subservice 36H is used to enable or disable the video output to the monitor display. When AL is 00H, video output, or video refresh, is enabled. When AL is 01H, video output is disabled. When the video output is disabled, the screen goes blank.

Video Service 13H, Subservice 00H

Write Character String (VGA Only)

Input:

AH   13H
AL   00H
BH   Page number
BL   Attribute
CX   Number of characters

DH	Row position
DL	Column position
ES:BP	Pointer to beginning of string

Output:

None

Description:

Video Service 13H, Subservice 00H is used to write a character string to the screen. The string is placed at the position specified in DH and DL. CX specifies the number of characters in the string. The string is written to the screen with the attributes defined in BL. ES:BP points to the character string. At the end of this service, the cursor remains at the beginning of the string.

Video Service 13H, Subservice 01H

Write Character String (EGA and VGA Only)

Input:

AH	13H
AL	01H
BH	Page number
BL	Attribute
CX	Number of characters
DH	Row position
DL	Column position
ES:BP	Pointer to beginning of string

Output:

None

Description:

Video Service 13H, Subservice 01H is used to write a character string to the screen. The string is placed at the position specified in DH and DL. CX specifies the number of characters in the string. The string is written to the screen with the attributes defined in BL. ES:BP points to the character string. At the end of this service, the cursor is positioned at the location following the last character in the string.

Video Service 13H, Subservice 02H

Write Character String (EGA and VGA Only)

Input:

AH	13H
AL	02H
BH	Page number
CX	Number of characters and attributes in string
DH	Row position
DL	Column position
ES:BP	Pointer to beginning of string

Output:

None

Description:

Video Service 13H, Subservice 02H is used to write a character string. ES:BP points to the beginning of the character string. The string is written to the screen beginning at the position specified in DH and DL. The string consists of alternate characters and attributes. The number of characters and attributes is defined in CX. After the service is completed, the cursor position remains at the position specified in DH and DL.

Video Service 13H, Subservice 03H

Write Character String (EGA and VGA Only)

Input:

AH	13H
AL	03H
BH	Page number
CX	Number of characters and attributes in string
DH	Row position
DL	Column position
ES:BP	Pointer to beginning of string

Output:

None

Description:

Video Service 13H, Subservice 03H is used to write a character string that consists of alternate characters and attributes. ES:BP points to the beginning of the character string. The string is written to the screen beginning at the position specified in DH and DL. The number of characters and attributes is defined in CX. When the service is ended, the cursor is positioned at the location following the last character in the string.

Video Service 1AH

Read or Write Display Combination Code (VGA Only)

Input:

AH	1AH
AL	00H = Read DCC
	01H = Write DCC
BH	Inactive DCC
BL	Active DCC

Note: DCC equals the display combination code.

Output:

AL	1AH = Call is valid
	Anything else = Call was not valid

Description:

Video Service 1AH is used to read or write a 2-byte display combination code. This service is a system function and, thus, is not ordinarily used.

Video Service 1BH

Return Functionality and State Data (VGA Only)

Input:

AH	1BH
BX	00H
ES:BP	Pointer to data buffer

Output:

AL	1BH = Call is valid
	Anything else = Call was not valid
ES:BP	Data buffer updated

Description:

Video Service 1BH is used to read the functionality and state table. This table contains information about the video mode and video hardware configuration.

Video Service 1CH

Save/Restore Video State (VGA Only)

Input:

AH	1CH
AL	00H = Return size of save/restore buffer
	01H = Save video state
	02H = Restore video state
CX	Bit 0 = Video HW state
	Bit 1 = Video data areas
	Bit 2 = Video DAC state and color registers
ES:BP	Pointer to save/restore buffer

Output:

AL	1CH = Call is valid
	Anything else = Call was not valid
BX	Block count for buffer size

Description:

Video Service 1CH is used to save or restore video data to a designated buffer. When AL is 00H, the information that describes the status of the video BIOS and hardware is returned. When AL is 01H, the current video state information is saved in the buffer pointed to by ES:BP. When AL is 02H, the previous video state is restored.

9

Microsoft C Graphics Functions

This chapter is a detailed reference guide for all Microsoft graphics functions. This guide contains a series of useful information ranging from the syntax to an example for each graphics function. The following information will help you get the most out of this reference guide.

Syntax: The syntax for each function is provided in this section. A brief description of each argument is also included.

Function: This section contains a very brief description of the function.

Files to Include: The include file needed for the function being described is listed in this section.

Compatibility: This section describes the function's compatibility with various operating systems. The operating systems considered for compatibility are DOS, OS/2, UNIX, and XENIX.

Description: A full description of the function is contained in this section.

Values Returned: The return values of the function are discussed here.

Related Functions: This section describes some of the Microsoft functions that are used with, or similar to, the function being described.

Similar Turbo C++ Functions: Turbo C++ functions that are used for similar purposes are described in this section.

Suggested Code Structure and Use: This section contains a functional description of the function's potential use. It also contains a code structure that illustrates a typical use of the function. This code structure is similar to pseudocode but provides a better feel for the way in which the function is used in a program. All necessary initializations of parameters, modes, and so on are listed along with the function to make it clear how to use the function properly.

Example: An example that uses the function is briefly described in this section. The code for the example is also listed.

_arc

Syntax:

```
short _far _arc (short x1, short y1, short x2, short y2,
                 short x3, short y3, short x4, short y4);
short x1, y1;      upper left corner of binding rectangle
short x2, y2;      lower right corner of binding rectangle
short x3, y3;      endpoint for starting vector
short x4, y4;      endpoint for ending vector
```

Function:

The _arc function draws an arc, which is a portion of the specified ellipse, in the current color using the view coordinate system.

Files to Include:

```
#include <graph.h>
```

Compatibility:

DOS

Description:

The _arc function draws a portion of the ellipse specified by the rectangular region x1, y1 and x2, y2. The x1 and y1 arguments specify the upper left corner of the rectangular region. The x2 and y2 arguments specify the lower right corner. The arc begins at the point where the ellipse intersects the vector that starts at the center of the rectangle and extends to the point x3, y3. The arc is then drawn counterclockwise in the current color until it reaches the vector that starts at the center of the rectangle and extends to the point x4, y4. The _arc function is not filled and uses solid lines only. The view coordinate system is used with this function. See figure 9.1.

Fig. 9.1. The _arc function.

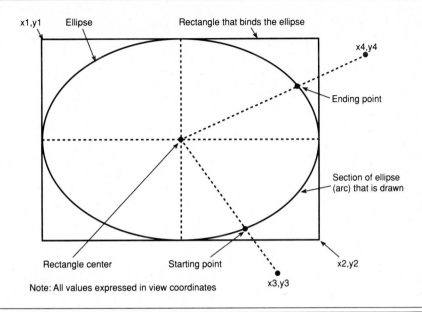

Note: All values expressed in view coordinates

Values Returned:

If successful, a nonzero value is returned. A zero is returned if an error is encountered.

Related Functions:

```
_setcolor      :      sets the current color
```

Similar Turbo C++ Functions:

```
arc  :  draws a circular arc
void far arc (int x, int y, int startangle,
             int endangle, int radius);
ellipse  :  draws an elliptical arc
void far ellipse (int x, int y, int startangle,
                 int endangle, int xradius, int yradius);
```

Suggested Code Structure and Use:

The _arc function is useful for creating complex shapes and curves. Several arcs can be connected for very complex graphics. The _arc function should be used with the view coordinate system.

```
#include <stdio.h>
#include <graph.h>
void main ()
{
_setvideomode ( mode ); /* set mode by graphics card */
        .
        .
        .
_arc (x1, y1, x2, y2, x3, y3, x4, y4); /* draw arc */
        .
        .
        .
_setvideomode (_DEFAULTMODE); /* resets graphics card */
}
```

Example:

This program demonstrates the operation of the _arc function. The program draws a portion of the ellipse defined by coordinates 30,30 and 289,169. See figure 9.2. The arc begins at the point where the vector that begins at the center of the ellipse and extends to 159,199 intersects the ellipse. The arc is then drawn in a counterclockwise direction until it intercepts the vector that begins at the center of the ellipse and extends to 289,0.

```
#include <graph.h>
#include <stdio.h>
void main ()
{
        /*  Initialization  */
_setvideomode (_MRES4COLOR);
_setbkcolor (_RED);
_rectangle (_GBORDER,0,0,319,199);
      /*  Draw arc    */
_arc (30,30,289,169,159,199,289,0);
_settextposition (22,10);
_outtext ("Press a Key to Exit");
      /*  Delay and exit  */
getch ();
_setvideomode (_DEFAULTMODE);
}
```

Fig. 9.2. Example _arc output.

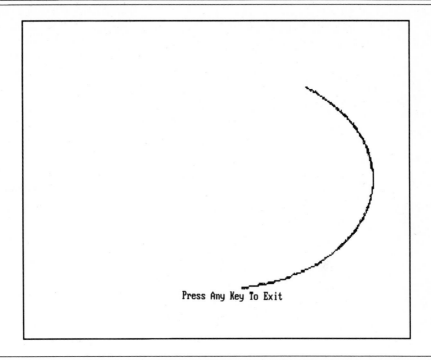

Press Any Key To Exit

_arc_w

Syntax:

```
short _far _arc_w (double x1, double y1, double x2,
                   double y2, double x3, double y3,
                   double x4, double y4);
double x1, y1;  upper left corner of binding rectangle
double x2, y2;  lower right corner of binding rectangle
double x3, y3;  endpoint for starting vector
double x4, y4;  endpoint for ending vector
```

Function:

The _arc_w function draws an arc, which is a portion of an ellipse, in the current window using the window coordinate system.

Files to Include:

```
#include <graph.h>
```

Compatibility:

DOS

Description:

The _arc_w function is similar to the _arc function, but uses the window coordinate system. Therefore, all arguments are expressed in window coordinates. The arc is drawn inside the binding rectangle specified by the x1,y1 and x2,y2 arguments. The x1 and y1 arguments identify the upper left corner of the binding rectangle; the x2 and y2 arguments identify the lower right corner of the binding rectangle. The arc begins at the point where it intersects the vector that begins at the center of the binding rectangle and extends to x3,y3. The arc is then drawn in a counterclockwise fashion, in the current color, until it intersects the vector that begins at the center of the binding rectangle and extends to x4,y4. The arc is drawn using a solid line and is not filled. See figure 9.3.

Fig. 9.3. The _arc_w function.

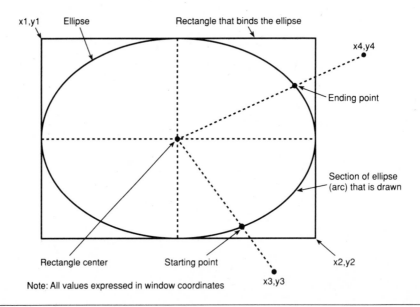

Values Returned:

If successful, a nonzero value is returned. If unsuccessful, a zero is returned.

Related Functions:

```
_setcolor        :        sets the current color
```

Similar Turbo C++ Functions:

None

Suggested Code Structure and Use:

The _arc_w function can be used anytime an arc must be drawn while using the window coordinate system. The _arc_w function is useful for creating simple or complex curves.

```
#include <stdio.h>
#include <graph.h>
void main ()
{
_setvideomode ( mode );  /* set video mode */
    .
    .
    .
_setviewport (x1,y1,x2,y2);  /* size viewport */
_setwindow (flag,x1,y1,x2,y2); /* window dimensions */
    .
    .
    .
_arc_w (x1,y1,x2,y2,x3,y3,x4,y4);
    .
    .
    .
_setvideomode (_DEFAULTMODE); /* reset and exit */
}
```

Example:

This program demonstrates the use of the _arc_w function. A viewport is set, then a window is set (both cover the entire screen). The dimensions of the window are set from -100.0 to 100.0 in both the x and y directions. An arc is then drawn inside the window. See figure 9.4.

```
#include <graph.h>
#include <stdio.h>
void main ()
{
     /*   Initialization   */
_setvideomode (_ERESCOLOR);
_rectangle (_GBORDER,0,0,639,349);
     /*   Set window   */
_setviewport (0,0,639,349);
_setwindow (0, -100.0, -100.0, 100.0, 100.0);
     /*   Draw arc   */
_arc_w (-80.0,-80.0,80.0,80.0,0.0,-80.0,0.0,80.0);
     /*   Delay and exit   */
_settextposition (23,30);
_outtext ("Press Any Key To Exit");
getch ();
_setvideomode (_DEFAULTMODE);
}
```

Fig. 9.4.   Example _arc_w output.

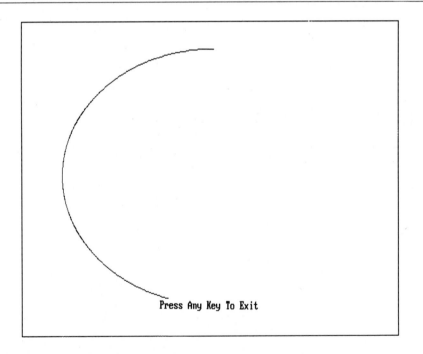

Press Any Key To Exit

_arc_wxy

Syntax:

```
short _far _arc_wxy(struct _wxycoord _far *xy1,
                struct _wxycoord _far *xy2,
                struct _wxycoord _far *xy3,
                struct _wxycoord _far *xy4);
struct _wxycoord _far *xy1;   upper left corner
struct _wxycoord _far *xy2;   lower right corner
struct _wxycoord _far *xy3;   endpoint for starting vector
struct _wxycoord _far *xy4;   endpoint for ending vector
```

Function:

The _arc_wxy function draws an arc, or portion of an ellipse, using the window coordinate system.

Files to Include:

```
#include <graph.h>
```

Compatibility:

DOS

Description:

The _arc_wxy function is identical to the _arc_w function, but the arguments are defined using a structure of type _wxycoord. The xy1 argument defines the upper left corner of the binding rectangle; the xy2 argument defines the lower right corner of the binding rectangle. The starting vector extends to the xy3 argument. The ending vector extends to the xy4 argument. The arc begins where the underlying ellipse intersects the starting vector. It is then drawn counterclockwise until it intersects the ending vector. See figure 9.5. The _arc_wxy function, like the _arc_w function, uses window coordinates, solid lines, and the current color.

Fig. 9.5. The _arc_wxy function.

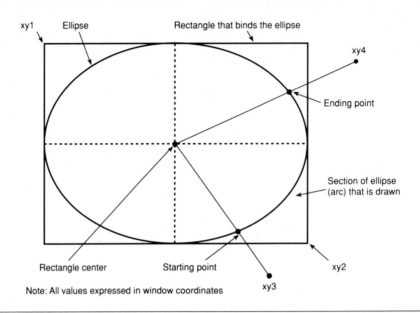

Values Returned:

If drawn successfully, a nonzero value is returned; otherwise, a zero is returned.

Related Functions:

```
_setcolor    :     sets the current color
```

Similar Turbo C++ Functions:

None

Suggested Code Structure and Use:

The _arc_wxy function can be used anywhere the _arc_w function is used. The only difference is in the way the arguments are defined. Sometimes, it is more convenient to use a structure rather than independent variables to pass the required arguments.

```
#include <stdio.h>
#include <graph.h>
void main ()
{
struct _wxycoord xy1, xy2, xy3, xy4;
_setvideomode ( mode );   /* set mode */
        .
     {assign values to the structure}
        .
_setviewport (x1, y1, x2, y2); /* size viewport */
_setwindow (flag, x1, y1, x2, y2); /* window dimensions*/
_arc_wxy (&xy1, &xy2, &xy3, &xy4);
        .
_setvideomode (_DEFAULTMODE); /* reset and exit */
}
```

Example:

The following program demonstrates the use of the _arc_wxy function by drawing an arc in the current window. The window dimensions are from -100.0 to 100.0 in both the x and y directions. See figure 9.6.

```
#include <graph.h>
#include <stdio.h>
void main ()
{
struct _wxycoord xy1, xy2, xy3, xy4;
xy1.wx = -80.0;
xy1.wy = -80.0;
xy2.wx = 80.0;
xy2.wy = 80.0;
xy3.wx = 0.0;
xy3.wy = -80.0;
xy4.wx = 0.0;
xy4.wy = 80.0;
_setvideomode (_ERESCOLOR);
_rectangle (_GBORDER,0,0,639,349);
     /* Open window */
_setviewport (0,0,639,349);
_setwindow (0,-100.0,-100.0,100.0,100.0);
```

289

```
      /* Draw arc */
_arc_wxy (&xy1, &xy2, &xy3, &xy4);
      /* Delay and exit */
_settextposition (23,30);
_outtext ("Press Any Key To Exit");
getch ();
_setvideomode (_DEFAULTMODE);
}
```

Fig. 9.6. Example _arc_wxy output.

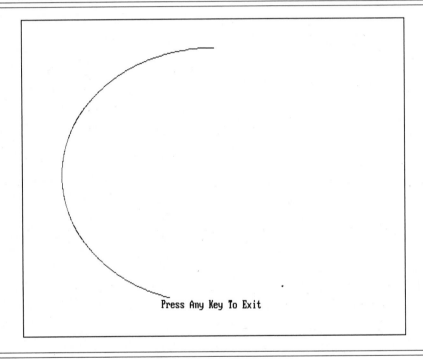

Press Any Key To Exit

_clearscreen

Syntax:

```
void _far _clearscreen (short area);
short area;      area to be cleared
```

Function:

The _clearscreen function clears the specified area and fills it with the current background color.

Files to Include:

```
#include <graph.h>
```

Compatibility:

DOS
OS/2

Description:

The area argument specifies the area to be cleared by the _clearscreen function. This area is cleared and filled with the current background color. Following are valid constants for the area argument:

_GCLEARSCREEN   Fills the entire screen with the background color.
_GVIEWPORT   Fills the current viewport with the background color.
_GWINDOW   Fills the current text window with the background color.

Values Returned:

There is no return value.

Related Functions:

```
_setbkcolor   :        sets the background color
```

Similar Turbo C++ Functions:

```
clrscr  :  clears the text window
void clrscr (void);
cleardevice  :  clears the graphics screen
void far cleardevice (void);
```

Suggested Code Structure and Use:

The _clearscreen function is useful for clearing a particular area. The following code structure demonstrates its use for clearing the entire screen. The examples in this section demonstrate the use of the _clearscreen function for clearing screens, viewports, and text windows.

```
#include <stdio.h>
#include <graph.h>
void main ()
{
_setvideomode ( mode ); /* set mode by graphics adapter */
        .
        .
        .
_clearscreen (_GCLEARSCREEN); /* clear screen */
        .
        .
        .
_setvideomode (_DEFAULTMODE); /* resets graphics card */
```

Screen

Example:

The following program clears the entire screen. It begins by filling the screen with various drawings. When a key is pressed, the background color is changed to red and the screen is cleared. To exit the program, press another key.

```
#include <stdio.h>
#include <graph.h>
void main ()
{
    /* Initialization */
_setvideomode (_MRES4COLOR);
_setbkcolor (_BLUE);
_rectangle (_GBORDER,0,0,319,199);
    /* Add features to the screen */
_setcolor (2);
_ellipse (_GFILLINTERIOR,30,30,289,139);
_settextposition (23,5);
_outtext ("Press Any Key to Clear Screen");
getch ();
```

```
      /* Clear screen with new background
         color (red) */
_setbkcolor (_RED);
_clearscreen (_GCLEARSCREEN);
      /* Delay and exit */
_settextposition (23,8);
_outtext ("Press Any Key to Exit");
getch ();
_setvideomode (_DEFAULTMODE);
}
```

Viewport

Example:

This example demonstrates the clearing of a viewport. A viewport is opened after initialization and filled with miscellaneous figures. When a key is pressed, the viewport is cleared. Note that the rectangle surrounding the viewport is not cleared. To end the program, press another key.

```
#include <stdio.h>
#include <graph.h>

void main ()
{
      /* Initialization */
_setvideomode (_MRES4COLOR);
_setbkcolor (_BLUE);
_rectangle (_GBORDER,0,0,319,199);
_settextposition (23,5);
_outtext ("Press Any Key to Clear Viewport");

      /* Open viewport */
_rectangle (_GBORDER,29,29,290,140);
_ellipse (_GFILLINTERIOR,40,40,279,129);
_setviewport (30,30,289,139);

      /* Clear viewport */
getch ();
_clearscreen (_GVIEWPORT);
      /* Set viewport to entire screen */
_setviewport (0,0,319,199);
_settextposition (23,5);
_outtext ("      Press Any Key to Exit          ");
```

```
                    /* Delay and exit */
getch ();
_setvideomode (_DEFAULTMODE);
}
```

Text Window

Example:

This program opens a text window and then uses the _clearscreen function with the
_GWINDOW argument to clear it.

```
#include <stdio.h>
#include <graph.h>
void main ()
{
    /* Initialization */
_setbkcolor (4L);
_clearscreen (_GWINDOW);

    /* Open text window and set background
       color of window to blue         */
_settextwindow (10,10,15,70);
_setbkcolor (1L);
_clearscreen (_GWINDOW);
_settextposition (3,12);
_outtext ("Press any Key to Clear Text Window");
    /* Delay--then clear text window */
getch ();
_clearscreen (_GWINDOW);
    /* Prompt for exit */
_settextwindow (1,1,25,80);
_settextposition (23,30);
_outtext ("Press Any Key to Exit");
    /* Delay and exit */
getch ();
_setvideomode (_DEFAULTMODE);
}
```

_displaycursor

Syntax:

```
short _far _displaycursor (short switch);
short switch;
```

Function:

In graphics mode, the **_displaycursor** function turns the solid text cursor on or off.

Files to Include:

```
#include <graph.h>
```

Compatibility:

DOS
OS/2

Description:

The **_displaycursor** function allows the programmer to turn the solid text cursor on or off while in graphics mode. The cursor, by default, is not displayed upon entering graphics mode. The following short integer switch arguments set the state of the cursor:

_GCURSORON   Turns on the text cursor.
_GCURSOROFF   Turns off the text cursor.

Values Returned:

The **_displaycursor** function returns the previous value of the cursor state (switch). No error return is provided.

Related Functions:

```
_settextcursor  :  sets the text cursor shape
```

Similar Turbo C++ Functions:

None

Suggested Code Structure and Use:

One use of the _displaycursor function is to turn the cursor on when prompting for user input. The following code structure illustrates how this _displaycursor function could be used in this way. The cursor should be turned off when leaving the function that turned it on, to prevent confusion in subsequent functions.

```
#include <stdio.h>
#include <graph.h>
void main ()
{
_setvideomode ( mode );   /* set mode by graphics card */
        .
        .
        .

_displaycursor (_GCURSORON);   /* turn solid cursor on */
        .
        .
        .

_displaycursor (_GCURSOROFF); /* turn off before exiting */
_setvideomode (_DEFAULTMODE); /* resets graphics card */
}
```

Example:

The following program uses the _MRES4COLOR video mode, which supports 24-by-40 text characters. The _displaycursor switch is set to on initially; therefore, the cursor is displayed. The program then accepts and echoes input from the keyboard. Pressing the 1 key will change the setting of the _displaycursor switch. Pressing the Esc key will exit the program.

```
#include <stdio.h>
#include <graph.h>
#define ESC 27
void main ()
{
 struct rccoord cursor_pos;
 int ch;
 int cursor_status;

 _setvideomode (_MRES4COLOR);
 _displaycursor (_GCURSORON);
 cursor_status = 1;             /* 0 for off, 1 for on */
 _settextposition (1,1);
 _outtext ("Cursor is presently on ");
```

```
_settextposition (2,1);
_outtext ("Enter a <1> to change cursor on or off");
_settextposition (4,1);
/*  Do loop for program execution--exits when ESC key
    is pressed   */
do
  {
    ch = getch ();

    cursor_pos = _gettextposition ();      /* retrieves current
                          text cursor position */
    /* The following statements change the cursor status flag
       and the current status of the _displaycursor function
       when <1> is pressed. */
    if (ch == '1')
    {
      cursor_status = cursor_status + 1;
      if (cursor_status > 1)
        cursor_status = 0;
      if (cursor_status == 0)
        {
         _settextposition (1,1);
         _outtext ("Cursor is presently off");
         _displaycursor (_GCURSOROFF);
        }
      if (cursor_status == 1)
        {
         _settextposition (1,1);
         _outtext ("Cursor is presently on ");
         _displaycursor (_GCURSORON);
        }
      _settextposition (cursor_pos.row, cursor_pos.col);
    }
    /*  The following statements change the value of the row
        and column variables in the cursor_pos structure.
        The column is incremented until it reaches 39, then
        it is reset to 1 and the row attribute is incremented. */
    cursor_pos.col++;
    if (cursor_pos.col > 39)
    {
     cursor_pos.col = 1;
     cursor_pos.row++;
    }
    putch (ch);
    _settextposition (cursor_pos.row, cursor_pos.col);
```

```
        }   while (ch != ESC);
      _setvideomode (_DEFAULTMODE); /* Reset */
    }
```

_ellipse

Syntax:

```
short _far _ellipse (short fillflag, short x1, short y1,
          short x2, short y2);
short   fillflag;          fill or border only
short x1, short y1;        upper left corner of rectangle
short x2, short y2;        lower right corner of rectangle
```

Function:

The _ellipse function draws an ellipse in the specified rectangular region using view coordinates.

Files to Include:

```
#include <graph.h>
```

Compatibility:

DOS

Description:

An ellipse with a border of the current color is drawn in the boundaries of the rectangle defined by x1,y1 and x2,y2. See figure 9.7. The x1 and y1 arguments define the upper left corner of the rectangle. The x2 and y2 arguments define the lower right corner of the rectangle. The fillflag argument determines whether the ellipse will be drawn with only a border or filled. The two valid fillflag arguments follow:

_GFILLINTERIOR   Fills the ellipse with the current fill pattern.
_GBORDER   Draws only the border; the ellipse is not filled.

If a horizontal or vertical line is described by the x1,y1 and x2,y2 arguments, no ellipse is drawn.

Fig. 9.7. The _ellipse function.

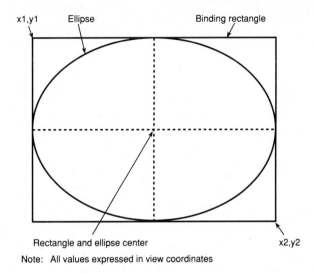

Note: All values expressed in view coordinates

Values Returned:

If drawn successfully, a nonzero value is returned; if unsuccesful, a zero is returned.

Related Functions:

```
_setcolor       :       sets the current color
_setfillmask    :       sets the current fill pattern
```

Similar Turbo C++ Functions:

```
ellipse   :   draws an elliptical arc
void far ellipse (int x, int y, int startangle,
                  int endangle, int xradius, int yradius);
fillellipse   :   draws and fills an ellipse
void far fillellipse (int x, int y, int xradius,
                  int yradius);
```

Suggested Code Structure and Use:

The _ellipse function is used for drawing circles and ellipses when using the view coordinate system. It may take some calculation or trial and error to create circles because the view coordinate system is not square in most modes. The following code structure demonstrates the use of the _ellipse function.

```
#include <stdio.h>
#include <graph.h>
void main ()
{
_setvideomode ( mode ); /* set mode by graphics adapter */
      .
      .
      .

_ellipse ( fillflag, x1, y1, x2, y2 ); /* draw ellipse */
      .
      .
      .

_setvideomode (_DEFAULTMODE); /* reset graphics card */
}
```

Example:

The following program demonstrates the uses of the _ellipse function. It begins by drawing an ellipse using the _GBORDER fillflag; thus, the ellipse is drawn with the current color and is not filled. Then the program draws a second ellipse using the _GFILLINTERIOR fillflag; this ellipse is filled. Upon completion, another ellipse is drawn over the first using a different current color and the _GBORDER fillflag. The result is an ellipse filled with white (Color 3) and surrounded by magenta (Color 2). Then the program draws a final ellipse, which is filled. See figure 9.8.

```
#include <stdio.h>
#include <graph.h>
void main ()
{
        /*   Initialization    */
_setvideomode (_MRES4COLOR);
_setbkcolor (_BLUE);
_rectangle (_GBORDER,0,0,319,199);
     /* Draw ellipse with border only  */
_ellipse (_GBORDER,20,20,70,159);
        /* Draw filled ellipse, then place
            colored border on it */
_ellipse (_GFILLINTERIOR,134,20,184,159);
_setcolor (2);
_ellipse (_GBORDER,134,20,184,159);
   /* Draw filled ellipse */
_ellipse (_GFILLINTERIOR,299,20,249,159);
_settextposition (22,10);
_outtext ("Press a Key to Exit");
```

```
        /* Delay and reset */
getch ();
_setvideomode (_DEFAULTMODE);
}
```

Figure 9.8. Example _ellipse output.

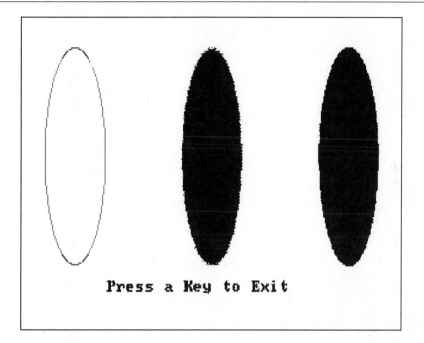

Press a Key to Exit

_ellipse_w

Syntax:

```
short _far _ellipse_w(short fillflag, double x1,
                double y1, double x2, double y2);
short fillflag;          fill or border only
double x1, y1;           upper left corner of rectangle
double x2, y2;           lower right corner of rectangle
```

Function:

The _ellipse_w function draws an ellipse in the current window using the window coordinate system.

Files to Include:

```
#include <graph.h>
```

Compatibility:

DOS

Description:

The _ellipse_w function creates an ellipse in the current window using the window coordinate system. The ellipse is drawn, using the current color and fill pattern, in the binding rectangle defined by x1,y1 and x2,y2. The x1 and y1 arguments identify the upper left corner of the binding rectangle; the x2 and y2 arguments identify the lower right corner of this rectangle. Figure 9.9 illustrates the use of these arguments. The ellipse can either be filled or drawn with only a border. The fillflag arguments follow:

_GFILLINTERIOR	Fills the ellipse with the current fill pattern.
_GBORDER	Draws only the border; the ellipse is not filled.

The _ellipse_w function uses the window coordinate system.

Fig. 9.9. The _ellipse_w function.

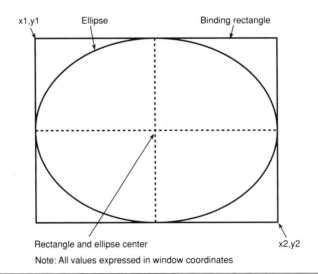

Note: All values expressed in window coordinates

Values Returned:

If drawn successfully, a nonzero value is returned; if unsuccessful, a zero is returned.

Related Functions:

```
_setcolor     :     sets the current color
_setfillmask  :     sets the fill pattern
```

Similar Turbo C++ Functions:

None

Suggested Code Structure and Use:

The _ellipse_w function is used to create circles or ellipses in the current window. A window must be set before the call to the _ellipse_w function is made. The following code structure illustrates one way to use the _ellipse_w function.

```
#include <graph.h>
#include <stdio.h>
void main ()
{
_setvideomode (mode);   /* set video mode */
        .
        .
        .
_setviewport (x1,y1,x2,y2); /* size viewport */
_setwindow (flag,x1,y1,x2,y2); /* window dimensions */
        .
        .
        .
_ellipse_w (fillflag,x1,y1,x2,y2);
        .
        .
        .
_setvideomode (_DEFAULTMODE); /* reset and exit */
}
```

Example:

The proper use of the _ellipse_w function is demonstrated in the following example. This program creates a window with dimensions of -100.0 to 100.0 in both the x and y directions and draws two ellipses in the window using the _ellipse_w function. See figure 9.10.

```
#include <graph.h>
#include <stdio.h>
void main ()
{
_setvideomode (_ERESCOLOR);
_rectangle (_GBORDER,0,0,639,349);
     /* Open window */
_setviewport (0,0,639,349);
_setwindow (0, -100.0, -100.0, 100.0, 100.0);
     /* Draw two ellipses */
_ellipse_w(_GBORDER, -75.0, -75.0, 75.0, 75.0);
_ellipse_w(_GFILLINTERIOR, -50.0, -50.0, 50.0, 50.0);
     /* Delay and exit */
_settextposition (23,30);
_outtext ("Press Any Key to Exit");
getch ();
_setvideomode (_DEFAULTMODE);
}
```

Fig. 9.10.   Example _ellipse_w output.

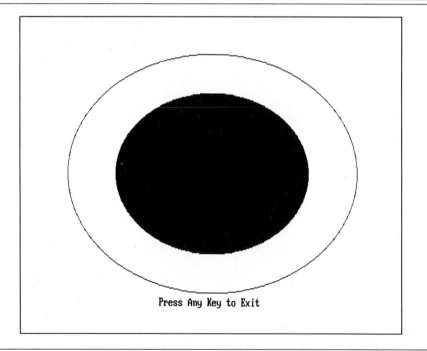

Press Any Key to Exit

_ellipse_wxy

Syntax:

```
short _far _ellipse_wxy(short fillflag, struct _wxycoord
        _far *xy1, struct _wxycoord _far *xy2);
short fillflag;                    fill or border
struct _wxycoord _far *xy1;        upper left corner
struct _wxycoord _far *xy2;        lower right corner
```

Function:

The _ellipse_wxy function produces an ellipse in the current color and window using the window coordinate system.

Files to Include:

```
#include <graph.h>
```

Compatibility:

DOS

Description:

The _ellipse_wxy function is like the _ellipse_w function, but the arguments are described in a structure of type _wxycoord. The xy1 argument defines the upper left corner of the binding rectangle for the ellipse. The xy2 argument defines the lower right corner of the binding ellipse. See figure 9.11. The fillflag argument is used to determine if the ellipse will be filled. The fillflag constants follow:

_GFILLINTERIOR   Fills the ellipse with the current fill pattern.
_GBORDER   Draws only the border; the ellipse is not filled.

The _ellipse_wxy function, like the _ellipse_w function, uses the window coordinate system.

Fig. 9.11. The _ellipse_wxy function.

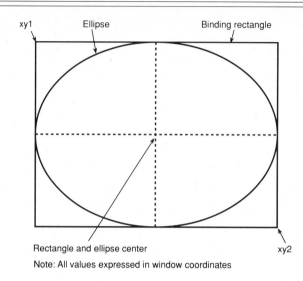

Note: All values expressed in window coordinates

Values Returned:

If successful, a nonzero value is returned; if unsuccessful, a zero is returned.

Related Functions:

```
_setcolor     :     set the current color
_setfillmask  :     sets the current fill pattern
```

Similar Turbo C++ Functions:

None

Suggested Code Structure and Use:

The _ellipse_wxy function can be used anywhere the _ellipse_w function is used. The ellipse_wxy function, however, uses structures of type _wxycoord to pass the required arguments. The following code structure illustrates the use of the _ellipse_wxy function.

```
#include <graph.h>
#include <stdio.h>
void main ()
{
struct _wxycoord xy1, xy2;
```

```
_setvideomode (mode); /* set video mode */
        .
        .
        .
_setviewport (x1, y1, x2 ,y2); /* size viewport */
_setwindow (flag, x1, y1, x2, y2); /*window dimensions*/
        .
        .
        .
    {assign values to xy1 and xy2 structures}
        .
        .
        .
_ellipse_wxy (fillflag, &xy1, &xy2);
        .
        .
        .
_setvideomode (_DEFAULTMODE); /* reset and exit */
}
```

Example:

The _ellipse_wxy function is used in the following program to create two concentric ellipses in the current window. See figure 9.12.

```
#include <graph.h>
#include <stdio.h>
void main ()
{
struct _wxycoord xy1, xy2;
_setvideomode (_ERESCOLOR);
_rectangle (_GBORDER,0,0,639,349);
      /* Open window */
_setviewport (0,0,639,349);
_setwindow (0, -100.0, -100.0, 100.0, 100.0);
      /* Draw two ellipses */
xy1.wx = -75.0;
xy1.wy = -75.0;
xy2.wx = 75.0;
xy2.wy = 75.0;
_ellipse_wxy (_GBORDER, &xy1, &xy2);
xy1.wx = -50.0;
xy1.wy = -50.0;
xy2.wx = 50.0;
xy2.wy = 50.0;
_ellipse_wxy (_GFILLINTERIOR, &xy1, &xy2);
      /* Delay and exit */
```

```
_settextposition (23,30);
_outtext ("Press Any Key to Exit");
getch ();
_setvideomode (_DEFAULTMODE);
}
```

Fig. 9.12. Example _ellipse_wxy output.

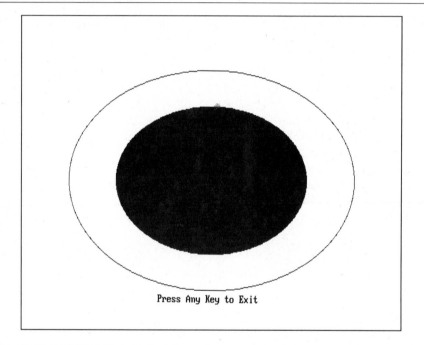

_floodfill

Syntax:

```
short _far _floodfill (short x, short y, short bordercolor);
short x, y;         starting point for fill
short bordercolor;  border color of fill area
```

Function:

The _floodfill function fills a bound area with the current color and fill pattern. This function uses the view coordinate system.

Files to Include:

```
#include <graph.h>
```

Compatibility:

DOS

Description:

The _floodfill function is used to fill an area bound by the value of the bordercolor argument. The area is filled with the current color and fill pattern. The x and y arguments define the view coordinates of the starting point for the fill. If this point is inside an area surrounded by the bordercolor, the area will be filled. If the point is outside the area, the background will be filled. If the point is on the border, no filling will be done. When the _floodfill function is called, the fill pattern is spread in all directions until the border color is reached. The boundary of the desired fill area must be solid with no breaks to prevent filling outside areas. The _floodfill function uses the view coordinate system.

Values Returned:

A nonzero value is returned when the function is successful. A zero is returned if the fill could not be completed or the starting point lies on the border color or outside the current clipping region.

Related Functions:

```
_setcolor      :      sets the current color
_setfillmask   :      sets the current 8 x 8 bit fill pattern
```

Similar C++ Functions:

```
floodfill  :  fills a bound area
void far floodfill (int x, int y, int border);
```

Suggested Code Structure and Use:

The _floodfill function is useful for filling a bound area when using the view coordinate system. The current color and fill pattern are used in the fill routine. Using this function, you can accomplish complex and detailed graphics. The following code structure illustrates how the _floodfill function could be used.

```
#include <stdio.h>
#include <graph.h>
unsigned char *(fillpattern [# of patterns]) =
  {"\x--\x--\x--\x--\x--\x--\x--\x--",
              .
              .
              .
   "\x--\x--\x--\x--\x--\x--\x--\x--"};
void main ()
{
_setvideomode ( mode ); /* set mode by adapter */
_setcolor ( bordercolor );  /* choose color for border */
         .
         .
         .
   { draw figure to fill with bordercolor }
         .
         .
         .
_setcolor ( fillcolor ); /* choose color for fill*/
_setfillmask ((char far *)(fillpattern [pattern #]));
                /* choose fill pattern */
_floodfill (x,y,bordercolor); /* fill area starting at x,y
                surrounded by bordercolor */
         .
         .
         .
_setvideomode (_DEFAULTMODE); /* reset */
}
```

Example:

The following example of the _floodfill function begins by drawing three rectangles. When a key is pressed, the first rectangle is filled with the current color. The fill point is set inside the rectangle. When another key is pressed, the program attempts to fill the second rectangle. The fill point is set on the border; therefore, no filling is done. Another keystroke demonstrates what happens when the fill point is outside the desired area.

```
#include <stdio.h>
#include <graph.h>
void main ()
{
    /*       Initialization       */
_setvideomode (_MRES4COLOR);
```

```
_setbkcolor (_BLUE);
_rectangle (_GBORDER,0,0,319,199);
    /*    Draw three rectangles  */
_rectangle (_GBORDER,20,20,70,159);
_rectangle (_GBORDER,134,20,184,159);
_rectangle (_GBORDER,249,20,299,159);
    /*    Fill first rectangle with
     Color 2 when key is pressed   */
_settextposition (22,2);
_outtext ("Press a key to fill first rectangle");
_settextposition (23,2);
_outtext ("Fill Point is inside rectangle");
getch ();
_setcolor (2);
_floodfill (21,21,3);
    /* Attempt to fill second rectangle
        with a fill point on the border    */
_settextposition (22,2);
_outtext ("Press a key to fill second rectangle");
_settextposition (23,2);
_outtext ("Fill Point is on rectangle border");
getch ();
_floodfill (134,20,3);
    /* Attempt to fill third rectangle
        with a fill point outside the rectangle */
_settextposition (22,2);
_outtext ("Press a Key to fill third rectangle  ");
_settextposition (23,2);
_outtext ("Fill Point is outside rectangle   ");
getch ();
_floodfill (300,20,3);
    /*    Print exit message  */
_settextposition (22,2);
_outtext ("Press a Key to exit             ");
_settextposition (23,2);
_outtext ("                      ");

/*  Delay and reset  */
getch ();
_setvideomode (_DEFAULTMODE);
}
```

_floodfill_w

Syntax:

```
short _far _floodfill_w (double x, double y,
                             short bordercolor);
double x, y;           starting point of the fill
short bordercolor;     border color of the fill area
```

Function:

The _floodfill_w function fills a bound area in the current window using the current color and fill pattern.

Files to Include:

```
#include <graph.h>
```

Compatibility:

DOS

Description:

The _floodfill_w function is used with the window coordinate system to fill a bound area with the current color and fill pattern. The x and y arguments define the window coordinates that mark the starting point of the fill. The starting point should lie inside the area to be filled. If the point is outside the boundary, the outside will be filled. If the point lies on the border, no filling will take place. It is important that the border be solid and only one color; otherwise, the results will be unpredictable.

Values Returned:

If the function is successful, a nonzero value is returned. If the fill is unsuccessful, or if the starting point lies on the bordercolor, or if the starting point lies outside the clipping region, a zero is returned.

Related Functions:

```
_setcolor      :     sets the current color
_setfillmask   :     sets the current fill pattern
```

Similar Turbo C++ Functions:

None

Suggested Code Structure and Use:

The _floodfill_w function is useful for filling bound areas when using the window coordinate system. You can create complex images using various colors and fill patterns with the _floodfill_w function.

```
#include <graph.h>
#include <stdio.h>
void main ()
{
_setvideomode (mode); /* set mode */
    .
    .
    .
_setviewport (x1,y1,x2,y2); /* size viewport */
_setwindow (flag,x1,y1,x2,y2); /* window dimensions */
    .
    .
    .
    { create image to be filled }
    .
    .
    .
_floodfill_w (x,y,bordercolor); /* flood area */
    .
    .
    .
_setvideomode (_DEFAULTMODE); /* reset and exit */
}
```

Example:

In this example program, the _floodfill_w function is used to fill a rectangle that is drawn using window coordinates. See figure 9.13. The border color of the rectangle, and thus the bound area, is Color 2. The fill color is Color 1.

```
#include <graph.h>
#include <stdio.h>
void main ()
{
_setvideomode (_ERESCOLOR);
_rectangle (_GBORDER,0,0,639,349);
    /* Open window */
_setviewport (0,0,639,349);
_setwindow (0,-100.0,-100.0,100.0,100.0);
    /* Draw rectangle and fill it */
_setcolor (2);
_rectangle_w (_GBORDER,-80.0,-80.0,80.0,80.0);
_setcolor (1);
```

```
_floodfill_w (0.0,0.0,2);
      /* Delay and exit */
_settextposition (23,30);
_outtext ("Press any Key To Exit");
getch ();
_setvideomode (_DEFAULTMODE);
}
```

Fig. 9.13. Example _floodfill_w output.

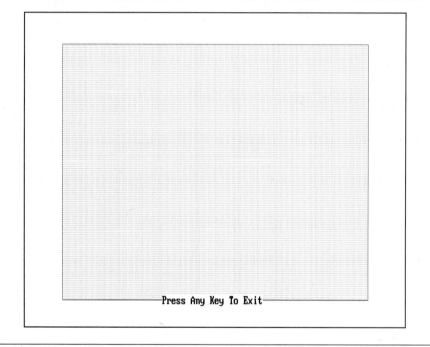

_getactivepage

Syntax:

```
short _far _getactivepage(void);
```

Function:

The _getactivepage function returns the number of the current active page.

Files to Include:

```
#include <graph.h>
```

Compatibility:

DOS

Description:

The _getactivepage function is used to retrieve the page number of the current active page. The current active page is the video page in memory to which all output is sent. All hardware modes support multiple pages of text but only some modes, when combined with sufficient video memory, support multiple pages of graphics. The _getvideoconfig function is useful for determining the number of pages available with the hardware in use.

Values Returned:

The number of the current active page is returned.

Related Functions:

```
_setactivepage      :       sets the active page
```

Similar Turbo C++ Functions:

```
setactivepage  :  sets the active page
void far setactivepage (int page);
```

Suggested Code Structure and Use:

The _getactivepage function is used to determine the page number of the active page. The active page is the location (page) in video memory to which graphics output is sent. The page number of the current active page is important, for example, to programmers who use multiple pages of graphics output for animation.

```
#include <graph.h>
#include <stdio.h>
void main ()
{
short pagenumber;
_setvideomode (mode);   /* set mode */
      .
```

```
        .
pagenumber = _getactivepage ();   /* get active page */
        .
        .
_setvideomode (_DEFAULTMODE); /* reset and exit */
}
```

Example:

This program demonstrates the proper use of the _getactivepage function. The active page is initially set to Page 1. The page number is then retrieved using the _getactivepage function and echoed on the screen. The active page is reset to Page 0 upon exiting the program. This program requires an EGA or VGA with sufficient memory to support multiple pages of graphics.

```
#include <stdio.h>
#include <graph.h>
void main ()
{
short pagenumber;
char buffer [80];
_setvideomode (_ERESCOLOR);
_rectangle (_GBORDER, 0, 0, 639, 349);
     /* Set, retrieve, and echo the
        active page number */
_setactivepage (1);
_clearscreen (_GCLEARSCREEN);
pagenumber = _getactivepage();
_settextposition (15,25);
sprintf (buffer, "The active page number is %d",
            pagenumber);
_outtext (buffer);
_settextposition (23,25);
_outtext ("Press Any Key To Continue");
_setvisualpage (1);
     /* Delay and exit */
getch ();
_setactivepage (0);
_setvisualpage (0);
_setvideomode (_DEFAULTMODE);
}
```

_getarcinfo

Syntax:

```
short _far _getarcinfo(struct xycoord _far *startvector,
                struct xycoord _far *endvector,
                struct xycoord _far *fillpoint);
struct xycoord _far *startvector;    starting point
struct xycoord _far *endvector;      ending point
struct xycoord _far *fillpoint;      fill point
```

Function:

The _getarcinfo function returns information on the arc most recently drawn by the _arc or _pie functions. The return values are expressed in viewport coordinates.

Files to Include:

```
#include <graph.h>
```

Compatibility:

DOS

Description:

The _getarcinfo function returns information on the most recent arc that has been drawn with the _arc or _pie functions. The starting, ending, and fill points of the arc are returned in a structure of type xycoord. These points are useful for modifying or recreating the arc. All points are returned in view coordinates.

Values Returned:

If successful in obtaining the information, a nonzero value is returned. If no arc has been successfully drawn since the last time the screen was cleared or a new videomode or viewport defined, a zero is returned.

Related Functions:

```
_arc     :    draws an arc in view coordinates
_pie     :    draws a wedge in view coordinates
```

Similar Turbo C++ Functions:

```
getarccoords  :  gets coordinates of last call to arc
void far getarccoords (struct arccoordstype
                    far *arccoords);
```

Suggested Code Structure and Use:

The _getarcinfo function is used to obtain information on the most recent arc drawn by any of the _pie or _arc functions. The returned values can be used to recreate or fill the arc. By knowing the endpoints of the arc, it is easier to blend the arc into other figures.

```
#include <graph.h>
#include <stdio.h>
void main ()
{
struct xycoord startvector, endvector, fillpoint;
_setvideomode ( mode ); /* set video mode */
    .
    .
    { draw arc with any of _arc or _pie functions }
    .
    .
_getarcinfo (&startvector, &endvector, &fillpoint);
    .
    .
_floodfill (fillpoint.xcoord,fillpoint.ycoord,
        bordercolor);  /* use arc info */
    .
    .
_setvideomode (_DEFAULTMODE);  /* reset and exit */
}
```

Example:

The _getarcinfo function is used in the following program to connect the endpoints of an arc, then fill it. See figure 9.14. Note that the _getarcinfo function returns view coordinates.

```
#include <graph.h>
#include <stdio.h>
void main ()
{
```

```
struct xycoord startvector, endvector, fillpoint;
_setvideomode (_ERESCOLOR);
_rectangle (_GBORDER,0,0,639,349);
      /* Draw arc and get info */
_arc (50,50,590,300,320,0,320,349);
_getarcinfo (&startvector, &endvector, &fillpoint);
      /* Connect endpoint and fill */
_moveto (startvector.xcoord, startvector.ycoord);
_lineto (endvector.xcoord, endvector.ycoord);
_setcolor (1);
_floodfill (fillpoint.xcoord, fillpoint.ycoord, 15);
      /*  Delay and exit */
_settextposition (23,30);
_outtext ("Press any Key to Exit");
getch ();
_setvideomode (_DEFAULTMODE);
}
```

Fig. 9.14.   Example _getarcinfo output.

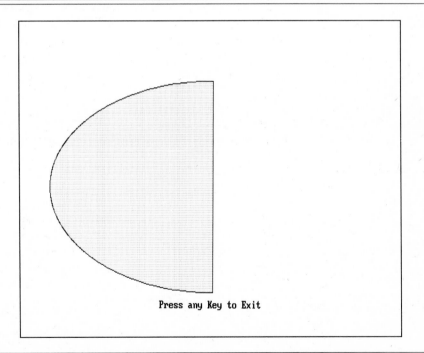

_getbkcolor

Syntax:

```
long _far _getbkcolor (void);
```

Function:

The _getbkcolor function returns the pixel value of the current background color.

Files to Include:

```
#include <graph.h>
```

Compatibility:

DOS
OS/2

Description:

The pixel value of the current background color is returned by the _getbkcolor function. The return value differs in form from text to graphics mode.

In graphics mode, the background color is set by the form

```
_setbkcolor (_BLUE);
```

The background color would be set to blue. See the _setbkcolor description for further information on setting various background colors. _BLUE represents a constant value; the _getbkcolor function, however, will not return this value. A 0 will be returned.

In text mode, the background color is set by the form

```
_setbkcolor (1L);
```

The background color would then be set to blue. Again, the description of _setbkcolor provides further information on setting background colors. Unlike the graphics mode, however, a call to _getbkcolor in text mode will return the value of the background color, which in this case is 1L. Table 9.1 will aid in the interpretation of background colors.

Table 9.1. *Background constants and values.*

Color	Pixel value for text modes	Color constant for graphics modes
Black	OL	_BLACK
Blue	1L	_BLUE
Green	2L	_GREEN
Cyan	3L	_CYAN
Red	4L	_RED
Magenta	5L	_MAGENTA
Brown	6L	_BROWN
White	7L	_WHITE
Dark gray	8L	_GRAY
Light blue	9L	_LIGHTBLUE
Light green	10L	_LIGHTGREEN
Light cyan	11L	_LIGHTCYAN
Light red	12L	_LIGHTRED
Light magenta	13L	_LIGHTMAGENTA
Yellow	14L	_LIGHTYELLOW
Bright white	15L	_BRIGHTWHITE

Values Returned:

A long integer which represents the current background color is returned. No error value is returned.

Related Functions:

```
_setbkcolor    : Sets the current background color
```

Similar Turbo C++ Functions:

```
getbkcolor  :  gets the background color
int far getbkcolor (void);
```

Suggested Code Structure and Use:

The _getbkcolor function is used to retrieve the current background color in text modes. Programmers often find this information useful. For example, you may want different color backgrounds for each text window. By retrieving the current background color and incrementing, the next text window can be set to another color. The following code structure illustrates the typical use of this command.

```
#include <stdio.h>
#include <graph.h>
void main ()
{
  long background_color; /* initialize variable to hold
                  the returned background color */
  _setvideomode ( mode );  /* set mode by graphics card */
        .
        .
        .
  _setbkcolor ( color );  /* set color by values described
        with this function  */
      .
      .
      .
  background_color = _getbkcolor ();
      .
      .
      .
  { use the background color information }
      .
      .
      .
  _setvideomode (_DEFAULTMODE);  /* reset graphics card */
}
```

Text Mode

Example:

This program demonstrates how the _getbkcolor function works in text mode. The program sets the background color to blue (1 L), and retrieves this color with the _getbkcolor function. This color is then printed on the screen. To exit the program, press any key.

```
#include <stdio.h>
#include <graph.h>
void main ()
{
long background_color;          /* stores background color  */
_setbkcolor (1L);  /* sets text background to blue */
_clearscreen (_GCLEARSCREEN);
background_color = _getbkcolor(); /*gets background color*/
```

```
printf ("The Background Color Is: %d\n\n",
          background_color);
printf ("Press Any Key to Return to Original Mode");
getch ();
_setbkcolor (OL); /* sets text background to black */
_clearscreen (_GCLEARSCREEN);
}
```

Graphics Mode

Example:

This program demonstrates how the _getbkcolor function works in graphics mode. The background color is set to blue (_BLUE), and this color is retrieved using the _getbkcolor function. This return value is then output to the screen. The output is 0—remember that in graphics mode, the _getbkcolor function returns a 0 instead of the value of the background color constant.

```
#include <stdio.h>
#include <graph.h>
void main ()
{
 long background_color;  /* for storage of background
               color   */
 char buffer [40];        /* for storage of text string */

 _setvideomode (_MRES4COLOR);
 _setbkcolor (_BLUE);
 background_color = _getbkcolor ();
 sprintf (buffer,"The Background Color Is: %d",
     background_color);
 _settextposition (5,1);
 _outtext (buffer);
 _settextposition (10,1);
 _outtext ("Press Any Key to Return to Original Mode");
 getch ();
 _setvideomode (_DEFAULTMODE);
}
```

_getcolor

Syntax:

```
short _far _getcolor (void);
```

Function:

The _getcolor function is used to retrieve the current color number as set by the _setcolor function.

Files to Include:

```
#include <graph.h>
```

Compatibility:

DOS

Description:

The current color number used for line drawing and area fill routines can be retrieved with the _getcolor function. Upon entering graphics mode, the current color is set to the default value, which is the highest numbered color from the current palette. Palettes vary by graphics mode and are discussed in detail under the _setcolor function. Tables 9.2 and 9.3 will help you interpret the return values.

Values Returned:

The current color number is returned. No error return is provided.

Related Functions:

```
_setcolor     :  used to set the current color
```

Similar Turbo C++ Functions:

```
getcolor  :  gets the current color
int far getcolor (void);
```

Table 9.2. *Default color palette for 16-color modes.*

Pixel value	Color
0	Black
1	Blue
2	Green
3	Cyan
4	Red
5	Magenta
6	Brown
7	White
8	Dark gray
9	Light blue
10	Light green
11	Light cyan
12	Light red
13	Light magenta
14	Yellow
15	Bright white

Table 9.3. *Color palettes.*

	Pixel value			
Palette number	Color 0	Color 1	Color 2	Color 3
Palettes in _MRES4COLOR mode				
0	Selectable	Green	Red	Brown
1	Selectable	Cyan	Magenta	Light gray
2	Selectable	Light green	Light red	Yellow
3	Selectable	Light cyan	Light magenta	White
CGA palettes in _MRESNOCOLOR mode				
0	Selectable	Blue	Red	Light gray
1	Selectable	Light blue	Light red	White
EGA palettes in _MRESNOCOLOR mode				
0	Selectable	Green	Red	Light gray
1	Selectable	Light green	Light red	Yellow
2	Selectable	Light cyan	Light red	Yellow
3	Selectable	Light green	Light red	Yellow

Suggested Code Structure and Use:

The _getcolor function retrieves the current color. It is often used to store the current color number before changing it. In this way, the current color can be reset to its original color upon exiting the function. The following code structure shows how this could be accomplished.

```
#include <stdio.h>
#include <graph.h>
void main ()
{
int current_color;   /*  stores the returned current
                 color /*
 _setvideomode ( mode ); /* set by graphics card */
 current_color = _getcolor (); /* retrieve current color */
         .
         .
         .
 _setcolor (current_color); /* resets current color to
                 original color  */
 _setvideomode (_DEFAULTMODE); /* resets graphics card */
}
```

Example:

This program draws a rectangle in the current (default) color, retrieves the value of this default color, and outputs the value to the screen. The current color is then set to another value and a rectangle is drawn using this color. This color value is then retrieved and output to the screen.

```
#include <stdio.h>
#include <graph.h>
void main ()
{
int current_color;      /*  Holds current color  */
char buffer [40];       /*  Formatted print buffer  */
    /*      Initialization     */
_setvideomode (_MRES4COLOR);
_setbkcolor (_BLUE);
_rectangle (_GFILLINTERIOR,240,20,300,80);
    /*      Retrieve current color     */
current_color = _getcolor ();
    /*      Print text and current color  */
_settextposition (4,2);
sprintf (buffer,"The Current Color Is : %d", current_color);
_outtext (buffer);
_settextposition (6,2);
```

```
_outtext ("Press Any Key to Continue");
getch ();
    /*     Reset and get current color */
_setcolor (1);
current_color = _getcolor ();
    /*     Print text and current color  */
_rectangle (_GFILLINTERIOR,240,180,300,120);
sprintf (buffer,"The New Current Color Is : %d",
        current_color);
_settextposition (18,2);
_outtext (buffer);
_settextposition (20,2);
_outtext ("Press Any Key to Continue");
    /*     Delay and exit      */
getch ();
_setvideomode (_DEFAULTMODE);
}
```

_getcurrentposition

Syntax:

```
struct xycoord _far _getcurrentposition (void);
```

Function:

The _getcurrentposition function returns the view coordinates of the current graphics cursor position.

Files to Include:

```
#include <graph.h>
```

Compatibility:

DOS

Description:

The current position of the graphics cursor is maintained internally by the graphics routines. The _getcurrentposition function returns the current position of this graphics cursor expressed in view coordinates. These x and y coordinates are returned in the xycoord structure, which is defined in graph.h. The position of the graphics cursor is updated by the _outgtext, _moveto, and _lineto functions.

```
struct xycoord
    {
     short xcoord;
     short ycoord;
    };
```

Values Returned:

The view coordinates of the graphics cursor position are returned. No error value is returned.

Related Functions:

```
_moveto    :    changes  the  position  of  the  graphics  cursor
_lineto    :    updates  the  graphics  cursor  after  drawing
```

Similar Turbo C++ Functions:

```
getx  :  gets  the  x  value  of  the  graphics  cursor
int  far  getx  (void);

gety  :  gets  the  y  value  of  the  graphics  cursor
int  far  gety  (void);
```

Suggested Code Structure and Use:

The _getcurrentposition function is useful when drawing figures relative to the current position of the graphics cursor. When developing a user interface, it is often desirable to create an image relative to a crosshair cursor that updates the location of the internal graphics cursor. When a particular key is pressed, a box, for example, can be drawn starting at the position of the crosshair cursor. Many graphics programs use this type of scheme. By obtaining the current position of the graphics cursor, it is easy to draw a figure relative to this cursor position.

```
#include <stdio.h>
#include <graph.h>
void main ()
```

```
{
struct xycoord cursorposition;  /* define structure for
                storing cursor coordinates*/
_setvideomode ( mode ); /* set mode by adapter */
         .

         .

         .

cursorposition = _getcurrentposition ();
         .

         .

         .

  { use the cursor information }
         .

         .

         .

_setvideomode (_DEFAULTMODE);
}
```

Example:

This program uses the _getcurrentposition function to retrieve the x and y position of
a crosshair cursor. See figure 9.15. The crosshair cursor is controlled by the keypad. The Num Lock
key must be on. The 4 key shifts the cursor left, the 8 key shifts the cursor up, the 6 key shifts the
cursor right, and the 2 key shifts the cursor down. Each time a key is pressed, the current position
of the center of this crosshair cursor, which is also the current position of the internal graphics
cursor, is printed on the screen. To end the program, press Esc.

```
#include <stdio.h>
#include <graph.h>
#define ESC 27
void main ()
{
int ch;
int x,y;
int oldx, oldy;
struct xycoord cursorposition;
char buffer [40];

    /* Initialization */
_setvideomode (_MRES4COLOR);
_setbkcolor (_BLUE);
_rectangle (_GBORDER,0,0,319,199);
    /* Draw initial cursor */
x = 155;
```

```
y = 95;
_moveto (x+5,y);
_lineto (x+5,y+10);
_moveto (x,y+5);
_lineto (x+10,y+5);
_moveto (x+5,y+5);
     /* Output initial setting of cursor position */
cursorposition = _getcurrentposition ();
sprintf (buffer, "X Position : %d", cursorposition.xcoord);
_settextposition (23,10);
_outtext (buffer);
sprintf (buffer, "Y Position : %d", cursorposition.ycoord);
_settextposition (24,10);
_outtext (buffer);

do
    {
    oldx = x;
    oldy = y;
    ch = getch ();
          /* Move cursor points */
    if (ch == '4')
     x = x - 5;
    if (ch == '8')
     y = y - 5;
    if (ch == '6')
     x = x + 5;
    if (ch == '2')
     y = y + 5;
      /* Check borders */
    if (y < 5)
     y = y + 5;
    if (y > 140)
     y = y - 5;
    if (x > 305)
     x = x - 5;
    if (x < 5)
     x = x + 5;
    _setcolor (0);
    _moveto (oldx+5,oldy);
    _lineto (oldx+5,oldy+10);
    _moveto (oldx,oldy+5);
    _lineto (oldx+10,oldy+5);
    _setcolor (3);
    _moveto (x+5,y);
```

```
    _lineto (x+5,y+10);
    _moveto (x,y+5);
    _lineto (x+10,y+5);
    _moveto (x+5,y+5);
    /* Output present setting of cursor position */
cursorposition = _getcurrentposition ();
sprintf (buffer, "X Position : %d", cursorposition.xcoord);
_settextposition (23,10);
_outtext (buffer);
_outtext ("          ");
sprintf (buffer, "Y Position : %d", cursorposition.ycoord);
_settextposition (24,10);
_outtext (buffer);
_outtext ("          ");
    } while (ch != ESC);
_setvideomode (_DEFAULTMODE);
}
```

Fig. 9.15. Example _getcurrentposition output.

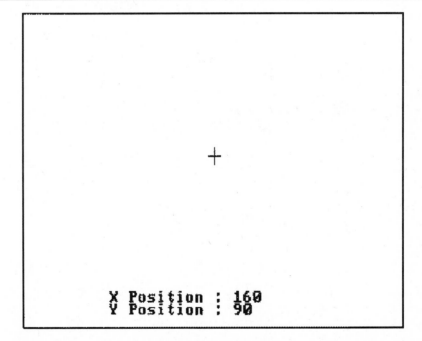

_getcurrentposition_w

Syntax:

```
struct _wxycoord _far _getcurrentposition_w(void);
```

Function:

The _getcurrentposition_w function returns the position of the graphics cursor expressed in window coordinates.

Files to Include:

```
#include <graph.h>
```

Compatibility:

DOS

Description:

The _getcurrentposition_w function is similar to the _getcurrentposition function, but the values are returned in a structure of type _wxycoord and are expressed as window coordinates. The position of the graphics cursor is updated by the _outgtext, _lineto_w, and _moveto_w functions.

Values Returned:

The position of the graphics cursor, expressed in window coordinates, is returned in a structure of type _wxycoord. This structure is shown in the following:

```
struct _wxycoord
{
double wx;
double wy;
}
```

Related Functions:

```
_moveto_w       :       moves the graphics cursor
_lineto_w       :       draws a line, moves cursor
```

Similar Turbo C++ Functions:

None

Suggested Code Structure and Use:

You use the _getcurrentposition_w function to obtain the current position of the graphics cursor when using window coordinates. After you obtain these window coordinates, text and other output can be positioned relative to them. The following code structure illustrates the method by which you can obtain these coordinates.

```
#include <graph.h>
#include <stdio.h>
void main ()
{
struct _wxycoord position;
_setvideomode (mode); /* set video mode */
      .
      .
_setviewport (x1,y1,x2,y2); /* size viewport */
_setwindow (flag,x1,y1,x2,y2); /* window dimensions */
      .
      .
position = _getcurrentposition_w ();
      .
    { use current position }
      .
      .
_setvideomode (_DEFAULTMODE); /* reset and exit */
}
```

Example:

The _getcurrentposition_w function is used in this program to obtain the current position of the graphics cursor, expressed in window coordinates. Next, the program calculates and draws an ellipse with a center at the current graphics position. See figure 9.16.

```
#include <graph.h>
#include <stdio.h>
void main ()
{
struct _wxycoord position;
_setvideomode (_ERESCOLOR);
_rectangle (_GBORDER,0,0,639,349);
```

```
                /* Open window */
_setviewport (0,0,639,349);
_setwindow (0,-100.0,-100.0,100.0,100.0);
                /* Draw line, and get position */
_moveto_w (-75.0,-75.0);
_lineto_w (75.0,75.0);
position = _getcurrentposition_w ();
                /* Use position to draw ellipse */
_ellipse_w (_GBORDER,position.wx-10.0,position.wy-10.0,
            position.wx+10.0,position.wy+10.0);
                /* Delay and exit */
_settextposition (23,30);
_outtext ("Press any Key to Exit");
getch ();
_setvideomode (_DEFAULTMODE);
}
```

Fig. 9.16. Example _getcurrentposition_w output.

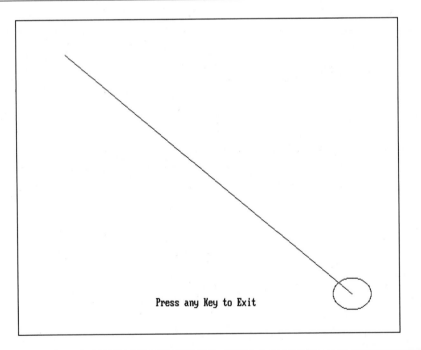

_getfillmask

Syntax:

```
unsigned char _far * _far _getfillmask (unsigned char
      _far *pattern);
unsigned char _far *pattern;        fill pattern
```

Function:

The _getfillmask function is used to get the current fill pattern. The fill pattern is an 8-by-8 pattern of bits that is used with the _floodfill, _rectangle, _ellipse, _polygon, and _pie functions. The _setfillmask function is used to set this 8-by-8 bit pattern.

Files to Include:

```
#include <graph.h>
```

Compatibility:

DOS

Description:

The _getfillmask function retrieves the current 8-by-8 bit pattern as set by the _setfillmask function. This 8-by-8 bit pattern is used for the _floodfill, _pie, _ellipse, _polygon, and _rectangle functions. The pattern is returned in eight characters; the address of these characters is provided in the pattern argument. The 8-by-8 bit pattern determines how the area will be filled. Each bit in the pattern represents a pixel. A 1 bit sets the corresponding pixel to the current color; a 0 bit leaves the pixel unchanged. A NULL pattern is the default setting. If no fill pattern is specified, the area is filled with a solid pattern of the current color. In other words, every pixel in the area to be filled is set to the current color.

Values Returned:

Eight characters are returned to the address provided in the pattern argument. NULL is returned if no pattern is specified.

Related Functions:

```
_setfillmask      :   specifies the current fill pattern
```

Similar Turbo C++ Functions:

```
getfillpattern  :  get the current fill pattern
void far getfillpattern (char far *pattern);
```

Suggested Code Structure and Use:

This code structure illustrates how the original fill pattern can be stored upon entering a function. It is good practice to then restore the fill pattern to the original fill pattern upon exiting a function.

```
#include <stdio.h>
#include <graph.h>
  /* sets the desired number of fill patterns  */
unsigned char * (pattern [ # of patterns ]) =
     {"\x--\x--\x--\x--\x--\x--\x--\x--",
                        .
                        .
                        .
        "\x--\x--\x--\x--\x--\x--\x--\x--"};
char *oldfillpattern = "00000000"; /* holder for old
                        pattern */
void main ()
{
 unsigned char far *originalpattern; /* holds original
                        pattern */
 _setvideomode ( mode ); /* set by graphics card */
 originalpattern = _getfillmask (oldfillpattern);  /* gets
                        original fill pattern  */
 _setfillmask ((char far *)(pattern [ pattern # ])); /* set
                        the new fill pattern */
        .
        .
        .
 _setfillmask (originalpattern); /* resets to original
                        pattern */
 _setvideomode (_DEFAULTMODE);  /* resets graphics card */
}
```

Example:

This example demonstrates how the _getfillmask function can be used to store previous fill patterns. First, the original pattern is stored. Then, two new fill patterns are set and used. Finally, the fill pattern is restored to the original and used. See figure 9.17.

```
#include <stdio.h>
#include <graph.h>
unsigned char * (fillpattern [2])=
{"\x55\xAA\x55\xAA\x55\xAA\x55\xAA",
 "\x20\x02\x80\x08\x20\x02\x80\x08"};
char *oldfillpattern = "00000000";  /* holder for old fill
                    pattern */
void main ()
{
unsigned char far *originalpattern;  /* variable for
                                original pattern  */
_setvideomode (_MRES4COLOR);
_setbkcolor (_BLUE);
_setcolor (3);
    /* store the original pattern set upon
       entering graphics mode */
originalpattern = _getfillmask (oldfillpattern);
    /*  set the fill pattern to pattern 1 an fill a
        rectangle on the top half of the screen */
_setfillmask ((char far *)(fillpattern [0]));
_rectangle (_GBORDER,0,0,319,99);
_floodfill (1,1,3);
     /* set the fill pattern to pattern 2 and fill
        a rectangle on the bottom half of the screen */
_setfillmask ((char far *)(fillpattern [1]));
_rectangle (_GBORDER,0,99,319,199);
_floodfill (1,100,3);
_setcolor (1);
/*  restore the fill pattern to the original pattern and
   fill a rectangle with the original pattern--the default
   pattern of a solid fill      */
_setfillmask (originalpattern);
_rectangle (_GBORDER,40,40,279,159);
_setcolor (2);
_floodfill (41,41,1);
_settextposition (12,10);
_outtext ("Press a key to exit");
    /*  delay and reset     */
getch ();
_setvideomode (_DEFAULTMODE);
}
```

Fig. 9.17. Example _getfillmask output.

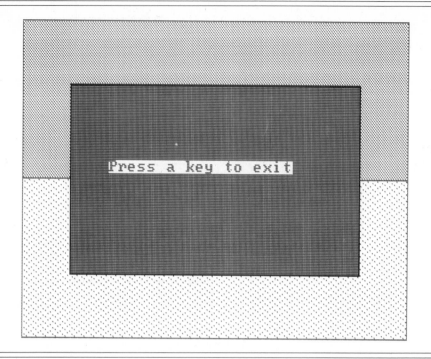

_getfontinfo

Syntax:

```
short _far _getfontinfo(struct _fontinfo _far
                        *fontbuffer);
struct _fontinfo _far *fontbuffer;   font information
```

Function:

The _getfontinfo function returns the characteristics of the current font in a structure of type _fontinfo.

Files to Include:

```
#include <graph.h>
```

Compatibility:

DOS

Description:

The _getfontinfo function returns the characteristics of the current font. The font information is returned in a structure of type _fontinfo; this structure follows. Table 9.4 will help you interpret the returned information.

```
struct _fontinfo
{
int type;
int ascent;
int pixwidth;
int pixheight;
int avgwidth;
char filename[81];
char facename[32];
}
```

Table 9.4. *Font information.*

Argument	Meaning
type	Vector (1) or bit-mapped (0) font
ascent	Top to bottom pixel distance
pixwidth	Character width in pixels
pixheight	Character height in pixels
avgwidth	Average character width
filename	Path and file name
facename	Font name

Values Returned:

The characteristics of the current font are returned in a structure of type _fontinfo. A -1 is returned if no font has been registered or loaded.

Related Functions:

```
_setfont          :    selects a font
_registerfonts    :    initializes fonts
```

Similar Turbo C++ Functions:

```
gettextsetting  :  gets information about the current font
```

```
void far gettextsettings (struct textsettingstype
                          far *texttypeinfo);
```

Suggested Code Structure and Use:

The _getfontinfo function returns information on the current font. You can use this
information to make sure that the correct font is in use. The following code structure illustrates the
method by which the font information is obtained.

```
#include <graph.h>
#include <stdio.h>
void main ()
{
struct _fontinfo information;
_setvideomode ( mode ); /* set video mode */
_registerfonts ("*.fon"); /* register fonts in current
                     directory */
_setfont ("t'courier' h12 w9 b f");  /* select courier
          font, 12x9 size */
_getfontinfo (&information);

     .
     { use font information }
     .
_setvideomode (_DEFAULTMODE); /* reset and exit */
}
```

Example:

This example demonstrates the use of the _getfontinfo function. The font information is
obtained after the fonts are registered and a font is selected. Then the pixel width and height are
displayed on the screen.

```
#include <graph.h>
#include <stdio.h>
void main ()
{
struct _fontinfo information;
char buffer [40];
_setvideomode (_ERESCOLOR);
_rectangle (_GBORDER,0,0,639,349);
     /* Register and set fonts */
_registerfonts ("*.fon"); /*files in current directory*/
_setfont ("t'courier' h12 w9 b f");
     /* Get and use font info */
```

```
_getfontinfo (&information);
sprintf (buffer,"Pixel Width : %d",
         information.pixwidth);
_settextposition (10,30);
_outtext (buffer);
sprintf (buffer, "Pixel Height : %d",
         information.pixheight);
_settextposition (15,30);
_outtext (buffer);
     /* Delay and exit */
_settextposition (23,30);
_outtext ("Press Any Key To Exit");
getch ();
_unregisterfonts ();
_setvideomode (_DEFAULTMODE);
}
```

_getgtextextent

Syntax:

```
short _far _getgtextextent(unsigned char _far *text);
unsigned char _far *text;     text to measure
```

Function:

The _getgtextextent function determines and returns the width of the text string to be printed in the current font.

Files to Include:

```
#include <graph.h>
```

Compatibility:

DOS

Description:

The _getgtextextent function is used to determine the width, in pixels, of a text string that will be output with the _outgtext function. When determining the width of the text, the characteristics of the current font are taken into account.

Values Returned:

The required width in pixels is returned if successful. A -1 is returned if a font has not been registered.

Related Functions:

```
_outgtext          :     outputs string of text
_setfont           :     selects the current font
_registerfonts     :     initializes available fonts
```

Similar Turbo C++ Functions:

```
textwidth  :  returns the width of a string in pixels
int far textwidth (char far *textstring);
```

Suggested Code Structure and Use:

The `_getgtextextent` function is used to determine the width of a text buffer given the current font. The returned value can be used, for example, to calculate a starting point for centering the text on the screen.

```
#include <graph.h>
#include <stdio.h>
void main ()
{
int width;
_setvideomode (mode);
_registerfonts ("*.fon");  /* register fonts */
_setfont ("t'courier' h12 w9 b f");
    .
    .
    .
width = _getgtextextent( buffer );
    .
    .
    { use width information }
    .
    .
    .
_unregisterfonts ();  /* free memory */
_setvideomode (_DEFAULTMODE);  /* reset and exit */
}
```

Example:

The _getgtextextent function is used in this example to determine the pixel width of a string of text. The returned value is then output to the screen using the current font and vector orientation. See figure 9.18.

```
#include <graph.h>
#include <stdio.h>
void main ()
{
int width;
char buffer [40];
_setvideomode (_ERESCOLOR);
_rectangle (_GBORDER,0,0,639,349);
     /* Register and set fonts */
_registerfonts ("*.fon");
_setfont ("t'courier' h12 w9 b f");
_setgtextvector (0,1);
     /* Determine width */
width = _getgtextextent("Length of this buffer is :  ");
sprintf(buffer,"Length of this buffer is : %d", width);
_moveto (312,290);
_outgtext (buffer);
     /* Delay and exit */
_settextposition (23,30);
_outtext ("Press Any Key To Exit");
getch ();
_unregisterfonts ();
_setvideomode (_DEFAULTMODE);
}
```

_getgtextvector

Syntax:

```
struct xycoord _far _getgtextvector(void);
```

Function:

The _getgtextvector function returns the direction of the vector used for font orientation in a structure of type xycoord.

Fig. 9.18. Example _getgtextextent output.

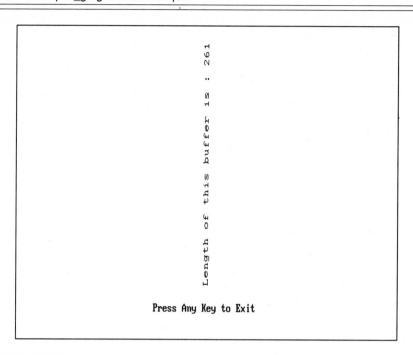

Files to Include:

```
#include <graph.h>
```

Compatibility:

DOS

Description:

The **_getgtextvector** function returns the orientation of the text vector. The text vector is used to determine the rotation of text output by the **_outgtext** function. The vector orientation is set by the **_setgtextvector** function. Table 9.5 will help you interpret the return values.

Table 9.5. *Vector orientation.*

Values for x,y	Orientation
1,0	Horizontal text (default)
0,1	Rotated 90 degrees counterclockwise
-1,0	Rotated 180 degrees counterclockwise
0,-1	Rotated 270 degrees counterclockwise

Values Returned:

The text direction vector, which determines the direction for font rotation, is returned in a structure of type `xycoord`. This structure follows.

```
struct xycoord
     {
     short xcoord;
     short ycoord;
     }
```

Related Functions:

```
_setgtextvector     :     sets the orientation vector
```

Similar Turbo C++ Functions:

```
gettextsettings  :  get font information including
                      direction of output
void far gettextsettings (struct textsettingstype
                      far *texttypeinfo);
```

Suggested Code Structure and Use:

The `_getgtextvector` function is used to determine the current orientation of the current text vector. This information is useful because you may want to maintain or change the current setting before displaying font text.

```
#include <graph.h>
#include <stdio.h>
void main ()
     {
```

```
struct xycoord orientation;
_setvideomode ( mode ); /* set video mode */
_registerfonts ("*.fon"); /* register fonts */
_setfont ("t'courier' h12 w9 b f"); /* set font */
_setgtextvector (0,1);
orientation = _getgtextvector (); /* get info */
          .
          .

   { use orientation information }

          .
          .
_setvideomode (_DEFAULTMODE); /* reset and exit */
}
```

Example:

The following program demonstrates the use of the _getgtextvector function. The function is used to obtain the current orientation of the text vector. Then this information is displayed using the current font and vector orientation. See figure 9.19.

```
#include <graph.h>
#include <stdio.h>
void main ()
{
struct xycoord orientation;
char buffer [40];
_setvideomode (_ERESCOLOR);
_rectangle (_GBORDER,0,0,639,349);
     /* Register and set fonts */
_registerfonts ("*.fon");
_setfont ("t'courier' h12 w9 b f");
_setgtextvector (0,1);
     /* Get and use orientation */
orientation = _getgtextvector ();
sprintf (buffer,"X Orientation : %d",
          orientation.xcoord);
_moveto (300,200);
_outgtext (buffer);
sprintf (buffer, "Y Orientation : %d",
          orientation.ycoord);
_moveto (330,200);
_outgtext (buffer);
     /* Delay and exit */
_settextposition (23,30);
```

```
_outtext ("Press Any Key to Exit");
getch ();
_unregisterfonts ();
_setvideomode (_DEFAULTMODE);
}
```

Fig. 9.19. Example _getgtextvector output.

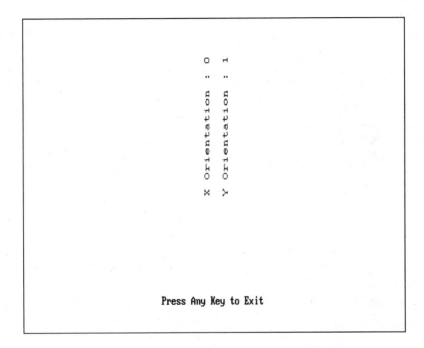

_getimage

Syntax:

```
void _far _getimage(short x1, short y1, short x2, short y2,
                    char _huge *image);
short x1, y1;            upper left corner of image
short x2, y2;            lower right corner of image
char _huge *image;      image buffer
```

Function:

The _getimage function stores a rectangular region of the screen when using the view coordinate system.

Files to Include:

```
#include <graph.h>
```

Compatibility:

DOS

Description:

When using the view coordinate system, you can store a rectangular region of the screen with the _getimage function. The region to be stored is defined by the rectangle x1,y1,x2,y2. The x1 and y1 arguments identify the upper left corner of the rectangle; the x2 and y2 arguments identify the lower right corner. The image is stored in a buffer; you can use the _imagesize function to determine the required buffer size.

Values Returned:

There is no return value.

Related Functions:

```
_imagesize    :    determines the number of bytes needed
                              to store an image
_putimage     :    places a stored image on the screen
```

Similar Turbo C++ Functions:

```
getimage  :  saves a screen image into memory

void far getimage (int left, int top, int right,
                   int bottom, void far *bitmap);
```

Suggested Code Structure and Use:

The _getimage function is useful for storing images that are needed later in the program. The method by which these images are placed on the screen (see the _putimage action arguments) determines their appearance. The following code structure illustrates the procedure for storing an image.

```
#include <stdio.h>
#include <graph.h>
#include <malloc.h>
char far *imagebuffer;
void main ()
{
_setvideomode ( mode ); /* set mode by adapter */
        .
        .
        .

   { Create image }
        .
        .
        .

imagebuffer = (char far *)malloc((unsigned int)
          _imagesize (x1,y1,x2,y2)); /* initialize
                             buffer size */
_getimage (x1,y1,x2,y2,imagebuffer); /* get image */
        .
        .
        .

_putimage (x,y,imagebuffer, action); /* place image */
        .
        .
        .

_setvideomode (_DEFAULTMODE); /* reset and exit */
}
```

Example:

This program demonstrates the use of the _g e t i m a g e function. After initialization, a rectangular image with a circular center is created. Then this image is stored using the _g e t i m a g e function. It is important to initialize the image buffer to the appropriate size before storing the image; the _i m a g e s i z e function will help establish a properly sized buffer. The stored image is then displayed in the four corners of the screen, as shown in figure 9.20.

```
#include <stdio.h>
#include <graph.h>
#include <malloc.h>
char far *imagebuffer;
void main ()
{
    /* Initialization */
_setvideomode (_MRES4COLOR);
```

```
_setbkcolor (_RED);
_rectangle (_GBORDER,0,0,319,199);
    /* Create image to be stored */
_rectangle (_GFILLINTERIOR,140,80,180,120);
_setcolor (1);
_ellipse (_GFILLINTERIOR,150,90,170,110);
    /* Save image */
imagebuffer = (char far *)malloc((unsigned int)
            _imagesize (140,80,180,120));
_getimage(140,80,180,120,imagebuffer);
    /* Put images on screen */
_putimage (20,20,imagebuffer,_GPSET);
_putimage (20,140,imagebuffer,_GPSET);
_putimage (260,20,imagebuffer,_GPSET);
_putimage (260,140,imagebuffer,_GPSET);
        /* Delay and exit */
_settextposition (23,10);
_outtext ("Press Any Key to Exit");
getch ();
_setvideomode (_DEFAULTMODE);
}
```

_getimage_w

Syntax:

```
void _far _getimage_w(double x1, double y1, double x2,
            double y2, char _huge *image);
double x1, y1;          upper left corner of image
double x2, y2;          lower right corner of image
char _huge *image;      image buffer
```

Function:

The _getimage_w function stores the image defined by window coordinates x1, y1 and x2, y2.

Files to Include:

```
#include <graph.h>
```

Compatibility:

DOS

Fig. 9.20. Example _getimage output.

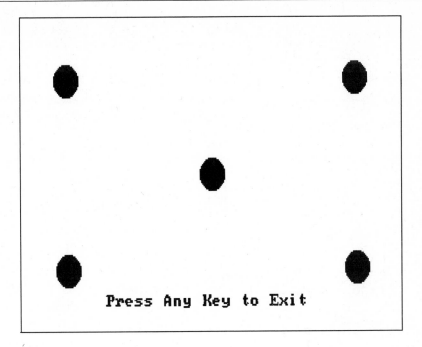

Description:

The **_getimage_w** function is similar to the **_getimage** function, but uses the window coordinate system. The **x1** and **y1** arguments define the upper left corner of the rectangular image. The **x2** and **y2** arguments define the lower right corner of the image. The **_imagesize_w** function is used with the **_getimage_w** function to determine the required size of the image buffer.

Values Returned:

There is no return value.

Related Functions:

```
_imagesize_w    :      determines size of image buffer
_putimage_w     :      used to place image buffer
```

Similar Turbo C++ Functions:

None

Suggested Code Structure and Use:

The _getimage_w function is used in the same way as the _getimage function. The only
difference is that the _getimage_w function uses the window coordinate system. The following
code structure demonstrates the use of the _getimage_w function.

```
#include <graph.h>
#include <stdio.h>
#include <malloc.h>
char far *imagebuffer;
void main ()
{
_setvideomode (mode); /* set mode */
_setviewport (x1,y1,x2,y2); /* size viewport */
_setwindow (flag,x1,y1,x2,y2); /* window dimensions */
      .
      .
      .
   { draw image to save }
      .
      .
      .
imagebuffer = (char far *)malloc((unsigned int)
      _imagesize_w(x1,y1,x2,y2)); /* size buffer */
_getimage_w (x1,y1,x2,y2,imagebuffer); /* get image */
_putimage_w (x1,y1,imagebuffer,action); /*place image*/
      .
      .
      .
_setvideomode (_DEFAULTMODE); /* reset and exit */
}
```

Example:

The following example demonstrates the use of the _getimage_w function to retrieve an image.
The retrieved image is placed on the screen four times. The window coordinate system is in use.

```
#include <graph.h>
#include <stdio.h>
#include <malloc.h>
char far *imagebuffer;
void main ()
{
_setvideomode (_ERESCOLOR);
_rectangle (_GBORDER,0,0,639,349);
```

```
_setviewport (0,0,639,349);
_setwindow (0,-100.0,-100.0,100.0,100.0);
     /* Draw image to save */
_setcolor (1);
_rectangle_w (_GFILLINTERIOR,-30.0,-30.0,30.0,30.0);
_setcolor (4);
_ellipse_w (_GFILLINTERIOR,-15.0,-15.0,15.0,15.0);
     /* Save image */
imagebuffer = (char far *)malloc((unsigned int)
     _imagesize_w (-30.0,-30.0,30.0,30.0));
_getimage_w (-30.0,-30.0,30.0,30.0,imagebuffer);
     /* Place image */
_putimage_w (-90.0,-90.0,imagebuffer,_GPSET);
_putimage_w (-90.0,30.0,imagebuffer,_GPSET);
_putimage_w (30.0,-90.0,imagebuffer,_GPSET);
_putimage_w (30.0,30.0,imagebuffer,_GPSET);
     /* Delay and exit */
_settextposition (23,30);
_outtext ("Press Any Key To Exit");
getch();
_setvideomode (_DEFAULTMODE);
}
```

_getimage_wxy

Syntax:

```
void _far _getimage_wxy(struct _wxycoord _far *xy1,
             struct _wxycoord _far *xy2,
             char _huge *image);
struct _wxycoord _far *xy1;   upper left corner of image
struct _wxycoord _far *xy2;   lower right corner of image
char _huge *image;            image buffer
```

Function:

The _getimage_wxy stores the image defined by the window coordinate pairs x y 1 and x y 2.

Files to Include:

```
#include <graph.h>
```

Compatibility:

DOS

Description:

The `_getimage_wxy` function is similar to the `_getimage_w` function. Both use the window coordinate system, but the methods by which the arguments are passed differ. When using the `_getimage_wxy` function, the rectangular image is defined by the coordinate pairs `xy1` and `xy2`. The `xy1` argument defines the upper left corner of the image; the `xy2` argument defines the lower right corner of the image. The `_imagesize_wxy` function is used with the `_getimage_wxy` function to determine the required size of the image buffer.

Values Returned:

There is no return value.

Related Functions:

```
_imagesize_wxy      :    determines size of buffer
_putimage_wxy       :    places an image
```

Similar Turbo C++ Functions:

None

Suggested Code Structure and Use:

The `_getimage_wxy` function is used for storing images in the window coordinate system. This function is similar to the `_getimage_w` function but uses a structure of type `_wxycoord` for its arguments. The following code demonstrates how the function can be used.

```
#include <graph.h>
#include <stdio.h>
#include <malloc.h>
char far *imagebuffer;
void main ()
{
struct _wxycoord corner1, corner2;
_setvideomode (mode); /* set video mode */
_setviewport (x1,y1,x2,y2); /* size viewport */
_setwindow (flag,x1,y1,x2,y2); /* window dimensions */
        .
        .
        .
    { draw image and specify the structure values }
        .
```

```
          .
          .
          .
imagebuffer = (char far *)malloc((unsigned int)
     _imagesize_wxy (&corner1,&corner2));
_getimage_wxy (&corner1,&corner2,imagebuffer);
_putimage_w (x1,y1,imagebuffer,action);
          .
          .
          .

_setvideomode (_DEFAULTMODE);
}
```

Example:

This program creates an image, stores it with the `_getimage_wxy` function, and places the
stored image in the four corners of the screen. See figure 9.21.

```
#include <graph.h>
#include <stdio.h>
#include <malloc.h>
char far *imagebuffer;
void main ()
{
struct _wxycoord corner1, corner2;
_setvideomode (_ERESCOLOR);
_rectangle (_GBORDER,0,0,639,349);
_setviewport (0,0,639,349);
_setwindow (0,-100.0,-100.0,100.0,100.0);
     /* Draw image to save */
_setcolor (1);
_rectangle_w (_GFILLINTERIOR,-30.0,-30.0,30.0,30.0);
_setcolor (4);
_ellipse_w (_GFILLINTERIOR,-15.0,-15.0,15.0,15.0);
     /* Save image */
corner1.wx = -30.0;
corner1.wy = -30.0;
corner2.wx = 30.0;
corner2.wy = 30.0;
imagebuffer = (char far *)malloc((unsigned int)
     _imagesize_wxy (&corner1, &corner2));
_getimage_wxy (&corner1,&corner2,imagebuffer);
     /* Place image */
_putimage_w (-90.0,-90.0,imagebuffer,_GPSET);
_putimage_w (-90.0,30.0,imagebuffer,_GPSET);
```

```
_putimage_w (30.0,-90.0,imagebuffer,_GPSET);
_putimage_w (30.0,30.0,imagebuffer,_GPSET);
    /* Delay and exit */
_settextposition (23,30);
_outtext ("Press Any Key To Exit");
getch();
_setvideomode (_DEFAULTMODE);
}
```

Fig. 9.21. Example _getimage_wxy output.

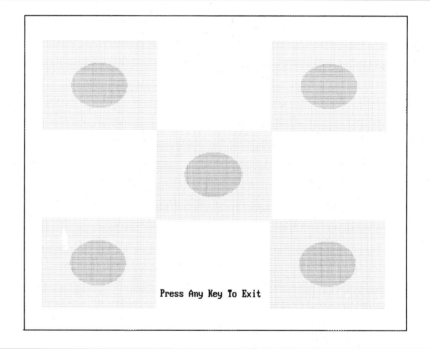

_getlinestyle

Syntax:

```
unsigned short _far _getlinestyle (void);
```

Function:

The `_getlinestyle` function returns the 16-bit pattern set by the `_setlinestyle` function.

Files to Include:

```
#include <graph.h>
```

Compatibility:

DOS

Description:

The 16-bit line pattern set by the `_setlinestyle` function is retrieved by the `_getlinestyle` function. The `_lineto`, `_polygon`, and `_rectangle` functions use this 16-bit pattern to draw straight lines. The appearance of the line is controlled by this pattern. A 1 bit sets the corresponding pixel to the current color; a 0 bit leaves the corresponding pixel unchanged. The default pattern is 0XFFFF; this corresponds to a solid line.

Values Returned:

A 16-bit unsigned integer is returned. The default pattern is returned when no pattern is specified.

Related Functions:

```
_setlinestyle   :   sets the 16-bit pattern used for
                    drawing straight lines
```

Similar Turbo C++ Functions:

```
getlinesettings  :  gets the current line style,
                    pattern, and thickness
void far getlinesettings (struct linesettingstype
                          far *lineinfo);
```

Suggested Code Structure and Use:

The `_getlinestyle` function retrieves the current line style. The most common use of this function is to store old line patterns. It is a good practice to store the current line pattern upon entering a function, then reset the current line pattern to the original pattern upon exiting the function. This is illustrated in the following code structure.

```
#include <stdio.h>
#include <graph.h>
  /* set line patterns  */
short linepattern [ # of patterns ] =
  {0x----,0x----, ... , 0x----};
void main ()
{
int oldlinepattern; /* holds the old line pattern */
 _setvideomode ( mode ); /* set by graphics card */
 oldpattern = _getlinestyle (); /* gets current line
                   pattern */
 _setlinestyle (linepattern [pattern #]); /* sets new line
                   pattern */

         .
         .
         .

 _setlinestyle (oldlinepattern); /* reset to original line
                             pattern before exiting */
 _setvideomode (_DEFAULTMODE); /* reset graphics card */
}
```

Example:

This program creates two line patterns. Next, upon entering the function, the program stores the current line pattern. The program then sets the current line pattern to pattern 1 and draws a line, then resets the current line pattern to pattern 2 and draws the new line. Finally, the program resets the current line pattern to the original line pattern and draws a line. See figure 9.22.

```
#include <stdio.h>
#include <graph.h>

short linepattern [2] = {0x8000, 0xFF18};

void main ()
{
int oldlinepattern;
_setvideomode (_MRES4COLOR);
_setbkcolor (_BLUE);
_rectangle (_GBORDER,0,0,319,199);
     /*  Save the default line pattern */
oldlinepattern = _getlinestyle ();
     /* Set line pattern to pattern 1 and draw a line  */
_setlinestyle (linepattern [0]);
_moveto (5,50);
```

```
_lineto (314,50);
    /* Set line pattern to pattern 2 and draw a line  */
_setlinestyle (linepattern [1]);
_moveto (5,100);
_lineto (314,100);
    /* Set line pattern to the original pattern (default)
        and draw a line */
_setlinestyle (oldlinepattern);
_moveto (5,150);
_lineto (314,150);
_settextposition (22,12);
_outtext ("Press a Key to Exit");
    /* Delay and reset   */
getch();
_setvideomode (_DEFAULTMODE);
}
```

Fig. 9.22. Example _getlinestyle output.

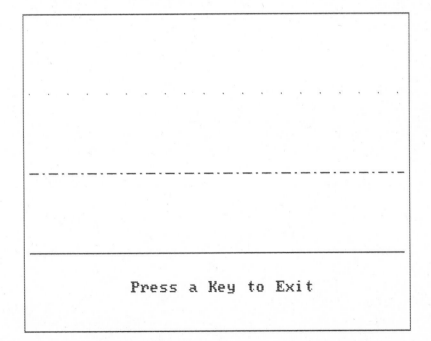

_getphyscoord

Syntax:

```
struct xycoord _far _getphyscoord(short x, short y);
short x, y;        view coordinates to convert
```

Function:

The _getphyscoord function converts view coordinates into physical coordinates and returns these physical coordinates.

Files to Include:

```
#include <graph.h>
```

Compatibility:

DOS

Description:

The _getphyscoord function returns the physical coordinates of a pixel located at view coordinates xcoord, ycoord. The origin of the physical coordinate system is at the upper left corner of the screen, as shown in Figure 9.23. The origin of the view coordinate system is at an arbitrary point defined by the _setvieworg function.

Values Returned:

A structure of type xycoord is defined in the header file graph.h. This structure follows:

```
struct xycoord
{
short xcoord;
short ycoord;
};
```

The view coordinates of the identified pixel are returned in this structure. No error value is returned.

Related Functions:

```
_getviewcoord    :    returns the view coordinates of a
                      pixel from its physical coordinates
```

Fig. 9.23. Coordinate systems.

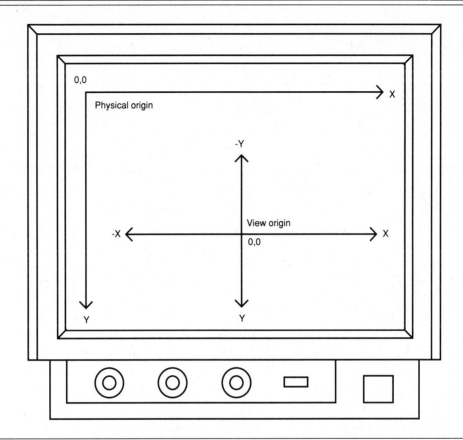

Similar Turbo C++ Functions:

None

Suggested Code Structure and Use:

Many drawing routines use view coordinates. The origin of the view coordinate system, however, is set to physical coordinates. It is often necessary to shift the view origin of a point expressed in view coordinates, especially in three-dimensional rotations. For this reason, it is useful to convert view coordinates into physical ones. The following code structure illustrates how this might be done.

```
#include <stdio.h>
#include <graph.h>
void main ()
```

```
{
 struct xycoord physxycoord; /* defines physxycoord as
                                structure of type xycoord */
 _setvideomode ( mode ); /* set mode by graphics card */
 _setvieworg (x,y); /* sets the view origin to physical
                        coordinates x,y */
      .
      .
      .

 physxycoord = _getphyscoord (x,y); /* get physical
                                        coordinates */
 _setvieworg (physxycoord.xcoord, physxycoord.ycoord);
        /* reset the view origin */
      .
      .
      .

 _setvideomode (_DEFAULTMODE); /* reset graphics card */
}
```

Example:

This program sets the view origin to physical coordinates 160,100. It then converts view coordinates 0,0 into physical coordinates and stores them in the physxycoord structure. The physical coordinates 160,100 are then output to the screen.

```
#include <stdio.h>
#include <graph.h>
void main ()
{
struct xycoord physxycoord;
char buffer [40];
    /* Initialization */
_setvideomode (_MRES4COLOR);
_setbkcolor (_BLUE);
_rectangle (_GBORDER,0,0,319,199);
   /* Set view origin to physical coordinates 160,100) */
_setvieworg(160,100);
    /* Save physical coordinates of view point 0,0
       in the physxycoord structure */
physxycoord = _getphyscoord(0,0);
    /* Print the results of the previous statement   */
sprintf (buffer, "Physical x for View x 0 is: %d",
 physxycoord.xcoord);
```

```
_settextposition (5,2);
_outtext (buffer);
sprintf (buffer, "Physical y for View y 0 is: %d",
 physxycoord.ycoord);
_settextposition (9,2);
_outtext (buffer);
_settextposition (22,12);
_outtext ("Press a Key to Exit");

    /* Delay and reset  */
getch ();
_setvideomode (_DEFAULTMODE);
}
```

_getpixel

Syntax:

```
short _far _getpixel(short x, short y);
short x, y;           view coordinates of point
```

Function:

The _getpixel function returns the pixel value of the specified view coordinates.

Files to Include:

```
#include <graph.h>
```

Compatibility:

DOS

Description:

The pixel value of the screen coordinates specified by the x and y arguments is determined through the _getpixel function. The current mode and palette must be considered when evaluating the returned value because the range of possible pixel values varies between adapters and modes. (See tables 9.2 and 9.3, under the _getcolor function, for help in interpreting the _getpixel return value.)

Values Returned:

The pixel value of the specified coordinates is returned if the coordinates lie in the current clipping region. A -1 is returned if this is not the case.

Related Functions:

```
_setpixel        :        sets a pixel to the current color
```

Similar Turbo C++ Functions:

```
getpixel : gets the color of the specified pixel
unsigned far getpixel (int x, int y);
```

Suggested Code Structure and Use:

The _getpixel function is useful for evaluating the status of a particular pixel. For example, suppose you need to identify and modify all pixels with a pixel value of 2 inside a given region, or area. The following code structure illustrates this use of the _getpixel function.

```
#include <stdio.h>
#include <graph.h>
void main ()
{
int pixelcolor;
_setvideomode ( mode ); /* set mode by adapter */
         .
         .
         .
pixelcolor = _getpixel (x,y); /* retrieve pixel value */
if (pixelcolor == ( color number ))
 {
  _setcolor ( new color );
  _setpixel (x,y);
 }
         .
         .
         .
_setvideomode (_DEFAULTMODE); /* reset */
}
```

Example:

This program uses the _getpixel function to determine the pixel value of each pixel on the screen. If the pixel value is 3, the pixel is set to Color 2.

```c
#include <stdio.h>
#include <graph.h>
#define ESC 27
void main ()
{
int pixelcolor;
int x, y;
    /* Initialization */
_setvideomode (_MRES4COLOR);
_setbkcolor (_BLUE);
_rectangle (_GBORDER,0,0,319,199);
x = 0;
y = 0;
    /* Add figures and colors to screen */
_ellipse (_GFILLINTERIOR,20,20,70,159);
_setcolor (2);
_ellipse (_GFILLINTERIOR,134,20,184,159);
_setcolor (3);
_ellipse (_GBORDER,134,20,184,159);
_ellipse (_GBORDER,249,20,299,159);
_setcolor (2);
_settextposition (23,5);
_outtext ("Press Any Key to Begin Conversion");
getch ();
    /* Evaluates pixel value for each pixel */
do
    {
    pixelcolor = _getpixel (x,y);
    if (pixelcolor == 3)
        _setpixel (x,y);
    x = x + 1;
    if (x == 320)
        {
        x = 0;
        y = y + 1;
        }
    } while (y != 200);
    /* Delay and exit */
_settextposition (22,5);
```

```
_outtext ("Conversion Complete");
_settextposition (23,5);
_outtext ("Press Any Key to Continue        ");
getch ();
_setvideomode (_DEFAULTMODE);
}
```

_getpixel_w

Syntax:

```
short _far _getpixel_w(double x, double y);
double x, y;   window coordinates of point
```

Function:

This function determines the pixel value of the specified window coordinates.

Files to Include:

```
#include <graph.h>
```

Compatibility:

DOS

Description:

The _getpixel_w function is similar to the _getpixel function but uses window coordinates. The pixel value of the x , y window coordinates is returned. Due to variations in hardware and video modes, the video mode, hardware, and palette in use must be taken into consideration when interpreting the returned pixel value. Tables 9.2 and 9.3, under the _getcolor function, are useful for interpreting the returned value. Also remember that the _remapallpalette and _remappalette functions can alter predefined palettes.

Values Returned:

The pixel value is returned if successful. A -1 is returned if unsuccessful.

Related Functions:

```
_setpixel_w    :    sets the specified pixel to the
                    current color (window coordinates)
```

Similar Turbo C++ Functions:

None

Suggested Code Structure and Use:

The _getpixel_w function is used to retrieve the pixel value of window coordinates. The following code structure illustrates the use of the **_getpixel_w** function.

```
#include <graph.h>
#include <stdio.h>
void main ()
{
int pixelvalue;
_setvideomode ( mode ); /* set video mode */
_setviewport (x1,y1,x2,y2); /* size viewport */
_setwindow (flag,x1,y1,x2,y2); /* set window dimensions */
        .
        .
        .
pixelvalue = _getpixel_w (x1,y1);
        .
        .
        .
        { Use pixel color information }
        .
        .
        .
_setvideomode (_DEFAULTMODE);
}
```

Example:

This example demonstrates the proper use of the **_getpixel_w** function. The program creates two ellipses inside the current window and retrieves the pixel value of the window coordinates 0.00,0.00. The retrieved pixel value is then printed on the screen, as shown in figure 9.24.

```
#include <graph.h>
#include <stdio.h>
void main ()
{
int pixelcolor;
char buffer [40];
```

```
_setvideomode (_ERESCOLOR);
_rectangle (_GBORDER,0,0,639,349);
     /* Open window */
_setviewport (0,0,639,349);
_setwindow (0, -100.0, -100.0, 100.0, 100.0);
_ellipse_w(_GBORDER, -75.0, -75.0, 75.0, 75.0);
_setcolor (4);
_ellipse_w(_GFILLINTERIOR, -50.0, -50.0, 50.0, 50.0);
     /* Obtain pixel value at 0.0,0.0 and output */
pixelcolor = _getpixel_w (0.0,0.0);
sprintf(buffer,"The Pixel Value at 0.0 - 0.0 :
               %d",pixelcolor);
_settextposition (3,22);
_outtext (buffer);
     /* Delay and exit */
_settextposition (23,30);
_outtext ("Press Any Key to Exit");
getch ();
_setvideomode (_DEFAULTMODE);
}
```

Fig. 9.24. Example _getpixel_w output.

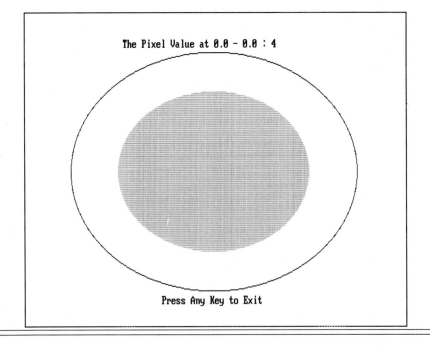

_gettextcolor

Syntax:

```
short _far _gettextcolor (void);
```

Function:

The _gettextcolor function returns the pixel value of the current text color.

Files to Include:

```
#include <graph.h>
```

Compatibility:

DOS
OS/2

Description:

The pixel value of the current text color is returned by the _gettextcolor function. This pixel value is used by the _outtext and _outmem functions to determine the color of text output. Table 9.6 provides pixel values for various text colors and attributes.

Table 9.6. *Predefined text colors.*

Pixel value for normal text	Pixel value for blinking text	Text color
0	16	Black
1	17	Blue
2	18	Green
3	19	Cyan
4	20	Red
5	21	Magenta
6	22	Brown
7	23	White
8	24	Dark gray
9	25	Light blue
10	26	Light green
11	27	Light cyan
12	28	Light red
13	29	Light magenta
14	30	Yellow
15	31	Bright yellow

Values Returned:

The current color, or pixel value, of the current text color is returned. No error value is returned.

Related Functions:

```
_settextcolor  : sets the current text color
```

Similar Turbo C++ Functions:

None

Suggested Code Structure and Use:

The _gettextcolor function is used for retrieving the current text color. This is useful when highlighting text. By retrieving and adding 16 to the current text color, then overwriting the text, the text will blink (this works only in certain modes). The following code structure illustrates the procedure for retrieving the current text color.

```
#include <stdio.h>
#include <graph.h>
void main ()
{
int textcolor;
_setvideomode ( mode ); /* set mode by adapter */
          .
          .
          .
textcolor = _gettextcolor ();
          .
          .
          .
   { use text color }
          .
          .
          .
_setvideomode (_DEFAULTMODE); /* reset */
}
```

Example:

This program outputs text in various text colors and retrieves these text colors with the _gettextcolor function. The text colors are then output to the screen.

```
#include <stdio.h>
#include <graph.h>
void main ()
{
int textcolor;
char buffer [40];
        /* Initialization */
_setbkcolor (4L);
_clearscreen (_GWINDOW);
        /* Set, retrieve, and output various
        text colors */
_settextposition (5,5);
textcolor = _gettextcolor ();
sprintf (buffer, "The Current Text Color Is: %d",
                textcolor);
_outtext (buffer);
_settextposition (20,5);
_outtext ("Press Any Key to Continue");
getch ();
_settextcolor (31);
_settextposition (10,5);
textcolor = _gettextcolor ();
sprintf (buffer, "The Current Text Color Is Now: %d",
                textcolor);
_outtext (buffer);
_settextposition (20,5);
_outtext ("Press Any Key to Continue");
getch ();
_settextcolor (16);
_settextposition (15,5);
textcolor = _gettextcolor ();
sprintf (buffer, "The Current Text Color Is Now: %d",
                textcolor);
_outtext (buffer);
    /* Delay and exit */
_settextposition (20,5);
_outtext ("Press Any Key to Exit      ");
getch ();
}
```

_gettextcursor

Syntax:

```
short _far _gettextcursor(void);
```

Function:

The _gettextcursor function determines the current cursor shape in text modes.

Files to Include:

```
include <graph.h>
```

Compatibility:

DOS
OS/2

Description:

The _gettextcursor function works only in text modes. When in text mode, the _gettextcursor function returns the attribute, or shape, of the text cursor. Table 9.7 will help you interpret the returned values.

Table 9.7. *Text cursor attributes.*

Attribute	Shape
0x0707	Underline
0x0007	Full block
0x0607	Double underline
0x2000	No cursor

Values Returned:

The cursor attribute is returned when successful; otherwise, a -1 is returned.

Related Functions:

```
_displaycursor  :  turns cursor display on/off
_settextcursor  :  sets the text cursor shape
```

Similar Turbo C++ Functions:

```
_setcursortype  :  selects cursor appearance
void _setcursortype (int cursortype);
```

Suggested Code Structure and Use:

The _gettextcursor function is used to retrieve the shape of the text cursor in text modes. This information is useful because it is a good practice to reset the cursor shape when exiting a function that alters the shape. The following code structure illustrates this use of the _gettextcursor function.

```
#include <stdio.h>
#include <graph.h>
void main ()
{
short cursorshape;
_clearscreen (_GCLEARSCREEN);
cursorshape = _gettextcursor (); /* get cursor shape */
            .
            .
            .
        _settextcursor ( shape ); /* set a cursor shape */
            .
            .
            .
_settextcursor(cursorshape); /* reset before exiting */
}
```

Example:

The _gettextcursor function is used in the following demonstration to retrieve the cursor shape upon entering the function. The cursor shape is changed, then reset to the original cursor shape upon exiting the function.

```
#include <graph.h>
#include <stdio.h>
void main ()
{
short oldcursorshape;
short newcursorshape;
newcursorshape = 0x0007;
      /* Get old shape and display cursor */
oldcursorshape = _gettextcursor ();
```

```
_clearscreen (_GCLEARSCREEN);
_displaycursor (_GCURSORON);
_settextposition (10,3);
_outtext ("Press Any Key To Change The Cursor Shape");
_settextposition (15,3);
    /* Delay and change cursor shape */
getch ();
_settextcursor (newcursorshape);
    /* Delay and exit */
_settextposition (23,3);
_outtext ("Press Any Key To Exit");
_settextposition (15,3);
getch ();
_settextcursor(oldcursorshape);
_clearscreen (_GCLEARSCREEN);
}
```

_gettextposition

Syntax:

```
struct rccoord _far _gettextposition(void);
```

Function:

The _gettextposition function returns the position of the text cursor.

Files to Include:

```
#include <graph.h>
```

Compatibility:

DOS
OS/2

Description:

The current row and column positions of the text cursor are returned in a structure of type rccoord when the _gettextposition function is called. The text cursor marks the starting point where text will be displayed. Its position is maintained internally by the graphics routines. Only the _outtext and _outmem functions use this position as a starting point. Font text output—which uses the graphics cursor for positioning and _outgtext for output—does use the text cursor position. The rccoord structure follows.

```
struct rccoord
  {
    short row;
    short col;
  }
```

Values Returned:

The current position of the text cursor is returned in a structure of type rccoord. No error value is returned.

Related Functions:

```
_settextposition   :   sets the position of the text
                       cursor
```

Similar Turbo C++ Functions:

```
wherex  :  gives column position of cursor
int wherex (void);
wherey  :  gives row position of cursor
int wherey (void);
```

Suggested Code Structure and Use:

The _gettextposition function returns the position of the text cursor. This is useful for positioning subsequent output relative to the position of the text cursor. Examples of uses are for the insertion or deletion of text. The following code structure illustrates the procedure for retrieving the current text cursor position.

```
#include <stdio.h>
#include <graph.h>
void main ()
{
struct rccoord cursorposition;
_setvideomode ( mode ); /* set mode by adapter */
       .
       .
       .
cursorposition = _gettextposition (); /* retrieve
```

```
                              current text cursor position */
                  .
                  .
                  .
         { use text cursor information }
                  .
                  .
                  .
      _setvideomode (_DEFAULTMODE);
      }
```

Example:

This program uses the _gettextposition function to output the row and column location of the text cursor. The text cursor is highlighted with the _displaycursor function and can be moved with the keypad. With the Num Lock key on, 8 moves the cursor up one row, 2 moves the cursor down one row, 4 moves the cursor one column to the left, and 6 moves the cursor one column to the right. Each time a key is pressed, the row and column displays are updated.

```
#include <stdio.h>
#include <graph.h>
#define ESC 27
void main ()
{
struct rccoord cursorposition;
char buffer [40];
int ch;
     /* Initialization */
_setvideomode (_MRES4COLOR);
_setbkcolor (_BLUE);
_displaycursor (_GCURSORON);
_settextposition (23,5);
_outtext ("Row : 1");
_settextposition (24,5);
_outtext ("Column : 1");
_settextposition (1,1);
do
     {
          /* Accept and process keypad input */
        cursorposition = _gettextposition ();
        ch = getch ();
        if (ch == '8')
          cursorposition.row = cursorposition.row - 1;
```

```
      if (ch == '2')
       cursorposition.row = cursorposition.row + 1;
      if (ch == '4')
       cursorposition.col = cursorposition.col - 1;
      if (ch == '6')
       cursorposition.col = cursorposition.col + 1;
          /* Check boundaries */
      if (cursorposition.row < 1)
       cursorposition.row = 1;
      if (cursorposition.row > 20)
       cursorposition.row = 20;
      if (cursorposition.col < 1)
       cursorposition.col = 1;
      if (cursorposition.col > 40)
       cursorposition.col = 40;
          /* Output status */
      _settextposition (23,5);
      sprintf (buffer, "Row : %d", cursorposition.row);
      _outtext (buffer);
      _outtext ("          ");
       settextposition (24,5);
      sprintf (buffer, "Column : %d", cursorposition.col);
       outtext (buffer);
       outtext ("          ");
      _settextposition (cursorposition.row,
            cursorposition.col);
      } while (ch != ESC);
   _setvideomode (_DEFAULTMODE);
   }
```

_gettextwindow

Syntax:

```
void _far _gettextwindow(short _far *r1, short _far *c1,
                short _far *r2, short _far *c2);
short _far *r1, *c1;    upper left row and column
short _far *r2, *c2;    lower right row and column
```

Function:

The _gettextwindow function retrieves the row and column values of the upper left and lower right corners of the current text window.

Files to Include:

```
#include <graph.h>
```

Compatibility:

DOS
OS/2

Description:

The _gettextwindow function retrieves the row and column values of the corners of the current rectangular text window. The r1 and c1 values identify the row and column numbers, respectively, of the upper left corner of the text window. The r2 and c2 arguments identify the lower right corner of the text window.

Values Returned:

There is no return value.

Related Functions:

```
_settextwindow      :        initializes a text window
```

Similar Turbo C++ Functions:

```
gettextinfo  :  get text mode information including the row
                and column coordinates for the text window
void gettextinfo (struct text_info *r);
```

Suggested Code Structure and Use:

The _gettextwindow function is used to retrieve the column and row positions of the current text window. The following code structure illustrates one method of obtaining these corner positions.

```
#include <stdio.h>
#include <graph.h>
void main ()
```

```
{
short r1, c1, r2, c2;
_setvideomode ( mode ); /* set video mode */
_settextwindow (row1,col1,row2,col2); /* set text window */
        .
        .
        .

_gettextwindow (&r1,&c1,&r2,&c2); /*get corner positions*/
        .
        .
        .
    { Use information }
        .
        .
        .
_setvideomode (_DEFAULTMODE);
}
```

Example:

The _gettextwindow function is used in this example to obtain the row and column positions of the corners of the current text window. These row and column positions are then output on the screen.

```
#include <graph.h>
#include <stdio.h>
void main ()
{
short r1, c1, r2, c2;
char buffer [40];
_setvideomode (_ERESCOLOR);
_rectangle (_GBORDER,0,0,639,349);
    /* Set text window and get window info */
_settextwindow (3,3,23,77);
_gettextwindow (&r1,&c1,&r2,&c2);
    /* Display window info */
_settextposition (1,1);
sprintf (buffer,"Upper Left Row Number : %d",r1);
_outtext (buffer);
_settextposition (6,1);
sprintf (buffer,"Upper Left Column Number : %d",c1);
_outtext (buffer);
_settextposition (11,1);
sprintf (buffer,"Lower Right Row Number : %d",r2);
```

```
_outtext (buffer);
_settextposition (16,1);
sprintf (buffer,"Lower Right Column Number : %d",c2);
_outtext (buffer);
    /* Delay and exit */
_settextposition (19,1);
_outtext ("Press Any Key To Exit");
getch ();
_setvideomode (_DEFAULTMODE);
}
```

_getvideoconfig

Syntax:

```
struct videoconfig _far * _far _getvideoconfig
        (struct videoconfig _far *graph_config);
struct videoconfig _far *graph_config;  configuration info
```

Function:

The `_getvideoconfig` function returns the configuration of the current graphics environment. The following information is returned through a structure of type `videoconfig`:

    number of pixels on the x-axis
    number of pixels on the y-axis
    number of rows of text available
    number of columns of text available
    number of colors
    number of bits per pixel
    number of available video pages
    current video mode
    display adapter
    display monitor
    size of video memory in kilobytes

Files to Include:

```
#include <graph.h>
```

Compatibility:

DOS
OS/2

Description:

Information about the current graphics environment is returned in a structure of type `videoconfig` when the `_getvideoconfig` function is called. This structure follows. Most of the returned values are easily interpreted. Tables 9.8, 9.9, and 9.10 will help you interpret the mode, adapter, and monitor information.

```
struct videoconfig
{
  short numxpixels;
  short numypixels;
  short numtextcols;
  short numtextrows;
  short numcolors;
  short bitsperpixel;
  short numvideopages;
  short mode;
  short adapter;
  short monitor;
  short memory;
};
```

Table 9.8. *Video modes.*

Mode	Constant	Meaning
_MAXRESMODE	-3	Highest resolution mode
_MAXCOLORMODE	-2	Most color mode
_DEFAULTMODE	-1	Original mode
_TEXTBW40	0	40-column text—16 shades of gray
_TEXTC40	1	40-column text—16 or 8 colors
_TEXTBW80	2	80-column text—16 shades of gray
_TEXTC80	3	80-column text—16 or 8 shads of gray
_MRES4COLOR	4	320x200—4 colors
_MRESNOCOLOR	5	320x200—4 shades of gray
_HRESBW	6	640x200—black and white
_TEXTMONO	7	80-column text—black and white
_HERCMONO	8	720x348—black and white
_MRES16COLOR	13	320x200—16 colors
_HRES16COLOR	14	640x200—16 colors

Table 9.8. *continues*

Table 9.8. cont. *Video modes.*

Mode	Constant	Meaning
_ERESNOCOLOR	15	640x350—black and white
_ERESCOLOR	16	640x350—16 colors
_VRES2COLOR	17	640x480—black and white
_VRES16COLOR	18	640x480—16 colors
_MRES256COLOR	19	320x200—256 colors
_ORESCOLOR	64	640x400—1 of 16 colors

Table 9.9. *Adapter values.*

Constant	Value	Meaning
_MDPA	0x0001	Monochrome Display Adapter
_CGA	0x0002	Color Graphics Adapter
_EGA	0x0004	Enhanced Graphics Adapter
_VGA	0x0008	Video Graphics Adapter
_MCGA	0x0010	Multicolor Graphics Array
_HGC	0x0020	Hercules Graphics Card
_OCGA	0x0042	Olivetti Color Graphics Adapter
_OEGA	0x0044	Olivetti Enhanced Graphics Adapter
_OVGA	0x0048	Olivetti Video Graphics Array

Table 9.10. *Monitor values.*

Constant	Value	Meaning
_MONO	0x0001	Monochrome
_COLOR	0x0002	Color or emulation
_ENHCOLOR	0x0004	Enhanced color
_ANALOGMONO	0x0008	Analog monochrome
_ANALOGCOLOR	0x0010	Analog color
_ANALOG	0x0018	Analog monochrome and color

Values Returned:

The information is returned in a structure of type `videoconfig`. No error value is returned.

Related Functions:

```
_setvideomode   :   used to set the current video mode
```

Similar Turbo C++ Functions:

```
gettextinfo  :  gets text mode information
void gettextinfo (struct text_info *r);
getgraphmode  :  returns the graphics mode
int far getgraphmode (void);
```

Suggested Code Structure and Use:

Information about the current graphics environment is important for programming. This information is easily obtained with the _getvideoconfig function. The following code structure illustrates how to retrieve and use this information.

```
#include <stdio.h>
#include <graph.h>
void main ()
{
struct videoconfig graphconfig; /* structure for storage of
                        returned values */
int bits_per_pixel;
_setvideomode ( mode ); /* set mode by graphics card */
_getvideoconfig (&graphconfig); /* get graphics info */
        .
        .
        .

bits_per_pixel = graphconfig.bitsperpixel; /* use info */
        .
        .
        .

_setvideomode (_DEFAULTMODE); /* reset graphics card */
}
```

Example:

This program demonstrates how to gather and use the information collected with the _getvideoconfig function. The information on the graphics environment is returned in the graphconfig structure. Then some of this information is printed on the screen, as shown in figure 9.25.

```
#include <stdio.h>
#include <graph.h>
void main ()
{
struct videoconfig graphconfig;
```

```
char buffer [40];
            /*    Initialization      */
_setvideomode (_MRES4COLOR);
_setbkcolor (_BLUE);
_rectangle (_GBORDER,0,0,319,199);
      /*    Get the current video configuration  */
_getvideoconfig (&graphconfig);
      /*    Print some of the values returned
            by _getvideoconfig */
sprintf (buffer,"Pixels on X Axis: %d",
         graphconfig.numxpixels);
_settextposition (2,2);
_outtext (buffer);
sprintf (buffer,"Pixels on Y Axis: %d",
         graphconfig.numypixels);
_settextposition (4,2);
_outtext (buffer);
sprintf (buffer,"Number of Text Columns: %d",
         graphconfig.numtextcols);
_settextposition (6,2);
_outtext (buffer);
sprintf (buffer,"Number of Text Rows: %d",
          graphconfig.numtextrows);
_settextposition (8,2);
_outtext (buffer);
sprintf (buffer,"Number of Colors: %d",
         graphconfig.numcolors);
_settextposition (10,2);
_outtext (buffer);
sprintf (buffer,"Bits Per Pixel: %d",
          graphconfig.bitsperpixel);
_settextposition (12,2);
_outtext (buffer);
sprintf (buffer,"Number Video Pages: %d",
          graphconfig.numvideopages);
_settextposition (14,2);
_outtext (buffer);
sprintf (buffer,"Video Memory: %d",
          graphconfig.memory);
_settextposition (16,2);
_outtext (buffer);
_settextposition (22,11);
_outtext ("Press a Key to Exit");
getch ();
_setvideomode (_DEFAULTMODE);
}
```

Fig. 9.25. Example _getvideoconfig output.

```
Pixels on X Axis: 320
Pixels on Y Axis: 200
Number of Text Columns: 40
Number of Text Rows: 25
Number of Colors: 4
Bits Per Pixel: 2
Number Video Pages: 1
Video Memory: 256



            Press a Key to Exit
```

_getviewcoord

Syntax:

```
struct xycoord _far _getviewcoord (short x, short y);
short x, y;    physical coordinates to convert
```

Function:

The _getviewcoord function converts physical coordinates into view coordinates and returns these view coordinates.

Files to Include:

```
#include <graph.h>
```

Compatibility:

DOS

Description:

The `_getviewcoord` function returns the view coordinates of a pixel located at physical coordinates `x, y`. The physical coordinate system has its origin in the upper left corner of the screen. The view coordinate system has its origin at an arbitrary point defined by the `_setvieworg` function, as shown in Figure 9.26.

Fig. 9.26. Coordinate systems.

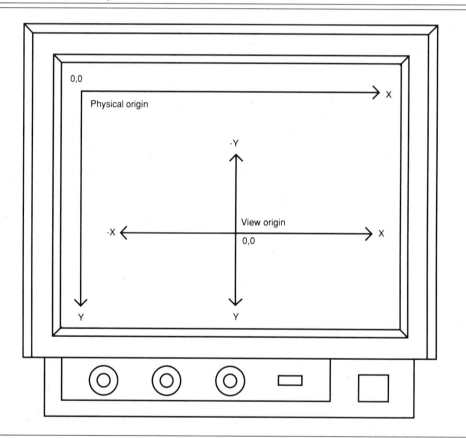

Values Returned:

A structure of type xycoord is defined in the header file graph.h. The view coordinates of the identified pixel are returned in this structure. No error value is returned.

```
struct xycoord
   {
   short xcoord;
   short ycoord;
   };
```

Related Functions:

_setvieworg   : sets the origin of the view
                      coordinate system
_getphyscoord   : gets the physical coordinates of a
                      pixel located at view coordinates x,y

Similar Turbo C++ Functions:

None

Suggested Code Structure and Use:

Because many drawing routines use view coordinates, it is often necessary to convert physical coordinates into view coordinates. This is usually accomplished with the _getviewcoord function. The following code structure illustrates how the _getviewcoord function can be used for this purpose.

```
#include <stdio.h>
#include <graph.h>
void main ()
{
 struct xycoord viewxycoord; /* defines viewxycoord as
                             structure of type xycoord */
 _setvideomode ( mode );  /* set mode by graphics card */
 _setvieworg (x,y); /* sets view origin to physical
                      coordinates x,y */
    .
    .
    .
 viewxycoord = _getviewcoord (x,y); /* get view
                  coordinates */
 moveto (viewxycoord.xcoord, viewxycoord.ycoord);  /* use
                  view coordinates */
    .
```

.
.

```
_setvideomode (_DEFAULTMODE); /* reset graphics card */
}
```

Example:

This program sets the view origin to physical coordinates 160,100. Then these physical coordinates are converted and stored in the viewxycoord structure. Finally, the view coordinates are output to the screen, as shown in figure 9.27.

```
#include <graph.h>
#include <stdio.h>
void main ()
{
struct xycoord viewxycoord;
char buffer [40];
          /* Initialization   */
_setvideomode (_MRES4COLOR);
_setbkcolor (_BLUE);
_rectangle (_GBORDER,0,0,319,199);
      /* Set view origin to physical coordinates 160,100 */
_setvieworg (160,100);
    /* Save the view coordinates of physical point 160,100
            in the viewxycoord structure */
viewxycoord = _getviewcoord (160,100);
          /* Print the results of the previous statement */
sprintf (buffer, "The x view coordinate for 160 is: %d",
      viewxycoord.xcoord);
_settextposition (5,2);
_outtext (buffer);
sprintf (buffer, "The y view coordinate for 100 is: %d",
      viewxycoord.ycoord);
_settextposition (9,2);
_outtext (buffer);
_settextposition (22,12);
_outtext ("Press a Key to Exit");
    /*    Delay and reset   */
getch ();
_setvideomode (_DEFAULTMODE);
}
```

Fig. 9.27. Example _getviewcoord output.

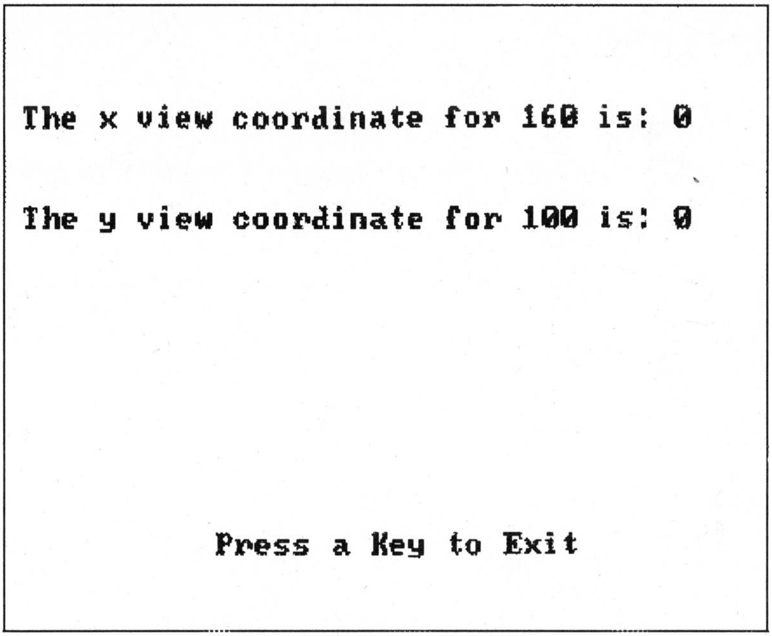

The x view coordinate for 160 is: 0

The y view coordinate for 100 is: 0

Press a Key to Exit

_getviewcoord_w

Syntax:

```
struct xycoord _far _getviewcoord_w(double x, double y);
double x, y;        window coordinates to convert
```

Function:

The _getviewcoord_w function converts the window coordinates specified by x and y to view coordinates.

Files to Include:

```
#include <graph.h>
```

Compatibility:

DOS

Description:

The `_getviewcoord_w` function converts the specified window coordinates into view coordinates. The x and y arguments identify the window coordinates that will be converted. The converted view coordinates are returned in a structure of type x y c o o r d.

Values Returned:

The translated view coordinates of the specified window coordinates are returned in a structure of type x y c o o r d. This structure follows:

```
struct xycoord
    {
    short xcoord;
    short ycoord;
    };
```

Related Functions:

```
_getviewcoord    :        converts physical coordinates
                          to view coordinates
```

Similar Turbo C++ Functions:

None

Suggested Code Structure and Use:

The specified window coordinates are converted to view coordinates and returned with the `_getviewcoord_w` function. This function is useful because the conversion of coordinates is necessary in almost all serious graphics program. The following code structure demonstrates the use of the `_getviewcoord_w` function.

```
#include <stdio.h>
#include <graph.h>
void main ()
{
struct xycoord coord;
_setvideomode ( mode ); /* set video mode */
_setviewport (x1,y1,x2,y2); /* size viewport */
_setwindow (flag,x1,y1,x2,y2); /* set window dimensions */
```

```
                .
                .
                .
coord = _getviewcoord_w (x, y); /* get view coordinates */
                .
                .
                .

    { Use Coordinates }
                .
                .
                .

_setvideomode (_DEFAULTMODE); /* reset and exit */
}
```

Example:

This program demonstrates how the _getviewcoord_w function can be used to convert the specified window coordinates to view coordinates. These view coordinates are then output to the screen, as shown in figure 9.28.

```
#include <graph.h>
#include <stdio.h>
void main ()
{
struct xycoord coord;
char buffer [40];
_setvideomode (_ERESCOLOR);
_rectangle (_GBORDER,0,0,639,349);
        /* Open window */
_setviewport (0,0,639,349);
_setwindow (0,-100.0,-100.0,100.0,100.0);
        /* Convert coordinates and output */
coord = _getviewcoord_w (0.0,0.0);
sprintf(buffer,"x view coordinate for 0.0 is
                        %d",coord.xcoord);
_settextposition(3,3);
_outtext (buffer);
sprintf(buffer,"y view coordinate for 0.0 is %d",
                        coord.ycoord);
_settextposition(8,3);
_outtext (buffer);
        /*  Delay and exit  */
_settextposition (23,3);
_outtext ("Press Any Key To Exit");
```

```
getch ();
_setvideomode (_DEFAULTMODE);
}
```

Fig. 9.28. Example _getviewcoord_w output.

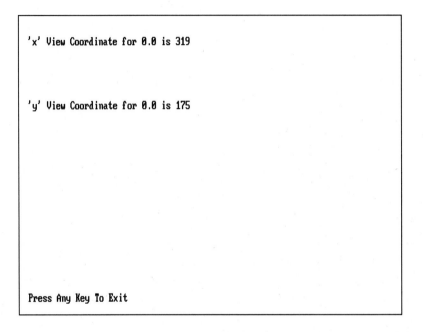

```
'x' View Coordinate for 0.0 is 319


'y' View Coordinate for 0.0 is 175










Press Any Key To Exit
```

_getviewcoord_wxy

Syntax:

```
struct xycoord _far _getviewcoord_wxy(struct _wxycoord
                _far *xy1);
struct _wxycoord _far *xy1;      window pair to convert
```

Function:

The _getviewcoord_wxy function converts the specified window coordinate pair into view coordinates.

Files to Include:

```
#include <graph.h>
```

Compatibility:

DOS

Description:

The _getviewcoord_wxy function translates window coordinates into view coordinates. The coordinates to be converted are specified by the xy1 coordinate pair. The resulting view coordinates are returned in a structure of type xycoord.

Values Returned:

The translated view coordinates are returned in a structure of type xycoord. This structure follows.

```
struct xycoord
    {
    short xcoord;
    short ycoord;

    };
```

Related Functions:

```
_getviewcoord      :      converts physical coordinates
                          to view coordinates
```

Similar Turbo C++ Functions:

None

Suggested Code Structure and Use:

The _getviewcoord_wxy function is used in the same way as the _getviewcoord_w function, but the coordinates to be converted are expressed in a coordinate pair. The following code structure illustrates the use of the _getviewcoord_wxy function for coordinate conversion.

```
#include <graph.h>
#include <stdio.h>
void main ()
```

```
{
struct xycoord vcoord;
struct _wxycoord wcoord;
_setvideomode ( mode ); /* set video mode */
_setviewport (x1,y1,x2,y2); /* size viewport */
_setwindow (flag,x1,y1,x2,y2); /* set window dimensions */
        .
        .
        .
wcoord.wx = 0.0;
wcoord.wy = 0.0;
vcoord = _getviewcoord_wxy (&wcoord);
        .
        .
        .
     { Use converted coordinates }
        .
        .
        .
_setvideomode (_DEFAULTMODE);
}
```

Example:

The `_getviewcoord_wxy` function is used in this example to convert the 0.0,0.0 window coordinates to view coordinates. Then these coordinates are output to the screen.

```
#include <graph.h>
#include <stdio.h>
void main ()
{
struct xycoord vcoord;
struct _wxycoord wcoord;
char buffer [40];
_setvideomode (_ERESCOLOR);
_rectangle (_GBORDER,0,0,639,349);
     /* Open window */
_setviewport (0,0,639,349);
_setwindow (0,-100.0,-100.0,100.0,100.0);
     /* Convert and output coordinates */
wcoord.wx = 0.0;
wcoord.wy = 0.0;
vcoord = _getviewcoord_wxy (&wcoord);
sprintf(buffer,"View x for 0.0 is %d",vcoord.xcoord);
```

```
_settextposition (3,5);
_outtext (buffer);
sprintf(buffer,"View y for 0.0 is %d",vcoord.ycoord);
_settextposition (10,5);
_outtext (buffer);
      /* Delay and exit */
_settextposition (23,5);
_outtext ("Press Any Key To Exit");
getch ();
_setvideomode (_DEFAULTMODE);
}
```

_getvisualpage

Syntax:

```
short _far _getvisualpage(void);
```

Function:
The _getvisualpage function returns the page number of the current visual page.

Files to Include:
```
#include <graph.h>
```

Compatibility:
DOS
OS/2

Description:
The page number of the current visual page is returned by the _getvisualpage function. The current visual page is the video page that is currently displayed on the screen. This page may differ from the screen to which graphics output is being sent (see the _setactivepage function). All types of video hardware support multiple text pages, but not all support multiple video pages. The _getvideoconfig function determines the availability of multiple graphics pages.

Values Returned:
The page number of the current visual page is returned.

Related Functions:

```
_getactivepage      :    gets page number of active page
_setvisualpage      :    sets the visual page number
_setactivepage      :    sets the active page number
```

Similar Turbo C++ Functions:

None

Suggested Code Structure and Use:

The _getvisualpage function is used to retrieve the page number of the video page that is currently displayed on the screen. Some applications use multiple pages of graphics information (if the hardware supports it). Therefore, it is important that the programmer has access to the page number information. By getting the current visual page number and incrementing, the next video page can then be displayed. The following code structure illustrates one method of obtaining the current visual page number.

```
#include <graph.h>
#include <stdio.h>
void main ()
{
short vispage;
_setvideomode ( mode );   /* set video mode */
_setactivepage ( page number );   /* set active page */
            .
            .
            .
    ( Draw on Active Page )
            .
            .
            .
_setvisualpage ( page number );   /* set visual page */
vispage = _getvisualpage ();   /* get visual page number */
            .
            .
            .
    ( Use visual page number }
            .
            .
            .
_setvideomode (_DEFAULTMODE); /* reset and exit */
}
```

Example:

The _getvisualpage function is used in the following example to obtain the page number of the current visual page. The active page is set to 1; subsequent graphics output is sent to a hidden page in video memory because the default visual page is page 0. After figures are drawn on page 1, the visual page is set to 1, and the visual page number is retrieved using the _getvisualpage function. Then the visual page number is output to the screen. Both the active and visual page numbers are reset to 0 before exiting the program.

```c
#include <graph.h>
#include <stdio.h>
void main ()
{
short vispage;
char buffer [40];
_setvideomode (_ERESCOLOR);
_rectangle (_GBORDER,0,0,639,349);
    /* Set active page to page 1,
        draw image, set visual page to 1 */
_setactivepage (1);
_clearscreen (_GCLEARSCREEN);
_rectangle (_GBORDER,0,0,639,349);
_rectangle (_GFILLINTERIOR,30,30,610,310);
_setvisualpage (1);
    /* Retrieve visual page number and output */
vispage = _getvisualpage ();
sprintf(buffer,"The Visual Page Number Is %d",vispage);
_settextposition (2,5);
_outtext (buffer);
    /* Delay and exit */
_settextposition (24,5);
_outtext ("Press Any Key To Exit");
getch ();
_setactivepage (0);
_setvisualpage (0);
_setvideomode (_DEFAULTMODE);
}
```

_getwindowcoord

Syntax:

```c
struct _wxycoord _far _getwindowcoord(short x, short y);
short x, y;                  view coordinates to convert
```

Function:

The _getwindowcoord function converts the view coordinates specified by x and y into window coordinates and returns these coordinates.

Files to Include:

```
#include <graph.h>
```

Compatibility:

DOS

Description:

The _getwindowcoord function converts view coordinates into window coordinates. The view coordinates to be converted are specified by the x and y arguments. The resulting window coordinates are returned in a structure of type _wxycoord.

Values Returned:

The window coordinates of the specified view coordinates are returned in a structure of type _wxycoord. This structure follows. No error value is returned.

```
structure _wxycoord
    {
    double wx;
    double wy;
    };
```

Related Functions:

```
_getviewcoord        : converts physical coordinates to
                       view coordinates
```

Similar Turbo C++ Functions:

None

Suggested Code Structure and Use:

The _getwindowcoord function is used to convert the specified view coordinates into window coordinates. This conversion is frequently required because the various coordinate systems overlay each other. The following code structure illustrates the use of the _getwindowcoord function.

```
#include <graph.h>
#include <stdio.h>
void main ()
{
struct _wxycoord wcoord;
_setvideomode ( mode ); /* set video mode */
_setviewport (x1,y1,x2,y2); /* size viewport */
_setwindow (flag,x1,y1,x2,y2); /* set window */
          .
          .
          .
wcoord =  _getwindowcoord (x,y);  /* convert coordinates */
          .
          .
          .
    { Use information }
          .
          .
          .
_setvideomode (_DEFAULTMODE); /* reset and exit */
```

Example:

The following example demonstrates the use of the **_getwindowcoord** function. This example opens a window, uses the **_getwindowcoord** function to convert view coordinates 319,175 to window coordinates, and outputs the window coordinates. See figure 9.29.

```
    #include <graph.h>
    #include <stdio.h>
    void main ()
    {
    struct _wxycoord wcoord;
    char buffer [40];
    _setvideomode (_ERESCOLOR);
    _rectangle (_GBORDER,0,0,639,349);
            /* Open window */
    _setviewport (0,0,639,349);
    _setwindow (0,-100.0,-100.0,100.0,100.0);

            /* Convert coordinates and output */
    wcoord = _getwindowcoord (319,175);
    sprintf(buffer,"x window coordinate for 319 is
                    %f",wcoord.wx);
    _settextposition (5,5);
```

399

```
_outtext (buffer);
sprintf(buffer,"y window coordinate for 175 is
                    %f",wcoord.wy);
_settextposition (15,5);
_outtext (buffer);
          /* Delay and exit */
_settextposition (23,5);
_outtext ("Press Any Key To Exit");
getch ();
_setvideomode (_DEFAULTMODE);
}
```

Fig. 9.29. Example _getwindowcoord output.

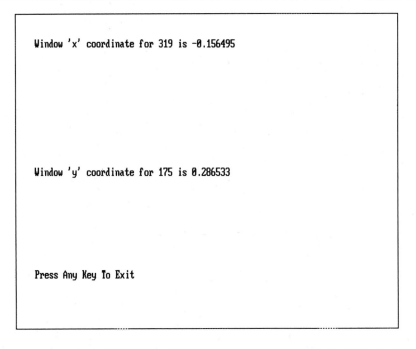

Window 'x' coordinate for 319 is -0.156495

Window 'y' coordinate for 175 is 0.286533

Press Any Key To Exit

_getwritemode

Syntax:

```
short _far _getwritemode(void);
```

Function:

The _getwritemode function returns the current logical write mode used by the _lineto, _rectangle, and _polygon functions.

Files to Include:

```
#include <graph.h>
```

Compatibility:

DOS

Description:

The _getwritemode function returns the current logical write mode as set by the _setwritemode function. The write mode specifies the means by which each pixel of a straight line will be drawn. Table 9.11 lists the logical constants for the write modes. The _GPSET write mode is the default value.

Table 9.11. *Write modes.*

Constant	Purpose
_GAND	The displayed pixels are the logical AND of the existing pixel values and the line pixel values.
_GOR	The displayed pixels are the logical OR of the existing pixel values and the line pixel values.
_GPRESET	The line is the negative of the stored line; each pixel is inverted before it is placed on the screen.
_GPSET	The line is placed on the screen exactly over all existing images.
_GXOR	The displayed pixels are the exclusive OR of the existing pixel values and the line pixel values.

Values Returned:

The current logical write mode is returned when successful; table 9.11 lists the possible return values. A -1 is returned if the function is unsuccessful.

Related Functions:

```
_setwritemode      :    selects the write mode
```

Similar Turbo C++ Functions:

```
setwritemode  :  sets the logical write mode for lines
void far setwritemode (int mode);
```

Suggested Code Structure and Use:

The _getwritemode function is used to retrieve the current write mode. The write mode determines the method by which straight lines will be drawn. The following code structure illustrates a method for obtaining the write mode.

```
#include <graph.h>
#include <stdio.h>
void main ()
{
short writemode;
_setvideomode ( mode ); /* set video mode */
_setwritemode ( _GPSET ); /* set a write mode */
        .
        .
        .

writemode = _getwritemode ();  /* retrieve write mode */
        .
        .
        .
    { Use write mode information }
        .
        .
        .
_setvideomode (_DEFAULTMODE); /* reset and exit */
}
```

Example:

The _getwritemode function is used in this example to retrieve the current write mode. The write mode is output to the screen along with an example of graphics output using this write mode. All five write modes are demonstrated. See figure 9.30.

```
#include <graph.h>
#include <stdio.h>
void main ()
{
short writemode;
char buffer [40];
_setvideomode (_ERESCOLOR);
_rectangle (_GBORDER,0,0,639,349);
     /* Set, get, and output write modes */
_setwritemode (_GPSET);
writemode = _getwritemode();
sprintf(buffer,"The write mode is %d",writemode);
_settextposition (3,5);
_outtext(buffer);
_moveto (320,30);
_lineto (620,30);
_setwritemode (_GPRESET);
writemode = _getwritemode ();
sprintf(buffer,"The write mode is %d",writemode);
_settextposition (8,5);
_outtext(buffer);
_moveto (320,105);
_lineto (620,105);
_setwritemode (_GXOR);
writemode = _getwritemode ();
sprintf(buffer,"The write mode is %d",writemode);
_settextposition (13,5);
_outtext(buffer);
_moveto (320,175);
_lineto (620,175);
_setwritemode (_GOR);
writemode = _getwritemode ();
sprintf(buffer,"The write mode is %d",writemode);
_settextposition (18,5);
_outtext(buffer);
_moveto (320,245);
_lineto (620,245);
_setwritemode (_GAND);
```

```
writemode = _getwritemode ();
sprintf(buffer,"The write mode is %d",writemode);
_settextposition (23,5);
_outtext(buffer);
_moveto (320,320);
_lineto (620,320);
     /* Delay and exit */
_settextposition (13,40);
_outtext ("Press Any Key to Exit");
getch ();
_setvideomode (_DEFAULTMODE);
}
```

Fig. 9.30.   Example _getwritemode output.

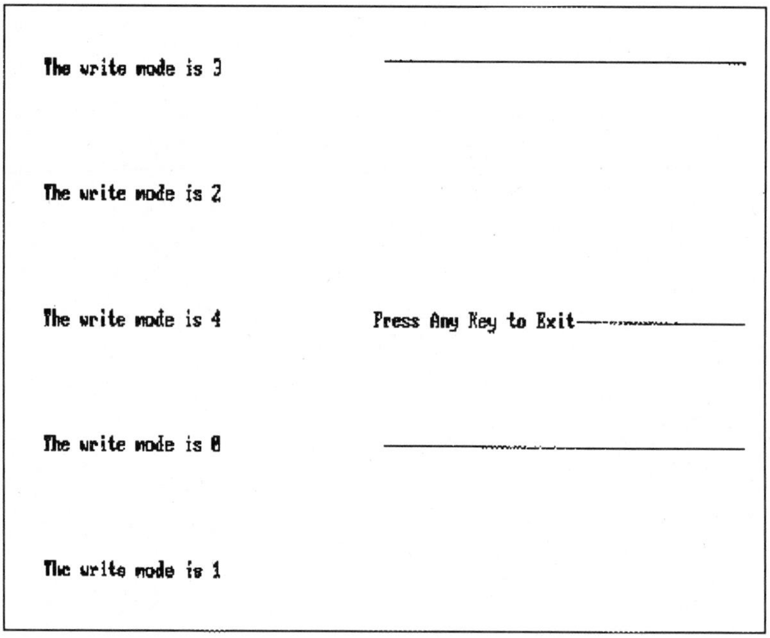

_grstatus

Syntax:

```
short _far _grstatus(void);
```

Function:

The _grstatus function determines if an error or warning was generated by the most recently called graphics function.

Files to Include:

```
#include <graph.h>
```

Compatibility:

DOS
OS/2

Description:

The _grstatus function provides the status of the most recently called graphics function. Both errors and warnings are returned. If the value returned is less than 0, an error occurred. A return value greater than 0 indicates a warning. Table 9.12 shows the constant values returned and their meaning.

Table 9.12. *Status information.*

Constant	Value
No errors or warnings	
_GROK	0
Warnings	
_GRNOOUTPUT	1
_GRCLIPPED	2
_GRPARAMETERALTERED	3
Errors	
_GRERROR	1
_GRMODENOTSUPPORTED	-2
_GRNOTINPROPERMODE	-3

Table 9.12. *continues*

Table 9.12. cont. *Status information.*

Constant	Value
_GRINVALIDPARAMETER	-4
_GRFONTFILENOTFOUND	-5
_GRINVALIDFONTFILE	-6
_GRCORRUPTEDFONTFILE	-7
_GRINSUFFICIENTMEMORY	-8
_GRINVALIDIMAGEBUFFER	-9

The following functions set the return value to _GROK because they do not provide errors:

_displaycursor
_getactivepage
_getgtextvector
_gettextcolor
_gettextposition
_gettextwindow
_getvideoconfig
_getvisualpage
_outmem
_outtext
_unregisterfonts
_wrapon

Table 9.13 contains a list of functions and the possible error and warning codes generated by each.

Table 9.13. *Error and warning code summary.*

Function	Error codes	Warning codes
_arc functions	_GRNOTINPROPERMODE _GRINVALIDPARAMETER	_GRNOOUTPUT _GRCLIPPED
_clearscreen	_GRNOTINPROPERMODE _GRINVALIDPARAMETER	
_ellipse functions	_GRNOTINPROPERMODE _GRINVALIDPARAMETER _GRINSUFFICIENTMEMORY	_GRNOOUTPUT _GRCLIPPED
_getarcinfo	_GRNOTINPROPERMODE	
_getcurrentposition functions	_GRNOTINPROPERMODE	
_getfontinfo	_GRERROR	
_getgtextextent	_GRERROR	
_getgtextvector	_GRPARAMETERALTERED	
_getimage	_GRNOTINPROPERMODE	_GRPARAMETERALTERED

Function	Error codes	Warning codes
_getphyscoord	_GRNOTINPROPERMODE	
_getpixel	_GRNOTINPROPERMODE	
_gettextcursor	_GRNOTINPROPERMODE	
_getviewcoord functions	_GRNOTINPROPERMODE	
_getwindowcoord	_GRNOTINPROPERMODE	
_getwritemode	_GRNOTINPROPERMODE	
_imagesize functions	_GRNOTINPROPERMODE	
_lineto functions	_GRNOTINPROPERMODE	_GRNOOUTPUT _GRCLIPPED
_moveto functions	_GRNOTINPROPERMODE	
_outgtext	_GRNOTINPROPERMODE	_GRCLIPPED _GRNOOUTPUT
_pie functions	_GRNOTINPROPERMODE _GRINVALIDPARAMETER _GRINSUFFICIENTMEMORY	_GRNOOUTPUT _GRCLIPPED
_polygon functions	_GRNOTINPROPERMODE _GRINVALIDPARAMETER _GRINSUFFICIENTMEMORY	_GRNOOUTPUT _GRCLIPPED
_putimage functions	_GRERROR _GRNOTINPROPERMODE _GRINVALIDPARAMETER _GRINVALIDIMAGEBUFFER	_GRPARAMETERALTERED _GRNOOUTPUT
_rectangle functions	_GRNOTINPROPERMODE _GRINVALIDPARAMETER _GRINSUFFICIENTMEMORY	_GRNOOUTPUT _GRCLIPPED
_registerfonts	_GRCORRUPTEDFONTFILE _GRFONTFILENOTFOUND _GRINSUFFICIENTMEMORY _GRINVALIDFONTFILE	
_scrolltextwindow		_GRNOOUTPUT
_selectpalette	_GRNOTINPROPERMODE _GRINVALIDPARAMETER	
_setactivepage	_GRINVALIDPARAMETER	
_setbkcolor	_GRINVALIDPARAMETER	_GRPARAMETERALTERED
_setcliprgn	_GRNOTINPROPERMODE	_GRPARAMETERALTERED
_setcolor	_GRNOTINPROPERMODE	_GRPARAMETERALTERED
_setfont	_GRERROR _GRFONTFILENOTFOUND _GRINSUFFICIENTMEMORY _GRPARAMETERALTERED	
_setgtextvector	_GRPARAMETERALTERED	
_settextcolor		_GRPARAMETERALTERED

Table 9.13. *continues*

Table 9.13. cont. *Error and warning code summary.*

Function	Error codes	Warning codes
_settextcursor	_GRNOTINPROPERMODE	
_settextposition		_GRPARAMETERALTERED
_settextrows	_GRINVALIDPARAMETER	_GRPARAMETERALTERED
_settextwindow		_GRPARAMETERALTERED
_setvideomode	_GRERROR	
	_GRMODENOTSUPPORTED	
	_GRINVALIDPARAMETER	
_setvideomoderows	_GRERROR	
	_GRMODENOTSUPPORTED	
	_GRINVALIDPARAMETER	
_setvieworg	_GRNOTINPROPERMODE	
_setviewport	_GRNOTINPROPERMODE	_GRPARAMETERALTERED
_setvisualpage	_GRINVALIDPARAMETER	
_setwindow	_GRNOTINPROPERMODE	_GRPARAMETERALTERED
	_GRINVALIDPARAMETER	
_setwritemode	_GRNOTINPROPERMODE	
	_GRINVALIDPARAMETER	

Values Returned:

The status of the most recently called graphics function is returned.

Related Functions:

See functions listed in table 9.13.

Similar Turbo C++ Functions:

```
graphresult  :  returns an error code for the last
                unsuccessful graphics operation
    int far graphresult (void);
```

Suggested Code Structure and Use:

The _grstatus function is used to determine the status of the most recently drawn graphics function. This function is very useful in determining why a graphics function failed. The following code structure illustrates the use of the _grstatus function.

```
#include <graph.h>
#include <stdio.h>
void main ()
{
```

```
short status;
_setvideomode ( mode );   /* set video mode */
                 .
                 .
                 .
     { Call a graphics function }
                 .
                 .
                 .
status = _grstatus ();   /* get status of the function */
                 .
                 .
                 .
     { Use the status information }
                 .
                 .
                 .
_setvideomode (_DEFAULTMODE); /* reset and exit */
}
```

Example:

This example uses the _g r s t a t u s function to obtain information on the status of the previously called _e l l i p s e function. If the status value is 0, no error occurred. If the status value is negative, an error occurred. A positive status value indicates a warning. A message indicating the status is output to the screen, as shown in figure 9.31.

```
#include <graph.h>
#include <stdio.h>
void main ()
{
short status;
_setvideomode (_ERESCOLOR);
_rectangle (_GBORDER,0,0,639,349);
     /* Draw and get status */
_ellipse (_GFILLINTERIOR,50,50,589,299);
status = _grstatus ();
     /* Output status */
_settextposition (3,3);
if (status == 0)
     _outtext ("There was no error or warning");
if (status < 0)
     _outtext ("There was an error");
if (status > 0)
```

```
        _outtext ("There was a warning");
        /* Delay and exit */
_settextposition (24,3);
_outtext ("Press Any Key To Exit");
getch ();
_setvideomode (_DEFAULTMODE);
}
```

Fig. 9.31. Example _grstatus output.

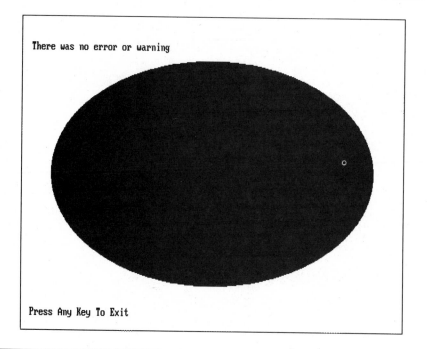

_imagesize

Syntax:

```
long _far _imagesize(short x1, short y1, short x2,
                     short y2);
short x1, y1;        upper left corner of image
short x2, y2;        lower right corner of image
```

Function:

The _imagesize function returns the number of bytes required to store a rectangular image when using the view coordinate system.

Files to Include:

```
#include <graph.h>
```

Compatibility:

DOS

Description:

The _imagesize function determines the number of bytes required to store an image in the rectangular region defined by the x1,y1 and x2,y2 arguments. The x1 and y1 arguments specify the upper left corner of the rectangular region; the x2 and y2 arguments specify the lower right corner. This function is useful in determining the storage area needed for the _getimage function. The alternate method is to use the following formulas:

```
x_width = abs(x1-x2) + 1;
y_width = abs(y1-y2) + 1;
imagesize = 4 + (((x_width * bitsperpixel + 7)/8)* y_width);
```

The bitsperpixel parameter can be determined by calling the _getvideoconfig function to retrieve the bitsperpixel field in a structure of type videoconfig.

Values Returned:

The required number of bytes to store the rectangular region is returned. No error value is returned.

Related Functions:

```
_getvideoconfig    :  used to get information on the current
                      graphics environment including the
                      bitsperpixel field
_getimage          :  saves an image
```

Similar Turbo C++ Functions:

```
imagesize  :  returns the number of bytes required to store
              a bit image
unsigned far imagesize (int left, int top, int right,
                        int bottom);
```

Suggested Code Structure and Use:

The _imagesize function is most commonly used to size the buffer in which an image is stored with the _getimage function. The following code structure illustrates this use.

```
#include <stdio.h>
#include <graph.h>
#include <malloc.h>
char far *imagebuffer;
void main ()
{
_setvideomode ( mode ); /* set mode by adapter */
        .
        .
        .
    { Draw image to be stored }
        .
        .
        .
imagebuffer = (char far *)malloc((unsigned int)
          _imagesize (x1,y1,x2,y2));
_getimage (x1,y1,x2,y2,imagebuffer);
        .
        .
        .
    { Use image }
        .
        .
        .
_setvideomode (_DEFAULTMODE);
}
```

Example:

This program uses the _imagesize function to size the buffer used to store an image. A figure is drawn, stored with help of the _imagesize function, and placed in another location on the screen.

```
#include <stdio.h>
#include <graph.h>
#include <malloc.h>
char far *imagebuffer;
void main ()
{
        /* Initialization */
```

```
_setvideomode (_MRES4COLOR);
_setbkcolor (_BLUE);
_rectangle (_GBORDER,0,0,319,199);
        /* Draw figure to save */
_rectangle (_GFILLINTERIOR,140,80,180,120);
_setcolor (2);
_rectangle (_GFILLINTERIOR,150,90,170,110);
        /* Save figure */
imagebuffer = (char far *)malloc((unsigned int)
      _imagesize (140,80,180,120));
_getimage (140,80,180,120,imagebuffer);
        /* Place image */
_putimage (140,20,imagebuffer,_GPSET);
        /* Delay and exit */
_settextposition (23,10);
_outtext ("Press Any Key to Exit");
getch ();
_setvideomode (_DEFAULTMODE);
}
```

_imagesize_w

Syntax:

```
long _far _imagesize_w(double x1, double y1, double x2,
                       double y2);
double x1, y1;          upper left corner of image
double x2, y2;          lower right corner of image
```

Function:

The _imagesize_w function determines the number of bytes required to store a rectangular image when using window coordinates.

Files to Include:

```
#include <graph.h>
```

Compatibility:

DOS

Description:

The _imagesize_w function calculates the number of bytes required to store a rectangular image. This function is most commonly used with the _getimage_w function to size the image buffer. Both of these functions use the window coordinate system. The x1 and y1 arguments describe the upper left corner of the rectangular image; the x2 and y2 arguments describe the lower right corner of this image.

Values Returned:

The number of bytes required to store the image is returned.

Related Functions:

```
_getimage_w        :          store a rectangular image
```

Similar Turbo C++ Functions:

None

Suggested Code Structure and Use:

The _imagesize_w function is used to calculate the buffer size required to save an image. This function is used when the rectangular image is defined by window coordinates. The following code structure illustrates the use of the _imagesize_w function.

```
#include <graph.h>
#include <stdio.h>
#include <malloc.h>
char far *imagebuffer;
void main ()
{
_setvideomode ( mode ); /* set mode by graphics hardware */
_setviewport (x1,y1,x2,y2); /* size viewport */
_setwindow (flag,x1,y1,x2,y2); /* set window dimensions */
            .
            .
            .
imagebuffer = (char far *)malloc((unsigned int)
              _imagesize_w (x1,y1,x2,y2));
_getimage_w = (x1,y1,x2,y2,imagebuffer);
_putimage_w = (x1,y1,imagebuffer,action);
            .
            .
            .
```

```
_setvideomode (_DEFAULTMODE); /* reset and exit */
}
```

Example:

The following example uses the **_imagesize_w** function to set the required size of the image buffer. The image buffer is used by the **_getimage_w** function to store the image. The stored image is then placed on the screen four times, as shown in figure 9.32.

```
#include <stdio.h>
#include <graph.h>
#include <malloc.h>
char far *imagebuffer;
void main ()
{
_setvideomode (_ERESCOLOR);
_rectangle (_GBORDER,0,0,639,349);
      /* Open window */
_setviewport (0,0,639,349);
_setwindow (0,-100.0,-100.0,100.0,100.0);
      /* Draw image to save */
_setcolor (14);
_rectangle_w(_GFILLINTERIOR,-30.0,-30.0,30.0,30.0);
_setcolor (4);
_rectangle_w (_GFILLINTERIOR,-20.0,-20.0,20.0,20.0);
_setcolor (2);
_rectangle_w (_GFILLINTERIOR,-10.0,-10.0,10.0,10.0);
      /* Get image */
imagebuffer = (char far *)malloc((unsigned int)
         _imagesize_w (-30.0,-30.0,30.0,30.0));
_getimage_w (-30.0,-30.0,30.0,30.0,imagebuffer);
      /* Place image */
_putimage_w (-90.0,-90.0,imagebuffer,_GPSET);
_putimage_w (-90.0,30.0,imagebuffer,_GPSET);
_putimage_w (30.0,-90.0,imagebuffer,_GPSET);
_putimage_w (30.0,30.0,imagebuffer,_GPSET);
      /* Delay and exit */
_settextposition (23,30);
_outtext ("Press Any Key To Exit");
getch ();
_setvideomode (_DEFAULTMODE);
}
```

Fig. 9.32. Example _imagesize_w output.

_imagesize_wxy

Syntax:

```
long _far _imagesize_wxy(struct _wxycoord _far *xy1,
                struct _wxycoord _far *xy2);
struct _wxycoord _far *xy1;  upper left corner of image
struct _wxycoord _far *xy2;  lower right corner of image
```

Function:

The `_imagesize_wxy` function determines the number of bytes required to store a rectangular image defined by window coordinates.

Files to Include:

```
#include <graph.h>
```

Compatibility:

DOS

Description:

The _imagesize_wxy function determines the number of bytes required to store a rectangular image when operating with the window coordinate system. The x y 1 coordinate pair describes the upper left corner of the rectangular image; the x y 2 coordinate pair describes the lower right corner of the image. The _imagesize_wxy function is commonly used to size the image buffer used by the _getimage_wxy function.

Values Returned:

The function returns the number of bytes required to store the image.

Related Functions:

```
_getimage_wxy          :          stores a rectangular image in the
                                   window coordinate system
```

Similar Turbo C++ Functions:

None

Suggested Code Structure and Use:

The following code structure illustrates the proper use of the _imagesize_wxy function. This function sizes an image buffer for use by the _getimage_wxy function.

```c
#include <graph.h>
#include <stdio.h>
#include <malloc.h>
char far *imagebuffer;
void main ()
{
struct _wxycoord corner1, corner2;
_setvideomode ( mode ); /* set video mode */
_setviewport (x1,y1,x2,y2); /* size viewport */
_setwindow (flag,x1,y1,x2,y2); /* set window dimensions */
          .
          .
          .
corner1.wx = -30.0;
corner1.wy = -30.0;
corner2.wx = 30.0;
corner2.wy = 30.0;
```

```
imagebuffer = (char far *)malloc((unsigned int)
            _imagesize_wxy (&corner1, &corner2));
_getimage_wxy (&corner1,&corner2,imagebuffer);
_putimage_w (x1,y1,imagebuffer,action);
        .
        .
        .

_setvideomode (_DEFAULTMODE);   /* reset and exit */
}
```

Example:

The _imagesize_wxy function is used in this example to size the image buffer used by the _getimage_wxy function. The image is then stored and output to the screen.

```
#include <stdio.h>
#include <graph.h>
#include <malloc.h>
char far *imagebuffer;
void main ()
{
struct _wxycoord corner1, corner2;
_setvideomode (_ERESCOLOR);
_rectangle (_GBORDER,0,0,639,349);
    /* Open window */
_setviewport (0,0,639,349);
_setwindow (0,-100.0,-100.0,100.0,100.0);
    /* Draw image to save */
_setcolor (14);
_rectangle_w(_GFILLINTERIOR,-30.0,-30.0,30.0,30.0);
_setcolor (4);
_rectangle_w (_GFILLINTERIOR,-20.0,-20.0,20.0,20.0);
_setcolor (2);
_rectangle_w (_GFILLINTERIOR,-10.0,-10.0,10.0,10.0);
    /* Get image */
corner1.wx = -30.0;
corner1.wy = -30.0;
corner2.wx = 30.0;
corner2.wy = 30.0;
imagebuffer = (char far *)malloc((unsigned int)
            _imagesize_wxy (&corner1, &corner2));
_getimage_wxy (&corner1,&corner2,imagebuffer);
```

```
        /* Place image */
_putimage_w (-90.0,-90.0,imagebuffer,_GPSET);
_putimage_w (-90.0,30.0,imagebuffer,_GPSET);
_putimage_w (30.0,-90.0,imagebuffer,_GPSET);
_putimage_w (30.0,30.0,imagebuffer,_GPSET);
        /* Delay and exit */
_settextposition (23,30);
_outtext ("Press Any Key To Exit");
getch ();
_setvideomode (_DEFAULTMODE);
}
```

_lineto

Syntax:

```
short _far _lineto(short x, short y);
short x, y;      endpoint for the line
```

Function:

The _lineto function draws a line from the graphics cursor to a specified point. This function uses view coordinates.

Files to Include:

```
#include <graph.h>
```

Compatibility:

DOS

Description:

A line is drawn from the graphics cursor to the point specified by the x and y arguments. The line is drawn using the current color and current line pattern. After the line is drawn, the graphics cursor is set to the x,y endpoint. The _lineto function is commonly used with the _moveto function to create complex images. Figure 9.33 illustrates the typical use of the _lineto function. Use the view coordinate system with this function.

Fig. 9.33. The _lineto function.

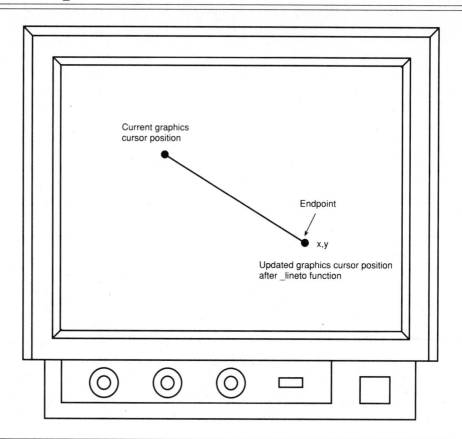

Values Returned:

A nonzero value is returned if the line is drawn successfully. A zero is returned if unsuccessful.

Related Functions:

```
_setcolor       :    sets the current color
_setlinestyle   :    sets the current line pattern for
                     straight lines
_moveto         :    moves the graphics cursor to a
                     specified point
```

Similar Turbo C++ Functions:

```
line   :  draws a line between two points
void far line (int x1, int y1, int x2, int y2);
linerel  :  draws a line a relative distance from the
             cursor position
void far linerel (int dx, int dy);
lineto  :  draws a line from the cursor to x,y
void far lineto (int x, int y);
```

Suggested Code Structure and Use:

The _lineto function is useful for creating complex images. When used with the _moveto function, intricate images can be created. The following code structure illustrates how the _moveto and _lineto functions are used.

```
#include <stdio.h>
#include <graph.h>
void main ()
{
_setvideomode ( mode ); /* set mode by adapter */
      .
      .
      .
_moveto (x,y);
_lineto (x,y);
      .
      .
      .
_setvideomode (_DEFAULTMODE); /* reset */
}
```

Example:

The following program uses the _lineto function to draw a line from the center of the screen to the cursor position. The cursor can be moved with the keypad when the Num Lock key is on. 8 moves the cursor up, 2 moves the cursor down, 4 moves the cursor left, and 6 moves the cursor right.

```
#include <stdio.h>
#include <graph.h>
#define ESC 27
void main ()
{
int ch;
```

421

```
int x,y;
int oldx, oldy;
struct xycoord cursorposition;
char buffer [40];

         /* Initialization */
_setvideomode (_MRES4COLOR);
_setbkcolor (_BLUE);
_rectangle (_GBORDER,0,0,319,199);
         /* Draw initial cursor */
x = 155;
y = 95;
_moveto (x+5,y);
_lineto (x+5,y+10);
_moveto (x,y+5);
_lineto (x+10,y+5);
_moveto (x+5,y+5);
         /* Output initial setting of cursor position */
cursorposition = _getcurrentposition ();
sprintf (buffer, "X Position : %d", cursorposition.xcoord);
_settextposition (23,10);
_outtext (buffer);
sprintf (buffer, "Y Position : %d", cursorposition.ycoord);
_settextposition (24,10);
_outtext (buffer);
do
{
     oldx = x;
     oldy = y;
     _moveto (160,100);
     _lineto (cursorposition.xcoord,cursorposition.ycoord);
     ch = getch ();
     _setcolor (0);
     _moveto (160,100);
     _lineto (cursorposition.xcoord,cursorposition.ycoord);
     _setcolor (3);
         /* Move cursor points */
     if (ch == '4')
      x = x - 5;
     if (ch == '8')
      y = y - 5;
     if (ch == '6')
```

```
       x = x + 5;
      if (ch == '2')
       y = y + 5;
          /* Check borders */
      if (y < 5)
       y = y + 5;
      if (y > 140)
       y = y - 5;
      if (x > 305)
       x = x - 5;
      if (x < 5)
       x = x + 5;
          /*  Move cursor  */
 _ setcolor (0);
 _moveto (oldx+5,oldy);
 _lineto (oldx+5,oldy+10);
 _moveto (oldx,oldy+5);
 _lineto (oldx+10,oldy+5);
 _setcolor (3);
 _moveto (x+5,y);
 _lineto (x+5,y+10);
 _moveto (x,y+5);
 _lineto (x+10,y+5);
 _moveto (x+5,y+5);
          /* Output present setting of cursor position */
   cursorposition = _getcurrentposition ();
   sprintf (buffer, "X Position : %d",
    cursorposition.xcoord);
   _settextposition (23,10);
   _outtext (buffer);
   _outtext ("         ");
   sprintf (buffer, "Y Position : %d",
    cursorposition.ycoord);
   _settextposition (24,10);
   _outtext (buffer);
   _outtext ("         ");


} while (ch != ESC);
_setvideomode (_DEFAULTMODE);
}
```

_lineto_w

Syntax:

```
short _far _lineto_w(double x, double y);
double x,y;        endpoint for the line
```

Function:

The _lineto_w function draws a line from the current position of the graphics cursor to the point specified by x,y. This function uses window coordinates.

Files to Include:

```
#include <graph.h>
```

Compatibility:

DOS

Description:

The _lineto_w function creates a line in the current window. The current color, current line pattern, and window coordinate system are used with this function. The x and y arguments identify the endpoint of the line. The line begins at the current position of the graphics cursor and extends to the endpoint. The position of the graphics cursor is then set to the location of the endpoint. The _lineto_w function is often used with the _moveto_w function to create complex images when operating in the window coordinate system.

Values Returned:

If the line is drawn successfully, a nonzero value is returned. If unsuccessful, a zero is returned.

Related Functions:

```
_setcolor          :     sets the current color
_setlinestyle      :     sets the current line pattern
_moveto_w          :     moves the graphics cursor to
                         the specified window coordinates
```

Similar Turbo C++ Functions:

None

Suggested Code Structure and Use:

The _lineto_w function is used to draw a line in the window coordinate system. The _lineto_w function is often used with the _moveto_w function to create complex images when using the window coordinate system. The following code structure illustrates the use of the _lineto_w function.

```
#include <graph.h>
#include <stdio.h>
void main ()
{
_setvideomode ( mode ); /* set mode by adapter */
_setviewport (x1,y1,x2,y2); /* size viewport */
_setwindow (flag,x1,y1,x2,y2); /* set window dimensions */
            .
            .
            .
_moveto_w (x,y); /* move graphics cursor */
_lineto_w (x,y); /* draw line to window coordinates x,y */
            .
            .
            .
_setvideomode (_DEFAULTMODE); /* reset and exit */
}
```

Example:

In the following example, the _lineto_w function is used with the _moveto_w function to create an image on the screen. See figure 9.34. The entire screen is set as a window with dimensions -100.0,-100.0, and 100.0,100.0.

```
#include <graph.h>
#include <stdio.h>
void main ()
{
_setvideomode (_ERESCOLOR);
_rectangle (_GBORDER,0,0,639,349);
     /* Open window */
_setviewport (0,0,639,349);
_setwindow (0,-100.0,-100.0,100.0,100.0);
     /* Draw image */
_moveto_w (0.0,0.0);
_lineto_w (-50.0,-50.0);
_lineto_w (0.0,-25.0);
_lineto_w (50.0,-50.0);
```

```
_lineto_w (0.0,0.0);
_lineto_w (50.0,-50.0);
_lineto_w (25.0,0.0);
_lineto_w (50.0,50.0);
_lineto_w (0.0,0.0);
_lineto_w (50.0,50.0);
_lineto_w (0.0,25.0);
_lineto_w (-50.0,50.0);
_lineto_w (0.0,0.0);
_lineto_w (-50.0,50.0);
_lineto_w (-25.0,0.0);
_lineto_w (-50.0,-50.0);
     /* Delay and exit */
_settextposition (24,5);
_outtext ("Press Any Key To Exit");
getch ();
_setvideomode (_DEFAULTMODE);
}
```

Fig. 9.34. Example _lineto_w output.

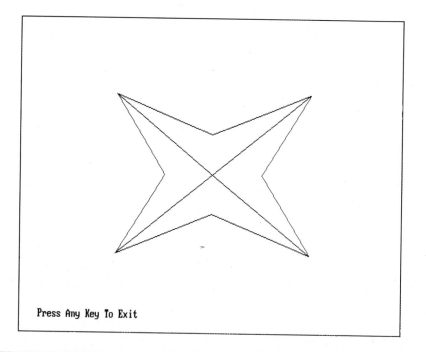

_moveto

Syntax:

```
struct xycoord _far _moveto(short x, short y);
short x, y;        view coordinates to place cursor
```

Function:

The _moveto function updates the graphics cursor position maintained internally by the graphics routines. This function uses the view coordinate system.

Files to Include:

```
#include <graph.h>
```

Compatibility:

DOS

Description:

When the _moveto function is called, the position of the graphics cursor is moved to the view coordinates specified by the x, y arguments. No drawing is done when the cursor is moved. This function is often used with the _lineto function to create complex images. Figure 9.35 illustrates the use of the _moveto function.

Values Returned:

The view coordinates of the previous graphics cursor position are returned in a structure of type xycoord. This structure follows.

```
struct xycoord
   {
   short xcoord;
   short ycoord;
   };
```

Related Functions:

```
_lineto    :    draws a line from the graphics cursor to the
                specified coordinates
```

Fig. 9.35. The _moveto function.

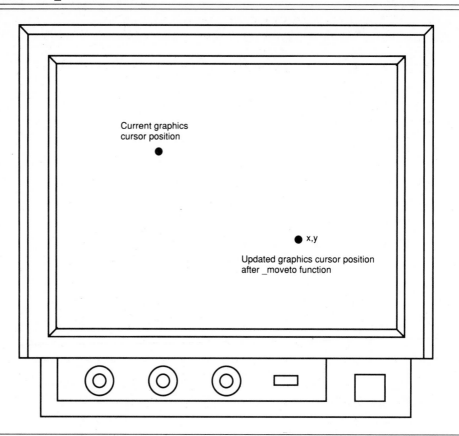

Similar Turbo C++ Functions:

```
moveto  :  moves the cursor to x,y
void far moveto (int x, int y);
```

Suggested Code Structure and Use:

The **_moveto** function (when used with the **_lineto** function) is useful for creating complex images. The following code structure illustrates this use.

```
#include <stdio.h>
#include <graph.h>
void main ()
{
_setvideomode ( mode ); /* set mode by adapter */
```

```
          .
          .
          .
   _moveto (x,y);
   _lineto (x,y);
          .
          .
          .
   _setvideomode (_DEFAULTMODE);
   }
```

Example:

This example creates a cursor that can be moved about the screen. A line is drawn from the cursor to the center of the screen. The **_moveto** function designates an endpoint for this line. This program accepts keypad input when the Num Lock key is on. 4 and 6 move the cursor left and right, respectively; 8 and 2 move the cursor up and down, respectively. Press Esc to end the program.

```
#include <stdio.h>
#include <graph.h>
#define ESC 27
void main ()
{
int ch;
int x,y;
int oldx, oldy;
struct xycoord cursorposition;
char buffer [40];

        /* Initialization */
_setvideomode (_MRES4COLOR);
_setbkcolor (_BLUE);
_rectangle (_GBORDER,0,0,319,199);
        /*      Draw initial cursor */
x = 155;
y = 95;
_moveto (x+5,y);
_lineto (x+5,y+10);
_moveto (x,y+5);
_lineto (x+10,y+5);
_moveto (x+5,y+5);
        /* Output initial setting of cursor position */
cursorposition = _getcurrentposition ();
sprintf (buffer, "X Position : %d", cursorposition.xcoord);
```

429

```
_settextposition (23,10);
_outtext (buffer);
sprintf (buffer, "Y Position : %d", cursorposition.ycoord);
_settextposition (24,10);
_outtext (buffer);

do
      {
      oldx = x;
      oldy = y;
      _moveto (160,100);
      _lineto (cursorposition.xcoord,cursorposition.ycoord);
      ch = getch ();
      _setcolor (0);
      _moveto (160,100);
      _lineto (cursorposition.xcoord,cursorposition.ycoord);
      _setcolor (3);
            /* Move cursor points */
      if (ch == '4')
       x = x - 5;
      if (ch == '8')
       y = y - 5;
      if (ch == '6')
       x = x + 5;
      if (ch == '2')
       y = y + 5;
            /* Check borders */
      if (y < 5)
       y = y + 5;
      if (y > 140)
       y = y - 5;
      if (x > 305)
       x = x - 5;
      if (x < 5)
       x = x + 5;
            /*  Move cursor  */
      _setcolor (0);
      _moveto (oldx+5,oldy);
      _lineto (oldx+5,oldy+10);
      _moveto (oldx,oldy+5);
      _lineto (oldx+10,oldy+5);
      _setcolor (3);
      _moveto (x+5,y);
```

```
          _lineto (x+5,y+10);
          _moveto (x,y+5);
          _lineto (x+10,y+5);
          _moveto (x+5,y+5);
                /* Output present setting of cursor position */
          cursorposition = _getcurrentposition ();
          sprintf (buffer, "X Position : %d",
           cursorposition.xcoord);
         _settextposition (23,10);
          _outtext (buffer);
          _outtext ("          ");
          sprintf (buffer, "Y Position : %d",
                  cursorposition.ycoord);
          _settextposition (24,10);
          _outtext (buffer);
          _outtext ("          ");

     } while (ch != ESC);
     _setvideomode (_DEFAULTMODE);
     }
```

_moveto_w

Syntax:

```
struct _wxycoord _far _moveto_w(double x, double y);
double x, y;      window coordinates to place cursor
```

Function:

The _moveto_w function moves the graphics cursor to the position specified by the x and y window coordinates.

Files to Include:

```
#include <graph.h>
```

Compatibility:

DOS

Description:

The _moveto_w function moves the graphics cursor. When the cursor is moved, no drawing takes place. The x and y arguments identify the window coordinates of the desired graphics cursor position. This function is often used with the _lineto_w function.

Values Returned:

The previous position of the graphics cursor, expressed in window coordinates, is returned in a structure of type _wxycoord. This structure follows.

```
struct _wxycoord
    {
    double wx;
    double wy;
    };
```

Related Functions:

```
    _lineto_w      :  draws a line using window coordinates
```

Similar Turbo C++ Functions:

None

Suggested Code Structure and Use:

The _moveto_w function is used to move the graphics cursor when the window coordinate system is in use. The _moveto_w function is often used with the _lineto_w function to create images. The following code structure illustrates the use of the _moveto_w function.

```
#include <graph.h>
#include <stdio.h>
void main ()
{
_setvideomode ( mode ); /* set mode by adapter in use */
_setviewport (x1,y1,x2,y2); /* size viewport */
_setwindow (flag,x1,y1,x2,y2); /* set window dimensions */
        .
        .
        .
```

```
_moveto_w (x,y); /* move graphics cursor */
_lineto_w (x,y); /* draw line */
      .
      .
      .
_setvideomode (_DEFAULTMODE);   /* reset and exit */
}
```

Example:

In the following example, the _moveto_w and _lineto_w functions are used to create an image in the window coordinate system. See figure 9.36.

```
#include <graph.h>
#include <stdio.h>
void main ()
{
_setvideomode (_ERESCOLOR);
_rectangle (_GBORDER,0,0,639,349);
      /* Open window */
_setviewport (0,0,639,349);
_setwindow (0,-100.0,-100.0,100.0,100.0);
      /* Draw image */
_moveto_w (50.0,50.0);
_lineto_w (-50.0,-50.0);
_moveto_w (50.0,-50.0);
_lineto_w (-50.0,50.0);
_moveto_w (0.0,50.0);
_lineto_w (0.0,-50.0);
_moveto_w (50.0,0.0);
_lineto_w (-50.0,0.0);
      /* Delay and exit */
_settextposition (24,5);
_outtext ("Press Any Key To Exit");
getch ();
_setvideomode (_DEFAULTMODE);
}
```

Fig. 9.36. Example _moveto_w output.

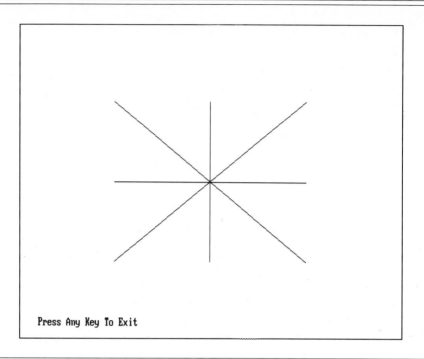

Press Any Key To Exit

_outgtext

Syntax:

```
void _far _outgtext(unsigned char _far *text);
unsigned char _far *text;          text string
```

Function:

The _outgtext function positions the text string on the screen, according to the current font and rotation.

Files to Include:

```
#include <graph.h>
```

Compatibility:

DOS

Description:

The _outgtext function places the specified text string at the current location of the graphics cursor using the current font, color, and vector orientation. The current graphics color, as set by the _setcolor function, is used to specify the color of font text output. The _outgtext function updates the position of the graphics cursor when printing is completed.

Values Returned:

There is no return value.

Related Functions:

```
_setcolor        :    sets the current color
_setfont         :    sets the current font
_setgtextvector  :    sets output vector orientation
```

Similar Turbo C++ Functions:

```
outtext   :  displays text at the current cursor position
void far outtext (char far *textstring);
outtextxy  :  displays a string starting at x, y
void far outtextxy (int x, int y, char far *textstring);
```

Suggested Code Structure and Use:

The _outgtext function is used to display font text. The following code structure illustrates the proper method for using the _outgtext function with registered and set fonts. (To display font text, the current font must be registered and set.)

```c
#include <graph.h>
#include <stdio.h>
void main ()
{
_setvideomode ( mode ); /* set mode by graphics adapter */
_registerfonts ("*.fon");  /* register fonts */
_setfont ("t'courier' h12 w9 b f");  /* select a font */
          .
          .
          .
```

```
_moveto (x,y); /* move cursor to place to start text */
_setgtextvector (0,0); /* set text vector orientation */
_outgtext ("Text String to Output"); /* output text */
            .
            .
            .
_unregisterfonts (); /* free memory */
_setvideomode (_DEFAULTMODE); /* reset and exit */
}
```

Example:

The _outgtext function is used in the following example to display text using the current font (courier) and various text vector orientations. See figure 9.37.

```
#include <graph.h>
#include <stdio.h>
void main ()
{
_setvideomode (_ERESCOLOR);
_rectangle (_GBORDER, 0, 0, 639, 349);
        /* Register and set fonts */
_registerfonts ("*.fon");
_setfont ("t'courier' h12 w9 b f");
        /* Output font text with different text
             vector orientations */
_moveto (70,30);
_setgtextvector (1,0);
_outgtext ("Font Text with Orientation 1,0");
_moveto (610,30);
_setgtextvector (0,-1);
_outgtext ("Font Text with Orientation 0,-1");
_moveto (570,320);
_setgtextvector (-1,0);
_outgtext ("Font Text with Orientation -1,0");
_moveto (30,320);
_setgtextvector (0,1);
_outgtext ("Font Text with Orientation 0, 1");
        /* Delay and exit */
_moveto (200,175);
_setgtextvector (1,0);
_outgtext ("Press Any Key To Exit");
```

```
    getch();
    _unregisterfonts ();
    _setvideomode (_DEFAULTMODE);
    }
```

Fig. 9.37.   Example _outgtext output.

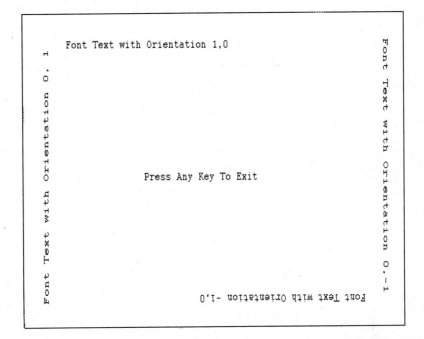

_outmem

Syntax:

```
void _far _outmem(unsigned char _far *text,
          short length);
unsigned char _far *text;          text string
short length;                      number of characters
```

Function:

The _outmem function places a specified number of characters on the screen. These characters are obtained from the text buffer.

Files to Include:

```
#include <graph.h>
```

Compatibility:

DOS
OS/2

Description:

The _outmem function is used to place on the screen a specified number of characters from a predefined text string. The text begins at the current position of the text cursor. The length argument defines the number of characters to output on the screen. The text argument refers to the text string from which these characters are obtained.

Values Returned:

There is no return value.

Related Functions:

```
_settextposition      :    positions the text cursor
```

Similar Turbo C++ Functions:

None

Suggested Code Structure and Use:

The _outmem function is used to output a specified number of characters from the specified string. The _outmem function is similar to the _outtext function but the number of output characters can be limited. The following code structure illustrates the use of the _outmem function.

```
#include <graph.h>
#include <stdio.h>
void main ()
{
```

```
_setvideomode ( mode ); /* set mode by adapter in use */
        .
        .
        .
_settextposition (row,column); /* set text cursor */
_outmem ("Output first 5 of text string",5);
        .
        .
        .
_setvideomode (_DEFAULTMODE); /* reset and exit */
}
```

Example:

The following example demonstrates the use of the _outmem function. A text string is defined,
but only the first 27 characters are output. Press any key to exit the program.

```
#include <stdio.h>
#include <graph.h>
void main ()
{
_setvideomode (_ERESCOLOR);
_rectangle (_GBORDER,0,0,639,349);
        /* Output the first 27 characters of string */
_settextposition (10,5);
_outmem ("No output after the period. No more output",27);
        /* Delay and exit */
_settextposition (23,5);
_outtext ("Press Any Key To Exit");
getch ();
_setvideomode (_DEFAULTMODE);
}
```

_outtext

Syntax:

```
void _far _outtext(unsigned char _far *textbuffer);
unsigned char far *textbuffer;              text string
```

439

Function:

The _outtext function is used to output text in text or graphics modes.

Files to Include:

```
#include <graph.h>
```

Compatibility:

DOS
OS/2

Description:

The _outtext function prints on the screen the null-terminated string pointed to by the textbuffer argument. The text is printed in the current text color starting at the location of the text cursor. Unlike other standard I/O routines, the _outtext function does not provide formatting. To output formatted text, first use the sprintf function to format the buffer, then use the _outtext function to print the buffer. The text cursor is updated to the next character location past the last character printed. If the text runs to the end of the line, it is either clipped or wrapped to the next line depending on the setting of the _wrapon function.

Values Returned:

There is no return value.

Related Functions:

```
_settextposition   :   sets the position of the text
                       cursor
_settextcolor      :   sets the current text color
_wrapon            :   determines if text will wrap to
                       next line
```

Similar Turbo C++ Functions:

```
outtext  :  displays text at current cursor position
void far outtext (char far *textstring);
outtextxy  :  displays text beginning at x,y
void far outtextxy (int x, int y, char far *textstring);
```

Suggested Code Structure and Use:

The _outtext function is useful for text output. The following code structure illustrates the use of the _outtext function for printing formatted text.

```
#include <stdio.h>
#include <graph.h>
void main ()
{
char buffer [line width];
_setvideomode ( mode ); /* set mode by adapter */
        .
        .
        .
sprintf (buffer, "Variable Value: %d", variable);
_settextposition (row,column);
_outtext (buffer);
        .
        .
        .
  _setvideomode (_DEFAULTMODE);
}
```

Example:

This program demonstrates the use of the _outtext function. The _wrapon function initially sets the text wrapping feature on, and a line of text is displayed to show the effects of this feature. Then the _wrapon function is used to turn the text wrapping feature off, and another line of text is displayed to demonstrate the effects.

```
#include <stdio.h>
#include <graph.h>
void main ()
{
        /* Initialization */
_setvideomode (_MRES4COLOR);
_setbkcolor (_RED);
        /* Set wrap feature on and
           display text */
_wrapon (_GWRAPON);
_settextposition (3,1);
_outtext ("This line demonstrates how text is wrapped
      to the next line when exceeding a line length");
```

```
                    /* Set wrap feature off and
                       display text */
_wrapon (_GWRAPOFF);
_settextposition (10,1);
_outtext ("This line will not wrap around at the
       end of the line");

                    /* Delay and exit */
_settextposition (24,8);
_outtext ("Press Any Key to Exit");
getch ();
_setvideomode (_DEFAULTMODE);
}
```

_pg_analyzechart

Syntax:

```
short _far _pg_analyzechart(chartenv _far *env, char
          _far * _far *categories, float _far
          *values, short number);
chartenv _far *env;                chart environment
char _far * _far *categories;      category variables
float _far *values;                data values
short number;                      number of values
```

Function:

The _pg_analyzechart function analyzes a single series of data, then fills the selected chart environment with default values for a specified type of chart.

Files to Include:

```
#include <pgchart.h>
```

Compatibility:

DOS

Description:

The _pg_analyzechart function analyzes a single series of data. The chart environment is then filled with default values for the specified chart type. The categories and values arguments are used to calculate all the variables created by the _pg_analyzechart function. Note: All Boolean flags should be set to TRUE prior to calling the _pg_analyzechart function.

Values Returned:

A zero is returned if successful. A nonzero value is returned if the function is unsuccessful.

Related Functions:

```
_pg_defaultchart      :      initializes variables for chart
_pg_initchart         :      initializes chart environment
```

Similar Turbo C++ Functions:

None

Suggested Code Structure and Use:

The _pg_analyzechart function is often used to test the current chart environment prior to displaying the chart. It is used also to fill the current chart evironment with default settings prior to customizing and displaying the chart. The following code structure illustrates the use of the _pg_analyzechart function for single series charts.

```
#include <pgchart.h>
#include <string.h>
#include <graph.h>
float _far values[# of values] = {5.0, ..., 4.0};
char _far *categories[# of values] = {"One", ..., "N"};
void main ()
{
chart env;
int charttest;        /* variable to test chart */
_setvideomode ( mode ); /* set mode */
_pg_initchart (); /* initialize chart environment */
_pg_defaultchart (&env, chart type, chart specs);
             .
             .
             .
charttest = _pg_analyzechart (&env,categories,values,
                              # of values);
if (charttest == 0)
```

```
        _pg_chart (&env, categories, values, # of values);
            .
            .
            .
    _setvideomode (_DEFAULTMODE);   /* reset and exit */
    }
```

Example:

The _pg_analyzechart function is used in the following example to test the current chart environment prior to drawing the chart. The default chart type is a column chart. The midterm grades of ten students are displayed, as shown in figure 9.38.

```
#include <pgchart.h>
#include <graph.h>
#include <stdio.h>
#include <string.h>
#define FALSE 0
#define TRUE 1
float _far values[10] = {87.0, 90.0, 82.0, 98.0, 71.0,
                         84.0, 78.0, 81.0, 74.0, 92.0};
char _far *categories[10]={"John","Jane","Jim","Sally",
                           "Sue","Rick","Kenny","Gary",
                           "Jill","Bob"};
void main ()
{
chartenv env;
int charttest;
_setvideomode (_ERESCOLOR);
    /* Initialize column chart environment */
_pg_initchart ();
_pg_defaultchart (&env, _PG_COLUMNCHART, _PG_PLAINBARS);
    /* Set titles
strcpy (env.maintitle.title, "Midterm Exam Scores");
strcpy (env.xaxis.axistitle.title, "Student");
strcpy (env.yaxis.axistitle.title, "Score");
env.xaxis.autoscale = TRUE;
env.yaxis.autoscale = TRUE;
    /* Test chart */
charttest = _pg_analyzechart(&env,categories,values,10);
    /* Draw chart if test okay */
if (charttest == 0)
        _pg_chart (&env, categories, values, 10);
    /* Delay and exit */
```

```
getch ();
_setvideomode (_DEFAULTMODE);
}
```

Fig. 9.38. Example _pg_analyzechart output.

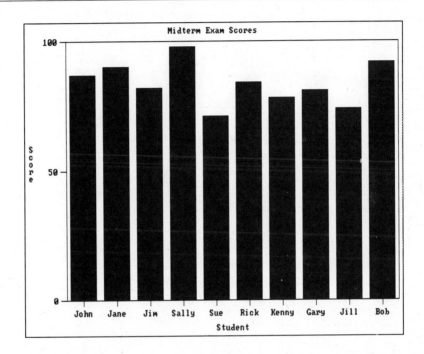

_pg_analyzechartms

Syntax:

```
short _far _pg_analyzechartms(chartenv _far *env, char
    _far * _far *categories, float _far *values,
    short numseries, short num, short arraydim,
    char _far * _far *serieslabels);
chartenv _far *env;                    chart environment
char _far * _far *categories;          category variables
float _far *values;                    data values
short numseries;                       number of series
short num;                             number of data values
short arraydim;                        row dimension
char _far * _far *serieslabels;        labels
```

445

Function:

The `_pg_analyzechartms` function analyzes a multiple series of data and fills the selected chart environment with default values for a multiseries chart of the selected type.

Files to Include:

```
#include <pgchart.h>
```

Compatibility:

DOS

Description:

The `_pg_analyzems` function is used to analyze a multiple series of data. It then fills the selected chart environment with default values for a selected multiseries chart. The `categories` and `values` arguments are used to calculate the variables of the selected chart.

Values Returned:

When successful, a zero is returned; otherwise, a nonzero value is returned.

Related Functions:

```
_pg_initchart        :        initializes the chart environment
```

Similar Turbo C++ Functions:

None

Suggested Code Structure and Use:

The `_pg_analyzechartms` function is often used to test the status of the current multiseries chart prior to drawing. The chart is used to fill the environment with the default settings prior to customizing it. The following code structure demonstrates the use of the `_pg_analyzechartms` function for testing the current environment.

```
#include <graph.h>
#include <string.h>
#include <pgchart.h>
float _far values[# of values] = {2.0, ..., 1.0};
char _far *categories[# of values] = {"One", ..., "N"};
char _far *series[# of series] = {"1",...,"N"};
void main ()
```

```
{
chartenv env;
int charttest;  /* variable for testing */
_setvideomode ( mode ); /* set video mode */
_pg_initchart (); /* initialize chart environment */
_pg_defaultchart (&env, chart type, chart specs);
            .
            .
            .

charttest = _pg_analyzechartms(&env,categories,values,
          # of series, # of values, # of rows, series);
if (charttest == 0)
      _pg_chartms(&env,categories,values,# of series,
                  # of values, # of rows, series);
            .
            .
            .

_setvideomode (_DEFAULTMODE);
}
```

Example:

The following example uses the _pg_analyzechartms function to test the current chart environment before displaying it. If the test is okay (the _pg_analyzechartms function returns a 0), the chart is drawn. See figure 9.39.

```
#include <string.h>
#include <stdio.h>
#include <graph.h>
#include <pgchart.h>
#define TRUE 1
#define FALSE 0
float _far values[20] = {87.0, 90.0, 82.0, 98.0, 71.0,
                         84.0, 78.0, 81.0, 74.0, 92.0,
                         77.0, 84.0, 91.0, 98.0, 77.0,
                         73.0, 83.0, 89.0, 90.0, 78.0};
char _far *students[10] = {"John","Jane","Jim","Sally",
                           "Sue","Rick","Kenny","Gary",
                           "Jill","Bob"};
char _far *test[2] = {"Midterm","Final"};
void main ()
{
chartenv env;
int charttest;
```

```
_setvideomode (_ERESCOLOR);
    /* Initialize column chart environment */
_pg_initchart();
_pg_defaultchart (&env, _PG_COLUMNCHART, _PG_PLAINBARS);
    /* Set titles */
strcpy (env.maintitle.title, "Test Scores");
strcpy (env.xaxis.axistitle.title, "Student");
strcpy (env.yaxis.axistitle.title, "Score");
env.xaxis.autoscale = TRUE;
env.yaxis.autoscale = TRUE;
    /* Test chart */
charttest = _pg_analyzechartms (&env,students,values,
            2,10,10,test);
    /* Draw chart if test okay */
if (charttest == 0)
        _pg_chartms(&env,students,values,2,10,10,test);
    /* Delay and exit */
getch ();
_setvideomode (_DEFAULTMODE);
}
```

Fig. 9.39. Example _pg_analyzechartms output.

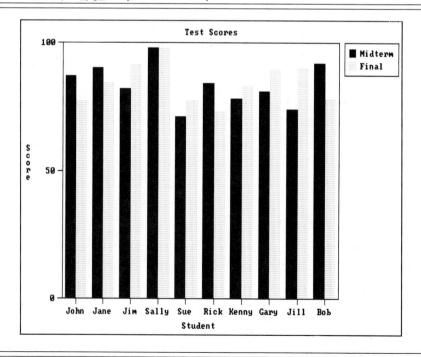

_pg_analyzepie

Syntax:

```
short _far _pg_analyzepie(chartenv _far *env, char _far *
    _far *categories, float _far *values, short _far
    *explode, short num);
chartenv _far *env;              chart environment
char _far * _far *categories;    category variables
float _far *values;              data values
short _far *explode;             explode flag
short num;                       number of data values
```

Function:

The _pg_analyzepie function analyzes a single series of data and fills the pie chart environment with the data contained in the values array.

Files to Include:

```
#include <pgchart.h>
```

Compatibility:

DOS

Description:

The _pg_analyzepie function is used to analyze a single series of data for a pie chart. Then the function fills the chart environment with the data values.

Values Returned:

If successful, a zero is returned; otherwise, a nonzero value is returned.

Related Functions:

```
_pg_chartpie      :      displays the pie chart
```

Similar Turbo C++ Functions:

None

Suggested Code Structure and Use:

The _pg_analyzepie function is often used to test the single series pie chart environment prior to displaying the chart. It is used also to fill the chart environment with the default values prior to customizing the chart. The following code structure illustrates the use of the _pg_analyzepie function to test a single series pie chart.

```
#include <graph.h>
#include <pgchart.h>
#include <string.h>
float _far values[# of values] = {4.0, ..., 2.0};
char _far *categories[# of values] = {"One", ..., "N"};
short _far explode[# of values] = {0, ..., 0};
void main ()
{
chartenv env;
int charttest;
_setvideomode ( mode ) /* set video mode */
_pginitchart (); /* initialize chart environment */
_pg_defaultchart (&env, chart type, chart specs);
          .
          .
          .
charttest = _pg_analyzepie(&env,categories,values,explode,
                           # of values);
if (charttest == 0)
    _pg_chartpie (&env,categories,values,explode,
                  # of values);
          .
          .
          .
_setvideomode (_DEFAULTMODE);
}
```

Example:

The _pg_analyzepie function is used in the following example to test the current pie chart environment. If a zero is returned, the pie chart is displayed on the screen, as shown in figure 9.40.

```
#include <graph.h>
#include <string.h>
#include <stdio.h>
#include <pgchart.h>
#define FALSE 0
#define TRUE 1
float _far values[6] = {35.0, 24.0, 19.0,
                        29.0, 31.0, 21.0};
char _far *categories[6] = {"Jim", "Sue", "Jack",
                            "Mary", "Bob", "Gary"};
short _far explode[6] = {1,0,0,0,0,0};
void main ()
{
chartenv env;
int charttest;
_setvideomode (_ERESCOLOR);
      /* Initialize pie chart environment */
_pg_initchart();
_pg_defaultchart (&env, _PG_PIECHART, _PG_PERCENT);
      /* Set titles */
strcpy (env.maintitle.title, "Sales Report");
      /* Test chart */
charttest = _pg_analyzepie (&env,categories,
                            values,explode,6);
```

```
                         /* Draw chart if test okay */
        if (charttest == 0)
             _pg_chartpie (&env,categories,values,explode,6);
             /* Delay and exit */
        getch ();
        _setvideomode (_DEFAULTMODE);
        }
```

Fig. 9.40. Example _pg_analyzepie output.

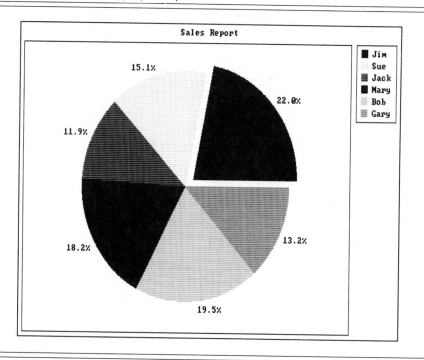

_pg_analyzescatter

Syntax:

```
short _far _pg_analyzescatter(chartenv _far *env, float
       _far *xvalues, float _far *yvalues, short num);
chartenv _far *env;            chart environment
float _far *xvalues;           x-axis data values
float _far *yvalues;           y-axis data values
short num;                     number of data values
```

Function:

The `_pg_analyzescatter` function analyzes a single series of data and fills the single series scatter chart environment.

Files to Include:

```
#include <pgchart.h>
```

Compatibility:

DOS

Description:

The `_pg_analyzescatter` function analyzes a single series of data for a scatter-type chart. The chart environment is then filled with the data points calculated from the x values and y values arguments. The `_pg_analyzescatter` function does not display the chart. Note: All Boolean flags should be set to TRUE before calling this function.

Values Returned:

A zero is returned when successful; otherwise, a nonzero value is returned.

Related Functions:

```
_pg_chartscatter      :  displays the scatter chart
_pg_initchart         :  initializes chart environment
```

Similar Turbo C++ Functions:

None

Suggested Code Structure and Use:

The `_pg_analyzescatter` function is often used to evaluate the scatter diagram environment before displaying the diagram. It is used also to fill the chart environment with default values before customizing the chart. The following code structure demonstrates the use of the `_pg_analyzescatter` function.

```
#include <stdio.h>
#include <string.h>
#include <graph.h>
#include <pgchart.h>

float _far xvalues[# of values] = {28.0, ..., 30.0};
```

```
float _far yvalues[# of values] = {120.0, ..., 58.0};
void main ()
{
chartenv env;
int charttest;
_setvideomode ( mode ); /* set video mode */
_pg_initchart (); /* initialize chart environment */
_pg_defaultchart (&env, _PG_SCATTERCHART, _PG_POINTONLY);
                    .
                    .
                    .
charttest = _pg_analyzescatter (&env,xvalues,
                yvalues,# of values);
if (charttest == 0)
    _pg_chartscatter (&env,xvalues,yvalues,# of values);
                    .
                    .
                    .
_setvideomode (_DEFAULTMODE);
}
```

Example:

The **_pg_analyzescatter** function is used in this example to test the scatter diagram environment before displaying it. If the **_pg_analyzescatter** function returns a zero, the diagram is displayed. See figure 9.41.

```
#include <stdio.h>
#include <string.h>
#include <graph.h>
#include <pgchart.h>
#define TRUE 1
#define FALSE 0
float _far xvalues[15] = { 28.0, 24.0, 16.0, 15.0, 27.0,
                           18.0, 20.0, 19.0, 12.0, 28.0,
                           13.0, 15.0, 29.0, 18.0, 11.0 };
float _far yvalues[15] = { 120.0, 75.0, 93.0, 90.0, 115.0,
                           48.0, 87.0, 95.0, 89.0, 108.0,
                           78.0, 89.0, 93.0, 119.0, 58.0};
void main ()
{
chartenv env;
int charttest;
_setvideomode (_ERESCOLOR);
```

```
      /* Initialize--set chart environment to scatter */
_pg_initchart ();
_pg_defaultchart (&env, _PG_SCATTERCHART, _PG_POINTONLY);
      /* Set titles */
strcpy (env.maintitle.title, "# of Sales vs.
                # of Customers");
strcpy (env.xaxis.axistitle.title, "Number of Sales");
strcpy (env.yaxis.axistitle.title, "Number of Customers");
env.xaxis.autoscale = TRUE;
env.yaxis.autoscale = TRUE;


      /* Test to see if valid */

charttest = _pg_analyzescatter (&env,xvalues,yvalues,15);
      /* Draw scatter diagram */
if (charttest == 0)
      _pg_chartscatter (&env, xvalues, yvalues, 15);
      /* Delay and exit */
getch ();
_setvideomode (_DEFAULTMODE);
}
```

_pg_analyzescatterms

Syntax:

```
short _far _pg_analyzescatterms(chartenv _far *env, float
      _far *xvalues, float _far *yvalues, short
      numseries, short num, short rowdim, char _far
      * _far *serieslabels);
chartenv _far *env;                 chart environment
float _far *xvalues;                x-axis values
float _far *yvalues;                y-axis values
short numseries;                    number of series
short num;                          number of data values
short rowdim;                       row dimension
char _far * _far *serieslabels;     label series
```

Fig. 9.41. Example _pg_analyzescatter output.

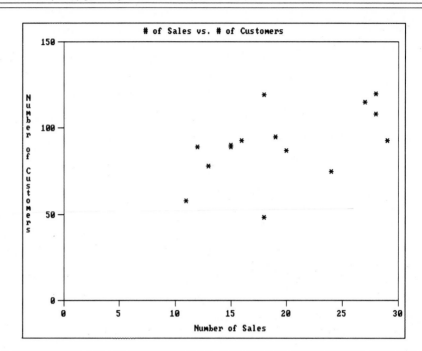

Function:

The **_pg_analyzescatterms** function analyzes a multiple series of data and fills the multiseries scatter chart environment.

Files to Include:

```
#include <pgchart.h>
```

Compatibility:

DOS

Description:

The **_pg_analyzescatterms** function is used to analyze a multiple series of data. After it analyzes the data, it fills the chart environment with the values calculated from the **xvalues** and **yvalues** arguments. This function does not display the chart. Note: All Boolean flags should be set to TRUE before calling this function.

Values Returned:

If successful, the function returns zero; if not successful, the function returns a nonzero value.

Related Functions:

```
_pg_chartscatterms     :  draws the scatter diagram
_pg_initchart          :  intializes the chart environment
```

Similar Turbo C++ Functions:

None

Suggested Code Structure and Use:

The _pg_analyzescatterms function is used to analyze the multiseries scatter diagram environment. This function is often used before displaying the chart to determine whether the environment is valid. It is used also to fill the environment with default values before customizing the chart. The following code structure demonstrates the use of the _pg_analzescatterms function.

```
#include <stdio.h>
#include <string.h>
#include <graph.h>
#include <pgchart.h>
float _far xvalues[# of values] = {28.0, ..., 30.0};
float _far yvalues[# of values] = {120.0, ..., 58.0};
char _far *series[# of series] = {"1", ..., "2"};
void main ()
{
chartenv env;
int charttest;
_setvideomode ( mode );  /* set video mode */
_pg_initchart ();    /* initialize chart environment */
_pg_defaultchart (&env, _PG_SCATTERCHART, _PG_POINTONLY);
env.xaxis.autoscale = TRUE;
env.yaxis.autoscale = TRUE;
          .
          .
          .
charttest = _pg_analyzescatterms(&env,xvalues,yvalues,
            # of series, # of values, row dim, series);
if (charttest == 0)
     _pg_chartscatterms (&env, xvalues, yvalues,
            # of series, # of values, row dim, series);
```

```
                    .
                    .
                    .
_setvideomode (_DEFAULTMODE);
}
```

Example:

This example demonstrates how the _pg_analzescatterms function can be used to evaluate the scatter diagram chart environment. If the _pg_analyzescatterms function returns a zero, the chart is drawn. See figure 9.42.

```
#include <stdio.h>
#include <string.h>
#include <graph.h>
#include <pgchart.h>
#define TRUE 1
#define FALSE 0
float _far xvalues[20] = { 28.0, 24.0, 16.0, 15.0, 27.0,
                           18.0, 20.0, 19.0, 12.0, 28.0,
                           26.0, 19.0, 27.0, 20.0, 14.0,
                           13.0, 15.0, 29.0, 18.0, 11.0 };
float _far yvalues[20] = { 120.0, 75.0, 93.0, 90.0, 115.0,
                           48.0, 87.0, 95.0, 89.0, 108.0,
                           75.0, 57.0, 104.0, 73.0, 99.0,
                           78.0, 89.0, 93.0, 119.0, 58.0};
char _far *store[2] = {"Store 1","Store 2"};
void main ()
{
chartenv env;
int charttest;
_setvideomode (_ERESCOLOR);
     /* Initialize chart--set scatter environment */
_pg_initchart ();
_pg_defaultchart (&env, _PG_SCATTERCHART, _PG_POINTONLY);
     /* Define titles */
strcpy (env.maintitle.title, "# of Sales vs. # of
               Customers");
strcpy (env.xaxis.axistitle.title, "Number of Sales");
strcpy (env.yaxis.axistitle.title, "Number of Customers");

env.xaxis.autoscale = TRUE;
env.yaxis.autoscale = TRUE;
     /* Analyze scatter diagram */
```

```
charttest = _pg_analyzescatterms(&env,xvalues,yvalues,
           2,10,10,store);
    /* Draw chart */
if (charttest == 0)
    _pg_chartscatterms (&env, xvalues, yvalues,
           2, 10, 10, store);
    /* Delay and exit */
getch ();
_setvideomode (_DEFAULTMODE);
}
```

Fig. 9.42. Example _pg_analyzescatterms output.

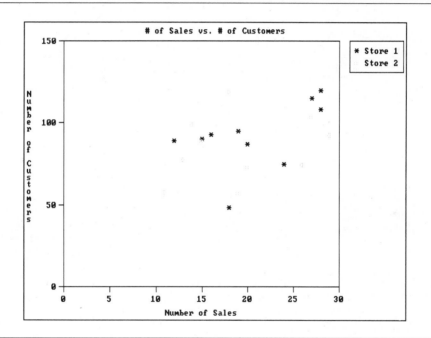

_pg_chart

Syntax:

```
short _far _pg_chart(chartenv _far *env, char _far * _far
       *categories, float _far *values, short num);
chartenv _far *env;                chart environment
```

```
char _far * _far *categories;        category variables
float _far *values;                  data values
short num;                           number of data values
```

Function:

The `_pg_chart` function displays the specified single series chart type.

Files to Include:

```
#include <pgchart.h>
```

Compatibility:

DOS

Description:

The `_pg_chart` function is used to display a single series chart. The `env` variable specifies the type of chart to be displayed. You may select a bar, column, or line chart. The `values` array contains the chart values. The `categories` array contains the labels for the values. The `num` argument specifies the number of data values contained in the data array.

Values Returned:

A zero is returned when successful; a nonzero value is returned when unsuccessful.

Related Functions:

```
_pg_initchart      :       initializes the environment
```

Similar Turbo C++ Functions:

None

Suggested Code Structure and Use:

The `_pg_chart` function is used to display a single series chart. The following code structure illustrates its use.

```
#include <graph.h>
#include <stdio.h>
#include <string.h>
#include <pgchart.h>
```

```
       float _far values[# of values] = {9.0, ..., 8.0};
       char _far *categories[# of values] = {"1", ...,"10"};
       void main ()
       {
       _setvideomode ( mode ); /* set mode */
       _pg_initchart();   /* initialize chart environment */
       _pg_defaultchart (&env,chart type, chart specs);
            .
            .
            .
       _pg_chart (&env,categories,values,# of values);
            .
            .
            .
       _setvideomode (_DEFAULTMODE);   /* reset and exit */
       }
```

Example:

The _pg_chart function is used in the following example to display the defined single series line chart. See figure 9.43.

```
#include <graph.h>
#include <stdio.h>
#include <string.h>
#include <pgchart.h>
#define TRUE 1
#define FALSE 0
float _far values[10] = {9.0, 11.0, 10.0, 9.0, 6.0,
                         10.0, 7.0, 6.0, 8.0, 7.0};
char _far *categories[10] = {"1","2","3","4","5","6",
                          "7","8","9","10"};
void main ()
{
chartenv env;
_setvideomode (_ERESCOLOR);
     /* Initialize line chart environment */
_pg_initchart();
_pg_defaultchart (&env,_PG_LINECHART,_PG_POINTANDLINE);
     /* Set titles */
strcpy (env.maintitle.title, "Gross Sales in Millions");
strcpy (env.xaxis.axistitle.title, "Store Number");
strcpy (env.yaxis.axistitle.title, "$ (Millions)");
env.xaxis.autoscale = TRUE;
```

```
env.yaxis.autoscale = TRUE;
    /* Draw chart */
_pg_chart (&env,categories,values,10);
    /* Delay and exit */
getch ();
_setvideomode (_DEFAULTMODE);
}
```

Fig. 9.43. Example _pg_chart output.

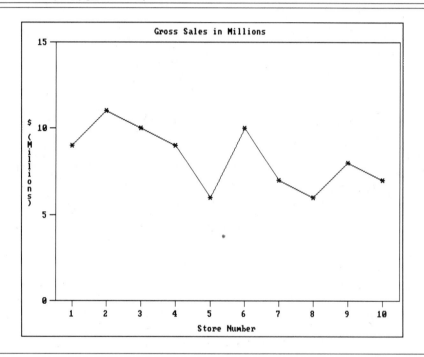

_pg_chartms

Syntax:

```
short _far _pg_chartms(chartenv _far *env, char _far *
      _far *categories, float _far *values, short
      numseries, short num, short arraydim,
      char _far * _far *serieslabels);
chartenv _far *env;                  chart environment
char _far * _far *categories;        category variables
```

```
float _far *values;            data values
short numseries;               number of series
short num;                     number of data values
short arraydim;                row dimension
char _far * _far *serieslabels;    labels for series
```

Function:

The _pg_chartms function displays the specified multiseries chart type.

Files to Include:

```
#include <pgchart.h>
```

Compatibility:

DOS

Description:

The _pg_chartms function is used to display a multiseries chart. The env argument specifies the type of chart to display. This can be a bar, column, or line chart. The num argument specifies the number of data points in each series. Each series must have the same number of data points. All data values are contained in the two-dimensional values array. The arraydim argument identifies the number of rows for the values array declaration. The following limitations must be taken into account when using this function: the maximum number of series is 10, and the arraydim argument must be equal to or larger than the num argument.

Values Returned:

A zero indicates success; a nonzero value indicates failure.

Related Functions:

```
_pg_initchart     :     initializes chart environment
```

Similar Turbo C++ Functions:

None

Suggested Code Structure and Use:

The _pg_chartms function is used to display the described multiseries chart environment. The following code structure illustrates the use of this function.

463

```
#include <graph.h>
#include <stdio.h>
#include <string.h>
#include <pgchart.h>

float _far values[# of values] = {9.0, ..., 10.0};
char _far *categories[# of values] = {"1", ..., "10"};
char _far *series[# of series] = {"1", ..., "2"};
void main ()
{
chartenv env;
_setvideomode ( mode );   /* set video mode */
_pg_initchart();    /* initialize chart environment */
_pg_defaultchart (&env,chart type, chart specs);
                      .
                      .
                      .
_pg_chartms (&env,categories,values,# of series, # of
                 values, # of rows, series);
                      .
                      .
                      .
_setvideomode (_DEFAULTMODE);
}
```

Example:

The _pg_chartms function is used in this example to draw a multiseries line chart. See figure 9.44.

```
#include <graph.h>
#include <stdio.h>
#include <string.h>
#include <pgchart.h>
#define TRUE 1
#define FALSE 0
float _far values[20] =
    {9.0, 11.0, 10.0, 9.0, 6.0, 10.0, 7.0, 6.0, 8.0, 7.0,
     8.0, 10.0, 7.0, 11.0, 6.0, 8.0, 9.0, 8.0, 8.0, 7.0};
char _far *categories[10] = {"1","2","3","4","5","6",
                             "7","8","9","10"};
char _far *year[2] = {"Year 1", "Year 2"};
void main ()
{
```

```
chartenv env;
_setvideomode (_ERESCOLOR);
     /* Initialize line chart environment */
_pg_initchart();
_pg_defaultchart (&env,_PG_LINECHART,_PG_POINTANDLINE);
     /* Set titles */
strcpy (env.maintitle.title, "Gross Sales in Millions");
strcpy (env.xaxis.axistitle.title, "Store Number");
strcpy (env.yaxis.axistitle.title, "$ (Millions)");
env.xaxis.autoscale = TRUE;
env.yaxis.autoscale = TRUE;
     /* Draw chart */
_pg_chartms (&env,categories,values,2,10,10,year);

     /* Delay and exit */
getch ();
_setvideomode (_DEFAULTMODE);
}
```

Fig. 9.44. Example _pg_chartms output.

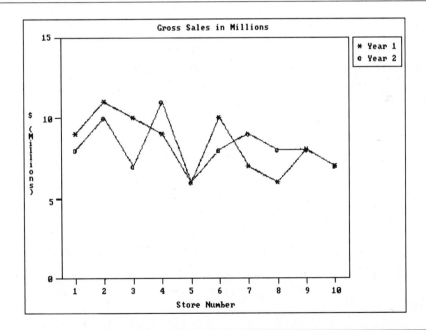

_pg_chartpie

Syntax:

```
short _far _pg_chartpie(chartenv _far *env, char _far *
        _far *categories, float _far *values, short _far
        *explode, short num);
chartenv _far *env;              chart environment
char _far * _far *categories;    category variables
float _far *values;              data values
short _far *explode;             explode flags
short num;                       number of data values
```

Function:

The _pg_chartpie function displays a pie chart from a single series of data.

Files to Include:

```
#include <pgchart.h>
```

Compatibility:

DOS

Description:

The _pg_chartpie function is used to display a single series pie chart. The data for the pie chart is contained in the values array. The categories array contains the labels for the pie chart values. The explode array identifies the pieces of the pie that will be exploded (removed slightly from the pie). A 1 in the explode array indicates that the corresponding piece will be exploded; a 0 indicates that the piece will not be exploded. The explode array should be dimensioned so that its length is greater than or equal to the num argument.

Values Returned:

A zero is returned if successful. A nonzero value is returned if unsuccessful.

Related Functions:

```
_pg_analyzepie        :    analyzes pie chart environment
_pg_initchart         :    initializes chart environment
```

Similar Turbo C++ Functions:

None

Suggested Code Structure and Use:

The _pg_chartpie function is used to display a single series pie chart. The following code structure demonstrates the use of this function.

```
#include <graph.h>
#include <string.h>
#include <stdio.h>
#include <pgchart.h>
float _far values[# of values] = {100.0, ..., 300.0};
char _far *categories[# of values] = {"1", ...,"6"};
short _far explode[# of values] = {0, ..., 0};
void main ()
{
chartenv env;
_setvideomode ( mode );  /* set video mode */
_pg_initchart();  /* initialize chart */
_pg_defaultchart (&env, chart type, chart specs);
          .
          .
          .
_pg_chartpie (&env,categories,values,explode,# of values);
          .
          .
          .
_setvideomode (_DEFAULTMODE);  /* reset and exit */
}
```

Example:

The following example creates a six-wedge pie chart. The _pg_chartpie function is used to display the chart. See figure 9.45.

```
#include <graph.h>
#include <string.h>
#include <stdio.h>
#include <pgchart.h>
#define FALSE 0
#define TRUE 1
float _far values[6] = {100.0, 150.0, 175.0, 50.0,
```

```
                              25.0, 100.0};
   char _far *categories[6] = {"Job 1", "Job 2", "Job 3",
                     "Job 4", "Job 5", "Job 6"};
   short _far explode[6] = {0,0,1,0,0,0};
   void main ()
   {
   chartenv env;
   _setvideomode (_ERESCOLOR);
        /* Initialize pie chart environment */
   _pg_initchart();
   _pg_defaultchart (&env, _PG_PIECHART, _PG_PERCENT);
        /* Set titles */
   strcpy (env.maintitle.title, "Manhour Report");
   strcpy (env.subtitle.title, "Percentage of Total per Job");
        /* Draw chart */
   _pg_chartpie (&env,categories,values,explode,6);
        /* Delay and exit */
   getch ();
   _setvideomode (_DEFAULTMODE);
   }
```

_pg_chartscatter

Syntax:

```
short _far _pg_chartscatter(chartenv _far *env, float
    _far *xvalues, float _far *yvalues, short num);
chartenv _far *env;            chart environment
float _far *xvalues;           x-axis values
float _far *yvalues;           y-axis values
short num;                     number of data values
```

Function:

The _pg_chartscatter function creates a single series scatter chart.

Files to Include:

```
#include <pgchart.h>
```

Fig. 9.45. Example _pg_chartpie output.

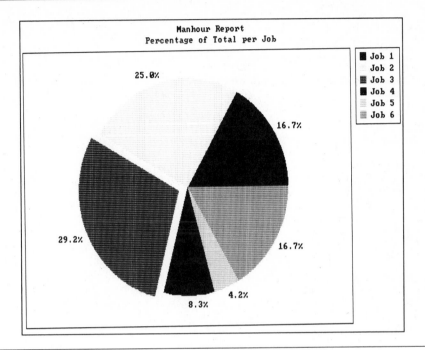

Compatibility:

DOS

Description:

The **_pg_chartscatter** function is used to display a single series scatter diagram. The **xvalues** array contains the data for the x coordinates of the diagram; the **yvalues** array contains the data for the y coordinates. Therefore, the first values in these arrays define the x and y coordinates for the first point. The **num** argument identifies the number of data in the chart.

Values Returned:

A zero indicates success; a nonzero value indicates failure.

Related Functions:

```
_pg_initchart        : initializes chart environment
```

Similar Turbo C++ Functions:

None

Suggested Code Structure and Use:

The _pg_chartscatter function is used to display the scatter diagram environment. The following code structure illustrates the use of the _pg_chartscatter function.

```
#include <stdio.h>
#include <string.h>
#include <graph.h>
#include <pgchart.h>
float _far xvalues[# of values] = {8.0, ..., 5.0};
float _far yvalues[# of values] = {200.0, ..., 800.0};
void main ()
{
chartenv env;
_setvideomode ( mode );  /* set video mode */
_pg_initchart ();  /* initialize chart environment */
_pg_defaultchart (&env, chart type, chart specs);
         .
         .
         .
_pg_chartscatter (&env, xvalues, yvalues, # of values);
         .
         .
         .
_setvideomode (_DEFAULTMODE);  /* reset and exit */
}
```

Example:

The _pg_chartscatter function is used in this example to display a scatter diagram (single series). In this example, the points on the chart are not connected, as shown in figure 9.46.

```
#include <stdio.h>
#include <string.h>
#include <graph.h>
#include <pgchart.h>
#define TRUE 1
#define FALSE 0
float _far xvalues[15] = { 8.0, 2.0, 6.0, 5.0, 7.0,
                           8.0, 0.0, 8.5, 2.0, 8.0,
                           3.0, 5.0, 8.5, 8.0, 1.0 };
```

```
float _far yvalues[15] = { 200.0,560.0,300.0,875.0,100.0,
                           800.0,700.0,500.0,875.0,800.0,
                           800.0,850.0,300.0,875.0,800.0};
void main ()
{
chartenv env;
_setvideomode (_ERESCOLOR);
     /* Initialize scatter chart environment */
_pg_initchart ();
_pg_defaultchart (&env, _PG_SCATTERCHART, _PG_POINTONLY);
     /* Set titles */
strcpy (env.maintitle.title, "# of Returns vs. #
               of Sales");
strcpy (env.xaxis.axistitle.title, "Number of
               Returns (x100)");
strcpy (env.yaxis.axistitle.title, "Number of
               Sales (x100)");
env.xaxis.autoscale = TRUE;
env.yaxis.autoscale = TRUE;
     /* Draw chart */
_pg_chartscatter (&env, xvalues, yvalues, 15);
     /* Delay and exit */
getch ();
_setvideomode (_DEFAULTMODE);
}
```

_pg_chartscatterms

Syntax:

```
short _far _pg_chartscatterms(chartenv _far *env, float
     _far *xvalues, float _far *yvalues, short
     numseries, short num, short rowdim, char _far
     * _far *serieslabels);
chartenv _far *env;                 chart environment
float _far *xvalues;                x-axis values
float _far *yvalues;                y-axis values
short numseries;                    number of series
short num;                          number of data values
short rowdim;                       row dimension
char _far * _far *serieslabels;     labels for series
```

Fig. 9.46. Example _pg_chartscatter output.

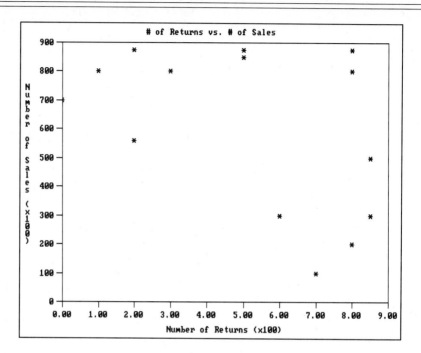

Function:

The **_pg_chartscatterms** function creates a multiseries scatter chart.

Files to Include:

```
#include <pgchart.h>
```

Compatibility:

DOS

Description:

The **_pg_chartscatterms** function is used to display a multiseries scatter diagram. The **xvalues** array contains the data for the x-axis of the diagram; the **yvalues** array contains the data for the y-axis. The data for each series is held in the columns for each array. For example, the first column in the **xvalues** array and the **yvalues** array contains information for the first series, the second column contains information for the second series, and so on. The num argument identifies the number of data in the chart. The numseries argument specifies the number of series. The serieslabels array holds the label names for each series.

Values Returned:

A zero is returned if successful; otherwise, a nonzero value is returned.

Related Functions:

```
_pg_initchart         :   initializes chart environment
_pg_chartscatter      :   display single series scatter charts
```

Similar Turbo C++ Functions:

None

Suggested Code Structure and Use:

The _pg_chartscatterms function is used to display a multiseries scatter diagram. The following example illustrates the use of this function.

```
#include <stdio.h>
#include <string.h>
#include <graph.h>
#include <pgchart.h>
float _far xvalues[# of values]={2800.0, ..., 3000.0};
float _far yvalues[# of values] = {6.0, ..., 5.0};
char _far *series[# of series] = {"1", ..., "2"};
void main ()
{
chartenv env;
_setvideomode ( mode );  /* set mode */
_pg_initchart ();  /* initialize chart environment */
_pg_defaultchart (&env, chart type, chart specs);
          .
          .
          .
_pg_chartscatterms (&env, xvalues, yvalues, # of series,
                    # of values, row dim, series);
          .
          .
          .
_setvideomode (_DEFAULTMODE);  /* reset and exit */
}
```

Example:

The _pg_chartscatterms function is used in this example to display a multiseries scatter diagram. See figure 9.47.

```c
#include <stdio.h>
#include <string.h>
#include <graph.h>
#include <pgchart.h>
#define TRUE 1
#define FALSE 0
float _far xvalues[20]={2800.0,2400.0,1600.0,1500.0,2700.0,
                        1800.0,2000.0,1900.0,1200.0,2800.0,
                        2600.0,1900.0,2700.0,2000.0,1400.0,
                        1300.0,1500.0,2875.0,1800.0,1100.0};
float _far yvalues[20] = { 6.0, 7.0, 8.7, 8.6, 5.0,
                           8.6, 7.0, 8.1, 8.3, 8.9,
                           7.4, 5.0, 4.2, 7.0, 8.2,
                           8.0, 2.4, 3.2, 1.0, 5.0};
char _far *store[2] = {"Plant 1","Plant 2"};
void main ()
{
chartenv env;
_setvideomode (_ERESCOLOR);
    /* Initialize scatter diagram environment */
_pg_initchart ();
_pg_defaultchart (&env, _PG_SCATTERCHART, _PG_POINTONLY);
    /* Set titles */
strcpy (env.maintitle.title, "# Produced vs.
             # of Defects");
strcpy (env.xaxis.axistitle.title, "Number Produced");
strcpy (env.yaxis.axistitle.title, "Number of
             Defects (x10)");
env.xaxis.autoscale = TRUE;
env.yaxis.autoscale = TRUE;

    /* Draw chart */
_pg_chartscatterms (&env, xvalues, yvalues,
                 2, 10, 10, store);
    /* Delay and exit */
getch ();
_setvideomode (_DEFAULTMODE);
}
```

Fig. 9.47. Example _pg_chartscatterms output.

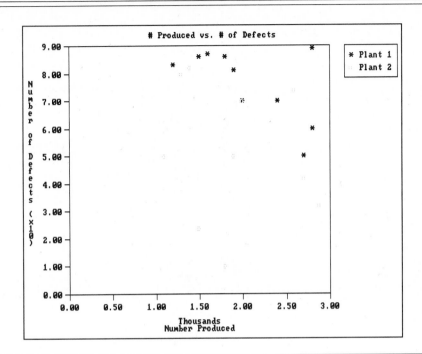

_pg_defaultchart

Syntax:

```
short _far _pg_defaultchart(chartenv _far *env, short
        charttype, short chartstyle);
chartenv _far *env;        chart environment
short charttype;           chart type
short chartstyle;          chart style
```

Function:

The **_pg_defaultchart** function initializes the variables required by the specified chart type.

Files to Include:

```
#include <pgchart.h>
```

Compatibility:

DOS

Description:

The `_pg_defaultchart` function is used to initialize the variables needed by the chart type specified in the `charttype` argument. The valid chart types and styles are shown in table 9.14. Because the title fields of the chart environment are cleared when the `_pg_defaultchart` function is called, titles should be reset after calling this function.

Table 9.14. *Presentation graphics chart types and styles.*

Constant	Type	Meaning
Bar chart types		
_PG_BARCHART	_PG_PLAINBARS	Side-by-side bars
	_PG_STACKEDBARS	Stacked bars
Column chart types		
_PG_COLUMNCHART	_PG_PLAINBARS	Side-by-side bars
	_PG_STACKEDBARS	Stacked bars
Line chart types		
_PG_LINECHART	_PG_POINTANDLINE	Points with lines
	_PG_POINTONLY	Points only
Pie chart types		
_PG_PIE_CHART	_PG_PERCENT	With percentages
	_PG_NOPERCENT	Without percentages
Scatter diagram types		
_PG_SCATTERCHART	_PG_POINTANDLINE	Points with lines
	_PG_POINTONLY	Points only

Values Returned:

A zero is returned when successful. A nonzero value indicates an error.

Related Functions:

```
_pg_initchart      :      initializes chart environment
```

Similar Turbo C++ Functions:

None

Suggested Code Structure and Use:

The _pg_defaultchart function is used anytime the chart environment is used. This function describes the type of chart to analyze and display. The following code structure demonstrates the use of this function.

```
#include <pgchart.h>
#include <graph.h>
#include <stdio.h>
#include <string.h>
float _far values[# of values] = {87.0, ..., 92.0};
char _far *categories[# of values] = {"John", ..., "Bob"};
void main ()
{
chartenv env;
_setvideomode ( mode );   /* set mode */
_pg_initchart ();   /* initialize chart evironment */
_pg_defaultchart (&env, chart type, chart specs);
          .
          .
          .
_pg_chart (&env, categories, values, # of values);
          .
          .
          .
_setvideomode (_DEFAULTMODE);   /* reset and exit */
}
```

Example:

The _pg_defaultchart function is used in the following example to set the default chart type to a column chart with plain bars. See figure 9.48.

```
#include <pgchart.h>
#include <graph.h>
#include <stdio.h>
#include <string.h>
#define FALSE 0
#define TRUE 1
float _far values[10] = {87.0, 90.0, 82.0, 98.0, 71.0,
                         84.0, 78.0, 81.0, 74.0, 92.0};
```

```
              char _far *categories[10] = {"John","Jane","Jim","Sally",
                                "Sue","Rick","Kenny","Gary",
                                "Jill","Bob"};
void main ()
{
chartenv env;
_setvideomode (_ERESCOLOR);
      /* Initialize column chart environment */
_pg_initchart ();
_pg_defaultchart (&env, _PG_COLUMNCHART, _PG_PLAINBARS);
      /* Set titles */
strcpy (env.maintitle.title, "Sales Commission ($1000's)");
strcpy (env.xaxis.axistitle.title, "Salesperson");
strcpy (env.yaxis.axistitle.title,"Total Sales Commissions");
env.xaxis.autoscale = TRUE;
env.yaxis.autoscale = TRUE;
      /* Draw chart */
_pg_chart (&env, categories, values, 10);

      /* Delay and exit */
getch ();
_setvideomode (_DEFAULTMODE);
}
```

_pg_getchardef

Syntax:

```
short _far _pg_getchardef(short charnum, unsigned char
                   _far  *chardef);
short charnum;               ASCII number
unsigned char _far *chardef;  8x8 bit map
```

Function:

The _pg_getchardef function gets the 8-by-8 pixel pattern for a specified ASCII number.

Files to Include:

```
#include <pgchart.h>
```

Fig. 9.48. Example _pg_defaultchart output.

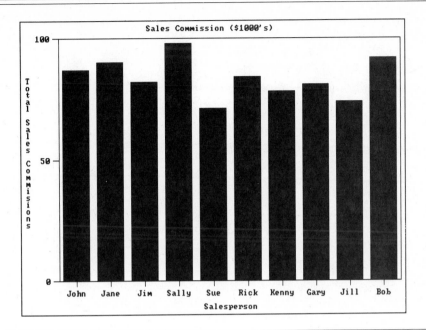

Compatibility:

DOS

Description:

The **_pg_getchardef** function retrieves the pixel pattern for an ASCII character. The **charnum** argument specifies the ASCII character to evaluate. The 8x8 bit pattern is returned in the **chardef** array. The returned bit pattern is for the default font used in only the chart environment. The current registered font for use with font text is not used. This function should be used in only the chart environment.

Values Returned:

A successful function call returns a zero; an unsuccessful call returns a nonzero value.

Related Functions:

```
_pg_setchardef    :    sets character definition
_pg_initchart     :    initializes chart environment
```

Similar Turbo C++ Functions:

None

Suggested Code Structure and Use:

The _pg_getchardef function is often used to retrieve the current bit pattern for an ASCII character before altering it. By doing this, the bit pattern can be reset when exiting the program or function. The following code structure illustrates this use of the _pg_getchardef function.

```
#include <graph.h>
#include <string.h>
#include <stdio.h>
#include <pgchart.h>
float _far values[6] = {100.0,150.0,175.0,50.0,25.0,100.0};
char _far *categories[6] = {"Job 1", "Job 2", "Job 3",
                            "Job 4", "Job 5", "Job 6"};
short _far explode[6] = {0,0,1,0,0,0};
void main ()
{
chartenv env;
unsigned char bitmap[8];
_setvideomode ( mode );
_pg_initchart();   /* initialize chart environment */
_pg_defaultchart (&env, chart type, chart specs);
            .
            .
            .
_pg_chartpie (&env,categories,values,explode,6);
_pg_getchardef (ASCII #,bitmap);   /* save bit map */
_pg_setchardef (ASCII #, new bit map); /* set new bit map */
            .
            .
            .
_pg_setchardef (ASCII #,bitmap);/*reset to old bit pattern*/
_setvideomode (_DEFAULTMODE); /* reset and exit */
}
```

Example:

The following example uses the _pg_getchardef function to retrieve the bit map of ASCII character 30. Figure 9.45 shows the exploded pie chart created by the listing; note the message on the right side of the figure.

```
#include <graph.h>
#include <string.h>
#include <stdio.h>
#include <pgchart.h>
#define FALSE 0
#define TRUE 1
float _far values[6] = {100.0,150.0,175.0,50.0,25.0,100.0};
char _far *categories[6] = {"Job 1", "Job 2", "Job 3",
                            "Job 4", "Job 5", "Job 6"};
short _far explode[6] = {0,0,1,0,0,0};
void main ()
{
chartenv env;
unsigned char bitmap[8];
_setvideomode (_ERESCOLOR);
     /* Initialize pie chart environment */
_pg_initchart();
_pg_defaultchart (&env, _PG_PIECHART, _PG_PERCENT);
     /* Set titles */
strcpy (env.maintitle.title, "Manhour Report");
strcpy (env.subtitle.title, "Percentage of Total per Job");
     /* Draw chart */
_pg_chartpie (&env,categories,values,explode,6);
     /* If bit map retrieved successfully,
        display message */
if (_pg_getchardef(30,bitmap) == 0)
     _pg_vlabelchart(&env,610,155,16,"Bit Map Retrieved");
     /* Delay and exit */
getch ();
_setvideomode (_DEFAULTMODE);
}
```

pg_getpalette

Syntax:

```
short _far _getpalette(paletteentry _far *palette);
paletteentry _far *palette;          palette structure
```

Function:

The _pg_getpalette function gets the current palette colors, line styles, fill patterns, and plot characters for all palettes.

Fig. 9.49. Example _pg_getchardef output.

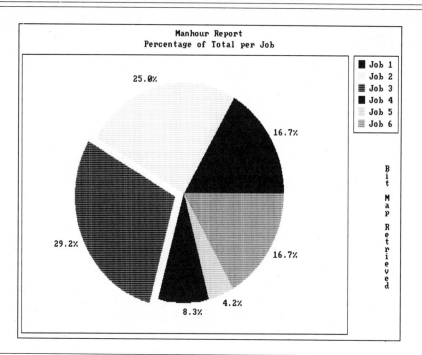

Files to Include:

```
#include <pgchart.h>
```

Compatibility:

DOS

Description:

The **_pg_getpalette** function retrieves the current palette colors, line styles, fill patterns, and characters for all palettes in the chart environment. This function should be used in only the chart environment.

Values Returned:

A zero is returned if successful. If the current palettes have not been initialized, the **_BADSCREENMODE** argument is returned.

Related Functions:

_pg_setpalette   :   sets the current palette for chart
                              environment

_pg_initchart   :   initializes chart environment

Similar Turbo C++ Functions:

None

Suggested Code Structure and Use:

The _pg_getpalette function returns the current palette features of the chart environment. This function is often used to load the palette features into a structure of type palettetype so that the features can be modified. These features are then made current through use of the _pg_setpalette function. The following code structure illustrates the use of the _pg_getpalette function.

```
#include <string.h>
#include <stdio.h>
#include <graph.h>
#include <pgchart.h>
float _far values[# of values] = {87.0, ..., 82.0};
char _far *categories[# of values] = {"John", ...", "Bob"};
char _far *series[# of series] = {"Midterm", ..., "Final"};
palettetype pal;
void main ()
{
chartenv env;
_setvideomode ( mode );  /* set video mode */
_pg_initchart();  /* initialize chart environment */
_pg_defaultchart (&env, chart type, chart specs);
        .
        .
        .
_pg_getpalette (pal); /* get palette features */
        .
        .
        .
     { change palette features }
        .
        .
        .
_pg_setpalette (pal);  /* set palette changes */
_pg_chartms(&env,categories,values,# of series, # of values,
```

```
                              row dim, series);
_pg_resetpalette();    /* reset palette */
_setvideomode (_DEFAULTMODE);   /* reset and exit */
}
```

Example:

The _pg_getpalette function is used in the following example to demonstrate how the palette can be changed. In this example, the first and second palette colors and line styles are modified. The chart is then drawn (yellow and green are the primary colors). The palette is reset before exiting.

```
#include <string.h>
#include <stdio.h>
#include <graph.h>
#include <pgchart.h>
#define TRUE 1
#define FALSE 0
float _far values[20] = {87.0, 90.0, 82.0, 98.0, 71.0,
                         84.0, 78.0, 81.0, 74.0, 92.0,
                         77.0, 84.0, 91.0, 98.0, 77.0,
                         73.0, 83.0, 89.0, 90.0, 78.0};
char _far *students[10] = {"John","Jane","Jim","Sally",
                           "Sue","Rick","Kenny","Gary",
                           "Jill","Bob"};
char _far *test[2] = {"Midterm","Final"};
palettetype pal;
void main ()
{
chartenv env;
_setvideomode (_ERESCOLOR);
     /* Initialize column chart environment */
_pg_initchart();
_pg_defaultchart (&env, _PG_COLUMNCHART, _PG_PLAINBARS);
     /* Set titles */
strcpy (env.maintitle.title, "Test Scores");
strcpy (env.xaxis.axistitle.title, "Student");
strcpy (env.yaxis.axistitle.title, "Score");

env.xaxis.autoscale = TRUE;
env.yaxis.autoscale = TRUE;
     /* Change palette */
_pg_getpalette (pal);
```

```
pal[1].color = 2;
pal[2].color = 14;
pal[1].style = 0xcccc;
pal[2].style = 0x3333;
_pg_setpalette (pal);
      /* Draw chart */
_pg_chartms(&env,students,values,2,10,10,test);
      /* Reset and exit */
_pg_resetpalette();
getch ();
_setvideomode (_DEFAULTMODE);
}
```

_pg_getstyleset

Syntax:

```
void _far _pg_getstyleset(unsigned short _far *styleset);
unsigned short _far *styleset;    current style set
```

Function:

The _pg_getstyleset function is used to retrieve the contents of the current style set.

Files to Include:

```
#include <pgchart.h>
```

Compatibility:

DOS

Description:

The _pg_getstyleset function retrieves the current style set. The style set is a global set of line styles used for borders, grids, and data connectors in the chart environment.

Values Returned:

There is no return value.

Related Functions:

```
_pg_setstyleset      :       set the style set
_pg_initchart        :       intialize chart environment
```

Similar Turbo C++ Functions:

None

Suggested Code Structure and Use:

The _pg_getstyleset function is used to retrieve the current style set before modifying it. The following code structure illustrates how the style set can be retrieved and modified. Note that the _pg_getstyleset and _pg_setstyleset functions are used before the _pg_defaultchart function is called.

```c
#include <string.h>
#include <stdio.h>
#include <graph.h>
#include <pgchart.h>
float _far values[# of values] = {87.0, ..., 82.0};
char _far *categories[# of values] = {"John", ..., "Bob"};
char _far *series[# of series] = {"Midterm", ..., "Final"};
styleset styles;
void main ()
{
chartenv env;
_setvideomode ( mode ); /* set video mode */
_pg_initchart();  /* initialize chart environment */
_pg_getstyleset (styles);  /* get style set */
styles[1] = 0x1111;        /* modify style set */
styles[2] = 0xEEEE;
_pg_setstyleset(styles);    /* set style set  */
_pg_defaultchart (&env, char type, chart specs);
              .
              .
              .

_pg_chartms(&env,categories,values,# of series,
            # of values, row dim, series);
              .
              .
              .

_pg_resetstyleset();             /* reset and exit */
_setvideomode (_DEFAULTMODE);
}
```

Example:

The following example uses the _pg_getstyleset function to retrieve the current style set prior to modifying it. The first and second line styles are modified, and the chart is drawn with these new line styles. The style set is reset before exiting.

```c
#include <string.h>
#include <stdio.h>
#include <graph.h>
#include <pgchart.h>
#define TRUE 1
#define FALSE 0
float _far values[20] = {87.0, 90.0, 82.0, 98.0, 71.0,
                         84.0, 78.0, 81.0, 74.0, 92.0,
                         77.0, 84.0, 91.0, 98.0, 77.0,
                         73.0, 83.0, 89.0, 90.0, 78.0};
char _far *students[10] = {"John","Jane","Jim","Sally",
                           "Sue","Rick","Kenny","Gary",
                           "Jill","Bob"};
char _far *test[2] = {"Midterm","Final"};
styleset styles;
void main ()
{
chartenv env;
_setvideomode (_ERESCOLOR);
_pg_initchart();
    /* Change style set */
_pg_getstyleset (styles);
styles[1] = 0x1111;
styles[2] = 0xEEEE;
_pg_setstyleset(styles);
_pg_defaultchart (&env, _PG_COLUMNCHART, _PG_PLAINBARS);
    /* Set titles */
strcpy (env.maintitle.title, "Test Scores");
strcpy (env.xaxis.axistitle.title, "Student");
strcpy (env.yaxis.axistitle.title, "Score");
env.xaxis.autoscale = TRUE;
env.yaxis.autoscale = TRUE;
    /* Draw chart */
_pg_chartms(&env,students,values,2,10,10,test);
    /* Delay and exit */
getch ();
_pg_resetstyleset();
_setvideomode (_DEFAULTMODE);
}
```

_pg_hlabelchart

Syntax:

```
short _far _pg_hlabelchart(chartenv _far *env, short x,
     short y, short color, char _far *label);
chartenv _far *env;                 chart environment
short x;                            x-coordinate
short y;                            y-coordinate
short color;                        text color
char _far *label;                   text label
```

Function:

The `_pg_hlabelchart` function is used to display horizontal text on the screen.

Files to Include:

```
#include <pgchart.h>
```

Compatibility:

DOS

Description:

The `_pg_hlabelchart` displays horizontal text in the chart environment. The x and y coordinates identify the starting points of the text string. These coordinates are specified relative to the upper left corner of the chart window. The text color is set by the `color` argument. The `label` argument identifies the text to be displayed.

Values Returned:

A zero indicates success; a nonzero value indicates failure.

Related Functions:

```
_pg_vlabelchart       :       display vertical text
_pg_initchart         :       intialize chart environment
```

Similar Turbo C++ Functions:

None

Suggested Code Structure and Use:

The _pg_hlabelchart function is used to display horizontal text on the chart. The _pg_hlabelchart function should be called after the chart is displayed on the screen. The following code structure demonstrates the use of this function.

```
#include <string.h>
#include <stdio.h>
#include <graph.h>
#include <pgchart.h>
float _far values[# of values] = {87.0, ..., 82.0};
char _far *categories[# of values] = {"John", ..., "Bob"};
char _far *series[# of series] = {"Midterm", ..., "Final"};
void main ()
{
chartenv env;
_setvideomode ( mode );  /* set video mode */
_pg_initchart();  /* initialize chart environment */
_pg_defaultchart (&env, chart type, chart specs);
          .
          .
          .
_pg_chartms(&env,categories,values,# of series,
          # of values, row dim, series);
          .
          .
          .
_pg_hlabelchart (&env,x,y,color, "Text Message");
          .
          .
          .
_setvideomode (_DEFAULTMODE);
}
```

Example:

The _pg_hlabelchart function is used in this example to display the message "Good Job! You All Passed" on the displayed chart. See figure 9.50.

```
#include <string.h>
#include <stdio.h>
#include <graph.h>
#include <pgchart.h>
#define TRUE 1
#define FALSE 0
```

```
float _far values[20] = {87.0, 90.0, 82.0, 98.0, 71.0,
                         84.0, 78.0, 81.0, 74.0, 92.0,
                         77.0, 84.0, 91.0, 98.0, 77.0,
                         73.0, 83.0, 89.0, 90.0, 78.0};
char _far *students[10] = {"John","Jane","Jim","Sally",
                           "Sue","Rick","Kenny","Gary",
                           "Jill","Bob"};
char _far *test[2] = {"Midterm","Final"};
void main ()
{
chartenv env;
_setvideomode (_ERESCOLOR);
    /* Initialize column chart */
_pg_initchart();
_pg_defaultchart (&env, _PG_COLUMNCHART, _PG_PLAINBARS);
    /* Set titles */
strcpy (env.maintitle.title, "Test Scores");
strcpy (env.xaxis.axistitle.title, "Student");
strcpy (env.yaxis.axistitle.title, "Score");
env.xaxis.autoscale = TRUE;
env.yaxis.autoscale = TRUE;
    /* Draw chart */
_pg_chartms(&env,students,values,2,10,10,test);
    /* Draw message in lower left corner */
_pg_hlabelchart (&env,20,335,16,"Good Job! You
                All Passed");
    /* Delay and exit */
getch ();
_setvideomode (_DEFAULTMODE);
}
```

_pg_initchart

Syntax:

```
short _far _pg_initchart(void);
```

Function:

The _pg_initchart function initializes the presentation graphics package.

Fig. 9.50. Example _pg_hlabelchart output.

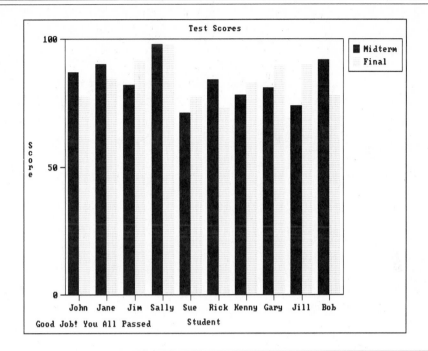

Files to Include:

```
#include <pgchart.h>
```

Compatibility:

DOS

Description:

The **_pg_initchart** function intializes the color pool, style pool, style set, palette modes, and font definitions in the presentation graphics package. This function is used with all programs that use the presentation graphics functions. This function should be used only after a graphics mode has been set and before other presentation graphics functions are called.

Values Returned:

A zero is returned if successful; otherwise, a nonzero value is returned.

Related Functions:

```
_pg_defaultchart        :       define default chart environment
```

Similar Turbo C++ Functions:

None

Suggested Code Structure and Use:

The _pg_initchart function is used to initialize the chart environment. It is used every time a chart will be displayed. The following code structure demonstrates the use of this function.

```c
#include <pgchart.h>
#include <graph.h>
#include <stdio.h>
#include <string.h>
float _far values[# of values] = {9.0, ..., 6.0};
char _far *categories[# of values] = {"1", ..., "20"};
void main ()
{
chartenv env;
_setvideomode ( mode );  /* set video mode */
_pg_initchart ();  /* initialize chart environment */
_pg_defaultchart (&env, chart type, chart specs);
            .
            .
            .
_pg_chart (&env, categories, values, # of values);
            .
            .
            .
_setvideomode (_DEFAULTMODE);  /* reset and exit */
}
```

Example:

The _pg_initchart function is used in this example to initialize the chart environment. A single series bar chart is drawn, as shown in figure 9.51.

```c
#include <pgchart.h>
#include <graph.h>
#include <stdio.h>
#include <string.h>
```

```
#define FALSE 0
#define TRUE 1
float _far values[20] = {9.0, 12.0, 6.0, 18.0, 13.0,
                         10.0, 14.0, 17.0, 8.0, 9.0,
                         11.0, 13.0, 9.0, 4.0, 7.0,
                         9.0, 11.0, 12.0, 7.0, 9.0};
char _far *categories[20] = {"1","2","3","4","5","6",
                "7","8","9","10","11","12","13","14",
                "15","16","17","18","19","20"};
void main ()
{
chartenv env;
_setvideomode (_ERESCOLOR);
    /* Initialize bar chart environment */
_pg_initchart ();
_pg_defaultchart (&env, _PG_BARCHART, _PG_PLAINBARS);
    /* Set titles */
strcpy (env.maintitle.title, "Cars Sold During
            20 Day Sale");
strcpy (env.xaxis.axistitle.title, "Cars Sold");
strcpy (env.yaxis.axistitle.title, "Day");
env.xaxis.autoscale = TRUE;
env.yaxis.autoscale = TRUE;
    /* Draw chart */
_pg_chart (&env, categories, values, 20);
    /* Delay and exit */
getch ();
_setvideomode (_DEFAULTMODE);
}
```

_pg_resetpalette

Syntax:

```
short _far _pg_resetpalette(void);
```

Function:

The _pg_resetpalette function returns all palette colors, line styles, fill patterns, and plot characters to their default values.

Fig. 9.51. Example _pg_initchart output.

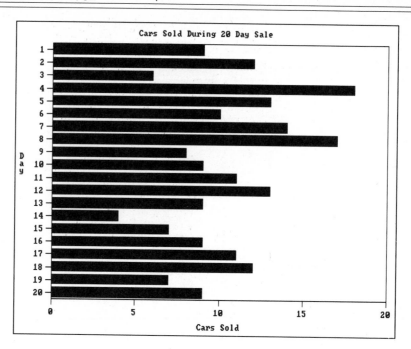

Files to Include:

```
#include <pgchart.h>
```

Compatibility:

DOS

Description:

The _pg_resetpalette function returns the palette colors, line styles, fill patterns, and plot characters to their default values given the current video mode in use. The presentation graphics palette used by this function is not the same palette used by the _setcolor function and other low-level graphics functions. The presentation graphics palette is used only for presentation graphics routines.

Values Returned:

A zero is returned if successful. If the screen mode is not valid, the _BADSCREENMODE argument is returned.

Related Functions:

```
_pg_setpalette      :  sets the chart environment palette
_pg_getpalette      :  gets the chart palette settings
```

Similar Turbo C++ Functions:

None

Suggested Code Structure and Use:

The _pg_resetpalette function is used to set all chart palette values to the default palette. Whenever the palette is modified, the _pg_resetpalette function should be called before exiting the function or program. The following code structure illustrates this use of the _pg_resetpalette function.

```
#include <string.h>
#include <stdio.h>
#include <graph.h>
#include <pgchart.h>
float _far values[# of values] = {87.0, ..., 78.0};
char _far *categories[# of values] = {"John", ..., "Bob"};
char _far *series[# of series] = {"Midterm", ..., "Final"};
palettetype pal;
void main ()
{
chartenv env;
_setvideomode ( mode ); /* set video mode */
_pg_initchart(); /* initialize chart environment */
_pg_defaultchart (&env, chart type, chart specs);
            .
            .
            .
_pg_getpalette (pal);      /* get, change, and set palette */
pal[1].color = 2;
pal[2].color = 14;
_pg_setpalette (pal);
            .
            .
            .
_pg_chartms(&env,categories,values,# of series,# of values,
```

495

```
                         row dim, series);
              .
              .
              .
_pg_resetpalette();                    /* reset and exit */
_setvideomode (_DEFAULTMODE);
}
```

Example:

This example modifies the chart palette. The _pg_resetpalette function is used to reset the palette to its default settings prior to exiting.

```
#include <string.h>
#include <stdio.h>
#include <graph.h>
#include <pgchart.h>
#define TRUE 1
#define FALSE 0
float _far values[20] = {87.0, 90.0, 82.0, 98.0, 71.0,
                         84.0, 78.0, 81.0, 74.0, 92.0,
                         77.0, 84.0, 91.0, 98.0, 77.0,
                         73.0, 83.0, 89.0, 90.0, 78.0};
char _far *students[10] = {"John","Jane","Jim","Sally",
                           "Sue","Rick","Kenny","Gary",
                           "Jill","Bob"};
char _far *test[2] = {"Midterm","Final"};
palettetype pal;
void main ()
{
chartenv env;
_setvideomode (_ERESCOLOR);
     /* Initialize column chart environment */
_pg_initchart();
_pg_defaultchart (&env, _PG_COLUMNCHART, _PG_PLAINBARS);
     /* Set titles */
strcpy (env.maintitle.title, "Test Scores");
strcpy (env.xaxis.axistitle.title, "Student");
strcpy (env.yaxis.axistitle.title, "Score");
env.xaxis.autoscale = TRUE;
env.yaxis.autoscale = TRUE;
     /* Change palette */
_pg_getpalette (pal);
pal[1].color = 2;
```

```
pal[2].color = 14;
pal[1].style = 0xcccc;
pal[2].style = 0x3333;
_pg_setpalette (pal);
     /* Draw chart */
_pg_chartms(&env,students,values,2,10,10,test);
     /* Reset and exit */
_pg_resetpalette();
getch ();
_setvideomode (_DEFAULTMODE);
}
```

_pg_resetstyleset

Syntax:

```
void _far _pg_resetstyleset(void);
```

Function:

The _pg_resetstyleset function resets the style set to its default values.

Files to Include:

```
#include <pgchart.h>
```

Compatibility:

DOS

Description:

The _pg_resetstyleset function returns the style set to its default values for the current screen mode. The style set is a set of global line styles used for borders, grids, and data connectors in the chart environment.

Values Returned:

There is no return value.

Related Functions:

```
_pg_setstyleset      :      set chart style set
_pg_initchart        :      initializes chart environment
```

Similar Turbo C++ Functions:

None

Suggested Code Structure and Use:

The `_pg_resetstyleset` function is used to reset the modified style set to its original default values. This function should be used before exiting the program or function. The following code structure illustrates the use of this function.

```c
#include <string.h>
#include <stdio.h>
#include <graph.h>
#include <pgchart.h>
float _far values[# of values] = {87.0, ..., 82.0};
char _far *categories[# of values] = {"John", ..., Bob"};
char _far *series[# of series] = {"Midterm", ..., "Final"};
styleset styles;
void main ()
{
chartenv env;
_setvideomode ( mode );  /* set video mode */
_pg_initchart();  /*  initialize chart environment  */
_pg_getstyleset (styles);  /* get, modify, and set */
styles[1] = 0x1111;          /*   style set */
styles[2] = 0xEEEE;
_pg_setstyleset(styles);
_pg_defaultchart (&env, _PG_COLUMNCHART, _PG_PLAINBARS);
             .
             .
             .
_pg_chartms(&env,categories,values,# of series,
         # of values, row dim, series);
             .
             .
             .
_pg_resetstyleset();   /* reset and exit */
_setvideomode (_DEFAULTMODE);
}
```

Example:

The _pg_resetstyleset function is used in this example to reset the altered style set values to the default. See figure 9.52. It is a good idea to reset style set values before exiting the function that modified them.

```c
#include <string.h>
#include <stdio.h>
#include <graph.h>
#include <pgchart.h>
#define TRUE 1
#define FALSE 0
float _far values[20] = {87.0, 90.0, 82.0, 98.0, 71.0,
                         84.0, 78.0, 81.0, 74.0, 92.0,
                         77.0, 84.0, 91.0, 98.0, 77.0,
                         73.0, 83.0, 89.0, 90.0, 78.0};
char _far *students[10] = {"John","Jane","Jim","Sally",
                           "Sue","Rick","Kenny","Gary",
                           "Jill","Bob"};
char _far *test[2] = {"Midterm","Final"};
styleset styles;
void main ()
{
chartenv env;
_setvideomode (_ERESCOLOR);
_pg_initchart();
     /* Change style set */
_pg_getstyleset (styles);
styles[1] = 0x1111;
styles[2] = 0xEEEE;
_pg_setstyleset(styles);
_pg_defaultchart (&env, _PG_COLUMNCHART, _PG_PLAINBARS);
     /* Set titles */
strcpy (env.maintitle.title, "Test Scores");
strcpy (env.xaxis.axistitle.title, "Student");
strcpy (env.yaxis.axistitle.title, "Score");
env.xaxis.autoscale = TRUE;
env.yaxis.autoscale = TRUE;
     /* Draw chart */
_pg_chartms(&env,students,values,2,10,10,test);
     /* Reset and exit */
getch ();
_pg_resetstyleset();
_setvideomode (_DEFAULTMODE);
}
```

Fig. 9.52.   Example _pg_resetstyleset output.

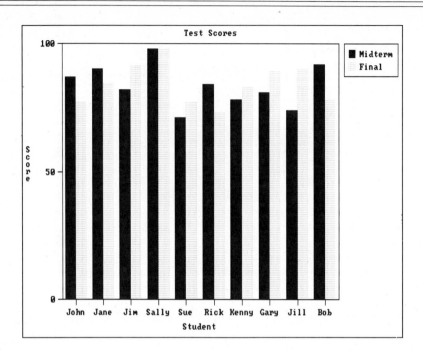

_pg_setchardef

Syntax:

```
short _far _pg_setchardef(short charnum, unsigned char
    _far *chardef);
short charnum;                          ASCII number
unsigned char _far *chardef;            8x8 bit map
```

Function:

The **_pg_setchardef** function is used to define the 8-by-8 bit pattern for the specified ASCII number.

Files to Include:

```
#include <pgchart.h>
```

Compatibility:

DOS

Description:

The _pg_setchardef function defines the 8-by-8 bit pattern used for the ASCII character specified by the charnum argument. The chardef array stores the 8-by-8 bit character pattern. The registered fonts are not altered by this function. Only the raster fonts used by the presentation graphics library are affected.

Values Returned:

A zero is returned if there were no errors. A nonzero value is returned if there was an error.

Related Functions:

```
_pg_getchardef      :      gets the character bit map
_pg_initchart       :      initializes chart environment
```

Similar Turbo C++ Functions:

None

Suggested Code Structure and Use:

The _pg_setchardef function is used to redefine the 8-by-8 bit pattern for a given ASCII character. The following code structure illustrates the use of the _pg_setchardef function.

```
#include <graph.h>
#include <string.h>
#include <stdio.h>
#include <pgchart.h>
float _far values[# of values] = {100.0, ..., 100.0};
char _far *categories[# of values] = {"1", ..., "6"};
short _far explode[# of values] = {0, ..., 0};
void main ()
{
chartenv env;
unsigned char bitmap[8]={0x--,0x--,0x--,0x--,
                         0x--,0x--,0x--,0x--};
_setvideomode ( mode );  /* set video mode */
_pg_initchart();  /* initialize chart environment */
_pg_defaultchart (&env, chart type, chart specs);
            .
            .
            .
```

```
_pg_chartpie (&env,categories,values,explode,# of values);
_pg_setchardef (ASCII #, bitmap);
              .
              .
              .
      { use new character }
              .
              .

_setvideomode (_DEFAULTMODE); /* reset and exit */
}
```

Example:

The _pg_setchardef function is used in this example to change the character 0 to a solid
8-by-8 bit pattern. Then the character is displayed on the right side of the screen.

```
#include <graph.h>
#include <string.h>
#include <stdio.h>
#include <pgchart.h>
#define FALSE 0
#define TRUE 1
float _far values[6] = {100.0, 150.0, 175.0,
                        50.0, 25.0, 100.0};
char _far *categories[6] = {"Job 1", "Job 2", "Job 3",
                          "Job 4", "Job 5", "Job 6"};
short _far explode[6] = {0,0,1,0,0,0};
void main ()
{
chartenv env;
unsigned char bitmap[8]={0xFF,0xFF,0xFF,0xFF,
                        0xFF,0xFF,0xFF,0xFF};
_setvideomode (_ERESCOLOR);
    /* Initialize pie chart environment */
_pg_initchart();
_pg_defaultchart (&env, _PG_PIECHART, _PG_PERCENT);
    /* Set titles */
strcpy (env.maintitle.title, "Manhour Report");
strcpy (env.subtitle.title, "Percentage of Total per Job");
    /* Draw chart */
_pg_chartpie (&env,categories,values,explode,6);
    /* Redefine 0 as solid block */
_pg_setchardef (48, bitmap);
```

```
      /* Use new character--results in solid bar */
_pg_vlabelchart(&env,610,155,16,"0000000000");
      /* Delay and exit */
getch ();
_setvideomode (_DEFAULTMODE);
}
```

_pg_setpalette

Syntax:

```
short _far _pg_setpalette(paletteentry _far *palette);
paletteentry _far *palette;        palette
```

Function:

The _pg_setpalette function is used to select the palette colors, line styles, fill patterns, and plot characters for all palettes.

Files to Include:

```
#include <pgchart.h>
```

Compatibility:

DOS

Description:

The _pg_setpalette function sets the palette colors, line styles, fill patterns, and plot characters for all presentation graphics palettes. This presentation graphics palette is used by the presentation graphics functions and differs from the palettes used by the _setcolor and other low-level graphics functions.

Values Returned:

A zero is returned if successful. If the new palettes are not valid, the _BADSCREENMODE argument is returned.

Related Functions:

```
_pg_getpalette        :      gets the chart palette
_pg_initchart         :      initializes chart environment
```

Similar Turbo C++ Functions:

None

Suggested Code Structure and Use:

The `_pg_setpalette` function sets changes made to the current palette. The `_pg_setpalette` function is used after the `_pg_getpalette` function is called and the palette changes are made.

```
#include <string.h>
#include <stdio.h>
#include <graph.h>
#include <pgchart.h>
float _far values[# of values] = {87.0, ..., 82.0};
char _far *categories[# of values] = {"John", ..., "Jim"};

char _far *series[# of series] = {"Midterm", ..., "Final"};
palettetype pal;
void main ()
{
chartenv env;
_setvideomode ( mode );   /* set video mode */
_pg_initchart();   /* initialize chart environment */
_pg_defaultchart (&env, chart type, chart specs);
               .
               .
               .
_pg_getpalette (pal);
pal[1].color = 2;
pal[2].color = 14;
pal[1].style = 0xcccc;
pal[2].style = 0x3333;
_pg_setpalette (pal);
               .
               .
               .
_pg_chartms (&env, categories, values, # of categories,
         # of values, row dim, series);
               .
               .
               .
_pg_resetpalette();
_setvideomode (_DEFAULTMODE);
}
```

Example:

The _pg_setpalette function is used in the following example to set the changes made in the current palette.

```c
#include <string.h>
#include <stdio.h>
#include <graph.h>
#include <pgchart.h>
#define TRUE 1
#define FALSE 0
float _far values[20] = {87.0, 90.0, 82.0, 98.0, 71.0,
                         84.0, 78.0, 81.0, 74.0, 92.0,
                         77.0, 84.0, 91.0, 98.0, 77.0,
                         73.0, 83.0, 89.0, 90.0, 78.0};
char _far *students[10] = {"John","Jane","Jim","Sally",
                           "Sue","Rick","Kenny","Gary",
                           "Jill","Bob"};
char _far *test[2] = {"Midterm","Final"};
palettetype pal;
void main ()
{
chartenv env;
_setvideomode (_ERESCOLOR);
     /* Initialize column chart environment */
_pg_initchart();
_pg_defaultchart (&env, _PG_COLUMNCHART, _PG_PLAINBARS);
     /* Set titles */
strcpy (env.maintitle.title, "Test Scores");
strcpy (env.xaxis.axistitle.title, "Student");
strcpy (env.yaxis.axistitle.title, "Score");
env.xaxis.autoscale = TRUE;
env.yaxis.autoscale = TRUE;
     /* Change palette */
_pg_getpalette (pal);
pal[1].color = 2;
pal[2].color = 14;
pal[1].style = 0xcccc;
pal[2].style = 0x3333;
_pg_setpalette (pal);
     /* Draw chart */
_pg_chartms(&env,students,values,2,10,10,test);
     /* Reset and exit */
_pg_resetpalette();
getch ();
```

```
_setvideomode (_DEFAULTMODE);
}
```

_pg_setstyleset

Syntax:

```
void _far _pg_setstyleset(unsigned short _far *styleset);
unsigned short _far *styleset;            new style set
```

Function:

The **_pg_setstyleset** function is used to select the current style set.

Files to Include:

```
#include <pgchart.h>
```

Compatibility:

DOS

Description:

The style set is set by the **_pg_setstyleset** function. This style set includes the line styles for borders, grids, and data connectors. The style set should be set before calling the **_pg_defaultchart** function but after a valid graphics mode has been set.

Values Returned:

There is no return value.

Related Functions:

```
_pg_getstyleset    :     gets the chart style set
_pg_initchart      :     initializes chart environment
```

Similar Turbo C++ Functions:

None

Suggested Code Structure and Use:

The _pg_setstyleset function is used to make the changes to the style set current. You should call the _pg_setstyleset function before calling the _pg_defaultchart function but after calling the _pg_getstyleset function and changing the style set. The following code structure illustrates the use of the _pg_setstyleset function.

```
#include <string.h>
#include <stdio.h>
#include <graph.h>
#include <pgchart.h>
float _far values[# of values] = {87.0, ..., 82.0};
char _far *categories[# of categories]={"John",...,"Jim"};
char _far *series[# of series] = {"Midterm", ..., "Final"};
styleset styles;
void main ()
{
chartenv env;
_setvideomode ( mode );  /* set video mode */
_pg_initchart();  /* initialize chart environment */
_pg_getstyleset (styles);
styles[1] = 0x1111;
styles[2] = 0xEEEE;
_pg_setstyleset(styles);
_pg_defaultchart (&env, chart type, chart specs);
        .
        .
        .
_pg_chartms(&env,categories,values,# of values,
           # of categories, row dim, series);
_pg_resetstyleset();
_setvideomode (_DEFAULTMODE);
}
```

Example:

The _pg_setstyleset function is used in this example to set the changes made to the style set. Then the changes to the style set are displayed.

```
#include <string.h>
#include <stdio.h>
#include <graph.h>
#include <pgchart.h>
#define TRUE 1
#define FALSE 0
```

```
float _far values[20] = {87.0, 90.0, 82.0, 98.0, 71.0,
                         84.0, 78.0, 81.0, 74.0, 92.0,
                         77.0, 84.0, 91.0, 98.0, 77.0,
                         73.0, 83.0, 89.0, 90.0, 78.0};
char _far *students[10] = {"John","Jane","Jim","Sally",
                           "Sue","Rick","Kenny","Gary",
                           "Jill","Bob"};
char _far *test[2] = {"Midterm","Final"};
styleset styles;
void main ()
{
chartenv env;
_setvideomode (_ERESCOLOR);
_pg_initchart();
     /* Change style set */
_pg_getstyleset (styles);
styles[1] = 0x1111;
styles[2] = 0xEEEE;
_pg_setstyleset(styles);
_pg_defaultchart (&env, _PG_COLUMNCHART, _PG_PLAINBARS);
     /* Set titles */
strcpy (env.maintitle.title, "Test Scores");
strcpy (env.xaxis.axistitle.title, "Student");
strcpy (env.yaxis.axistitle.title, "Score");
env.xaxis.autoscale = TRUE;
env.yaxis.autoscale = TRUE;
     /* Draw chart */
_pg_chartms(&env,students,values,2,10,10,test);
     /* Reset and exit */
getch ();
_pg_resetstyleset();
_setvideomode (_DEFAULTMODE);
}
```

_pg_vlabelchart

Syntax:

```
short _far _pg_vlabelchart(chartenv _far *env, short x,
     short y, short color, char _far *text);
chartenv _far *env;              chart environment
short x;                         x-coordinate
short y;                         y-coordinate
```

```
short color;                    text color
char _far *text;                text label
```

Function:

The _pg_vlabelchart function is used to display vertical text on the screen.

Files to Include:

```
#include <pgchart.h>
```

Compatibility:

DOS

Description:

The _pg_vlabelchart function diplays vertical text when using presentation graphics functions. The x and y arguments specify the starting point of the text in relationship to the upper left corner of the chart window. The color argument specifies the color of the text. The text string to be displayed is described by the text argument.

Values Returned:

A zero is returned when successful; a nonzero value indicates an error.

Related Functions:

```
_pg_hlabelchart      :   displays horizontal text
```

Similar Turbo C++ Functions:

None

Suggested Code Structure and Use:

The _pg_vlabelchart function is used to place text on the screen vertically. When using this function, first draw the chart, then write the text. The following code structure illustrates the use of the _pg_vlabelchart function.

```
#include <pgchart.h>
#include <graph.h>
#include <stdio.h>
```

```
#include <string.h>
float _far values[# of values] = {9.0, ..., 6.0};
char _far *categories[# of categories] = {"1", ..., "3"};
void main ()
{
chartenv env;
_setvideomode ( mode );  /* set video mode */
_pg_initchart ();  /* initialize chart environment */
_pg_defaultchart (&env, chart type, chart specs);
                    .
                    .
                    .
_pg_chart (&env, categories, values, # of values);
                    .
                    .
                    .
_pg_vlabelchart (&env, x, y, color, " Text String ");
_setvideomode (_DEFAULTMODE); /* reset and exit */
}
```

Example:

The _pg_vlabelchart function is used to display a message on the bar chart. The message is shown on the right side of the chart, as shown in figure 9.53.

```
#include <pgchart.h>
#include <graph.h>
#include <stdio.h>
#include <string.h>
#define FALSE 0
#define TRUE 1
float _far values[20] = {9.0, 12.0, 6.0, 18.0, 13.0,
                         10.0, 14.0, 17.0, 8.0, 9.0,
                         11.0, 13.0, 9.0, 4.0, 7.0,
                         9.0, 11.0, 12.0, 7.0, 9.0};
char _far *categories[20] = {"1","2","3","4","5","6",
            "7","8","9","10","11","12","13","14",
            "15","16","17","18","19","20"};
void main ()
{
chartenv env;
_setvideomode (_ERESCOLOR);
        /* Initialize bar chart environment */
```

```
_pg_initchart ();
_pg_defaultchart (&env, _PG_BARCHART, _PG_PLAINBARS);
    /*  Set title  */
strcpy (env.maintitle.title, "Cars Sold During
                            20 Day Sale");
strcpy (env.xaxis.axistitle.title, "Cars Sold");
strcpy (env.yaxis.axistitle.title, "Day");
env.xaxis.autoscale = TRUE;
env.yaxis.autoscale = TRUE;
    /* Draw chart */
_pg_chart (&env, categories, values, 20);
    /* Draw message on right side of screen */
_pg_vlabelchart (&env,595,50,16,"Total Sales
                Goal = 150 Cars");
    /* Delay and exit */
getch ();
_setvideomode (_DEFAULTMODE);
}
```

Fig. 9.53. Example _pg_vlabelchart output.

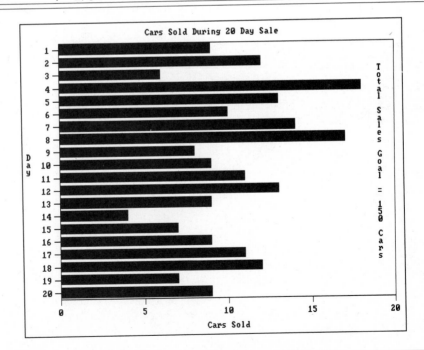

_pie

Syntax:

```
short far _pie(short fillflag, short x1, short y1,
        short x2, short y2, short x3, short y3,
        short x4, short y4);
short fillflag;                fill flag
short x1, y1;                  upper left corner of rectangle
short x2, y2;                  lower right corner of rectangle
short x3, y3;                  endpoint for starting vector
short x4, y4;                  endpoint for ending vector
```

Function:

The _pie function draws a pie-like wedge of an ellipse contained in the specified rectangular region. This function uses the view coordinate system.

Files to Include:

```
#include <graph.h>
```

Compatibility:

DOS

Description:

A pie-like wedge of the ellipse contained in the specified rectangular region is drawn when the _pie function is called. See figure 9.54. The rectangular region is defined by the x1, y1 and x2, y2 arguments. The x1 and y1 arguments define the upper left corner of the rectangular region. The x2 and y2 arguments define the lower right corner of this rectangle. The fillflag argument specifies whether the wedge will be drawn with only a border or filled. The two legal constants for the fillflag argument follow:

_GFILLINTERIOR	Fills the wedge with the current color and fill pattern.
_GBORDER	Draws only the border.

The arc of the wedge begins where the vector connecting the center of the rectangle and the point defined by the x3 and y3 arguments intersects the ellipse bound by the rectangular region. The arc is drawn counterclockwise in the current color until it reaches the vector that connects the center of the rectangle and the point defined by the x4 and y4 arguments. The vectors are also drawn in the current color beginning at the center of the rectangle and extending to the point where the vector intersects the ellipse.

Fig. 9.54. The _pie function.

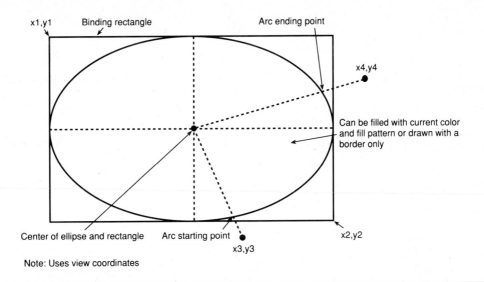

Note: Uses view coordinates

Values Returned:

A nonzero value is returned if drawn successfully; a zero is returned if unsuccessful.

Related Functions:

```
_setcolor     :     sets the current color
_setfillmask  :     sets the current fill pattern
```

Similar Turbo C++ Functions:

```
pieslice  :  draws and fills a pie slice
void far pieslice (int x, int y, int startangle,
                   int endangle, int radius);
```

Suggested Code Structure and Use:

The _pie function is used most commonly for creating pie charts independent of the chart environment. This function easily permits both normal pie charts and exploded pie charts. The following code structure illustrates the procedure for using the _pie function.

```
#include <stdio.h>
#include <graph.h>
void main ()
{
_setvideomode ( mode ); /* set mode by adapter */
         .
         .
         .
pie (fillflag,x1,y1,x2,y2,x3,y3,x4,y4); /* create pie */
         .
         .
         .
_setvideomode (_DEFAULTMODE);
}
```

Example:

This program creates a pie chart divided into quarters. The **_pie** function is used to create four sections of the pie; each section has a different pattern. See figure 9.55.

```
#include <stdio.h>
#include <graph.h>
void main ()
{
     /* Initialization */
_setvideomode (_MRES4COLOR);
_rectangle (_GBORDER,0,0,319,199);
_setbkcolor (_BLUE);
     /* Draw filled pie */
_pie (_GFILLINTERIOR,100,40,220,160,100,40,100,160);
     /* Draw filled pie with border */
_setcolor (1);
_pie (_GFILLINTERIOR,100,40,220,160,100,160,220,160);
_setcolor (3);
_pie (_GBORDER,100,40,220,160,100,160,220,160);
     /* Draw filled pie with border */
_setcolor (2);
_pie (_GFILLINTERIOR,100,40,220,160,220,160,220,40);
_setcolor (3);
_pie (_GBORDER,100,40,220,160,220,160,220,40);
     /* Draw bordered pie */
_pie (_GBORDER,100,40,220,160,220,40,100,40);
     /* Delay and exit */
_settextposition (23,8);
```

```
_outtext ("Press Any Key to Exit");
getch ();
_setvideomode (_DEFAULTMODE);
}
```

Fig. 9.55.   Example _pie output.

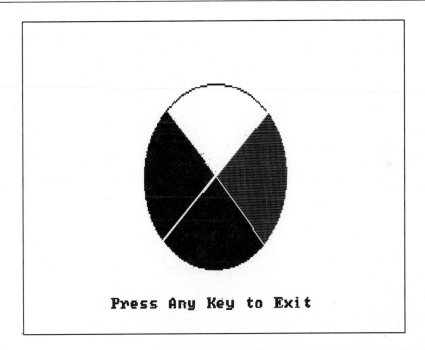

Press Any Key to Exit

_pie_w

Syntax:

```
short _far _pie_w(short fillflag, double x1, double y1,
      double x2, double y2, double x3,
      double y3, double x4, double y4);
short fillflag;            fill flag
double x1, y1;             upper left corner of rectangle
double x2, y2;             lower right corner of rectangle
double x3, y3;             endpoint for starting vector
double x4, y4;             endpoint for ending vector
```

Function:

The _pie_w function creates a pie-shaped wedge using the window coordinate system.

Files to Include:

```
#include <graph.h>
```

Compatibility:

DOS

Description:

The _pie_w function is used to create a pie-shaped wedge when using the window coordinate system. The fillflag argument indicates the way in which the pie will be drawn. The valid fillflag arguments follow:

_GFILLINTERIOR	Fills the wedge with the current color and fill pattern.
_GBORDER	Draws only the border.

The x1 and y1 arguments specify the upper left corner of the rectangle that binds the elliptical arc. The x2 and y2 arguments specify the lower right corner of this rectangle. The x3 and y3 arguments mark the endpoint of the starting vector. The arc begins where the underlying ellipse intersects the starting vector. The x4 and y4 arguments mark the endpoint of the ending vector. The arc ends where the underlying ellipse intersects the ending vector. Both the starting and ending vectors originate at the center of the binding rectangle. See figure 9.56. The current color and fill pattern are used with this function.

Values Returned:

The _pie_w function returns a nonzero value if successfully drawn. If not drawn successfully, a zero is returned.

Related Functions:

```
_pie_wxy     :     draw wedge in window coordinates
```

Similar Turbo C++ Functions:

None

Fig. 9.56. The _pie_w function.

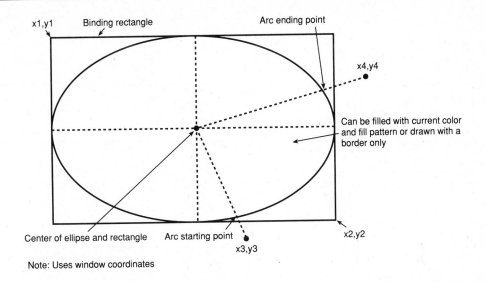

Note: Uses window coordinates

Suggested Code Structure and Use:

The **_pie_w** function is used to draw a pie-like wedge when using window coordinates. The following code structure illustrates the use of this function.

```
#include <graph.h>
#include <stdio.h>
void main ()
{
_setvideomode ( mode );  /* set video mode */
_setviewport (x1,y1,x2,y2);   /* size viewport */
_setwindow (flag,x1,y1,x2,y2); /* set window dimensions */
            .
            .
            .
_pie_w (fillflag,x1,y1,x2,y2,x3,y3,x4,y4); /* draw pie */
            .
            .
            .
_setvideomode (_DEFAULTMODE);  /* reset and exit */
}
```

Example:

The _pie_w function is used in this example to create a four-wedge pie chart. Alternate wedges of the pie are filled, as shown in figure 9.57.

```
#include <graph.h>
#include <stdio.h>
void main ()
{
_setvideomode (_ERESCOLOR);
_rectangle (_GBORDER,0,0,639,349);
    /* Open window */
_setviewport (0,0,639,349);
_setwindow (0,-100.00,-100.0,100.0,100.0);
    /* Draw pie */
_pie_w (_GBORDER,-75.0,-75.0,75.0,75.0,0.0,
                -100.0,-100,0.0);
_pie_w (_GFILLINTERIOR,-75.0,-75.0,75.0,75.0,
                -100.0,0.0,0.0,100);
_pie_w (_GBORDER,-75.0,-75.0,75.0,75.0,0.0,
                100.0,100.0,0.0);
_pie_w (_GFILLINTERIOR,-75.0,-75.0,75.0,75.0,
                100.0,0.0,0.0,-100.0);
    /* Delay and exit */
_settextposition (23,5);
_outtext ("Press Any Key To Exit");
getch ();
_setvideomode (_DEFAULTMODE);
}
```

_pie_wxy

Syntax:

```
short _far _pie_wxy(short fillflag, struct _wxycoord _far
    *xy1, struct _wxycoord _far *xy2, struct
    _wxycoord _far *xy3, struct _wxycoord _far *xy4);
short fillflag;          fill flag
struct _wxycoord *xy1;   upper left corner of rectangle
struct _wxycoord *xy2;   lower right corner of rectangle
struct _wxycoord *xy3;   endpoint for starting vector
struct _wxycoord *xy4;   endpoint for ending vector
```

Fig. 9.57. Example _pie_w output.

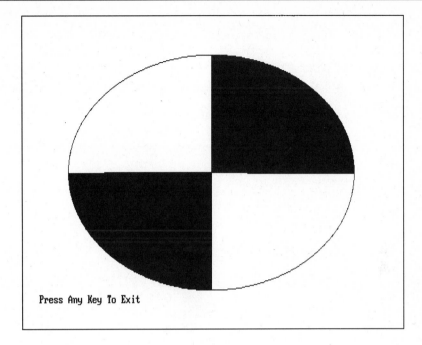

Function:

The **_pie_wxy** function creates a pie-like wedge in the specified rectangular region. This function uses the window coordinate system.

Files to Include:

```
#include <graph.h>
```

Compatibility:

DOS

Description:

The **_pie_wxy** function is used to create a pie-shaped wedge when using the window coordinate system. The **fillflag** argument indicates the way in which the pie will be drawn. The valid **fillflag** arguments follow:

_GFILLINTERIOR   Fills the wedge with the current color and fill pattern.
_GBORDER   Draws only the border.

The x y 1 coordinate pair specifies the upper left corner of the rectangle that binds the elliptical arc. The x y 2 coordinate pair specifies the lower right corner of this rectangle. The x y 3 coordinate pair marks the endpoint of the starting vector. The arc begins where the underlying ellipse intersects the starting vector. The x y 4 coordinate pair marks the endpoint of the ending vector. The arc ends where the underlying ellipse intersects the ending vector. Both the starting and ending vectors originate at the center of the binding rectangle. See figure 9.58. The current color and fill pattern are used with this function.

Fig. 9.58. The _pie_wxy function.

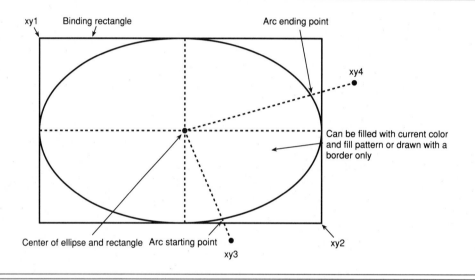

Values Returned:

If successful, a nonzero value is returned; otherwise, zero is returned.

Related Functions:

```
_pie_w     :      draws a wedge using window coordinates
```

Similar Turbo C++ Functions:

None

Suggested Code Structure and Use:

The _pie_wxy function is used to draw pie-like wedges when using the window coordinate system. The _pie_w function performs the same function but does not use a structure for its arguments. The following code structure illustrates the use of the _pie_wxy function.

```
#include <graph.h>
#include <stdio.h>
void main ()
{
struct _wxycoord xy1, xy2, xy3, xy4;
_setvideomode ( mode );  /* set video mode */
_setviewport (x1,y1,x2,y2);  /* size viewport */
_setwindow (flag,x1,y1,x2,y2); /* set window dimensions */
          .
          .
          .
xy1.wx = -75.0;
xy1.wy = -75.0;
xy2.wx = 75.0;
xy2.wy = 75.0;
xy3.wx = 25.0;
xy3.wy = -100.0;
xy4.wx = 65.0;
xy4.wy = -100.0;
_pie_wxy (fillflag,&xy1,&xy2,&xy3,&xy4);
          .
          .
          .
_setvideomode (_DEFAULTMODE);  /* reset and exit */
}
```

Example:

The _pie_wxy function is used in the following example to create a pie-like wedge. See figure 9.59.

```
#include <graph.h>
#include <stdio.h>
void main ()
{
struct _wxycoord xy1, xy2, xy3, xy4;
_setvideomode (_ERESCOLOR);
_rectangle (_GBORDER,0,0,639,349);
      /* Open window */
```

```
_setviewport (0,0,639,349);
_setwindow (0,-100.00,-100.0,100.0,100.0);
      /* Draw pie */
xy1.wx = -75.0;
xy1.wy = -75.0;
xy2.wx = 75.0;
xy2.wy = 75.0;
xy3.wx = 25.0;
xy3.wy = -100.0;
xy4.wx = 65.0;
xy4.wy = -100.0;
_pie_wxy (_GFILLINTERIOR,&xy1,&xy2,&xy3,&xy4);
      /* Delay and exit */
_settextposition (23,5);
_outtext ("Press Any Key To Exit");
getch ();
_setvideomode (_DEFAULTMODE);
}
```

Fig. 9.59. Example _pie_wxy output.

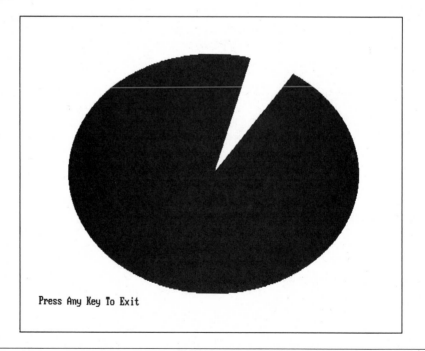

_polygon

Syntax:

```
short _far _polygon(short fillflag, struct xycoord
        _far *points, short numpoints);
short fillflag;                      fill flag;
struct xycoord _far *points;         points for polygon
short numpoints;                     number of points
```

Function:

The _polygon function creates a polygon using the current color and fill pattern. The view coordinate system is used with this function.

Files to Include:

```
#include <graph.h>
```

Compatibility:

DOS

Description:

The polygon function displays a polygon, or multisided figure, when using the view coordinate system. The fillflag argument is used to determine whether the figure will be filled. The valid fillflag arguments for the _polygon function follow:

_GFILLINTERIOR   Fills the polygon with the current color and fill pattern.
_GBORDER   Draws only the border.

The points array contains a series of structures that specify the points that define the polygon. These points are connected with straight lines to form the polygon. The numpoints argument specifies the number of points in the polygon and array. The polygon is drawn using the current color, fill pattern, write mode, and line style.

Values Returned:

If any portion of the polygon is drawn, a nonzero value is returned. If nothing is drawn, a zero is returned.

Related Functions:

```
_setcolor        :    sets the current color
_setwritemode    :    sets the current write mode
_setfillmask     :    sets the current fill pattern
_setlinestyle    :    sets the current line style
```

Similar Turbo C++ Functions:

```
drawpoly  :  draws the outline of a polygon
void far drawpoly (int numpoints, int far *polypoints);
fillpoly  :  draws and fills a polygon
void far fillpoly (int numpoints, int far *polypoints);
```

Suggested Code Structure and Use:

The _polygon function is used to create a figure with multiple sides when using the view coordinate system. The following code structure illustrates the use of this function.

```
#include <graph.h>
#include <stdio.h>
void main ()
{
struct xycoord figure[# of points];
_setvideomode ( mode );  /* set video mode */
        .
        .
        .
figure[0].xcoord = 300;
figure[0].ycoord = 175;
figure[1].xcoord = 40;
figure[1].ycoord = 75;
figure[2].xcoord = 600;
figure[2].ycoord = 75;
figure[3].xcoord = 340;
figure[3].ycoord = 175;
figure[4].xcoord = 600;
figure[4].ycoord = 275;
figure[5].xcoord = 40;
figure[5].ycoord = 275;
_polygon (fillflag,figure,# of points);
        .
        .
        .
_setvideomode (_DEFAULTMODE);  /* reset and exit */
}
```

524

Example:

The _polygon function is used in this example to create a six-sided figure, as shown in figure 9.60. The figure is not filled.

```
#include <graph.h>
#include <stdio.h>
void main ()
{
struct xycoord figure[6];
_setvideomode (_ERESCOLOR);
_rectangle (_GBORDER,0,0,639,349);
          /* Draw figure */
figure[0].xcoord = 300;
figure[0].ycoord = 175;
figure[1].xcoord = 40;
figure[1].ycoord = 75;
figure[2].xcoord = 600;
figure[2].ycoord = 75;
figure[3].xcoord = 340;
figure[3].ycoord = 175;
figure[4].xcoord = 600;
figure[4].ycoord = 275;
figure[5].xcoord = 40;
figure[5].ycoord = 275;
_polygon (_GBORDER,figure,6);
      /* Delay and exit */
_settextposition (23,5);
_outtext ("Press Any Key To Exit");
getch ();
_setvideomode (_DEFAULTMODE);
}
```

_polygon_w

Syntax:

```
short _far _polygon_w(short fillflag, double _far
     *points, short numpoints);
short fillflag;                fill flag
double _far *points;           points for polygon
short numpoints;               number of points
```

Fig. 9.60. Example _polygon output.

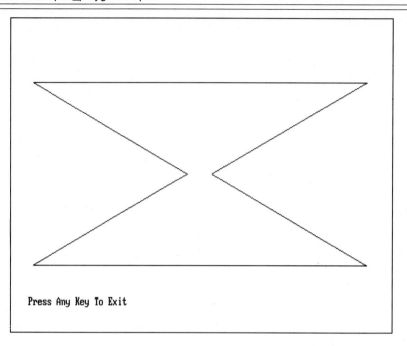

Press Any Key To Exit

Function:

The **_polygon_w** function creates a polygon using the current color and fill pattern. This function uses the window coordinate system.

Files to Include:

```
#include <graph.h>
```

Compatibility:

DOS

Description:

The **_polygon_w** function displays a polygon, or multisided figure, when using the window coordinate system. The **fillflag** argument is used to determine whether the polygon will be filled. The constants for the **fillflag** argument follow:

_GFILLINTERIOR   Fills the polygon with the current color and fill pattern.
_GBORDER   Draws only the border.

The points array contains the x and y coordinates for the points in the polygon. Because the _polygon_w function does not use a structure, the array must be twice the size of the number of points in the polygon. For example, a 6-point polygon needs an array of dimension size 12. The first two entries in the array contain the first x and y coordinate pair, the next two entries contain the second x and y coordinate pair, and so on. The numpoints argument identifies the number of points in the polygon. The current fill pattern, color, write mode, and line style are used with this function.

Values Returned:

If any part of the polygon is drawn, a nonzero value is returned; otherwise, a zero is returned.

Related Functions:

```
_setcolor        :    sets the current color
_setfillmask     :    sets the current fill pattern
_setwritemode    :    sets the current write mode
_setlinestyle    :    sets the current line style
```

Similar Turbo C++ Functions:

None

Suggested Code Structure and Use:

The _polygon_w function is used to display a multisided figure when using the window coordinate system. The following code structure demonstrates the use of this function.

```
#include <graph.h>
#include <stdio.h>
void main ()
{
double figure[# of points] = {-70.0, ..., -70.0};
_setvideomode ( mode );  /* set video mode */
_setviewport (x1,y1,x2,y2); /* size viewport */
_setwindow (flag,x1,y1,x2,y2); /* set window dimensions */
        .
        .
        .

_polygon_w (fillflag,figure,# of points);
        .
        .
        .
```

```
_setvideomode (_DEFAULTMODE);   /* reset and exit */
}
```

Example:

In the following example, an octagon is drawn with the _polygon_w function. See figure 9.61. The window coordinate system is in use.

```
#include <graph.h>
#include <stdio.h>
void main ()
{
double figure[16] = {-70.0,-35.0,  -35.0,-70.0,
                       35.0,-70.0,   70.0,-35.0,
                       70.0,35.0,       35.0,70.0,
                      -35.0,70.0,   -70.0,35.0};
_setvideomode (_ERESCOLOR);
_rectangle (_GBORDER,0,0,639,349);
     /* Open window */
_setviewport (0,0,639,349);
_setwindow (0,-100.0,-100.0,100.0,100.0);
     /* Draw polygon */
_polygon_w (_GBORDER,figure,8);
     /* Delay and exit */
_settextposition (23,5);
_outtext ("Press Any Key To Exit");
getch ();
_setvideomode (_DEFAULTMODE);
}
```

_polygon_wxy

Syntax:

```
short _far _polygon_wxy(short fillflag, struct _wxycoord
     _far *points, short numpoints);
short fillflag;                          fill flag
struct _wxycoord _far *points;           polygon points
short numpoints;                         number of points
```

Fig. 9.61. Example _polygon_w output.

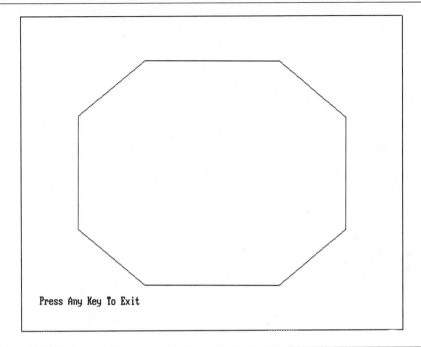

Press Any Key To Exit

Function:

The **_polygon_wxy** function creates a polygon using the current color and fill pattern. The window coordinate system is used with this function.

Files to Include:

```
#include <graph.h>
```

Compatibility:

DOS

Description:

The **_polygon_wxy** function is used to display a polygon, or multisided figure, when using the window coordinate system. The **points** array contains a series of structures that describe the x and y coordinates of the points of the polygon. The **numpoints** argument describes the number of points in the polygon and the array. The **fillflag** argument determines whether the polygon will be filled. The constants for the **fillflag** argument follow:

_GFILLINTERIOR   Fills the polygon with the current color and fill pattern.
_GBORDER   Draws only the border.

When displaying the _polygon_wxy function, the current color, write mode, line style, and fill pattern are used.

Values Returned:

If anything is drawn, a nonzero value is returned; otherwise, a zero is returned.

Related Functions:

```
_setcolor        :     sets the current color
_setwritemode    :     sets the current write mode
_setfillmask     :     sets the current fill pattern
_setlinestyle    :     sets the current line pattern
```

Similar Turbo C++ Functions:

None

Suggested Code Structure and Use:

The _polygon_wxy function is used to create a multisided figure when using the window coordinate system. This function has the same results as the _polygon_w function but uses a structure for its arguments. The following code structure illustrates the use of the _polygon_wxy function.

```
#include <graph.h>
#include <stdio.h>
void main ()
{
struct _wxycoord points[# of points];
_setvideomode ( mode );  /* set video mode */
_setviewport (x1,y1,x2,y2); /* size viewport */
_setwindow (flag,x1,y1,x2,y2); /* set window coordinates */
            .
            .
            .
points[0].wx = -70.0;
points[0].wy = -35.0;
points[1].wx = -35.0;
points[1].wy = -70.0;
points[2].wx = 35.0;
points[2].wy = -70.0;
```

```
_polygon_wxy (fillflag,points,# of points);
        .
        .
        .
_setvideomode (_DEFAULTMODE);   /* reset and exit */
}
```

Example:

The following example displays an octagon using the **_polygon_wxy** function. See figure 9.62. The window coordinate system is in use.

```
#include <graph.h>
#include <stdio.h>
void main ()
{
struct _wxycoord points[8];
_setvideomode (_ERESCOLOR);
_rectangle (_GBORDER,0,0,639,349);
        /* Open window */
_setviewport (0,0,639,349);
_setwindow (0,-100.0,-100.0,100.0,100.0);
        /* Define and draw polygon */
points[0].wx = -70.0;
points[0].wy = -35.0;
points[1].wx = -35.0;
points[1].wy = -70.0;
points[2].wx = 35.0;
points[2].wy = -70.0;
points[3].wx = 70.0;
points[3].wy = -35.0;
points[4].wx = 70.0;
points[4].wy = 35.0;
points[5].wx = 35.0;
points[5].wy = 70.0;
points[6].wx = -35.0;
points[6].wy = 70.0;
points[7].wx = -70.0;
points[7].wy = 35.0;
_polygon_wxy (_GBORDER,points,8);
        /* Delay and exit */
_settextposition (23,5);
_outtext ("Press Any Key To Exit");
```

```
getch ();
_setvideomode (_DEFAULTMODE);
}
```

Fig. 9.62. Example _polygon_wxy output.

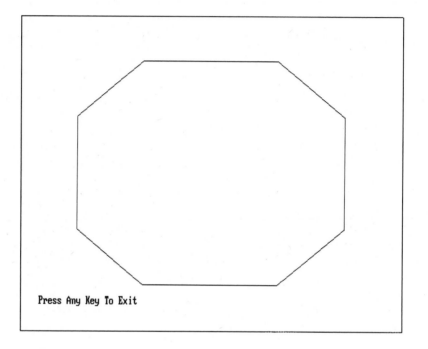

Press Any Key To Exit

_putimage

Syntax:

```
void _far _putimage(short x, short y, char _huge *image,
      short action);
short x, y;                  upper left corner of image
char _huge *image;           image buffer
short action;                method for placing image
```

Function:

The _putimage function places on the screen an image stored by the _getimage function. The _putimage function uses the view coordinate system.

Files to Include:

```
#include <graph.h>
```

Compatibility:

DOS

Description:

A rectangular image that has been stored by the _getimage function can be placed on the screen with the _putimage function. The x and y arguments identify the view coordinates where the upper left corner of the image will be placed. The image argument identifies the address of the buffer where the image is stored. The action argument, which is chosen from one of the five constants listed in table 9.15, identifies how the image will be placed on the screen.

Table 9.15. *Action arguments for the _putimage function.*

Constant	Purpose
_GAND	The displayed pixels are the logical AND of the existing pixel values and the transferred pixel values.
_GOR	The displayed pixels are the logical OR of the existing pixel values and the transferred pixel values.
_GPRESET	The image is the negative of the stored image; each pixel is inverted before it is placed on the screen.
_GPSET	The image is placed on the screen exactly as it was stored.
_GXOR	The displayed pixels are the exclusive OR of the existing pixel values and the transferred pixel values.

Values Returned:

No value is returned.

Related Functions:

```
_getimage :    stores a rectangular image
```

Similar Turbo C++ Functions:

```
putimage  :  outputs a bit image to the screen
void far putimage (int left, int top, void far *bitmap,
                      int op);
```

Suggested Code Structure and Use:

The _putimage function places a stored image on the screen. The following code structure illustrates how an image is stored and placed on the screen.

```
#include <stdio.h>
#include <graph.h>
#include <malloc.h>
char far *imagebuffer;
void main ()
{
_setvideomode ( mode ); /* set mode by adapter */
    .
    .
    .
  { draw image to be stored }
    .
    .
    .
imagebuffer = (char far *)malloc((unsigned int)
_imagesize(x1,y1,x2,y2));
_getimage (x1,y1,x2,y2,imagebuffer);
_putimage (x,y,imagebuffer, action);
    .
    .
    .
_setvideomode (_DEFAULTMODE);
}
```

Example:

The _putimage function is used in this program to place an image stored in imagebuffer on the left and right sides of the screen.

```
#include <stdio.h>
#include <graph.h>
#include <malloc.h>
char far *imagebuffer;
```

```
void main ()
{
        /* Initialization */
_setvideomode (_MRES4COLOR);
_setbkcolor (_RED);
_rectangle (_GBORDER,0,0,319,199);
        /* Create image to be stored */
_rectangle (_GFILLINTERIOR,140,80,180,120);
_setcolor (1);
_ellipse (_GFILLINTERIOR,150,90,170,110);
        /* Save image */
imagebuffer = (char far *)malloc((unsigned int)
      _imagesize (140,80,180,120));
_getimage(140,80,180,120,imagebuffer);
        /* Put images on screen */
_putimage (20,80,imagebuffer,_GPSET);
_putimage (260,80,imagebuffer,_GPSET);
        /* Delay and exit */
_settextposition (23,10);
_outtext ("Press Any Key to Exit");
getch ();
_setvideomode (_DEFAULTMODE);
}
```

_putimage_w

Syntax:

```
void _far _putimage_w(double x, double y, char _huge
      *image, short action);
double x, y;              upper left corner of image
char _huge *image;        image buffer
short action;             method for placing image
```

Function:

The `_putimage_w` function places a stored image on the screen at the specified window coordinates.

Files to Include:

```
#include <graph.h>
```

Compatibility:

DOS

Description:

The _putimage_w function places a stored image at the specified window coordinates. The x and y arguments define the position where the upper left corner of the image will be placed. The image argument is the pointer to the buffer where the image is stored. The action argument determines the method used for placing the image on the screen. The constants for the action argument are shown in table 9.15, under the _putimage function.

Values Returned:

There is no return value.

Related Functions:

```
_getimage_w       :  stores an image using window coordinates
_imagesize_w      :  sizes an image using window coordinates
```

Similar Turbo C++ Functions:

None

Suggested Code Structure and Use:

The _putimage_w function is used to place a stored image on the screen when using the window coordinate system. The following code structure illustrates the use of the _putimage_w function.

```
#include <stdio.h>
#include <graph.h>
#include <malloc.h>
char far *imagebuffer;
void main ()
{
_setvideomode ( mode );  /* set video mode */
_setviewport (x1,y1,x2,y2);  /* size viewport */
_setwindow (flag,x1,y1,x2,y2); /* set window dimensions */
            .
            .
            .
        { draw image to store }
            .
            .
            .
```

```
imagebuffer = (char far *)malloc((unsigned int)
      _imagesize_w (x1,y1,x2,y2));
_getimage_w (x1,y1,x2,y2,imagebuffer);
          .
          .
          .
_putimage_w (x,y,imagebuffer,_GPSET);
          .
          .
          .
_setvideomode (_DEFAULTMODE);  /* reset and exit */
}
```

Example:

In the following example, an image is drawn in the center of the screen and stored. Then the image is placed in the upper left corner of the screen with the **_putimage_w** function. See figure 9.63.

```
#include <stdio.h>
#include <graph.h>
#include <malloc.h>
char far *imagebuffer;
void main ()
{
          /* Initialization */
_setvideomode (_ERESCOLOR);
_rectangle (_GBORDER,0,0,639,349);
      /* Open window */
_setviewport (0,0,639,349);
_setwindow (0,-100.0,-100.0,100.0,100.0);
          /* Create image to be stored */
_rectangle_w (_GFILLINTERIOR,-20.0,-20.0,20.0,20.0);
_setcolor (1);
_ellipse_w (_GFILLINTERIOR,-10.0,-10.0,10.0,10.0);
          /* Save image */
imagebuffer = (char far *)malloc((unsigned int)
      _imagesize_w (-20.0,-20.0,20.0,20.0));
_getimage_w (-20.0,-20.0,20.0,20.0,imagebuffer);
          /* Put images on screen */
_putimage_w (-70.0,-70.0,imagebuffer,_GPSET);
          /* Delay and exit */
_settextposition (23,10);
_outtext ("Press Any Key to Exit");
```

```
getch ();
_setvideomode (_DEFAULTMODE);
}
```

Fig. 9.63. Example _putimage_w output.

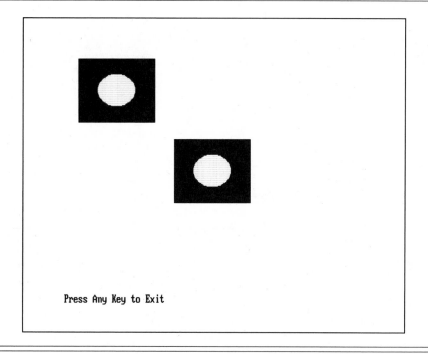

_rectangle

Syntax:

```
short _far _rectangle(short fillflag, short x1, short y1,
     short x2, short y2);
short fillflag;        fill flag
short x1, y1;          upper left corner of image
short x2, y2;          lower right corner of image
```

Function:

The _rectangle function is used to draw a rectangle with the current color and line style. This function uses the view coordinate system.

Files to Include:

```
#include <graph.h>
```

Compatibility:

DOS

Description:

A rectangle of the current color and line pattern is drawn when the _rectangle function is called. The upper left corner is defined by the x1 and y1 arguments. The lower right corner is defined by the x2 and y2 arguments. The fillflag argument determines whether the rectangle will be filled. The constants for the fillflag argument follow:

_GFILLINTERIOR   Fills the rectangle with the current color and fill pattern.
_GBORDER   Draws only the border.

See figure 9.64. If a rectangle will be filled later with the _floodfill function, a solid line pattern must be used.

Fig. 9.64. The _rectangle function.

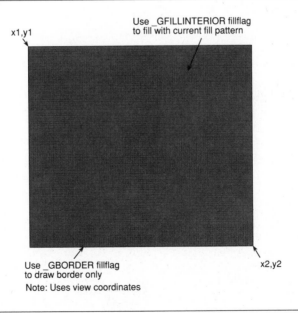

Use _GFILLINTERIOR fillflag
to fill with current fill pattern

x1,y1

Use _GBORDER fillflag
to draw border only

Note: Uses view coordinates

x2,y2

Values Returned:

A nonzero value is returned if the rectangle is drawn successfully. A zero is returned if unsuccessful.

Related Functions:

```
_setcolor         :        sets the current color
_setlinestyle     :        sets the current line pattern
_setfillmask      :        sets the current fill pattern
```

Similar Turbo C++ Functions:

```
rectangle : draws a rectangle
void far rectangle (int left, int top, int right,
                    int bottom);
bar  :  draws a two-dimensional bar
void far bar (int left, int top, int right, int bottom);
bar3d  :   draws a three-dimensional bar
void far bar3d (int left, int top, int right, int bottom,
                int depth, int topflag);
```

Suggested Code Structure and Use:

The _rectangle function is useful for creating rectangles and squares. The availability of different line styles and fill patterns makes this function very versatile. The following code structure illustrates a typical use of the _rectangle function.

```
#include <stdio.h>
#include <graph.h>
void main ()
{
_setvideomode ( mode ); /* set mode by adapter */
     .
     .
     .
_rectangle ( fill flag, x1, y1, x2, y2);
     .
     .
     .
_setvideomode (_DEFAULTMODE); /* reset */
}
```

Example:

The following example demonstrates several ways that the _rectangle function can be used. The first rectangle is drawn with the _GFILLINTERIOR fillflag argument, using a 50% fill patttern. The next two rectangles are drawn using the _GBORDER fillflag argument. Both of these rectangles use a different line pattern. See figure 9.65.

```
#include <stdio.h>
#include <graph.h>
short linepattern [3] =
        { 0x8000, 0xFF00, 0xC0C0 };
unsigned char *(fillpattern [2]) =
        {"\x55\xAA\x55\xAA\x55\xAA\x55\xAA",
    "\xFF\xFF\xFF\xFF\xFF\xFF\xFF\xFF"};
void main ()
{
        /* Initialization */
_setvideomode (_MRES4COLOR);
_setbkcolor (_RED);
_rectangle (_GBORDER,0,0,319,199);
        /* Draw rectangle filled 50% */
_setfillmask ((char far *)(fillpattern [0]));
_rectangle (_GFILLINTERIOR,10,10,309,40);
        /* Draw rectangle with dashed border */
_setfillmask ((char far *)(fillpattern [1]));
_setlinestyle (linepattern [3]);
_rectangle (_GBORDER,10,50,309,80);
        /* Draw rectangle with dashed border */
_setlinestyle (linepattern [2]);
_rectangle (_GBORDER,10,90,309,120);
        /* Delay and reset */
_settextposition (23,10);
_outtext ("Press Any Key to Exit");
getch();
_setvideomode (_DEFAULTMODE);
}
```

_rectangle_w

Syntax:

```
short _far _rectangle_w(short fillflag, double x1, double
    y1, double x2, double y2);
short fillflag;          fill flag
double x1, y1;           upper left corner of rectangle
double x2, y2;           lower right corner of rectangle
```

Fig. 9.65. Example _rectangle output.

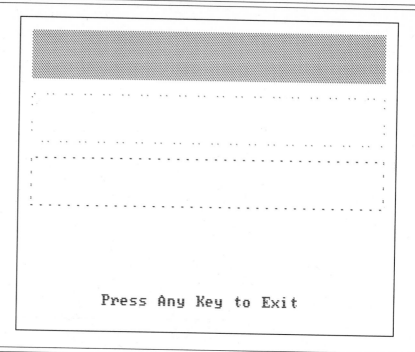

Press Any Key to Exit

Function:

The **_rectangle_w** function draws a rectangle using the current color, line style, and write mode. This function uses the window coordinate system.

Files to Include:

```
#include <graph.h>
```

Compatibility:

DOS

Description:

The **_rectangle_w** function displays a rectangle on the screen when using the window coordinate system. The **x1** and **y1** arguments describe the upper left corner of the rectangle. The **x2** and **y2** arguments describe the lower right corner of the argument. The **fillflag** argument is used to determine whether the rectangle will be filled. The constants for the **fillflag** argument follow:

_GFILLINTERIOR   Fills the rectangle with the current color and fill pattern.
_GBORDER   Draws only the border.

See figure 9.66. When the rectangle is displayed, the current color, fill pattern, write mode, and line style are used.

Fig. 9.66.   The _rectangle_w function.

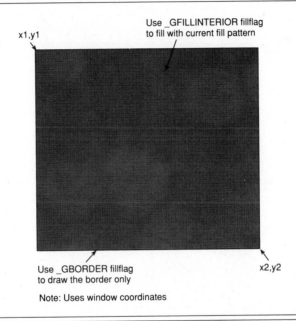

Values Returned:

If any part of the rectangle is drawn, a nonzero value is returned; otherwise, a zero is returned.

Related Functions:

```
_setcolor       :       sets the current color
_setwritemode   :       sets the current write mode
_setlinestyle   :       sets the current line pattern
_setfillmask    :       sets the current fill pattern
```

Similar Turbo C++ Functions:

None

Suggested Code Structure and Use:

The _rectangle_w function creates rectangles when using the window coordinate system. The following code structure demonstrates the use of this function.

```
#include <stdio.h>
#include <graph.h>
void main ()
{
_setvideomode ( mode );  /* set video mode */
_setviewport (x1,y1,x2,y2); /* size viewport */
_setwindow (flag,x1,y1,x2,y2); /* set window dimensions */
        .
        .
        .

_rectangle_w (fillflag,x1,y1,x2,y2);
        .
        .
        .

_setvideomode (_DEFAULTMODE);  /* reset and exit */
}
```

Example:

The _rectangle_w function is used in this example to draw overlaying rectangles. See figure 9.67. The window coordinate system is in use.

```
#include <stdio.h>
#include <graph.h>
void main ()
{
_setvideomode (_ERESCOLOR);
_rectangle (_GBORDER,0,0,639,349);
    /* Open window */
_setviewport (0,0,639,349);
_setwindow (0,-100.0,-100.0,100.0,100.0);
    /*   Draw rectangles */
_setcolor (14);
_rectangle_w (_GFILLINTERIOR,-75.0,-75.0,75.0,75.0);
_setcolor (4);
_rectangle_w (_GFILLINTERIOR,-60.0,-60.0,60.0,60.0);
_setcolor (2);
_rectangle_w (_GFILLINTERIOR,-45.0,-45.0,45.0,45.0);
_setcolor (1);
```

```
_rectangle_w (_GFILLINTERIOR,-30.0,-30.0,30.0,30.0);
      /* Delay and exit */
_settextposition (23,5);
_outtext ("Press Any Key To Exit");
getch ();
_setvideomode (_DEFAULTMODE);
}
```

Fig. 9.67. Example _rectangle_w output.

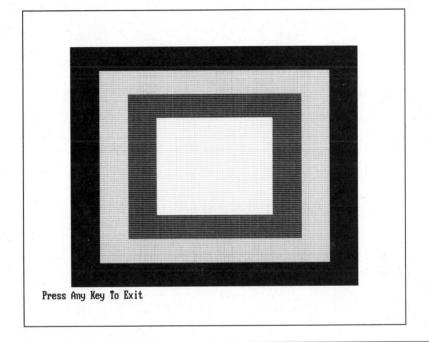

_rectangle_wxy

Syntax:

```
short _far _rectangle_wxy(short fillflag, struct
     _wxycoord _far *xy1, struct _wxycoord
     _far *xy2);
short fillflag;                    fill flag
struct _wxycoord _far *xy1;        upper left corner
struct _wxycoord _far *xy2;        lower right corner
```

Function:

The _rectangle_wxy function creates a rectangle using the current color, line style, fill pattern, and write mode. This function uses the window coordinate system.

Files to Include:

```
#include <graph.h>
```

Compatibility:

DOS

Description:

The _rectangle_wxy function displays a rectangle when using the window coordinate system. The upper left and lower right corners are described in a structure of type wxycoord:

```
struct _wxycoord
    {
    double wx;
    double wy;
    };
```

The upper left corner is described by the xy1 argument; the lower right corner is described by the xy2 argument. The fillflag argument determines whether the rectangle will be filled. The constants for the fillflag argument follow:

_GFILLINTERIOR	Fills the rectangle with the current color and fill pattern.
_GBORDER	Draws only the border.

See figure 9.68. The rectangle is displayed using the current color, line style, write mode, and fill pattern.

Values Returned:

If any part of the rectangle is drawn, a nonzero value is returned. If nothing is drawn, a zero is returned.

Related Functions:

```
_setcolor        :      sets the current color
_setfillmask     :      sets the current fill pattern
```

Fig. 9.68. The _rectangle _wxy function.

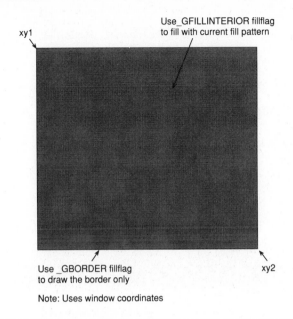

xy1

Use_GFILLINTERIOR fillflag
to fill with current fill pattern

Use _GBORDER fillflag
to draw the border only

xy2

Note: Uses window coordinates

Similar Turbo C++ Functions:

None

Suggested Code Structure and Use:

The _rectangle_wxy function is used to create rectangles when using the window coordinate system. The _rectangle_w function produces the same results as the _rectangle_wxy function but the arguments differ. The following code structure demonstrates the proper use of the _rectangle_wxy function.

```
#include <stdio.h>
#include <graph.h>
void main ()
{
struct _wxycoord corner1, corner2;
_setvideomode ( mode );      /* set video mode */
_setviewport (x1,y1,x2,y2); /* size viewport */
_setwindow (flag,x1,y1,x2,y2); /* set window dimensions */
        .
        .
        .
```

```
corner1.wx = -75.0;
corner1.wy = -75.0;
corner2.wx = 75.0;
corner2.wy = 75.0;
_rectangle_wxy (fillflag,&corner1,&corner2);
        .
        .
        .
_setvideomode (_DEFAULTMODE);  /* reset and exit */
}
```

Example:

This example uses the _rectangle_wxy function to display a series of rectangles. The window coordinate system is in use.

```
#include <stdio.h>
#include <graph.h>
void main ()
{
struct _wxycoord corner1, corner2;
_setvideomode (_ERESCOLOR);
_rectangle (_GBORDER,0,0,639,349);
    /* Open window */
_setviewport (0,0,639,349);
_setwindow (0,-100.0,-100.0,100.0,100.0);
    /* Draw rectangles */
_setcolor (14);
corner1.wx = -75.0;
corner1.wy = -75.0;
corner2.wx = 75.0;
corner2.wy = 75.0;
_rectangle_wxy (_GFILLINTERIOR,&corner1,&corner2);
_setcolor (4);
corner1.wx = -60.0;
corner1.wy = -60.0;
corner2.wx = 60.0;
corner2.wy = 60.0;
_rectangle_wxy (_GFILLINTERIOR,&corner1,&corner2);
_setcolor (2);
corner1.wx = -45.0;
corner1.wy = -45.0;
corner2.wx = 45.0;
corner2.wy = 45.0;
```

```
_rectangle_wxy (_GFILLINTERIOR,&corner1,&corner2);
_setcolor (1);
corner1.wx = -30.0;
corner1.wy = -30.0;
corner2.wx = 30.0;
corner2.wy = 30.0;
_rectangle_wxy (_GFILLINTERIOR,&corner1,&corner2);
       /* Delay and exit */
_settextposition (23,5);
_outtext ("Press Any Key To Exit");
getch ();
_setvideomode (_DEFAULTMODE);
}
```

_registerfonts

Syntax:

```
short _far _registerfonts(unsigned char _far *pathname);
unsigned char _far *pathname;   path name for font files
```

Function:

The _registerfonts function initializes the font graphics system.

Files to Include:

```
#include <graph.h>
```

Compatibility:

DOS

Description:

The _registerfonts function is used to register and intialize the font graphics system. You must register all fonts used in the program before calling any other font-related function, such as _getgtextextent, _setfont, _outgtext, and _unregisterfonts. When the _registerfonts function is called, the font header information in the specified font files are read and placed in memory. The pathname argument is used to describe the path and file name of the font (.FON) files. DOS wildcard characters (such as *) can be used. Each registered font uses about 140 bytes of memory. The _unregisterfonts function should be called before exiting the program so that all memory is freed before exiting. Table 9.16 describes the available font files and their contents.

Table 9.16 *Font files.*

File name	Typeface	Size in pixels	Mapping	Spacing
COURB.FON	Courier	10 x 8, 12 x 9, 15 x 12	Bit	Fixed
HELVB.FON	Helvetica	10 x 5, 12 x 7, 15 x 8, 18 x 9, 22 x 12, 28 x 16	Bit	Proportional
MODERN.FON	Modern	Scaled	Vector	Proportional
ROMAN.FON	Roman	Scaled		
SCRIPT.FON	Script	Scaled	Vector	Proportional
TMSRB.FON	Times Roman	10 x 5, 12 x 6, 15 x 8, 16 x 9, 20 x 12, 26 x 16	Bit	Proportional

Values Returned:

The number of fonts registered is returned if the function is successful. Otherwise, a negative value is returned.

Related Functions:

```
_outgtext          :     display font text output
_setfont           :     selects a registered font for use
```

Similar Turbo C++ Functions:

```
installuserfont  :  loads a font file
int far installuserfont (char far *pathname);
```

Suggested Code Structure and Use:

The _registerfonts function is used to register the desired font. The following code structure illustrates the use of the _registerfonts function to register the fonts in the current directory.

```
#include <graph.h>
#include <stdio.h>
void main ()
{
_setvideomode ( mode );  /* set video mode */
_registerfonts ("*.fon");  /* register fonts */
_setfont ("t'courier' h12 w9 b f"); /* set fonts */
```

```
            .
            .
            .
       { use fonts }
            .
            .
            .

_unregisterfonts ();        /* free memory */
_setvideomode (_DEFAULTMODE);  /* reset and exit */
}
```

Example:

The _registerfonts function is used to register the fonts in the current directory. The font files must be in the current directory for this example to work. The font is set to the Courier font and a message is displayed.

```
#include <graph.h>
#include <stdio.h>
void main ()
{
_setvideomode (_ERESCOLOR);
_rectangle (_GBORDER, 0, 0, 639, 349);
     /* Register and set fonts */
_registerfonts ("*.fon");
_setfont ("t'courier' h12 w9 b f");
     /* Display message */
_moveto (30,175);
_outgtext ("The fonts are registered.  Courier font
               in use");
     /* Delay and exit */
_settextposition (23,30);
_outtext ("Press Any Key to Exit");
getch();
_unregisterfonts ();
_setvideomode (_DEFAULTMODE);
}
```

_remapallpalette

Syntax:

```
short _far _remapallpalette (long _far *colors);
long _far *colors;          array of colors
```

Function:

When used with EGA, MCGA, or VGA, _remapallpalette reassigns all available pixel values. As a result, the entire EGA, MCGA, or VGA palette is redefined.

Files to Include:

```
#include <graph.h>
```

Compatibility:

DOS

Description:

The _remapallpalette function redefines the EGA, MCGA, or VGA palette. The colors argument points to an array of color numbers that contains the maximum number of colors supported by the current video mode. A list of predefined colors is in table 9.2, under the _getcolor function.

Values Returned:

If successful, a -1 is returned. Otherwise, a 0 is returned, indicating an error.

Related Functions:

```
_remappalette    :      redefines the relationship of the
                        value contained in a pixel and
                        the color displayed
```

Similar Turbo C++ Functions:

```
setallpalette  :  changes all palette colors
void far setallpalette (struct palettetype far * palette);
```

Suggested Code Structure and Use:

The _remapallpalette function redefines the entire palette, thus creating a customized palette. It is a good practice to have the original palette available so that you can restore the palette upon leaving the function. The following code structure illustrates this use of the _remapallpalette function. When you use this function, it is important to remember that all changes are immediately visible.

```
#include <stdio.h>
#include <graph.h>
/* used to restore to original palette */
long originalpalette [16] =
```

```
      {_BLACK, _BLUE, _GREEN, _CYAN, _RED, _MAGENTA, _BROWN,
      _WHITE, _GRAY, _LIGHTBLUE, _LIGHTGREEN, _LIGHTCYAN,
      _LIGHTRED, _LIGHTMAGENTA, _LIGHTYELLOW, _BRIGHTWHITE};
      /* used to set new palette */
long newcolorpalette [16] =
   { identify the order of colors desired };
void main ()
{
_setvideomode ( mode ); /* set mode by graphics card */
_remapallpalette (newcolorpalette); /* define the new
                          palette */
       .
       .
       .
_remapallpalette (originalpalette); /* reset the current
         palette to the original palette */
_setvideomode (_DEFAULTMODE); /* reset graphics card */
}
```

Example:

This program demonstrates the _remapallpalette function. It begins by creating a new color palette that is the reverse order of the default palette. Then sixteen rectangle are drawn and filled with the default palette. When a key is pressed, the new color palette is implemented. The results (Color 0 becomes Color 15 and vice versa, Color 1 becomes Color 14 and vice versa, and so on) are displayed, as shown in figure 9.69.

```
     #include <stdio.h>

#include <graph.h>
/* Create a new palette--this one reverses the order
      of the default palette     */
long newcolorpalette [16] =
        { _BRIGHTWHITE, _LIGHTYELLOW, _LIGHTMAGENTA,
_LIGHTRED,
        _LIGHTCYAN, _LIGHTGREEN, _LIGHTBLUE, _GRAY,
        _WHITE, _BROWN, _MAGENTA, _RED,
        _CYAN, _GREEN, _BLUE, _BLACK};
void main ()
{
int x;
int color;
        /* Initialization   */
```

```
_setvideomode (_ERESCOLOR);
_rectangle (_GBORDER,0,0,639,349);
        /* Draw two rows of eight rectangles  */
for (x=20; x<581; x=x+80)
        {
        _rectangle (_GBORDER,x,20,x+40,155);
        _rectangle (_GBORDER,x,195,x+40,330);
        }
color = 0;
    /* Fill the top row with the first eight colors of the
        predefined palette  */
for (x=21; x<582; x=x+80)
        {
        _setcolor (color);
        _floodfill (x,21,15);
        color = color + 1;
        }
      /* Fill the bottom row with the last eight colors of the
        predefined palette */
for (x=21; x<582; x=x+80)
        {
        _setcolor (color);
        _floodfill (x,196,15);
        color = color + 1;
        }
        /* Print message      */
_settextposition (13,23);
_outtext ("Press Any Key to Change Palette");
        /* Delay */
getch ();
        /* Redefine the colors in the palette to
          those in newcolorpalette */
_remapallpalette (newcolorpalette);
        /* Delay and reset */
getch ();
_setvideomode (_DEFAULTMODE);
}
```

Fig. 9.69. Example _remapallpalette output.

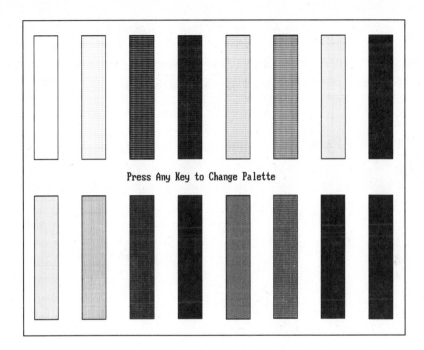

Press Any Key to Change Palette

_remappalette

Syntax:

```
long _far _remappalette (short pixel_value, long color);
short pixel_value;      pixel value to redefine
long color;            new color
```

Function:

The _remappalette function is used to remap a pixel value to the specified color. The _remappalette function works in only an EGA, an MCGA, or a VGA hardware environment.

Files to Include:

```
#include <graph.h>
```

Compatibility:

DOS

Description:

In an EGA, an MCGA or a VGA environment, the _remappalette function redefines the relationship between a particular pixel value and its color. This function is similar to the _remapallpalette function but only remaps one pixel value. The predefined colors are listed in table 9.2, under the _getcolor function.

Values Returned:

When an EGA, an MCGA, or a VGA is present, the _remappalette function returns the previous color number of the specified pixel. Otherwise, a -1 is returned to indicate an error.

Related Functions:

```
_remapallpalette    :    redefines all pixel values in a
                         palette
```

Similar Turbo C++ Functions:

```
setpalette  :  changes one palette color
void far setpalette (int colornum, int color);
```

Suggested Code Structure and Use:

The _remappalette function is useful for changing one of the colors in the palette. For example, you can change all green pixels to red with one call. Like other functions that alter default values, it is a good practice to reset the palette before exiting. The following code structure makes the default palette available for both the _remappalette and the _remapallpalette functions. The _remapallpalette function in this structure is used to restore the palette to its default setting. When using these functions, it is important to remember that any change is immediately visible.

```
#include <stdio.h>
#include <graph.h>
 /* identifies the predefined palette */
long originalpalette [16] =
  {_BLACK, _BLUE, _GREEN, _CYAN, _RED, _MAGENTA, _BROWN,
   _WHITE, _GRAY, _LIGHTBLUE, _LIGHTGREEN, _LIGHTCYAN,
   _LIGHTRED, _LIGHTMAGENTA, _LIGHTYELLOW, _BRIGHTWHITE};
void main ()
{
```

```
_setvideomode ( mode ); /* set mode by graphics card */
_remappalette (pixel_value, originalpalette [color #]);
        /* sets the pixel value to one of the colors in
           the original palette array */

              .
              .
              .

_remapallpalette (originalpalette); /* reset to original
                                       palette */
_setvideomode (_DEFAULTMODE); /* reset graphics card */
}
```

Example:

This program demonstrates the use of the _remappalette function. The program creates a colors array so that all predefined colors are easily available for use. Sixteen rectangles are drawn, each filled with one of the predefined colors. See figure 9.70. Each time a key is pressed, two colors are remapped, starting with Colors 0 and 15 (that is, Colors 0 and 15 are reversed), until all colors have been remapped. To exit the program, press q.

```
#include <stdio.h>
#include <graph.h>
    /* Create an array with available colors */
long colors [16] =
    { _BLACK, _BLUE, _GREEN, _CYAN,
    _RED, _MAGENTA, _BROWN, _WHITE,
    _GRAY, _LIGHTBLUE, _LIGHTGREEN, _LIGHTCYAN,
    _LIGHTRED, _LIGHTMAGENTA, _LIGHTYELLOW, _BRIGHTWHITE };
void main ()
{
int ch;
int x;
int color;
int color1;
    /* Initialization  */
_setvideomode (_ERESCOLOR);
_rectangle (_GBORDER,0,0,639,349);
    /* Draws two rows of eight rectangles   */
for (x=20; x<581; x=x+80)
    {
    _rectangle (_GBORDER,x,20,x+40,155);
    _rectangle (_GBORDER,x,195,x+40,330);
    }
color = 0;
```

```
      /*Fills the top row with the first eight colors from
       the predefined palette   */
   for (x=21; x<582; x=x+80)
      {
      _setcolor (color);
      _floodfill (x,21,15);
      color = color + 1;
      }
   /* Fills the bottom row with the last eight colors from the

               predefined palette */
   for (x=21; x<582; x=x+80)
      {
      _setcolor (color);
      _floodfill (x,196,15);
      color = color + 1;
      }
      /* Prints message */
   _settextposition (13,13);
   _outtext ("Press a Key to Alternate Various Colors - 'q'
            to Quit");
   color = 0;
    /* Alternates two colors, starting at 0 and 15, when a
       key is pressed. The loop ends when q is pressed */
   do {
       ch = getch ();
       color1 = 15 - color;
       _remappalette (color, colors [color1]);
       _remappalette (color1, colors [color]);
       color = color + 1;
      } while (ch != 'q');
      /* Reset  */
   _setvideomode (_DEFAULTMODE);
   }
```

_scrolltextwindow

Syntax:

```
   void _far _scrolltextwindow(short numlines);
   short numlines;       number of lines to scroll
```

Fig. 9.70. Example _remappalette output.

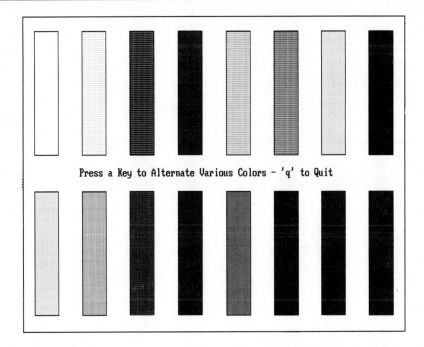

Press a Key to Alternate Various Colors – 'q' to Quit

Function:

The _scrolltextwindow function scrolls the current text window either up or down a specified number of lines.

Files to Include:

```
#include <graph.h>
```

Compatibility:

DOS
OS/2

Description:

The text window is scrolled either up or down using the _scrolltextwindow function. The numlines argument specifies the number of lines to scroll. If numlines is a positive number, the window is scrolled up the indicated number of lines. If numlines is a negative number, the window is scrolled down the indicated number of lines. When numlines is 0, the window is not affected. When the num lines argument exceeds the height of the current window, the window is cleared. The following two constants have been set for use with this function:

_GSCROLLUP   When this constant equals 1, scroll up one line.
_GSCROLLDOWN   When this constant equals -1, scroll down one line.

Values Returned:

There is no return value.

Related Functions:

```
_settextwindow  :  defines the current text window
```

Similar Turbo C++ Functions:

```
insline  :  inserts a blank line in the text window
void insline (void);
delline  :  deletes a line in the text window
void delline (void);
```

Suggested Code Structure and Use:

The _scrolltextwindow function is used to scroll the current text window. The following code structure illustrates the use of this function.

```
#include <stdio.h>
#include <graph.h>
void main ()
{
_setvideomode ( mode );  /* set video mode */
    .
    .
    .
_settextwindow (r1,c1,r2,c2);  /* set text window */
    .
    .
    .
_scrolltextwindow (# of lines);  /* scroll text */
    .
    .
    .
```

```
_setvideomode (_DEFAULTMODE);   /* reset and exit */
}
```

Example:

The _scrolltextwindow function is used in this example to scroll up the text in the window. Each time a key is pressed, the text is scrolled up. To end the program, press Esc.

```
#include <stdio.h>
#include <graph.h>
void main ()
{
int ch;
_setvideomode (_ERESCOLOR);
_rectangle (_GBORDER,0,0,639,349);
/* Text to scroll */
_settextposition (24,25);
_outtext ("Text to Scroll");
/* Set text window */
_settextwindow (2,2,24,79);
/* Scroll up one line with each
   keystroke--press Esc to exit  */
do
{
ch = getch ();
_scrolltextwindow (_GSCROLLUP);
} while (ch != 27);
/* Reset and exit */
_setvideomode (_DEFAULTMODE);
}
```

_selectpalette

Syntax:

```
short _far _selectpalette (short palette_number);
short palette_number;                   palette number
```

Function:

The _selectpalette function is used to choose one of the four predefined palettes when in _MRES4COLOR or _MRESNOCOLOR video mode.

Files to Include:

```
#include <graph.h>
```

Compatibility:

DOS

Description:

One of four predefined palettes can be selected with the _selectpalette function when in the _MRES4COLOR or _MRESNOCOLOR video mode. A palette contains four colors. Color 0 is a selectable color (see the _setbkcolor function); Colors 1, 2, and 3 are predefined and set. There are four palletes in the _MRES4COLOR mode; these palettes are the same in CGA and EGA environments. In _MRESNOCOLOR mode, various shades of gray are produced on black-and-white displays; colors are produced on color displays. The number of palettes and the colors available on each palette vary between CGA and EGA. See table 9.3, under the _getcolor function.

Values Returned:

The previous palette number is returned by the _selectpalette function. No error value is returned.

Related Functions:

```
_setbkcolor     : set Color 0 to a specified color
```

Similar Turbo C++ Functions:

```
initgraph       : initializes the video mode and palette
void far initgraph (int far *graphdriver,
int far *graphmode, char far *pathtodriver);
```

Suggested Code Structure and Use:

The _selectpalette function allows the user to choose between palettes of available colors while in _MRES4COLOR and _MRESNOCOLOR modes. The following code structure illustrates how the function would be used.

```
#include <stdio.h>
#include <graph.h>
void main ()
```

```
{
_setvideomode ( mode ); /* _MRES4COLOR or _MRESNOCOLOR */
_selectpalette (palette number); /* choose palette */
    .
    .
    .
_setvideomode (_DEFAULTMODE); /* reset graphics card */
}
```

Example:

This program draws four rectangles and fills them with the four available colors in the palette. See figure 9.71. When a key is pressed, the next palette is activated. To exit the program, press x. It is important to remember that Color 0 is selectable from the sixteen predefined colors. Remember also that the selection of a palette makes it immediately visible.

```
#include <stdio.h>
#include <graph.h>
void main ()
{
int palette;
int ch;
    /* Initialization   */
_setvideomode (_MRES4COLOR);
_rectangle (_GBORDER,0,0,319,199);
_setbkcolor (_BLUE);
/* Divide screen into four equivalent rectangles */
_rectangle (_GBORDER,0,0,159,99);
_rectangle (_GBORDER,0,99,159,199);
_rectangle (_GBORDER,160,0,319,99);
_rectangle (_GBORDER,160,99,319,199);
/* Fill the rectangles with the four palette colors   */
_setcolor (0);
_floodfill (1,1,3);
_setcolor (1);
_floodfill (1,100,3);
_setcolor (2);
_floodfill (161,1,3);
_setcolor (3);
_floodfill (161,100,3);
    /* Print message   */
_settextposition (12,3);
_outtext ("Press any key to change palettes");
_settextposition (13,12);
```

```
_outtext ("Press 'x' to exit");
palette = 1;
/* Change to the next palette when a key is pressed  */
/* Exit when x is pressed                            */
do
    {
    ch = getch ();
    _selectpalette (palette);
    palette = palette + 1;
    if (palette > 3)
      palette = 0;
    }      while (ch != 'x');
    /* Reset */
_setvideomode (_DEFAULTMODE);
}
```

Fig. 9.71. Example _selectpalette output.

_setactivepage

Syntax:

```
short _far _setactivepage (short page);
short page;      page number
```

Function:

The _setactivepage function provides the capability to store multiple pages of graphics or text in video memory.

Files to Include:

```
#include <graph.h>
```

Compatibility:

DOS

Description:

The _setactivepage function requires sufficient video memory for multiple page storage. When the _setactivepage function is called, the specified page, or section of memory, is identified as the area where graphics operations will be performed. For example, the CGA has only 16K of RAM, and therefore can support only one graphics page. In text mode, however, it can support multiple pages because text modes require less memory per page. EGA and VGA can be equipped with extra memory to support multiple pages of high-resolution graphics in graphics mode.

The _setactivepage function is used with the _setvisualpage function to alternate pages of text or graphics. The most common use of these functions is for animation. Graphics operations are performed on a nonvisual screen with the _setactivepage function. When the operations are completed, the page is made visual with the _setvisualpage function. Then the process is repeated. See the example for a demonstration of this technique.

Values Returned:

If successful, the page number of the previous active page is returned. If the function fails, a negative value is returned.

Related Functions:

```
_setvisualpage :    sets the current display page
```

Similar Turbo C++ Functions:

```
setactivepage  :  sets active page for graphics output
void far setactivepage (int page);
```

Suggested Code Structure and Use:

The _setactivepage function lets the user draw on a nonvisual section of memory. There must be sufficient video memory to perform this function successfully. (Use _getvideoconfig to see whether there is enough video memory.) The following code structure illustrates how a function might be structured to draw on a nonvisual page and then make the page visible. You could repeat this type of structure as many times as required.

```
#include <stdio.h>
#include <graph.h>
void main ()
{
_setvideomode ( mode ); /* set mode by graphics card */
_setactivepage (1); /* get ready to draw on nonvisual
        page 1 */
        .
        .
        .
   { draw on page 1 }
        .
        .
        .
_setvisualpage (1); /* show page 1 */
_setactivepage (0); /* get ready to draw on nonvisual
            page 0 */
        .
        .
        .
   { draw on page 0 }
        .
        .
        .
_setvisualpage (0); /* show page 0 */
_setvideomode (_DEFAULTMODE); /* reset graphics card */
}
```

Example:

This program demonstrates how two pages of graphics can be flipped, and how graphics can be drawn on a nonvisual page. The program begins by drawing an ellipse on the default visual and active page 0. It then sets the active page to 1 (nonvisual) and draws a rectangle. When a key is pressed, the pages alternate. This continues with each keystroke until you press x.

```
#include <stdio.h>
#include <graph.h>
void main ()
{
int ch;
int page;
/*    Initialization--this program requires an EGA or
 VGA with sufficient memory to support
 multiple graphics pages */
_setvideomode (_ERESCOLOR);
      /* Draw page 0 */
_rectangle (_GBORDER,0,0,639,349);
_ellipse (_GBORDER,100,100,540,250);
_setcolor (4);
_floodfill (320,175,15);
_settextposition (23,15);
_outtext ("Page 0 : Press Any Key for Next Page - 'x'
     for exit");
    /* Draw page 1 */
_setactivepage (1);
_clearscreen (_GCLEARSCREEN);
_setcolor (15);
_rectangle (_GBORDER,0,0,639,349);
_rectangle (_GBORDER,100,100,540,250);
_setcolor (1);
_floodfill (320,175,15);
_settextposition (23,15);
_outtext ("Page 1 : Press Any Key for Next Page -
     'x' for exit");
page = 0;
    /* Flip between pages--exit on x   */
do {
   _setvisualpage (page);
   ch = getch ();
   page = page + 1;
   if (page > 1)
     page = 0;
  } while (ch != 'x');
```

```
            /* Reset */
  _setvideomode (_DEFAULTMODE);
  }
```

_setbkcolor

Syntax:

```
long _far _setbkcolor (long color);
long color;            desired color
```

Function:

The _setbkcolor function sets the background color to the specified color.

Files to Include:

```
#include <graph.h>
```

Compatibility:

DOS
OS/2

Description:

The _setbkcolor function sets the background color to the pixel value specified in the color argument. The color argument differs between text and graphics mode. An index from the current palette is used in text mode; a mnemonic constant is used in graphics mode. The predefined values for the background colors as defined in graph.h are shown in table 9.1, under the _getbkcolor function.

The _setbkcolor function immediately changes the background color in graphics mode. In text mode, however, only the output produced after the _setbkcolor function has been executed is affected. A call to the _clearscreen function clears the text screen and changes the background to the color specified in the _setbkcolor function.

The _setbkcolor function is used also to specify Color 0 in CGA palettes. See table 9.3, under the _getcolor function, for more information on CGA palettes. The _remappalette function can be used to reset Color 0 in EGA and VGA environments.

Values Returned:

The _setbkcolor function returns the long integer index or value of the old background color. No error value is returned.

Related Functions:

```
_getbkcolor          :   gets the current background color
_remapallpalette     :   redefines the entire palette
_remappalette        :   redefines one pixel value
```

Similar Turbo C++ Functions:

```
setbkcolor  :  sets the current background color
void far setbkcolor (int color);
```

Graphics Mode

Suggested Code Structure and Use:

The _setbkcolor function is used to select one of 16 colors for the background. In graphics mode, the color selection is visible immediately. The following code structure can be used when implementing this function in graphics mode.

```
#include <stdio.h>
#include <graph.h>
long backcolor [16] =
  {_BLACK, _BLUE, _GREEN, _CYAN, _RED, _MAGENTA, _BROWN,
   _WHITE, _GRAY, _LIGHTBLUE, _LIGHTGREEN, _LIGHTCYAN,
   _LIGHTRED, _LIGHTMAGENTA, _LIGHTYELLOW, _BRIGHTWHITE};
void main ()
{
_setvideomode ( mode ); /* set mode by graphics card */
_setbkcolor (backcolor [color #]); /* choose a color */
        .
        .
        .
_setvideomode (_DEFAULTMODE); /* reset graphics mode */
}
```

Example:

This program demonstrates the various background colors in graphics modes. The program initializes an array which makes the background color easily available. When a key is pressed the background color changes. This is repeated until x is pressed.

```
#include <stdio.h>
#include <graph.h>
        /* Initialize colors for use by do loop  */
long backcolor [16] =
    {_BLACK, _BLUE, _GREEN, _CYAN, _RED, _MAGENTA,
        BROWN, _WHITE, _GRAY, _LIGHTBLUE, _LIGHTGREEN,
        _LIGHTCYAN, _LIGHTRED, _LIGHTMAGENTA,
        _LIGHTYELLOW, _BRIGHTWHITE};
void main ()
{
int color;
int ch;
    /* Initialization   */
_setvideomode (_MRES4COLOR);
_rectangle (_GBORDER,0,0,319,199);
    /* Print messages    */
_settextposition (11,2);
_outtext ("Press any key to change background");
_settextposition (13,2);
_outtext ("Press 'x' to exit");
color = 0;
/* Change background color when a key is pressed.
    Exit when x is pressed */
do {
    _setbkcolor (backcolor [color]);
    ch = getch ();
    color = color + 1;
    if (color > 15)
  color = 0;
 }  while (ch != 'x');
    /* Reset */
_setvideomode (_DEFAULTMODE);
}
```

Text Mode

Suggested Code Structure and Use:

The _setbkcolor function is used to select one of 16 colors for the background. In text mode, the color is not immediately visible. Only subsequent output is affected. To change the entire background, you should make a call to _clearscreen. The following code structure can be used when implementing this function in text modes.

```
#include <stdio.h>
#include <graph.h>
long backcolor [16] =
  { 0L, 1L, 2L, 3L, 4L, 5L, 6L, 7L, 8L, 9L, 10L, 11L,
    12L, 13L, 14L, 15L};
void main ()
{
_setvideomode ( mode ); /* set mode by graphics card */
_setbkcolor (backcolor [color #]}; /* choose color */
_clearscreen (area); /* clears screen or window */
        .
        .
        .

_setvideomode (_DEFAULTMODE); /* reset graphics card */
}
```

Example:

The following example demonstrates the procedure for setting the background color while in text modes. The _clearscreen function with the _GWINDOW area argument is used since only subsequent text output is affected by the _setbkcolor function while in text modes.

```
#include <stdio.h>
#include <graph.h>
    /* Establish array of colors */
long backcolor [16] =
    {0L, 1L, 2L, 3L, 4L, 5L, 6L, 7L, 8L,
     9L, 10L, 11L, 12L, 13L, 14L, 15L};
void main ()
{
int color;
int ch;
color = 0;
do
    {
    _setbkcolor (backcolor [color]);
    _clearscreen (_GWINDOW);
    _settextposition (11,2);
    _outtext ("Press Any Key to Change Background");
    _settextposition (13,2);
    _outtext ("Press 'x' to Exit");
```

```
        ch = getch ();
        color = color + 1;
        if (color > 15)
        color = 0;
        } while (ch != 'x');
    _setvideomode (_DEFAULTMODE);
    }
```

_setcliprgn

Syntax:

```
void _far _setcliprgn (short x1, short y1, short x2,
                short y2);
short x1, y1;                    upper left corner of region
short x2, y2;                    lower right corner of region
```

Function:

The _setcliprgn function clips the graphic output that exceeds the boundaries of the rectangular region defined by the points x1,y1 and x2,y2.

Files to Include:

```
#include <graph.h>
```

Compatibility:

DOS

Description:

The _setcliprgn function limits graphic output to the rectangular region defined by x1,y1 and x2,y2. The x1 and y1 parameters define the upper left corner of the clipping region. The x2 and y2 parameters define the lower right corner of the clipping region. These parameters are described by their physical coordinates. Unlike the _setviewport function, the _setcliprgn function does not alter the view coordinate system. The _setcliprgn function affects only subsequent graphic calls; previous output is unaffected. Figures 9.72 and 9.73 illustrate the use of the _setcliprgn function.

Fig. 9.72. The _setcliprgn function.

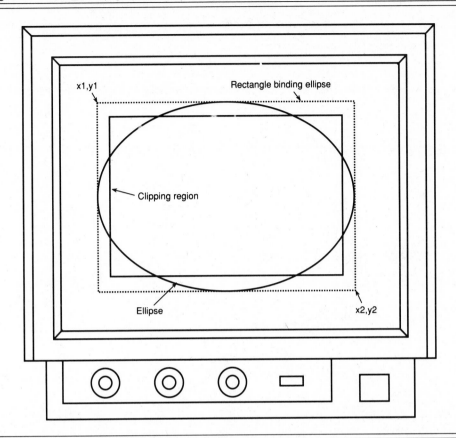

Values Returned:

No value is returned.

Related Functions:

```
_setviewport   : sets a clipping region while redefining
                 the origin of the view coordinate
                 system
_settextwindow : similar to the _setcliprgn function
                 but it is used with text output
```

Fig. 9.73. Resulting _setcliprgn output.

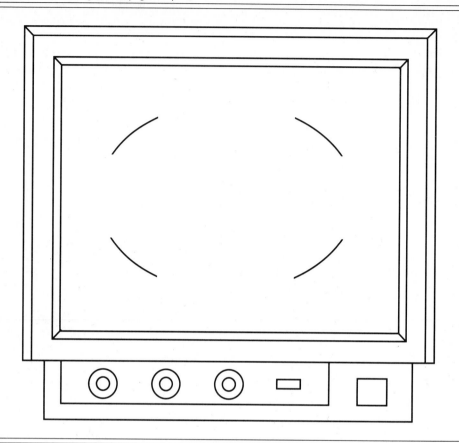

Similar Turbo C++ Functions:

```
setviewport  :  sets the current viewport--can be specified
                to clip at the viewport's border
void far setviewport (int left, int top, int right,
                      int bottom, int clip);
```

Suggested Code Structure and Use:

The _setcliprgn function is commonly used to restrict graphics output to a specified area. This is useful when only portions of subsequent output need to be displayed. The following code structure illustrates the common use of the _setcliprgn function.

```
#include <stdio.h>
#include <graph.h>
void main ()
{
_setvideomode ( mode ); /* set mode by adapter */
            .
            .
            .
_setcliprgn (x1,y1,x2,y2); /* set clipping region */
            .
            .
            .
_setvideomode (_DEFAULTMODE); /* reset */
}
```

Example:

This program demonstrates the use of the _setcliprgn function. An ellipse is drawn without being clipped. When a key is pressed, the ellipse is erased and redrawn partially outside the clipping region. The resulting output is four arcs, as shown in figure 9.74.

```
#include <stdio.h>
#include <graph.h>
void main ()
{
    /* Initialization */
_setvideomode (_MRES4COLOR);
_rectangle (_GBORDER,0,0,319,199);
_setbkcolor (_BLUE);
    /* Draw ellipse */
_ellipse (_GBORDER,50,50,270,150);
    /* Print messages */
_settextposition (23,2);
_outtext ("Press Key to Draw Clipped Ellipse");
    /* Delay */
getch ();
/* Delete previous ellipse, draw clipped ellipse  */
_setcolor (0);
_ellipse (_GBORDER,50,50,270,150);
_setcliprgn (60,60,260,140);
_setcolor (3);
_ellipse (_GBORDER,50,50,270,150);
    /* Delay and reset */
_settextposition (23,2);
```

```
_outtext ("Press Any Key to Continue          ");
getch ();
_setvideomode (_DEFAULTMODE);
}
```

Fig. 9.74. Example _setcliprgn output.

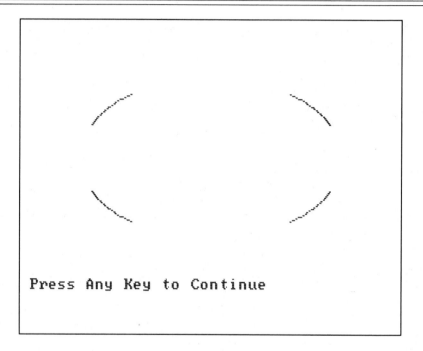

Press Any Key to Continue

_setcolor

Syntax:

```
short _far _setcolor (short color);
short color;          desired color
```

Function:

The _setcolor function sets the current color to the specified color.

Files to Include:

```
#include <graph.h>
```

Compatibility:

DOS

Description:

When the _setcolor function is called, the current color is set to the color specified in the color argument. The _arc, _ellipse, _floodfill, _lineto, _pie, _rectangle, and _setpixel functions use the current color as the default color. Upon entering graphics mode, the current color is set to the highest color number in the current color palette. If the color argument is outside the legal range of values in the current palette, the current color is set to the highest numbered color in the palette.

Due to differences in palettes, the actual color displayed by any one color argument depends on the current palette. For example _setcolor (1); in _MRES4COLOR mode with a current palette of 0 sets the current color to green. In _ERESCOLOR mode, however, _setcolor (1); sets the current color to blue. The available predefined colors for each palette are described in tables 9.2 and 9.3, under the _getcolor function. It is important to remember that calls to the _remappalette and _remapallpalette functions alter some of these predefined colors.

Values Returned:

When successful, the pixel value of the previous color is returned; otherwise, a -1 is returned.

Related Functions:

```
_getcolor :     returns the current color
```

Similar Turbo C++ Functions:

```
setcolor  :  sets the current color
void far setcolor (int color);
```

Suggested Code Structure and Use:

The _setcolor function is very useful for creating multicolored graphic displays. Because each drawing function (for example, _arc and _lineto) uses the current color, it is possible to create very detailed images. The most important consideration in using the _setcolor function is the current palette because there is a limited number of colors available in each palette. The following coded number structure illustrates the use of the _setcolor function.

```
#include <stdio.h>
#include <graph.h>
void main ()
{
_setvideomode ( mode ); /* set mode by adapter */
        .
        .
        .
_setcolor ( color ); /* select a color from the current
                palette */
        .
        .
        .
_setvideomode (_DEFAULTMODE); /* reset */
}
```

Example:

The following program uses the _setcolor function to select the three nonbackground colors available in the current palette. After a color is selected, an ellipse is drawn using this color. See figure 9.75.

```
#include <stdio.h>
#include <graph.h>
void main ()
{
int color;
    /* Initialization */
_setvideomode (_MRES4COLOR);
_rectangle (_GBORDER,0,0,319,199);
_setbkcolor (_RED);
    /* Draw three ellipses with the three nonbackground
        colors  */
_setcolor (1);
_ellipse (_GBORDER,25,25,294,174);
_setcolor (2);
_ellipse (_GBORDER,50,50,269,149);
_setcolor (3);
_ellipse (_GBORDER,75,75,244,124);
_settextposition (22,10);
_outtext ("Press a Key to Exit");
```

```
    /* Delay and reset */
getch ();
_setvideomode (_DEFAULTMODE);
}
```

Fig. 9.75. Example _setcolor output.

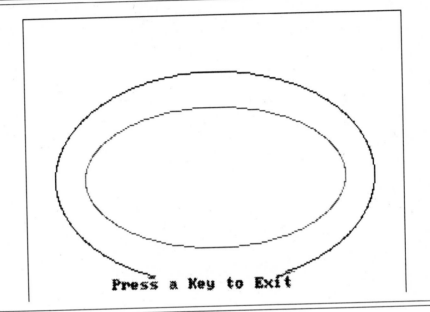

Press a Key to Exit

_setfillmask

Syntax:

```
void _far _setfillmask (unsigned char _far *fillpattern);
unsigned char _far *fillpattern;        fill pattern
```

Function:

The `_setfillmask` function defines an 8-by-8 bit pattern used for fill routines in the `_floodfill`, `_rectangle`, `_ellipse`, `_polygon`, and `_pie` functions.

Files to Include:

```
#include <graph.h>
```

Compatibility:

DOS

Description:

The 8-by-8 bit pattern used for filling an area in the _floodfill, _rectangle, _ellipse, _polygon, and _pie functions is defined through the _setfillmask function. The fillpattern argument defines this 8-by-8 bit pattern. Each character in the argument represents eight bits, or a row. The eight characters represent 8 rows, thus the 8-by-8 bit area. A 1 bit sets the corresponding pixel to the current color. A 0 bit leaves the corresponding pixel unchanged. The 8-by-8 bit pattern is repeated over the entire portion of the area to be filled. Upon entering graphics mode, the default fill pattern is

```
\xFF\xFF\xFF\xFF\xFF\xFF\xFF\xFF
```

This is a solid fill pattern.

Values Returned:

There is no return value.

Related Functions:

```
_getfillmask    :        returns the current fill pattern
```

Similar Turbo C++ Functions:

```
setfillpattern  :  selects a user-defined fill pattern
void far setfillpattern (char far *upattern, int color);
```

Suggested Code Structure and Use:

The _setfillmask function is used to set the current fill pattern for use by the drawing routines that use a fill pattern. With a limited number of colors, you can produce various shades of each color by creating several fill patterns. The following code structure demonstrates the procedure for using this function.

```
#include <stdio.h>
#include <graph.h>
unsigned char *(fillpattern [number of patterns])=
   {"\x--\x--\x--\x--\x--\x--\x--\x--",
                   .
                   .
                   .
```

```
        "\x--\x--\x--\x--\x--\x--\x--\x--"};
void main ()
{
_setvideomode ( mode ); /* set mode by adapter */
                .

                .

                .
_setfillmask ((char far *)(fillpattern [pattern #]));
                .

                .

                .
_setvideomode (_DEFAULTMODE); /* reset */
}
```

Example:

This program defines thirteen fill patterns, then draws sixteen rectangles. Each rectangle is then filled with one of the thirteen fill patterns, as shown in figure 9.76.

```
#include <stdio.h>
#include <graph.h>
/* Initialization of fill patterns */
unsigned char *(fillpattern [13])=
  {"\x00\x00\x00\x00\x00\x00\x00\x00",    /* 0% fill      */
   "\x00\x20\x00\x00\x00\x02\x00\x00",    /* 3% fill      */
   "\x20\x00\x02\x00\x80\x00\x08\x00",    /* 6% fill      */
   "\x20\x02\x80\x08\x20\x02\x80\x08",    /* 12.5% fill   */
   "\x44\x11\x44\x11\x44\x11\x44\x11",    /* 25% fill     */
   "\xAA\x44\xAA\x11\xAA\x44\xAA\x11",    /* 37.5% fill   */
   "\x55\xAA\x55\xAA\x55\xAA\x55\xAA",    /* 50% fill     */
   "\x55\xBB\x55\xEE\x55\xBB\x55\xEE",    /* 62.5% fill   */
   "\xBB\xEE\xBB\xEE\xBB\xEE\xBB\xEE",    /* 75% fill     */
   "\xDF\xFF\x7F\xF7\xDF\xFD\x7F\xF7",    /* 87.5% fill   */
   "\xDF\xFF\xFD\xFF\x7F\xFF\xF7\xFF",    /* 94% fill     */
   "\xFF\xDF\xFF\xFF\xFF\xFD\xFF\xFF",    /* 97% fill     */
   "\xFF\xFF\xFF\xFF\xFF\xFF\xFF\xFF"};   /* 100% fill    */
void main ()
{
int color;
int x;
_setvideomode (_MRES4COLOR);
_setbkcolor (_BLUE);
_rectangle (_GBORDER,0,0,319,199);
color = -1;
```

```
            /* Draw 16 rectangles      */
for (x=5; x<276; x=x+45)
      {
      _rectangle (_GBORDER,x,20,x+40,90);
       rectangle (_GBORDER,x,110,x+40,180);
      }
            /* Fill top rectangles      */
for (x=6; x<277; x=x+45)
      {
      color = color + 1;
       setfillmask ((char far *)(fillpattern [color]));
       floodfill (x,21,3);
            }
      /* Fill bottom rectangles */
for (x=6; x<232; x=x+45)
      {
      color = color + 1;
      _setfillmask ((char far *)(fillpattern [color]));
      _floodfill (x,111,3);
            }
_settextposition (24,10);
_outtext ("Press a Key to Exit");
      /*  Delay and reset  */
getch ();
_setvideomode (_DEFAULTMODE);
}
```

_setfont

Syntax:

```
short _far _setfont(unsigned char _far *options);
unsigned char _far *options;      font characteristics
```

Function:

The _setfont function is used to specify the set of registered fonts to use.

Files to Include:

```
#include <graph.h>
```

Fig. 9.76. Example _setfillmask output.

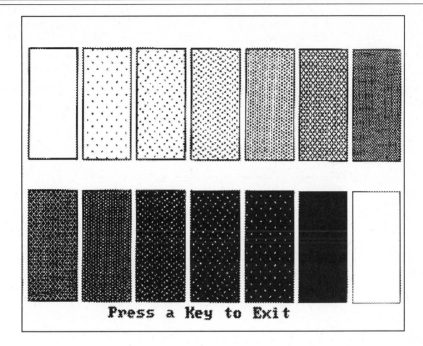

Press a Key to Exit

Compatibility:

DOS

Description:

The **_setfont** function selects one font from the set of registered fonts. The **options** string describes the characteristics of the font. The registered font that matches the characteristics in the **options** string, if found, is made the current font. All subsequent calls to the **_outgtext** function use this font.

The characteristics in table 9.17 can be specified in the **options** string. Spaces should be used to separate the options in the **options** string. When selecting options, mutually exclusive options (**f** and **p**, or **r** and **v**) are ignored. If the **b** option is selected and a font has been registered, the font that best fits the characteristics will be set. The **nx** option should be used alone. Table 9.18 lists the font names and descriptions for the **fontname** option. For a list of available font files and corresponding font sizes, see table 9.16, under the **_registerfonts** function.

Table 9.17. *The _setfont options.*

Characteristic	Description
t'fontname'	Name of font to use
hx	Character height—x is height in pixels
wy	Character width—y is width in pixels
f	Fixed-space font—don't use with p option
p	Proportional font—don't use with f option
v	Vector font—don't use with r option
r	Raster-mapped font—don't use with v option
b	Select the font with the best fit
nx	Choose font number x

Table 9.18. *Font descriptions.*

Fontname option	Description
Courier	Fixed-width, bit-mapped, serifs
Helv	Sans serif, proportional, bit-mapped
Tms Rmn	Proportional, bit-mapped, serifs
Script	Proportional, vector-mapped
Modern	Proportional, vector-mapped, no serifs
Roman	Proportional, vector-mapped, serifs

Values Returned:

When successful, 0 is returned. If no font is registered or a request for a specific font fails, -1 is returned.

Related Functions:

```
_registerfonts   :   registers the specified fonts
_outgtext        :   displays font text
```

Similar Turbo C++ Functions:

```
settextstyle : sets the text characteristics
void far settextstyle (int font, int direction,
                       int charsize);
```

Suggested Code Structure and Use:

The _setfont function is used to select a registered font for subsequent font text output. The following code structure illustrates one method for registering, setting, and using fonts. The font files should be in the current directory when compiling this example.

```
#include <graph.h>
#include <stdio.h>
void main ()
{
_setvideomode ( mode );   /* set video mode */
_registerfonts ("*.fon");   /* register fonts */
_setfont ("t'roman' h15 w9 p v"); /* select a font */
        .
        .
        .
_moveto (x,y); /* mark starting point for text */
_outgtext ("Text to Display");
        .
        .
        .
_unregisterfonts (); /* free memory */
_setvideomode (_DEFAULTMODE);   /* reset and exit */
}
```

Example:

The following example uses the _setfont function to select the Roman proportional font. Then a message is displayed in this font.

```
#include <graph.h>
#include <stdio.h>
void main ()
{
struct _fontinfo information;
char buffer [40];
_setvideomode (_ERESCOLOR);
_rectangle (_GBORDER, 0, 0, 639, 349);
     /* Register and select font */
_registerfonts ("*.fon");
_setfont ("t'roman' h15 w9 p v");
     /* Display font text */
_moveto (130,150);
_outgtext ("The Roman Vector Font Is Registered
```

```
                    And In Use");
        /* Delay and exit */
_settextposition (23,30);
_outtext ("Press Any Key to Exit");
getch();
_unregisterfonts ();
_setvideomode (_DEFAULTMODE);
}
```

_setgtextvector

Syntax:

```
struct xycoord _far _setgtextvector(short x, short y);
short x, y;              coordinates for text direction
```

Function:

The _setgtextvector function defines the vector orientation for text output.

Files to Include:

```
#include <graph.h>
```

Compatibility:

DOS

Description:

The _setgtextvector function sets the text vector orientation for font text output. The x and y arguments define the orientation for the vector; see table 9.19.

Table 9.19. *Vector orientation.*

Values for x,y	Orientation
1,0	Horizontal text (default)
0,1	Rotated 90 degrees counterclockwise
-1,0	Rotated 180 degrees counterclockwise
0,-1	Rotated 270 degrees counterclockwise

Values Returned:

The orientation of the previous vector is returned in a structure of type x y c o o r d. This structure follows.

```
structure xycoord
  {
  short xcoord;
  short ycoord;
  };
```

Related Functions:

```
_outgtext            :  displays font text output
```

Similar Turbo C++ Functions:

```
settextstyle  :  set the text characteristics including
                 direction of output
void far settextstyle (int fonts, int direction,
                       int charsize);
```

Suggested Code Structure and Use:

The _setgtextvector function is used to determine the method in which font text will be displayed. The possible orientations are horizontal (normal), rotated 90 degrees counterclockwise, rotated 180 degrees counterclockwise, and rotated 270 degrees counterclockwise. The following code structure illustrates the use of the _setgtextvector function.

```
#include <graph.h>
#include <stdio.h>
void main ()
{
int width;
_setvideomode (_ERESCOLOR);  /* set video mode */
_registerfonts ("*.fon");  /* register fonts */
_setfont ("t'courier' h12 w9 b f"); /* select a font */
         .
         .
         .
_setgtextvector (x,y);  /* set orientation */
_moveto (x,y);  /* starting point for text */
_outgtext ("Text to display");
```

```
        .
        .
        .
_unregisterfonts ();   /* free memory */
_setvideomode (_DEFAULTMODE);   /* reset and exit */
}
```

Example:

The _setgtextvector function is used in this example to set the vector orientation. Text is displayed using all of the possible vector orientations, as shown in figure 9.77.

```
#include <graph.h>
#include <stdio.h>
void main ()
{
int width;
_setvideomode ( mode );
     /* Register and select fonts */
_registerfonts ("*.fon");
_setfont ("t'courier' h12 w9 b f");
     /*  Display text using various vector orientations *
_moveto (330,170);
_setgtextvector (1,0);
_outgtext ("0 Degrees");
_moveto (315,165);
_setgtextvector (0,1);
_outgtext ("90 Degrees");
_moveto (310,180);
_setgtextvector (-1,0);
_outgtext ("180 Degrees");
_moveto (325,185);
_setgtextvector (0,-1);
_outgtext ("270 Degrees");
     /* Delay and exit */
_moveto (30,330);
_setgtextvector (1,0);
_outgtext ("Press Any Key to Exit");
getch();
_unregisterfonts ();
_setvideomode (_DEFAULTMODE);
}
```

Fig. 9.77. Example _setgtextvector output.

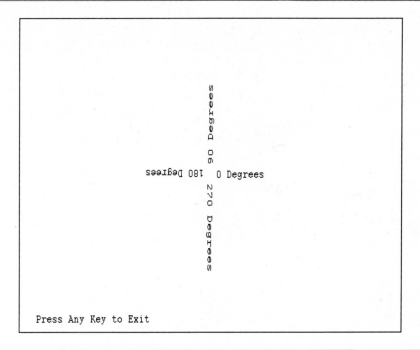

_setlinestyle

Syntax:

```
void _far _setlinestyle (unsigned short linepattern);
unsigned short linepattern;          line pattern
```

Function:

The _setlinestyle function defines a 16-bit line pattern for the straight lines used by the
_lineto and _rectangle functions.

Files to Include:

```
#include <graph.h>
```

Compatibility:

DOS

589

Description:

The _setlinestyle function controls the appearance of the straight lines used by the _lineto and _rectangle functions. The 16-bit linepattern argument defines the pattern for the straight lines. The lines can be dashed or solid. Upon entering graphics mode, the line pattern is set to the default value of 0xFFFF, which corresponds to a solid line. The line pattern is a 16-bit pattern; a 1 bit sets the corresponding pixel to the current color, and a 0 bit leaves the corresponding pixel unchanged. In Chapter 3, the section on drawing and line patterns describes various line patterns and their definitions.

Values Returned:

There is no return value.

Related Functions:

```
_getlinestyle   :         returns the current line pattern
```

Similar Turbo C++ Functions:

```
setlinestyle  :  sets the current line width and style
void far setlinestyle (int linestyle, unsigned upattern,
                        int thickness);
```

Suggested Code Structure and Use:

The _setlinestyle function is used to identify the current line style. These line styles are then used to draw straight lines. The following code structure illustrates the use of the _setlinestyle function.

```
#include <stdio.h>
#include <graph.h>
short linepattern [number of patterns] =
      {0x----,
         .
         .
         .
         0x----};
void main ()
{
_setvideomode ( mode ); /* set mode by adapter */
```

```
                  .
                  .
                  .
      _setlinestyle (linepattern [pattern #]);
                  .
                  .
                  .
      _setvideomode (_DEFAULTMODE);
      }
```

Example:

The following example demonstrates the use of the **_setlinestyle** function. Initially, nineteen line patterns are established. Then each of these patterns is used to create a line, as shown in figure 9.78.

```
      #include <stdio.h>
      #include <graph.h>
                    /* Line pattern number */
      short linepattern [19] =
       { 0x8000,          /*     1     */
         0xC000,          /*     2     */
         0xE000,          /*     3     */
         0xF000,          /*     4     */
         0xF800,          /*     5     */
         0xFC00,          /*     6     */
         0xFE00,          /*     7     */
         0xFF00,          /*     8     */
         0x8080,          /*     9     */
         0xC0C0,          /*    10     */
         0xE0E0,          /*    11     */
         0xF0F0,          /*    12     */
         0x8888,          /*    13     */
         0xCCCC,          /*    14     */
         0xDDDD,          /*    15     */
         0xE4E4,          /*    16     */
         0xF6F5,          /*    17     */
         0xFF18,          /*    18     */
         0xFFFF };        /*    19     */
      void main ()
      {
      int y, i;
      _setvideomode (_MRES4COLOR);
      _setbkcolor (_BLUE);
```

591

```
_rectangle (_GBORDER,0,0,319,199);
y = 9;
    /* Draw lines with different patterns */
for (i=0; i<19; i++)
    {
    _setlinestyle (linepattern [i]);
    _moveto (5,y);
    _lineto (314,y);
    y = y + 10;
    }
_settextposition (24,10);
_outtext ("Press a Key to Exit");
    /* Delay and reset  */
getch ();
_setvideomode (_DEFAULTMODE);
}
```

Fig. 9.78. Example _setlinestyle output.

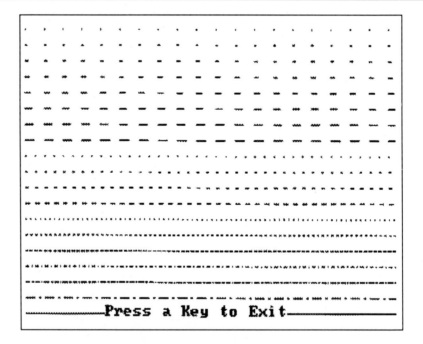

_setpixel

Syntax:

```
short _far _setpixel(short x, short y);
short x, y;    pixel coordinates to set to current color
```

Function:

The _setpixel function sets the specified pixel to the current color. This function uses the view coordinate system.

Files to Include:

```
#include <graph.h>
```

Compatibility:

DOS

Description:

When the _setpixel function is called, the pixel specified by the x and y arguments is set to the current color. The specified pixel is set to the current color only if the pixel lies within the current clipping region. The x and y coordinates of the pixel are described in view coordinates. Tables 9.2 and 9.3, under the _getcolor function, will help you set the appropriate color according to the mode.

Values Returned:

If the function is successful, the previous color (pixel value) of the specified pixel is returned. If the function is unsuccessful, a -1 is returned.

Related Functions:

```
_setcolor      :        sets the current color
_getpixel      :        retrieves the pixel value of the
                        specified pixel
```

Similar Turbo C++ Functions:

```
putpixel :  plots a pixel at a specified point
void far putpixel (int x, int y, int color);
```

Suggested Code Structure and Use:

The _setpixel function is useful for setting a specific pixel to a color. This function can be used to add specific detail to displays but is impractical for filling large areas. The following code structure illustrates the use of this function.

```
#include <stdio.h>
#include <graph.h>
void main ()
{
_setvideomode ( mode ); /* set mode by adapter */
        .
        .
        .
_setpixel (x,y); /* set pixel to current color */
        .
        .
        .
_setvideomode (_DEFAULTMODE); /* reset */
}
```

Example:

The following program demonstrates the use of the _setpixel function. Each pixel on the screen is evaluated with the _getpixel function. If the pixel value is 3, the _setpixel function sets the pixel to Color 2.

```
#include <stdio.h>
#include <graph.h>
#define ESC 27
void main ()
{
int pixelcolor;
int x, y;
    /* Initialization */
_setvideomode (_MRES4COLOR);
_setbkcolor (_BLUE);
_rectangle (_GBORDER,0,0,319,199);
x = 0;
y = 0;
    /* Add figures and colors to screen */
_rectangle (_GFILLINTERIOR,20,20,70,159);
_setcolor (2);
_rectangle (_GFILLINTERIOR,134,20,184,159);
_setcolor (3);
```

```
_rectangle (_GBORDER,134,20,184,159);
_rectangle (_GBORDER,249,20,299,159);
_setcolor (2);
_settextposition (23,5);
_outtext ("Press Any Key to Begin Conversion");
getch ();
    /* Evaluate pixel value for each pixel */
do
    {
    pixelcolor = _getpixel (x,y);
    if (pixelcolor == 3)
     _setpixel (x,y);
    x = x + 1;
    if (x == 320)
{
    x = 0;
    y = y + 1;
}
} while (y != 200);
    /* Delay and exit */
_settextposition (22,5);
_outtext ("Conversion Complete");
_settextposition (23,5);
_outtext ("Press Any Key to Continue          ");
getch ();
_setvideomode (_DEFAULTMODE);
}
```

_setpixel_w

Syntax:

```
short _far _setpixel_w(double x     , double y);
double x, y;   pixel coordinates to set to current color
```

Function:

The _setpixel_w function sets the specified pixel to the current color. This function uses the window coordinate system.

Files to Include:

```
#include <graph.h>
```

Compatibility:

DOS

Description:

The _setpixel_w function sets the pixel at window coordinates x , y to the current color. If the point specified by the x and y arguments lies outside the clipping region, the pixel is not changed.

Values Returned:

If the function is successful, the previous color of the specified pixel is returned; otherwise, a -1 is returned.

Related Functions:

```
_getpixel_w      :        gets the current color of a pixel
```

Similar Turbo C++ Functions:

None

Suggested Code Structure and Use:

The _setpixel_w function sets the pixel that corresponds to the window coordinates x , y to the current color. The resulting output is limited to one pixel; therefore, single points can easily be added where needed. The following code structure illustrates the use of the _setpixel_w function.

```
#include <stdio.h>
#include <graph.h>
void main ()
{
_setvideomode ( mode );  /* set video mode */
_setviewport (x1,y1,x2,y2); /* size viewport */
_setwindow (flag,x1,y1,x2,y2); /* window dimensions */
        .
        .
        .
```

```
_setcolor ( color ); /* set current color */
_setpixel_w (x,y);
          .
          .
          .
_setvideomode (_DEFAULTMODE);  /* reset and exit */
}
```

Example:

The `_setpixel_w` function is used in this example to display a series of points that begin in the upper left corner of the window and extend diagonally to the lower right corner of the window.

```c
#include <stdio.h>
#include <graph.h>
void main ()
{
double x,y;
_setvideomode (_ERESCOLOR);
_rectangle (_GBORDER,0,0,639,349);
     /* Open window */
_setviewport (0,0,639,349);
_setwindow (0,0.0,0.0,100.0,100.0);
     /* Draw points */
y = 4.0;
for ( x=10.0; x<100.0; x=x+10.0)
{
 _setpixel_w (x,y);
 y = y + 10.0;
}
     /* Delay and exit */
_settextposition (23,5);
_outtext ("Press Any Key to Continue");
getch ();
_setvideomode (_DEFAULTMODE);
}
```

_settextcolor

Syntax:

```
short _far _settextcolor(short color);
short color;     text color
```

Function:

The _settextcolor function defines the current text color.

Files to Include:

```
#include <graph.h>
```

Compatibility:

DOS
OS/2

Description:

The current text color is defined by the _settextcolor function. The color argument specifies the pixel value, or color, of the text used by the _outtext and _outmem functions. Font text color is not changed because font text color is set with the _setcolor function. The pixel values and their corresponding colors are shown in table 9.6, under the _gettextcolor function. (Pixel values 16-31 represent blinking text, and their colors are for use only in text modes.) These color are for use in text modes only.

Values Returned:

The pixel value of the previous text color is returned. No error value is returned.

Related Functions:

```
_gettextcolor   :         returns the current text color
```

Similar Turbo C++ Functions:

```
textcolor  :  sets the text color in text mode
void textcolor (int newcolor);
```

Suggested Code Structure and Use:

The _settextcolor function is useful for displaying text in different colors. The following code structure illustrates the normal use of the _settextcolor function.

```
#include <stdio.h>
#include <graph.h>
void main ()
{
```

```
_setvideomode ( mode ); /* set mode by adapter */
        .
        .
        .
_settextcolor ( text color ); /* set current text color */
        .
        .
        .
_setvideomode (_DEFAULTMODE); /* reset */
}
```

Example:

The following program demonstrates the use of the _settextcolor function. All available text colors are printed on the text screen.

```
#include <stdio.h>
#include <graph.h>
void main ()
{
int color;
int row;
char buffer [40];
          /* Initialization */
_setbkcolor (4L);
_clearscreen (_GWINDOW);
color = 0;
row = 5;
          /* Demonstrate the available
             text colors */
do
{
    _settextposition (row,15);
    _settextcolor (color);
     sprintf (buffer, "Color: %d",color);
    _outtext (buffer);
    _settextposition (row,60);
    _settextcolor (color+16);
     sprintf (buffer, "Color: %d",color+16);
    _outtext (buffer);
    color = color + 1;
    row = row + 1;
} while (color != 16);
    /* Delay and exit */
```

```
_settextposition (23,8);
_outtext ("Press Any Key to Exit");
getch();
_setvideomode (_DEFAULTMODE);
}
```

_settextcursor

Syntax:

```
short _far _settextcursor(short shape);
short shape;              cursor shape
```

Function:

The _settextcursor function defines the shape of the cursor in text modes.

Files to Include:

```
#include <graph.h>
```

Compatibility:

DOS
OS/2

Description:

The _settextcursor sets the shape of the text cursor in text modes. The shape argument is used to describe the attributes of the cursor. Table 9.20 lists the four shapes, or attributes, for use by the _settextcursor function.

Table 9.20. *Text cursor attributes.*

Attribute	Shape
0x0707	Underline
0x0007	Full block
0x0607	Double underline
0x2000	No cursor

Values Returned:

If successful, the previous shape of the cursor is returned. If unsuccessful, a -1 is returned.

Related Functions:

```
_gettextcursor        :        retrieves the text cursor shape
```

Similar Turbo C++ Functions:

```
    _setcursortype  :  sets the cursor appearance
    void _setcursortype (int cur_t);
```

Suggested Code Structure and Use:

The _settextcursor function is used to change the cursor attribute, or shape, of the text cursor. The following code structure illustrates the use of this function.

```
#include <graph.h>
#include <stdio.h>
void main ()
{
short oldcursorshape;
short newcursorshape;
newcursorshape = 0x0007;
oldcursorshape = _gettextcursor (); /* get old cursor */
_clearscreen (_GCLEARSCREEN);
_displaycursor (_GCURSORON);  /* display cursor */
        .
        .
        .
_settextcursor (newcursorshape); /* set new cursor shape */
        .
        .
        .
_settextcursor(oldcursorshape); /* reset to old cursor */
_clearscreen (_GCLEARSCREEN);
}
```

Example:

The function is used in this example to set a new text cursor shape. The old cursor shape is retrieved with the _gettextcursor function and displayed. Next, the _settextcursor function sets the new cursor shape. Before exiting the program, the _settextcursor function restores the old cursor shape.

```
#include <graph.h>
#include <stdio.h>
void main ()
{
short oldcursorshape;
short newcursorshape;
newcursorshape = 0x0007;  /* new shape */
     /* Get old cursor and display it */
oldcursorshape = _gettextcursor ();
_clearscreen (_GCLEARSCREEN);
_displaycursor (_GCURSORON);
_settextposition (10,3);
_outtext ("Press Any Key To Change The Cursor Shape");
_settextposition (15,3);
     /* Set new cursor  */
getch ();
_settextcursor (newcursorshape);
     /* Delay, reset cursor, and exit */
_settextposition (23,3);
_outtext ("Press Any Key To Exit");
_settextposition (15,3);
getch ();
_settextcursor(oldcursorshape);
_clearscreen (_GCLEARSCREEN);
}
```

_settextposition

Syntax:

```
struct rccoord _far _settextposition (short row, short col);
short row, col;            new row and column position
```

Function:

The _settextposition function positions the text cursor at the specified row and column.

Files to Include:

```
#include <graph.h>
```

Compatibility:

DOS
OS/2

Description:

The position of the text cursor is set by the _settextposition function. The row and column of the text cursor are maintained internally and are specified in the row and col arguments of the _settextposition function. Subsequent text output from the _outtext and _outmem functions will begin at the updated text position. Font text is not affected because font text uses the graphics cursor for positioning.

Values Returned:

The _settextposition function returns the previous text cursor position in a structure of type rccoord. This structure follows.

```
struct rccoord
  {
  short row;
  short col;
  };
```

Related Functions:

```
_gettextposition    :    retrieves the current position of
                         the text cursor
```

Similar Turbo C++ Functions:

```
gotoxy : positions cursor in text window
void gotoxy (int x, int y);
```

Suggested Code Structure and Use:

The _settextposition function is useful for placing the text cursor at a desired row and column location. The following code structure illustrates the use of this function.

```
#include <stdio.h>
#include <graph.h>
void main ()
{
_setvideomode ( mode ); /* set mode by adapter */
        .
        .
        .
_settextposition (row,column); /* place text cursor */
        .
        .
        .
_setvideomode (_DEFAULTMODE); /* reset */
}
```

Example:

The following program uses the _settextposition function to move the text cursor. With the Num Lock key on, the text cursor can be moved using the keypad. The 4, 6, 8, and 2 keys move the cursor left, right, up, and down, respectively. Press Esc to end the program.

```
#include <stdio.h>
#include <graph.h>
#define ESC 27
void main ()
{
struct rccoord cursorposition;
char buffer [40];
int ch;
     /* Initialization */
_setvideomode (_MRES4COLOR);
_setbkcolor (_BLUE);
_displaycursor (_GCURSORON);
_wrapon (_GWRAPOFF);
_settextposition (23,5);
_outtext ("Row : 1");
_settextposition (24,5);
_outtext ("Column : 1");
_settextposition (1,1);
do
```

```
   {
        /* Accept and process keypad input */
   cursorposition = _gettextposition ();
   ch = getch ();
   if (ch == '8')
     cursorposition.row = cursorposition.row - 1;
   if (ch == '2')
     cursorposition.row = cursorposition.row + 1;
   if (ch == '4')
      cursorposition.col = cursorposition.col - 1;
   if (ch == '6')
      cursorposition.col = cursorposition.col + 1;
   if (ch == '5')
     {
     _outtext ("<- Old Position - New Position ->");
     cursorposition.col = cursorposition.col + 33;
     }
        /* Check boundaries */
   if (cursorposition.row < 1)
     cursorposition.row = 1;
   if (cursorposition.row > 20)
     cursorposition.row = 20;
   if (cursorposition.col < 1)
      cursorposition.col = 1;
   if (cursorposition.col > 40)
     cursorposition.col = 40;
        /* Output status */
   _settextposition (23,5);
   sprintf (buffer, "Row : %d", cursorposition.row);
   _outtext (buffer);
   _outtext ("          ");
   _settextposition (24,5);
   sprintf (buffer, "Column : %d", cursorposition.col);
   _outtext (buffer);
   _outtext ("          ");
   _settextposition (cursorposition.row,
        cursorposition.col);
   } while (ch != ESC);
_setvideomode (_DEFAULTMODE);
}
```

_settextrows

Syntax:

```
short _far _settextrows(short numrows);
short numrows;              number of text rows desired
```

Function:

The _settextrows function is used to specify the number of rows to use in the current video mode.

Files to Include:

```
#include <graph.h>
```

Compatibility:

DOS
OS/2

Description:

The _settextrows function is used to request a specified number of text rows for the current video mode. If the number of text rows requested is not available for that mode, the _settextrows function sets an appropriate number of text rows and returns that value. The _MAXTEXTROWS constant can be used for the numrows argument to set the maximum number of text rows available given the current mode. The maximum number of rows is 50 for VGA, 43 for EGA, and 25 for all other modes. In graphics modes, which support 30 or 60 rows, the _MAXTEXTROWS constant will set 60 rows.

Values Returned:

When successful, the number of rows actually set is returned. A zero is returned when there is an error.

Related Functions:

```
_setvideomoderows     :     sets video mode and number of
                            text rows
```

Similar Turbo C++ Functions:

None

Suggested Code Structure and Use:

The _settextrows function is used to set the desired number of text rows for the given video mode. The following code structure illustrates the use of this function.

```
#include <graph.h>
#include <stdio.h>
void main ()
{
_setvideomode ( mode );   /* set video mode */
_settextrows ( # of rows ); /* request a number of rows */
            .
            .
            .
_setvideomode (_DEFAULTMODE); /* reset and exit */
}
```

Example:

The _settextrows function is used in this example to request 35 text rows. Because the _ERESCOLOR video mode does not support 35 text rows, the text row number is set to 25 and displayed. (25 is the number of rows that the _ERESCOLOR mode can support.)

```
#include <graph.h>
#include <stdio.h>
void main ()
{
int rows;
char buffer [40];
        /* Set video mode, request 35 rows, save the
           number of text rows actually set */
_setvideomode (_ERESCOLOR);
rows = _settextrows (35);
_rectangle (_GBORDER,0,0,639,349);
        /* Display the number of text rows actually set */
_settextposition (10,5);
if (rows !=0)
        sprintf (buffer,"The Actual Number of Rows
                Set Was : %d", rows);
if (rows == 0)
        sprintf (buffer,"Error : %d", rows);
_outtext (buffer);
        /* Delay and exit */
_settextposition (23,5);
_outtext ("Press Any Key To Exit");
```

```
getch ();
_setvideomode (_DEFAULTMODE);
}
```

_settextwindow

Syntax:

```
void _far _settextwindow(short r1, short c1, short r2,
              short c2);
short r1, c1;        upper left corner of window
short r2, c2;        lower right corner of window
```

Function:

The _settextwindow function opens a text window for subsequent text output.

Files to Include:

```
#include <graph.h>
```

Compatibility:

DOS
OS/2

Description:

A text window is specified by the row and column coordinates $r1, c1$ and $r2, c2$. The $r1$ and $c1$ arguments specify the upper left corner of the window; the $r2$ and $c2$ arguments specify the lower right corner of the window. See figure 9.79. All subsequent text cursor positioning is relative to the upper left corner of the text window. When the window is full, the top line scrolls out of view.

Values Returned:

No values are returned.

Related Functions:

```
_outtext            :    displays text
_settextposition    :    positions the text cursor
```

Fig. 9.79. The _settextwindow function.

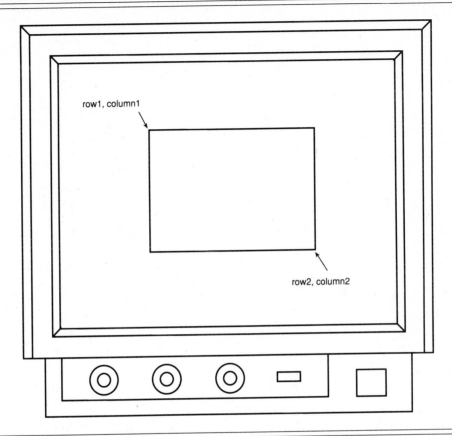

Similar Turbo C++ Functions:

```
window   :  sets the active text mode window
void window (int left, int top, int right, int bottom);
```

Suggested Code Structure and Use:

The _settextwindow function is useful for creating pop-up windows that bind text input. The following code structure illustrates the use of the _settextwindow function.

```
#include <stdio.h>
#include <graph.h>
void main ()
{
```

```
_setvideomode ( mode ); /* set mode by adapter */
        .
        .
        .
_settextwindow (row1, column1, row2, column2);
        .
        .
        .
_setvideomode (_DEFAULTMODE); /* reset */
}
```

Example:

This program demonstrates the _settextwindow function. A text window is opened and text is printed in the window, as shown in figure 9.80. The _wrapon function is on.

```
#include <stdio.h>
#include <graph.h>
void main ()
{
_setvideomode (_MRES4COLOR);
_setbkcolor (_BLUE);
_rectangle (_GBORDER,0,0,319,199);
_wrapon (_GWRAPON);
_settextwindow (5,10,15,30);
_outtext ("This message demonstrates the use of the
_settextwindow function.");
_outtext ("Press Any Key to Exit");
getch ();
_setvideomode (_DEFAULTMODE);
}
```

_setvideomode

Syntax:

```
short _far _setvideomode(short videomode);
short videomode;            desired mode
```

Function:

The _setvideomode function is used to select an appropriate display mode for the current hardware and display configuration.

Fig. 9.80. Example _settextwindow output.

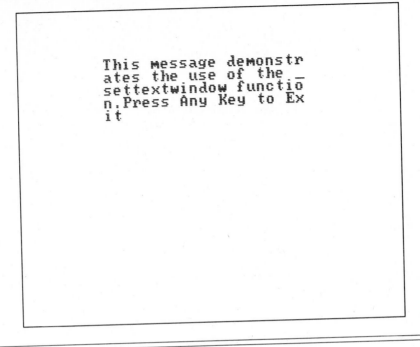

Files to Include:

```
#include <graph.h>
```

Compatibility:

DOS
OS/2

Description:

The screen or display mode is set by the _setvideomode function. The modes listed in table 9.8, under the _getvideoconfig function, are provided. Only certain modes are available for some adapters.

Values Returned:

If the specified video mode is supported by the current hardware and display, a nonzero value that indicates the number of text rows available is returned. Otherwise, a zero is returned.

Related Functions:

```
_getvideoconfig      :    returns the current video
                          configuration
```

Similar Turbo C++ Functions:

```
initgraph  :  initializes the graphics system
void far initgraph (int far *graphdriver,
          int far *graphmode, char far *pathtodriver);
textmode   :  sets a text mode
void textmode (int newmode);
```

Suggested Code Structure and Use:

The _setvideomode function is vital to the proper functioning of a graphics program. The _setvideomode function permits the selection of a graphics mode that best supports the application. It is important to reset the video mode to _DEFAULTMODE when exiting the program to avoid conflicts with video modes in other programs.

```
#include <stdio.h>
#include <graph.h>
void main ()
{
_setvideomode ( mode ); /* set mode by adapter */
          .
          .
          .
_setvideomode (_DEFAULTMODE); /* reset on exit */
}
```

Example:

In this program, the _setvideomode function is used to set different video modes. The same graphics are put on each screen, but depending on the mode, the graphics will appear different. See figure 9.81.

```
#include <stdio.h>
#include <graph.h>
void main ()
{
        /* _MRES4COLOR mode */
_setvideomode (_MRES4COLOR);
_setbkcolor (_BLUE);
```

```
_setcolor (2);
_ellipse (_GFILLINTERIOR,30,30,299,169);
_rectangle (_GBORDER,0,0,319,199);
_settextposition (23,8);
_outtext ("Press Any Key to Continue");
getch();
          /* _MRESNOCOLOR mode */
_setvideomode (_MRESNOCOLOR);
_setbkcolor (_BLUE);
_setcolor (2);
_ellipse (_GFILLINTERIOR,30,30,299,169);
_rectangle (_GBORDER,0,0,319,199);
_settextposition (23,8);
_outtext ("Press Any Key to Continue");
getch();
          /* _HRESBW mode */
_setvideomode (_HRESBW);
_setbkcolor (_BLUE);
_setcolor (2);
_ellipse (_GFILLINTERIOR,30,30,299,169);
_rectangle (_GBORDER,0,0,319,199);
_settextposition (23,8);
_outtext ("Press Any Key to Continue");
getch();
_setvideomode (_DEFAULTMODE);
}
```

_setvideomoderows

Syntax:

```
short _far _setvideomoderows(short videomode,
                   short numrows);
short videomode;        video mode
short numrows;          number of text rows desired
```

Function:

The _setvideomoderows function is used to set the video mode and number of text rows for a particular hardware and display configuration.

Fig. 9.81. Example _setvideomode output.

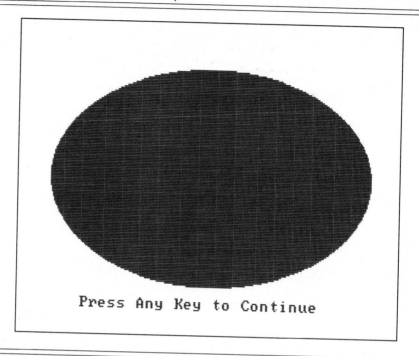

Press Any Key to Continue

Files to Include:

```
#include <graph.h>
```

Compatibility:

DOS
OS/2

Description:

The _setvideomoderows function sets the video mode and specifies the number of text rows desired. The videomode argument, as selected from table 9.8 (under the _getvideoconfig function), specifies the desired video mode. The numrows argument requests a number of text rows. If you use the _MAXTEXTROWS constant for the numrows argument, the _setvideomoderows function sets 50 text rows for VGA, 43 for EGA, and 25 for all others. In graphics modes that support 30 or 60 rows, 60 rows will be set when using the _MAXTEXTROWS constant. The _setvideomoderows function has the same effect as calling the _setvideomode and _settextrows functions in turn.

Values Returned:

The number of text rows actually set for the requested video mode is returned. If an error occurs, a zero is returned.

Related Functions:

```
_setvideomode    :    sets the video mode
_settextrows     :    requests a number of text rows
```

Similar Turbo C++ Functions:

```
initgraph  :  initializes the graphics system
void far initgraph (int far *graphdriver,
          int far *graphmode, char far *pathtodriver);
textmode   :  sets a text mode
void textmode (int newmode);
```

Suggested Code Structure and Use:

The _setvideomoderows function performs the same functions as the combined _setvideomode and _settextrows functions. The following code structure illustrates the use of this function.

```
#include <graph.h>
#include <stdio.h>
void main ()
{
_setvideomoderows (mode, # of text rows);
          .
          .
          .
_setvideomode (_DEFAULTMODE);  /* reset and exit */
}
```

Example:

The _setvideomoderows function is used to set the video mode and request 35 text rows. The actual number of text rows set is stored in the rows argument and displayed.

```
#include <graph.h>
#include <stdio.h>
void main ()
{
```

```
int rows;
char buffer [40];
    /* Set video mode, request 35 text rows */
rows = _setvideomoderows (_ERESCOLOR,35);
_rectangle (_GBORDER,0,0,639,349);
    /* Display actual number of text rows set */
_settextposition (10,5);
if (rows !=0)
    sprintf (buffer,"The Actual Number of Rows
        Set Was : %d", rows);
if (rows == 0)
    sprintf (buffer,"Error : %d", rows);
_outtext (buffer);
    /* Delay and exit */
_settextposition (23,5);
_outtext ("Press Any Key To Exit");
getch ();
_setvideomode (_DEFAULTMODE);
}
```

_setvieworg

Syntax:

```
struct xycoord _far _setvieworg(short x, short y);
short x, y;       coordinates of new view origin
```

Function:

The _setvieworg function places the view origin at the physical coordinates x,y.

Files to Include:

```
#include <graph.h>
```

Compatibility:

DOS

Description:

The origin of the view coordinate system is defined by the _setvieworg function. The x and y arguments define the physical point at which the view origin will be placed. All view points will be shifted the corresponding direction and distance.

The physical coordinate system has its origin located in the upper left corner of the screen (see Figure 9.82). Through use of the _setvieworg function, the view coordinate system has its origin placed at the physical coordinates specified by the x and y arguments (see Figure 9.83). The view origin can be placed at any physical point.

Fig. 9.82. The physical coordinate system.

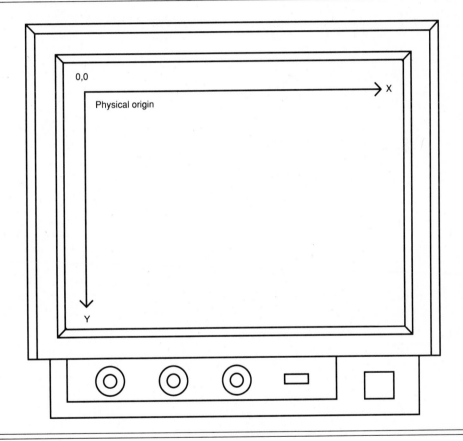

Fig. 9.83. The view coordinate system.

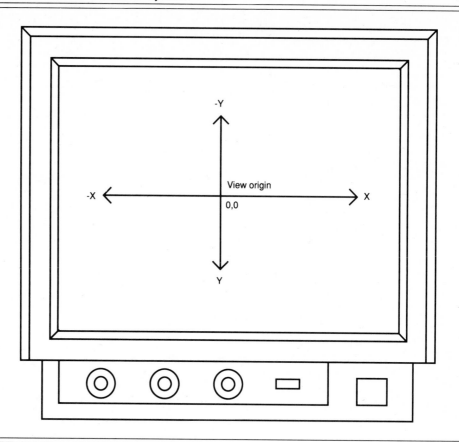

Values Returned:

The previous view origin is returned in a structure of type x y c o o r d. This structure follows.

```
struct xycoord
    {
    short xcoord;
    short ycoord;
    };
```

Related Functions:

```
_getviewcoord   :        converts physical coordinates to view
_getphyscoord   :        converts view coordinates to physical
                         coordinates
```

Similar Turbo C++ Functions:

None

Suggested Code Structure and Use:

The _setvieworg function is most useful for two- and three-dimensional rotations. By setting the view origin at the rotation point and executing the rotation algorithms, the screen appears to rotate about the view origin. The location of the view origin, set by the _setvieworg function, defines the point where rotation will occur. The following code structure illustrates the use of the _setvieworg function.

```
#include <stdio.h>
#include <graph.h>

void main ()
{
_setvideomode ( mode ); /* set mode by adapter */
      .
      .
      .
_setvieworg (x,y); /* set view origin */
      .
      .
      .
_setvideomode (_DEFAULTMODE); /* reset */
}
```

Example:

The following example uses the _setvieworg function to demonstrate the effects of moving the view origin. One ellipse is drawn. Then the view origin is reset and the ellipse is drawn again. The resulting output is two ellipses, one on each side of the screen.

```
#include <stdio.h>
#include <graph.h>
void main ()
{
```

```
                    /* Initialization */
        _setvideomode (_MRES4COLOR);
        _setbkcolor (_BLUE);
        _rectangle (_GBORDER,0,0,319,199);
                    /* Draw an ellipse with logical
                        origin at 0,0 */
        _ellipse (_GBORDER,20,20,70,159);
                    /* Draw same ellipse with view
                        origin at 230,0 */
        _setvieworg (230,0);
        _ellipse (_GBORDER,20,20,70,159);
                    /* Delay and exit */
        _settextposition (23,8);
        _outtext ("Press Any Key to Continue");
        getch ();
        _setvideomode (_DEFAULTMODE);
        }
```

_setviewport

Syntax:

```
void _far _setviewport(short x1, short y1, short x2,
short y2);
short x1, y1;        upper left corner of viewport
short x2, y2;        lower right corner of viewport
```

Function:

The _setviewport function sets a rectangular clipping region. This function has the same effect as the _setcliprgn function but sets the view origin to the upper left corner of the clipping region.

Files to Include:

```
#include <graph.h>
```

Compatibility:

DOS

Description:

The x1,y1 and x2,y2 arguments of the _setviewport function define the rectangular clipping region. Subsequent graphics calls with points outside this region will be clipped at the rectangle's border. The _setviewport function is similar to the _setcliprgn function but relocates the origin of the view coordinate system to the upper left corner of the viewport. The x1 and y1 arguments define the upper left corner of the viewport; the x2 and y2 arguments define the lower right corner. See figure 9.84. You can use the _setwindow function to set the dimensions of the viewport.

Fig. 9.84. The _setviewport function.

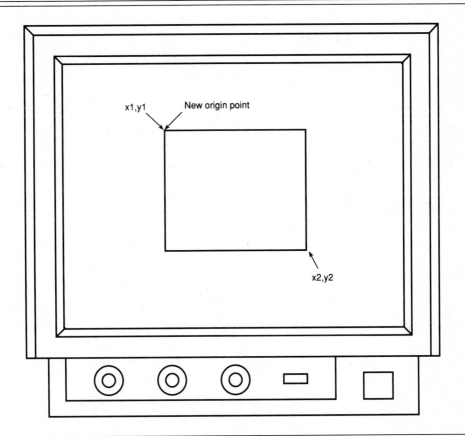

Values Returned:

No values are returned.

Related Functions:

```
_setcliprgn      :  defines a rectangular clipping region
_setvieworg      :  sets the view origin
```

Similar Turbo C++ Functions:

```
setviewport      :  sets the current viewport
void far setviewport (int left, int top, int right,
                      int bottom, int clip);
```

Suggested Code Structure and Use:

The _setviewport function is useful for setting clipping regions with the view origin at the upper left corner. The following code structure illustrates the use of the _setviewport function.

```
#include <stdio.h>
#include <graph.h>
void main ()
{
_setvideomode ( mode ); /* set mode by adapter */
     .
     .
     .
_setviewport (x1,y1,x2,y2); /* open viewport */
     .
     .
     .
_setvideomode (_DEFAULTMODE); /* reset and exit */
}
```

Example:

The following program demonstrates the use of the _setviewport function. A viewport is opened and a rectangle and an ellipse are drawn inside the viewport, as shown in figure 9.85. Press any key to end the program.

```
#include <stdio.h>
#include <graph.h>
void main ()
{
_setvideomode (_MRES4COLOR);
_setbkcolor (_RED);
_rectangle (_GBORDER,0,0,319,199);
          /* Open viewport */
_setviewport (20,20,120,120);
_rectangle (_GBORDER,0,0,100,100);
_ellipse (_GBORDER,0,0,100,100);
getch ();
_setvideomode (_DEFAULTMODE);
}
```

Fig. 9.85. Example _setviewport output.

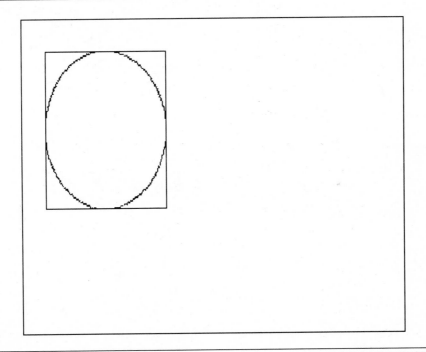

_setvisualpage

Syntax:

```
short _far _setvisualpage(short page);
short page;          page number
```

Function:

The _setvisualpage function defines the current video page to be displayed on the screen. This function works in text modes and in EGA and VGA graphics modes if sufficient video memory is available on the adapter.

Files to Include:

```
#include <graph.h>
```

Compatibility:

DOS

Description:

In video adapters with sufficient memory to support multiple text or graphics pages, the _setvisualpage function can be used to select a particular video page, or section of memory, to be displayed. The default page number is 0. See the _setactivepage description for further information on memory requirements.

Values Returned:

The page number of the previous display page is returned if the _setvisualpage function is successful. If unsuccessful, a negative value is returned.

Related Functions:

```
_setactivepage :     selects the video page for subsequent
                     output
```

Similar Turbo C++ Functions:

```
setvisualpage  :  sets the visual page number
void far setvisualpage (int page);
```

Suggested Code Structure and Use:

The _setvisualpage function is useful when used with the _setactivepage function. Output can be produced on a nonvisual page with the _setactivepage function and made visible with the _setvisualpage function. The following code structure illustrates the use of the _setvisualpage function.

```
#include <stdio.h>
#include <graph.h>
void main ()
{
_setvideomode ( mode ); /* set mode by adapter */
         .
         .
         .

_setactivepage (1); /* set to nonvisual page */
         .
         .
         .

   { produce output on nonvisual page }
         .
         .
         .

_setvisualpage (1); /* make page visible */
         .
         .
         .

_setvideomode (_DEFAULTMODE); /* reset */
}
```

Example:

This program demonstrates the practice of creating graphics on a nonvisual page. The page is then made visible with the _setvisualpage function.

```
#include <stdio.h>
#include <graph.h>
void main ()
{
_setvideomode (_ERESCOLOR);
_setbkcolor (_BLUE);
_rectangle (_GBORDER,0,0,639,349);
_ellipse (_GFILLINTERIOR,40,40,599,319);
```

```
_settextposition (22,3);
_outtext ("Press Any Key to Change Pages");
getch ();
           /* Draw on nonvisual page */
_setactivepage (1);
_clearscreen (_GCLEARSCREEN);
_setbkcolor (_RED);
_rectangle (_GBORDER,0,0,639,349);
_ellipse (_GFILLINTERIOR,40,40,599,319);
_settextposition (22,10);
_outtext ("Press Any Key to Exit");
           /* Set visual page to 1 */
_setvisualpage (1);
getch ();
_setvideomode (_DEFAULTMODE);
}
```

_setwindow

Syntax:

```
short _far _setwindow(short invertflag, double x1,
     double y1, double x2, double y2);
short invertflag;        invert flag
double x1, y1;           upper left corner of window
double x2, y2;           lower right corner of window
```

Function:

The _setwindow function defines a virtual window by which all subsequent output using window coordinates will be bound.

Files to Include:

```
#include <graph.h>
```

Compatibility:

DOS

Description:

The _setwindow function defines the window bound by the specified coordinates. The x1, y1 arguments describe the upper left corner of the window; the x2, y2 arguments define the lower right corner. The invertflag argument sets the direction of the window coordinate system. If the invertflag argument is set to TRUE (1), the y coordinates decrease from the top of the screen to the bottom. If invertflag is set to FALSE (0), the y coordinates increase from the top of the screen to the bottom (as in the physical and view coordinate systems). The window dimensions set by this function apply only to the current viewport. The _setwindow function has no effect on the chart environment text or font text.

Values Returned:

A nonzero value is returned if successful. A zero is returned if unsuccessful.

Related Functions:

```
_setviewport      :       sets the viewport
```

Similar Turbo C++ Functions:

None

Suggested Code Structure and Use:

The _setwindow function is used to set the dimensions of the current viewport. The following code structure illustrates the use of this function.

```
#include <graph.h>
#include <stdio.h>
void main ()
{
_setvideomode ( mode );   /* set video mode */
_setviewport (x1,y1,x2,y2); /* size viewport */
_setwindow (flag,x1,y1,x2,y2); /* set window dimensions */
    .
    .
    .
_setvideomode (_DEFAULTMODE);   /* reset and exit */
}
```

Example:

The _setwindow function is used in this example to set the current viewport (which is defined by the view coordinates 50,50,590,300) to dimensions -100.0,-100.0,100.0,100.0. A rectangle and an ellipse are then displayed in this window, as shown in figure 9.86.

```
#include <graph.h>
#include <stdio.h>
void main ()
{
_setvideomode (_ERESCOLOR);
_rectangle (_GBORDER,0,0,639,349);
      /*  Open window  */
_setviewport (50,50,590,300);
_setwindow (0,-100.0,-100.0,100.0,100.0);
      /* Draw figures */
_setcolor (1);
_rectangle_w (_GBORDER,-100.0,-100.0,100.0,100.0);
_setcolor (4);
_ellipse_w (_GFILLINTERIOR,-90.0,-90.0,90.0,90.0);
      /* Delay and exit */
_settextposition (23,5);
_outtext ("Press Any Key To Exit");
getch ();
_setvideomode (_DEFAULTMODE);
}
```

_setwritemode

Syntax:

```
short _far _setwritemode(short writemode);
short writemode;     write mode for lines
```

Function:

The _setwritemode function identifies the logical write mode used to draw straight lines.

Files to Include:

```
#include <graph.h>
```

Fig. 9.86.   Example _setwindow output.

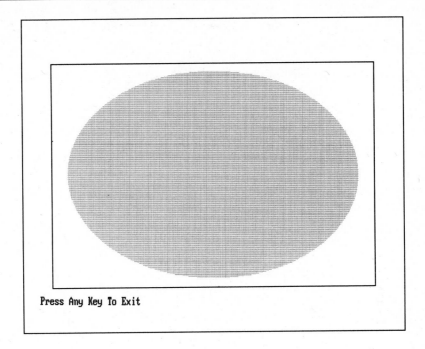

Compatibility:

DOS

Description:

The _setwritemode is used to determine the logical write mode for drawing straight lines. This function affects the output from the _lineto and _rectangle functions. The writemode argument is selected from the values in table 9.11, under the _getwritemode function.

Values Returned:

The previous write mode is returned if successful. A -1 indicates an error.

Related Functions:

```
_getwritemode      :        retrieves the current write mode
```

Similar Turbo C++ Functions:

```
setwritemode  :  sets the writing mode for line drawing
void far setwritemode (int mode);
```

Suggested Code Structure and Use:

The _setwritemode is used to set the logical write mode for displaying straight lines. The following code structure illustrates the use of this function.

```
#include <graph.h>
#include <stdio.h>
void main ()
{
_setvideomode ( mode );   /* set video mode */
          .
          .
          .
_setwritemode ( write mode );
          .
          .
          .
      { use write mode }
          .
          .
          .
_setvideomode (_DEFAULTMODE);  /* reset and exit */
}
```

Example:

The _setwritemode function is used in this example to demonstrate the results of the various line modes. The program draws a line in each write mode.

```
#include <graph.h>
#include <stdio.h>
void main ()
{
_setvideomode (_ERESCOLOR);
_setcolor (1);
_rectangle (_GFILLINTERIOR,0,0,639,349);
```

```
          /* Set write modes and draw a line with each */
_setcolor (15);
_setwritemode (_GPSET);
_moveto (20,30);
_lineto (620,30);
_setwritemode (_GPRESET);
_moveto (20,105);
_lineto (620,105);
_setwritemode (_GXOR);
_moveto (20,175);
_lineto (620,175);
_setwritemode (_GOR);
_moveto (20,245);
_lineto (620,245);
_setwritemode (_GAND);
_moveto (20,320);
_lineto (620,320);
     /* Delay and exit */
_settextposition (24,5);
_outtext ("Press Any Key to Exit");
getch ();
_setvideomode (_DEFAULTMODE);
}
```

_unregisterfonts

Syntax:

```
void _far _unregisterfonts(void);
```

Function:

The _unregisterfonts function frees the memory allocated to fonts by the _registerfonts function.

Files to Include:

```
#include <graph.h>
```

Compatibility:

DOS

Description:

The _unregisterfonts function is used to free the memory allocated to the registered fonts. All header information and font data are removed.

Values Returned:

There is no return value.

Related Functions:

```
_registerfonts    :        registers the specified fonts
```

Similar Turbo C++ Functions:

None

Suggested Code Structure and Use:

The _unregisterfonts function is used to free the memory allocated to the registered fonts. This function should be used before exiting any program that registers fonts. The following code structure illustrates the use of this function.

```
#include <graph.h>
#include <stdio.h>
void main ()
{
_setvideomode ( mode );  /* set video mode */
             .
             .
             .
_registerfonts ("*.fon"); /* register fonts */
_setfont ("t'courier' h12 w9 b f"); /* select a font */
             .
             .
             .
_moveto (x,y); /* starting point for font output */
_outgtext ("Font Text Output");
             .
             .
             .
```

```
_unregisterfonts ();   /* free memory */
_setvideomode (_DEFAULTMODE); /* reset and exit */
}
```

Example:

The _unregisterfonts function is used before exiting this program to free the memory allocated to the registered fonts.

```
#include <graph.h>
#include <stdio.h>
void main ()
{
_setvideomode (_ERESCOLOR);
_rectangle (_GBORDER, 0, 0, 639, 349);
    /* Register and select fonts */
_registerfonts ("*.fon");
_setfont ("t'courier' h12 w9 b f");
    /* Display text */
_moveto (30,175);
_outgtext ("The fonts are registered.  Courier
            font in use");
    /* Delay and exit */
_settextposition (23,30);
_outtext ("Press Any Key to Exit");
getch();
_unregisterfonts ();
_setvideomode (_DEFAULTMODE);
}
```

_wrapon

Syntax:

```
short _far _wrapon(short wrapflag);
short wrapflag;             wrap flag
```

Function:

The _wrapon function is used to control the way text is handled when it reaches the edge of the text window.

Files to Include:

```
#include <graph.h>
```

Compatibility:

DOS
OS/2

Description:

When using the _outtext function to output text, the wrapflag argument in the _wrapon function determines how the text is handled when it reaches the edge of the text window. The legal constants for the wrapflag argument follow:

_GWRAPON   Text after the end of the text line is wrapped to the next line.
_GWRAPOFF   Text will not extend past the end of the line. The last character is overwritten.

This function has no effect on presentation or font text.

Values Returned:

The previous value of the wrapflag argument is returned. No error value is returned.

Related Functions:

```
_settextwindow     :    sets a text window for text outpu
_outtext           :    used to display a string of text
```

Similar Turbo C++ Functions:

None

Suggested Code Structure and Use:

The _wrapon function is useful for establishing the method by which text responds when reaching the border of the current text window. The following code structure illustrates the use of this function.

```
#include <stdio.h>
#include <graph.h>
void main ()
{
```

```
_setvideomode ( mode ); /* set mode by adapter */
        .
        .
        .
_wrapon ( wrapflag );
        .
        .
        .
_setvideomode (_DEFAULTMODE); /* reset */
}
```

Example:

This program demonstrates the effects of the _wrapon function. One line of text is output with the _GWRAPON argument, and the other is output with the _GWRAPOFF argument.

```
#include <stdio.h>
#include <graph.h>
void main ()
{
_setvideomode (_MRES4COLOR);
_setbkcolor (_RED);
_wrapon (_GWRAPON);
          /* Demo wrap feature on */
_settextposition (5,2);
_outtext (" This line of text will wrap to the next line");
          /* Demo wrap feature off */
_wrapon (_GWRAPOFF);
_settextposition (10,2);
_outtext (" This line of text will not wrap
          to next line ");
          /* Delay and exit */
_settextposition (23,10);
_outtext ("Press Any Key to Exit");
getch ();
_setvideomode (_DEFAULTMODE);
}
```

Bibliography

Adams, Lee: *High Performance CAD Graphics in C,* Windcrest Books, Blue Ridge Summit, Pennsylvania, 1989.

Adams, Lee: *High-Speed Animation and Simulation for Microcomputers,* TAB Books, Inc., Blue Ridge Summit, Pennsylvania, 1987.

Barkakati, Nabajyoti: *The Waite Group's Microsoft C Bible,* Howard W. Sams and Company, Indianapolis, Indiana, 1988.

Campbell, John L.: *Inside OS/2: The Complete Programmer's Reference,* TAB Books, Inc., Blue Ridge Summit, Pennsylvania, 1988.

Charette, Robert N.: *Software Engineering Environments: Concepts and Technology,* Intertext Publications, Inc., New York, New York, 1986.

Ferraro, Richard F.: *Programmer's Guide to the EGA and VGA Cards,* Addison-Wesley Publishing Company, Reading, Massachusetts, 1988.

Howard, Bill: "Supplementing the Keyboard: Point and Shoot Devices," *PC Magazine,* August 1987, pp. 95-96.

Hsu, Jeffrey: *Microcomputer Programming Languages,* Hayden Book Company, Hasbrouck Heights, New Jersey, 1986.

Microsoft C Advanced Programming Techniques, Microsoft Corporation, 1990.

Microsoft C Reference, Microsoft Corporation, 1990.

Microsoft C Run-Time Library Reference, Microsoft Press, Redmond, Washington, 1990.

Microsoft QuickC Compiler for IBM Personal Computers and Compatibles, Microsoft Corporation, 1987.

Norton, Peter and John Socha: *Peter Norton's Assembly Language Book for the IBM PC,* Brady Books, New York, New York, 1986.

Norton, Peter and Richard Wilton: *The New Peter Norton Programmer's Guide to the IBM PC and PS/2,* Microsoft Press, Redmond, Washington, 1988.

Petzold, Charles: "Understanding and Using Bezier Splines in OS/2 Graphics," *PC Magazine,* 14 November 1989, pp. 409-420.

Rosch, Winn L.: "Digitizing Tablets Pointing the Way to Easier Input," *PC Magazine,* 28 November 1989, pp. 227-234.

Stevens, Roger T.: *Graphics Programming in C,* M&T Books, Redwood City, California, 1989.

Turbo C++: Library Reference, Borland International, 1990.

Index

Symbols

0% fill pattern, 66, 67
00H (Set Video Mode) BIOS video service, 245-246
01H (Set Cursor Size) BIOS video service, 246-247
02H (Set Cursor Position) BIOS video service, 247
03H (Read Cursor Position) BIOS video service, 247-248
04H (Read Light Pen Position) BIOS video service, 248
05H (Set Active Display Page) BIOS video service, 249
06H (Scroll Active Window Up) BIOS video service, 249
07H (Scroll Active Window Down) BIOS video service, 250
08H (Read Character and Attribute) BIOS video service, 250-251
09H (Write Character and Attribute) BIOS video service, 251
0AH (Write Character) BIOS video service, 251-252
0BH (Set Color Palette) BIOS video service, 252
0CH (Write Pixel) BIOS video service, 252-253
0DH (Read Pixel) BIOS video service, 253
0EH (Write TTY Character) BIOS video service, 253-254
0FH (Get Current Video Mode) BIOS video service, 254
0x8000 line pattern, 41-42
0x8080 line pattern, 46-47
0x8888 line pattern, 50
0xAAAA line pattern, 51
0xC000 line pattern, 42-43
0xC0C0 line pattern, 47-48
0xCCCC line pattern, 50-51
0xE000 line pattern, 43
0xE0E0 line pattern, 48
0xE4E4 line pattern, 51
0xEEEE line pattern, 51
0xF000 line pattern, 43
0xF0F0 line pattern, 48
0xF6F6 line pattern, 52
0xF800 line pattern, 44
0xF8F8 line pattern, 49
0xFC00 line pattern, 44
0xFCFC line pattern, 49
0xFE00 line pattern, 44
0xFEFE line pattern, 49
0xFF00 line pattern, 44
0xFF18 line pattern, 52
0xFF80 line pattern, 45
0xFFC0 line pattern, 45
0xFFE0 line pattern, 45
0xFFF0 line pattern, 45
0xFFF8 line pattern, 46
0xFFFC line pattern, 46
0xFFFE line pattern, 46
0xFFFF line pattern, 52
100% fill pattern, 72

10H BIOS video service
  00H subservice (Set Palette Register), 254-255
  01H subservice (Set Overscan Register), 255
  02H subservice (Set Palette and Overscan Register), 255
  03H subservice (Toggle Blinking or Intensity), 256
  07H subservice (Read VGA Palette Register), 256
  08H subservice (Read Overscan Register VGA Only), 257
  08H subservice (Read Overscan Register VGA Only), 257
  09H subservice (Read VGA Palette and Overscan Register), 257
  10H subservice (Set Individual VGA Color Register), 258
  12H subservice (Set Block of Color Registers), 258
  13H subservice (Select Color Page), 259
  15H subservice (Read Individual Color Register), 259
  17H subservice (Read Block of Color Registers), 260
  1AH subservice (Read Current Color Page Number), 260
  1BH subservice (Sum Color Values to Gray Scale), 261
11H BIOS video service
  00H subservice (Load Font), 261
  01H subservice (Load ROM 8-by-14 Character Set), 262
  02H subservice (Load ROM 8-by-8 Character Set), 262
  03H subservice (Set Block Specifier), 263
  04H subservice (Load ROM 8-by-16 Character Set), 263
  10H subservice (Load Font), 264
  11H subservice (Load ROM 8-by-14 Character Set), 264
  12H subservice (Load ROM 8-by-8 Character Set), 265
  14H subservice (Load ROM 8-by-16 Character Set), 265
  20H subservice (Load Character Pointer), 266
  20H subservice (Select Alternate Print Screen Routine), 270
  21H subservice (Load Character Pointer), 266
  22H subservice (Load Graphics ROM 8-by-14 Character Set), 267
  23H subservice (Load Graphics ROM 8-by-8 Character Set), 267
  24H subservice (Load Graphics ROM 8-by-16 Character Set), 268
  30H subservice (Return Character Generator Data), 268-269
12.5% fill pattern, 68
12H BIOS video service
  10H subservice (Get Video Information), 269
  20H subservice (Select Alternate Print Screen Routine), 269
  30H subservice (Set Scan Lines for Alphanumeric Modes), 270
  31H subservice (Default Palette Loading during Mode Set), 270, 271
  32H subservice (Video Enable or Disable), 271
  33H subservice (Sum to Gray Scale), 271-272
  34H subservice (Cursor Emulation), 272
  35H subservice (Display Switch), 272-273
  36H subservice (Video Screen On or Off), 273
13H BIOS video service
  00H subservice (Write Character String), 273-274
  01H subservice (Write Character String), 274
  02H subservice (Write Character String), 275
  03H subservice (Write Character String), 275-276
1AH (Read or Write Display Combination Code) BIOS video service, 276
1BH (Return Functionality and State Data) BIOS video service, 276-277
1CH (Save/Restore Video State) BIOS video service, 277
25% fill pattern, 69
3% fill pattern, 66-67
37.5% fill pattern, 69
50% fill pattern, 69
6% fill pattern, 68
62.5% fill pattern, 70
75% fill pattern, 70
80286 microprocessor, 4
  protected mode, 4
  real mode, 4
80386 microprocessor, 4-5
80486 microprocessor, 5
8086 microprocessor, 4
8088 microprocessor, 4
87.5% fill pattern, 71
94% fill pattern, 71
97% fill pattern, 72

A

active pages, 190-192
airbrush effects in filling shapes, 76-78
animation
    active pages, 190-192
    collecting images, 189-190
    full-screen animation, 190-201
    partial-screen animation, 201-209
        hidden images, 205-209
    placing complex images, 211-214
    placing images on background, 209-211
    speed, 215
    visual pages, 190-192
_arc function, 58-61, 280-283
_arc_w function, 58-61, 283-286
_arc_wxy function, 58-61, 287-290
arcs, 58-59
    complex curves
        _arc functions, 60-61
        Bezier curve, 62-64
        straight line approximation, 61-62
aspect ratio, 35-36
autoscale element (axistype structure), 187
autosize element (legendtype structure), 188
axiscolor element (axistype structure), 186
axistitle element (axistype structure), 186
axistype structure, 186-187
    autoscale element, 187
    axiscolor element, 186
    axistitle element, 186
    grid element, 186
    gridstyle element, 186
    labeled element, 186
    logbase element, 186
    rangetype element, 186
    scalefactor element, 187
    scalemax element, 187
    scalemin element, 187
    scaletitle element, 187
    ticdecimals element, 187
    ticformat element, 187
    ticinterval element, 187

B

background element (windowtype structure), 187

bar charts, 153
    multiple data series, 153-159
    _PG_PLAINBARS option, 153-157
    _PG_STACKEDBARS option, 153, 158-159
    single data series, 153-156
Bezier curves, 62-64
BIOS video services
    00H (Set Video Mode), 245-246
    01H (Set Cursor Size), 246-247
    02H (Set Cursor Position), 247
    03H (Read Cursor Position), 247-248
    04H (Read Light Pen Position), 248
    05H (Set Active Display Page), 249
    06H (Scroll Active Window Up), 249
    07H (Scroll Active Window Down), 250
    08H (Read Character and Attribute), 250-251
    09H (Write Character and Attribute), 251
    0AH (Write Character), 251-252
    0BH (Set Color Palette), 252
    0CH (Write Pixel), 252-253
    0DH (Read Pixel), 253
    0EH (Write TTY Character), 253-254
    0FH (Get Current Video Mode), 254
    10H
        subservice 00H (Set Palette Register), 254-255
        subservice 01H (Set Overscan Register), 255
        subservice 02H (Set Palette and Overscan Registers), 255
        subservice 03H (Toggle Blinking or Intensity), 256
        subservice 07H (Read VGA Palette Register), 256
        subservice 08H (Read Overscan Register VGA Only), 257
        subservice 09H (Read VGA Palette and Overscan Registers), 257
        subservice 10H (Set Individual VGA Color Register), 258
        subservice 12H (Set Block of Color Registers, 258
        subservice 13H (Select Color Page), 259
        subservice 15H (Read Individual Color Register), 259
        subservice 17H (Read Block of Color Registers), 260
        subservice 1AH (Read Current Color Page Number), 260
        subservice 1BH (Sum Color Values to Gray Scale), 261

11H
    subservice 00H (Load Font), 261
    subservice 01H (Load ROM 8-by-14 Character
        Set), 262
    subservice 02H (Load ROM 8-by-8 Character
        Set), 262
    subservice 03H (Set Block Specifier), 263
    subservice 04H (Load ROM 8-by-16 Character
        Set), 263
    subservice 10H (Load Font), 264
    subservice 11H (Load ROM 8-by-14 Character
        Set), 264
    subservice 12H (Load ROM 8-by-8 Character
        Set), 265
    subservice 14H (Load ROM 8-by-16 Character
        Set), 265
    subservice 20H (Load Character Pointer), 266
    subservice 21H (Load Character Pointer), 266
    subservice 22H (Load Graphics ROM 8-by-14
        Character Set), 267
    subservice 23H (Load Graphics ROM 8-by-8
        Character Set), 267
    subservice 24H (Load Graphics ROM 8-by-16
        Character Set), 268
    subservice 30H (Return Character Generator
        Data), 268-269
12H
    subservice 10H (Get Video Information), 269
    subservice 20H (Select Alternate Print Screen
        Routine), 269-270
    subservice 30H (Set Scan Lines for
        Alphanumeric Modes), 270
    subservice 31H (Default Palette Loading during
        Mode Set), 270-271
    subservice 32H (Video Enable or Disable), 271
    subservice 34H (Cursor Emulation), 272
    subservice 35H (Display Switch), 272-273
    subservice 36H (Video Screen On or Off), 273
    subservices 33H (Sum to Gray Scale), 271-272
13H
    subservice 00H (Write Character String), 273-
        274
    subservice 01H (Write Character String), 274
    subservice 02H (Write Character String), 275
    subservice 03H (Write Character String), 275-
        276
1AH (Read or Write Display Combination Code),
    276

1BH (Return Functionality and State Data), 276-
    277
1CH (Save/Restore Video State), 277
border element (windowtype structure), 187
bordercolor element (windowtype
    structure), 188
borderstyle element (windowtype
    structure), 188

C

CGA (Color Graphics Adapter), 6-7
    _HRESBW high-resolution mode, 6
    _MRES4COLOR medium-resolution mode, 6-7
    _MRESNOCOLOR medium-resolution mode, 6-7
    composite color monitors, 9
    composite monochrome monitors, 9
    RGB monitors, 9
character pool for presentation graphics, 182-184
character sets
    defining, 104-105
        example characters, 117-144
        filled characters, 108-111
        multicolored characters, 113-115
        scaleable fonts, 105-107
        shaded characters, 111-113
        shadowed characters, 116-118
        unfilled characters, 107-109
chartenv structure, 184-185
    chartstyle element, 184
    charttype element, 184
    chartwindow element, 185
    datawindow element, 185
    legend element, 185
    maintitle element, 185
    subtitle element, 185
    xaxis element, 185
    yaxis element, 185
charts
    bar *see* bar charts
    column *see* column charts
    drawing *see* presentation graphics
    line *see* line charts
    pie *see* pie charts
    stacked bar *see* bar charts
chartstyle element (chartenv structure),
    184
charttype element (chartenv structure),
    184
chartwindow element (chartenv structure),
    185

circles, 56-58
_clearscreen function, 290-294
clipping regions, 37, 93-95
collecting images for animation, 189-190
color pool for presentation graphics, 181-182
colors
    _MRES4COLOR graphics mode, 88-89
    font text type, 103
    lines, 37
    _MRESNOCOLOR graphics mode, 89-90
    predefined text colors, 103
    raster font text type, 103
    retrieving pixel color, 37
    setting pixel color, 36
    standard character set text type, 103
column charts, 159-160
    multiple data series, 161-165
    _PG_PLAINBARS option, 160-163
    _PG_STACKEDBARS option, 164-165
    single data series, 160-161
complex curves
    _arc functions, 60-61
    Bezier curve, 62-64
    straight line approximation, 61-62
composite color monitors, 9
composite monochrome monitors, 9
constants
    _GBORDER, 53-57, 80
    _GFILLINTERIOR, 53, 57, 80
    _GWRAPOFF, 99
    _GWRAPON, 99
conversion between coordinate systems, 32-33
coordinate systems
    converting, 32-33
    moving graphics cursor, 33-35
    physical, 30, 218-219
    text cursor, 98-99
    three-dimensional, 230-231
    two-dimensional, 217-218
    view, 31, 32, 218-219
    window, 32, 218
cos function, 218
COURB.FON file, 101
Courier font, 101
CPU *see* microprocessors
Cursor Emulation (12H, subservice 34H) BIOS video
    service, 272
customizing presentation graphics environment, 181
    character pool, 182-84

color pool, 181-182
pattern pool, 182-184
style pool, 182-184

D
dashed lines, 41-52
data series
    multiple
        bar charts, 153-159
        column charts, 161-165
        line charts, 176-180
        scatter diagram charts, 169-173
    single
        bar charts, 153-156
        column charts, 160-161
        line charts, 173-177
        scatter diagram charts, 166-169
datawindow element (chartenv structure),
    185
Default Palette Loading during Mode Set (12H,
    subservice 31H) BIOS video services, 270-
    271
defining character sets, 104-105
    example characters, 117-144
    filled characters, 108-111
    multicolored characters, 113-115
    scaleable fonts, 105-107
    shaded characters, 111-113
    shadowed characters, 116-118
    unfilled characters, 107-109
digitizer tablets, 11-14
direct drive monochrome monitors, 8
Display Switch (12H, subservice 35H) BIOS video
    service, 272-273
_displaycursor function, 295-298
displaying
    font text, 102
    percentages in pie charts, 150-152
DOS, 5
drawing
    arcs, 58-59
    complex curves
        _arc functions, 60-61
        Bezier curve, 62-64
        straight line approximation, 61-62
    circles, 56-58
    ellipses, 56-58
    lines, 37-40
        color, 37

filling shapes with `_floodfill` function, 39
`_moveto` function, 38
`_moveto_w` function, 38
pie charts, 79-84
    exploded pie charts, 84-88
polygons, 55-56
rectangles, 52-54
squares, 52-54
wedge shapes, 79-88

E

EGA (Enhanced Graphics Adapter), 7-8
    _ERESCOLOR mode, 7
    _ERESNOCOLOR mode, 7
    _HRES16COLOR mode, 7
    _MRES16COLOR mode, 7
    direct drive monochrome monitor, 8
`_ellipse` function, 298-301
`_ellipse_w` function, 56-58, 301-304
`_ellipse_wxy` function, 56-58, 305-308
ellipses, 56-58
    rotating in two dimensions, 227-231
_ERESCOLOR graphics mode, 7
_ERESNOCOLOR graphics mode, 7
error codes, 406-408
exploded pie charts, 84-88, 150-154

F

fill patterns
    0% fill, 66-67
    3% fill, 66-67
    6% fill, 68
    12.5% fill, 68
    25% fill, 69
    37.5% fill, 69
    50% fill, 69
    62.5% fill, 70
    75% fill, 70
    87.5% fill, 71
    94% fill, 71
    97% fill, 72
    100% fill, 72
filling shapes
    `_floodfill` functions, 64-65
    fill patterns, 65-72
    halftoning, 72-75
        airbrushing, 76-78
        indistinct horizons, 74-76

shading, 72-75
    airbrushing, 76-78
    indistinct horizons, 74-76
`_floodfill` function, 39, 64-65, 108-111, 308-311
`_floodfill_w` function, 39, 64-65, 312-314
fonts
    color, 103
    Courier font, 101
    creating, 104-105
        example characters, 117-144
        filled characters, 108-111
        multicolored characters, 113-115
        scalable fonts, 105-107
        shaded characters, 111-113
        shadowed characters, 116-118
        unfilled characters, 107-109
    displaying, 102
    font text type, 98-101
    Helvetica font, 101
    Modern font, 101
    registering fonts, 102
    Roman font, 101
    Script font, 101
    selecting registered fonts, 102
full-screen animation, 190-201
functions
    `_arc`, 58-61, 280-283
    `_arc_w`, 58-61, 283-286
    `_arc_wxy`, 58-61, 287-290
    `_clearscreen`, 290-294
    `cos`, 218
    `_displaycursor`, 295-298
    `_ellipse`, 56-58, 227-231, 298-301
    `_ellipse_w`, 56-58, 301-304
    `_ellipse_wxy`, 56-58, 305-308
    error codes, 406-408
    `_floodfill`, 39, 64-65, 108-111, 308-311
    `_floodfill_w`, 39, 64-65, 312-314
    `_getactivepage`, 314-316
    `_getarcinfo`, 61, 317-319
    `_getbkcolor`, 320-323
    `_getcolor`, 324-327
    `_getcurrentposition`, 35, 327-331
    `_getcurrentposition_w`, 35, 332-334
    `_getfillmask`, 335-338
    `_getfontinfo`, 338-341
    `_getgtextextent`, 341-343
    `_getgtextvector`, 343-347

_getimage, 201-209, 347-350
_getimage_w, 350-353
_getimage_wxy, 353-356
_getlinestyle, 356-359
_getphyscoord, 32, 360-363
_getpixel, 37, 363-366
_getpixel_w, 37, 366-368
_gettextcolor, 369-371
_gettextcursor, 372-374
_gettextposition, 374-377
_gettextwindow, 377-380
_getvideoconfig, 35, 380-385
_getviewcoord, 32-33, 385-389
_getviewcoord_w, 33, 389-392
_getviewcoord_wxy, 33, 392-395
_getvisualpage, 395-397
_getwindowcoord, 33, 397-400
_getwritemode, 401-404
_grstatus, 405-410
_imagesize, 410-413
_imagesize_w, 413-416
_imagesize_wxy, 416-419
_lineto, 34-40, 419-423
_lineto_w, 34-40, 424-426
_moveto, 33, 38, 102, 427-431
_moveto_w, 33, 38, 431-434
_outgtext, 98, 102, 434-437
_outmem, 97, 100-101, 437-439
_outtext, 97, 100-101, 439-442
_pg_analyzechart, 442-445
_pg_analyzechartms, 445-448
_pg_analyzepie, 449-451
_pg_analyzescatter, 452-456
_pg_analyzescatterms, 455-459
_pg_chart, 153, 160, 173, 459-462
_pg_chartms, 153, 160, 173, 462-465
_pg_chartpie, 150, 466-469
_pg_chartscatter, 165, 468-472
_pg_chartscatterms, 165, 471-475
_pg_defaultchart, 148, 475-479
_pg_getchardef, 478-482
_pg_getpalette, 103, 481-485
_pg_getstyleset, 485-487
_pg_hlabelchart, 98, 488-491
_pg_initchart, 148, 490-494
_pg_resetpalette, 493-497
_pg_resetstyleset, 497-500
_pg_setchardef, 500-503
_pg_setpalette, 103, 503-506

_pg_setstyleset, 506-508
_pg_vlabelchart, 98, 508-511
_pie, 79-88, 512-515
_pie_w, 79-88, 515-518
_pie_wxy, 79-88, 518-523
_polygon, 55-56, 224-227, 523-526
_polygon_w, 55-56, 525-529
_polygon_wxy, 55-56, 528-532
_putimage, 201-211, 532-535
_putimage_w, 535-538
_rectangle, 52-55, 221-225, 538-542
_rectangle_w, 52-55, 541-545
_rectangle_wxy, 52-55, 545-549
_registerfonts, 102, 549-551
_remapallpalette, 551-555
_remappalette, 555-559
_scrolltextwindow, 558-561
_selectpalette, 89-90, 561-564
_setactivepage, 190-192, 565-568
_setbkcolor, 88, 568-572
_setcliprgn, 93-95, 572-576
_setcolor, 36-37, 90, 103,113-115, 576-579
_setfillmask, 111-113, 579-583
_setfont, 102, 582-586
_setgtextvector, 102, 586-589
_setlinestyle, 37-38, 589-592
_setpixel, 36, 593-595
_setpixel_w, 36, 595-597
_settextcolor, 103, 597-600
_settextcursor, 600-602
_settextposition, 98, 602-605
_settextrows, 606-608
_settextwindow, 144, 608-611
_setvideomode, 610-614
_setvideomoderows, 613-616
_setvieworg, 31-32, 616-620
_setviewport, 32, 91-93, 620-623
_setvisualpage, 190-192, 624-626
_setwindow, 32, 626-629
_setwritemode, 628-631
sin, 218
sprintf, 100
_unregisterfonts, 631-633
_wrapon, 99-100, 633-635

G

_GAND argument, 203, 211-214
_GBORDER constant, 53-54, 57-80
Get Current Video Mode (0FH) BIOS video service,
    254

Get Video Information (12H, subservice 10H) BIOS video service, 269
_getactivepage function, 314-316
_getarcinfo function, 61, 317-319
_getbkcolor function, 320-323
_getcolor function, 324-327
_getcurrentposition function, 35, 327-331
_getcurrentposition_w function, 35, 332-334
_getfillmask function, 335-338
_getfontinfo function, 338-341
_getgtextextent function, 341-343
_getgtextvector function, 343-347
_getimage function, 201-209, 347-350
_getimage_w function, 350-353
_getimage_wxy function, 353-356
_getlinestyle function, 356-359
_getphyscoord function, 32, 360-363
_getpixel function, 37, 363-366
_getpixel_w function, 37, 366-368
_gettextcolor function, 369-371
_gettextcursor function, 372-374
_gettextposition function, 98, 374-377
_gettextwindow function, 377-380
_getvideoconfig function, 35, 380-385
_getviewcoord function, 32-33, 385-389
_getviewcoord_w function, 33, 389-392
_getviewcoord_wxy function, 392-395
_getviewcoord_wxy functions, 33
_getvisualpage function, 395-397
_getwindowcoord function, 33, 397-400
_getwritemode function, 401-404
_GFILLINTERIOR constant, 53, 57-80
_GOR argument, 203, 211-214
_GPRESET argument, 203
_GPSET argument, 203
graphics adapters
    see video subsystems, 6
graphics cursor, 33-35
graphics modes
    _MRES4COLOR, 88-89
    _MRESNOCOLOR, 89-90
_GRCLIPPED error code, 406-407
_GRCORRUPTEDFONTFILE error code, 407
_GRERROR error code, 406-408
_GRFONTFILENOTFOUND error code, 407
grid element (axistype structure), 186
gridstyle element (axistype structure), 186

_GRINSUFFICIENTMEMORY error code, 406-407
_GRINVALIDIMAGEBUFFER error code, 407
_GRINVALIDPARAMETER error code, 406-408
_GRMODENOTSUPPORTED error code, 408
_GRNOOUTPUT error code, 406-407
_GRNOTINPROPERMODE error code, 406-408
_GRPARAMETERALTERED error code, 406-408
_grstatus function, 405-410
_GWRAPOFF constant, 99
_GWRAPON constant, 99
_GXOR argument, 203

H
halftoning shapes, 72-75
    airbrushing, 76-78
    indistinct horizons, 74-76
HELVB.FON file, 101
Helvetica font, 101
hidden images in partial screen animation, 205-209
hidden surface removal in three-dimensional drawing, 240-241
_HRES16COLOR graphics mode, 7
_HRESBW graphics mode, 6

I
_imagesize function, 410-413
_imagesize_w function, 413-416
_imagesize_wxy function, 416-419
initializing presentation graphics environment, 147-148
input devices
    digitizer tablet, 11-14
    keyboard, 10
    light pen, 13-14
    mouse, 10-11
    trackball, 10-11

J
justify element (titletype structure), 185

K
keyboard, 10

L
labeled element (axistype structure), 186
legend element (chartenv structure), 185
legend element (legendtype structure), 188
legendtype structure, 188
    autosize element, 188

`legend` element, 188
`legendwindow` element, 188
`place` element, 188
`textcolor` element, 188
`legendwindow` element (`legendtype`
     structure), 188
light pens, 13-14
line charts, 173
    multiple data series, 176-180
    _PG_POINTANDLINE option, 175-180
    _PG_POINTONLY option, 173-179
    single data series, 173-177
lines, 37-40
    clipping region, 37
    color, 37
    dashed lines, 41-52
    filling shapes with `_floodfill` function, 39
    `_moveto` function, 38
    `_moveto_w` function, 38
`_lineto` function, 34, 37-40, 419-423
`_lineto_w` function, 34, 37-40, 424-426
Load Character Pointer (11H, subservice 20H) BIOS
    video service, 266
Load Character Pointer (11H, subservice 21H) BIOS
    video service, 266
Load Font (11H, subservice 00H) BIOS video
    service, 261
Load Font (11H, subservice 10H) BIOS video
    service, 264
Load Graphics ROM 8-by-14 Character Set (11H,
    subservice 22H) BIOS video service, 267
Load Graphics ROM 8-by-16 Character Set (11H,
    subservice 24H) BIOS video service, 268
Load Graphics ROM 8-by-8 Character Set (11H,
    subservice 23H) BIOS video service, 267
Load ROM 8-by-14 Character Set (11H, subservice
    01H) BIOS video service, 262
Load ROM 8-by-14 Character Set (11H, subservice
    11H) BIOS video service, 264
Load ROM 8-by-16 Character Set (11H, subservice
    04H) BIOS video service, 263
Load ROM 8-by-16 Character Set (11H, subservice
    14H) BIOS video service, 265
Load ROM 8-by-8 Character Set (11H, subservice
    02H) BIOS video service, 262
Load ROM 8-by-8 Character Set (11H, subservice
    12H) BIOS video service, 265
`logbase` element (`axistype` structure), 186

M

`maintitle` element (`chartenv` structure),
    185
MCGA (Multi Color Graphics Adapter)
    _MRES256COLOR graphics mode, 8
MCGA (Multi Color Graphics Array), 8
    _VRES2COLOR mode, 8
MDA (Monochrome Display Adapter)
    direct drive monochrome monitor, 8
microprocessors, 3
    80286, 4
    80386, 4-5
    80486, 5
    8086, 4
    8088, 4
Modern font, 101
MODERN.FON file, 101
monitors
    aspect ratio, 35-36
    composite color, 9
    composite monochrome, 9
    direct drive monochrome, 8
    RGB, 9
    variable-frequency, 9
mouse, 10-11
`_moveto` function, 33, 38, 102, 427-431
`_moveto_w` function, 33, 38, 431-434
moving graphics cursor, 33-35
_MRES16COLOR graphics mode, 7
_MRES256COLOR graphics mode, 8
_MRES4COLOR graphics mode, 6
    colors available, 88-89
_MRESNOCOLOR graphics mode, 6-7
    colors available, 89-90
MS-DOS *see* DOS
multiple data series
    bar charts, 153-159
    column charts, 161-165
    line charts, 176-180
    scatter diagram charts, 169-173

O

operating systems
    MS-DOS, 5
    OS/2, 5, 6
orientation, text vector orientation, 102
OS/2 operating system, 5-6
    protected mode, 5
    real mode, 5

_outgtext function, 98, 102, 434-437
_outmem function, 97, 100-101, 437-439
_outtext function, 97, 100-101, 439-442

P

partial-screen animation, 201-209
  hidden images, 205-209
pattern pool for presentation graphics, 182-184
percentages
  displaying
    pie charts, 150-152
_pg_analyzechart function, 442-445
_pg_analyzechartms function, 445-448
_pg_analyzepie function, 449-451
_pg_analyzescatter function, 452-456
_pg_analyzescatterms function, 455-459
_pg_chart function, 153, 160, 173, 459-462
_pg_chartms function, 153, 160, 173, 462-465
_pg_chartpie function, 150, 466-469
_pg_chartscatter function, 165, 468-472
_pg_chartscatterms function, 165, 471-475
_pg_defaultchart function, 148, 475-479
_pg_getchardef function, 478-482
_pg_getpalette function, 103, 481-485
_pg_getstyleset function, 485-487
_pg_hlabelchart function, 98, 488-491
_pg_initchart function, 148, 490-494
_PG_PLAINBARS bar chart option, 153-157
_PG_PLAINBARS column chart option, 160-163
_PG_POINTANDLINE line chart option, 175-180
_PG_POINTANDLINE scatter diagram charts
    option, 167-173
_PG_POINTONLY line chart option, 173-179
_PG_POINTONLY scatter diagram charts option,
    166-171
_pg_resetpalette function, 493-497
_pg_resetstyleset function, 497-500
_pg_setchardef function, 500-503
_pg_setpalette function, 103, 503-506
_pg_setstyleset function, 506-508
_PG_PLAINBARS bar chart option, 153
_PG_STACKEDBARS bar chart option, 158-159
_PG_STACKEDBARS column chart option,
    164-165
_pg_vlabelchart function, 98, 508-511
pgchart.h header file, 181
physical coordinate system, 30, 218-219
  conversion to other coordinate systems, 32-33
pie charts, 79-84, 150

displaying percentages, 150-152
exploded pie charts, 84-88, 150-154
single data series, 150-154
_pie function, 79-88, 512-515
_pie_w function, 79-88, 515-518
_pie_wxy function, 79-88, 518-523
pixels
  retrieving color, 37
  setting color, 36
  size, 36
place element (legendtype structure), 188
_polygon function, 55-56, 224-227, 523-526
_polygon_w function, 55-56, 525-529
_polygon_wxy function, 55-56, 528-532
polygons, 55-56
  rotating in two dimensions, 224-227
positioning text cursor, 98
predefined text colors, 103
presentation graphics
  bar charts, 153-159
  chartenv structure, 184-185
  column charts, 159-165
  customizing environment, 181
    character pool, 182-184
    color pool, 181-182
    pattern pool, 182-184
    style pool, 182-184
  initializing environment, 147-148
  line charts, 173-180
  pie charts, 150-154
  program structure, 149-150
  scatter diagram charts, 165-173
protected mode
  80286 microprocessor, 4
  OS/2 operating system, 5
_putimage function, 201-211, 532-535
  _GAND argument, 211-214
  _GOR arguement, 211- 214
  _GOR argument, 203
  _GPSET argument, 203
  _GXOR argument, 203
  _GAND argument, 203
  _GPRESET argument, 203
_putimage_w function, 535-538

R

rangetype element (axistype structure),
    186
raster font text type, 98

color, 103

Read Block of Color Register (10H, subservice 17H) BIOS video service, 260

Read Character and Attribute (08H) BIOS video service, 250-251

Read Current Color Page Number (10H, 1AH) BIOS video service, 260

Read Cursor Position (03H) BIOS video service, 247-248

Read EGA Palette Register (10H, subservice 07H) BIOS video service, 256

Read Individual Color Register (10H, subservice 15H) BIOS video service, 259

Read Light Pen Position (04H) BIOS video service, 248

Read or Write Display Combination Code (1AH) BIOS video service, 276

Read Overscan Register VGA only (10H, subservice 08H) BIOS video service, 257

Read Pixel (0DH) BIOS video service, 253

Read VGA Palette and Overscan Registers (10H, subservice 09H) BIOS video service, 257

real mode
    80286 microprocessor, 4
    OS/2 operating system, 5

_rectangle function, 52-55, 221-225, 538-542

_rectangle_w function, 52-55, 541-545

_rectangle_wxy function, 52-55, 545-549

rectangles, 52-54
    rotating in three dimensions, 232-240
    rotating in two dimensions, 221-225

_registerfonts function, 102, 549-551

registering fonts, 102

_remapallpalette function, 551-553

_rempallpalette function, 554-555

_remappalette function, 555-559

removing hidden surfaces from three-dimensional drawings, 240-241

retrieving pixel color, 37

retrieving position of text cursor, 98

Return Character Generator Data (11H, subservice 30H) BIOS video service, 268-269

Return Functionality and State Data (1BH) BIOS video service, 276-277

RGB monitors, 9

ROM BIOS video services, 245-277

Roman font, 101

ROMAN.FON file, 101

rotating
    coordinate pairs in two dimensions, 217-221
        formulas, 218-219
    ellipses in two dimensions, 227-231
    objects in three dimensions, 231-240
    polygons in two dimensions, 224-227
    rectanges
    rectangles
        in two dimensions, 221-225
        in three dimensions, 232-240

S

Save/Restore Video State (1CH) BIOS video service, 277

scalefactor element (axistype structure), 187

scalemax element (axistype structure), 187

scalemin element (axistype structure), 187

scaletitle element (axistype structure), 187

scatter diagram charts, 165
    multiple data series, 169-173
    _PG_POINTANDLINE option, 167-173
    _PG_POINTONLY option, 166-171
    single data series, 166-169

Script font, 101

SCRIPT.FON file, 101

Scroll Active Window Down (07H) BIOS video service, 250

Scroll Active Window Up (06H) BIOS video service, 249

_scrolltextwindow function, 558-561

Select Alternate Print Screen Routine (12H, subservice 20H) BIOS video service, 269-270

Select Color Page (10H, subservice 13H) BIOS video service, 259

selecting registered fonts, 102

_selectpalette function, 89-90, 561-564

Set Active Display Page (05H) BIOS video service, 249

Set Block of Color Registers (10H, subservice 12H) BIOS video service, 258

Set Block Specifier (11H, subservice 03H) BIOS video service, 263

Set Color Palette (0BH) BIOS video service, 252
Set Cursor Position (02H) BIOS video service, 247
Set Cursor Size (01H) BIOS video service, 246-247
Set Individual VGA Color Register (10H, subservice 10H) BIOS video service, 258
Set Overscan Register (10H, subservice 01H) BIOS video service, 255
Set Palette and Overscan Register (10H, subservice 02H) video service, 255
Set Palette Register (10H, subservice 00H) BIOS video service, 254-255
Set Scan Lines for Alphanumeric Modes (12H, subservice 30H) BIOS video service, 270
Set Video Mode (00H) BIOS video service, 245-246
_setactivepage function, 190-192, 565-568
_setbkcolor function, 88, 568-572
_setcliprgn function, 93-95, 572-576
_setcolor function, 36-37, 90, 103, 113-115, 576-579
_setfillmask function, 111-113, 579-583
_setfont function, 102, 582-586
_setgtextvector function, 102, 586-589
_setlinestyle function, 37-38, 589-592
_setpixel function, 36, 593-595
_setpixel_w function, 36, 595-597
_settextcolor function, 103, 597-600
_settextcursor function, 600-602
_settextposition function, 98, 602-605
_settextrows function, 606-608
_settextwindow function, 144, 608-611
_setvideomode function, 610-614
_setvideomoderows function, 613-616
_setvieworg function, 31-32, 616-620
_setviewport function, 32, 91-93, 620-623
_setvisualpage function, 190-192, 624-626
_setwindow function, 32, 626-629
_setwritemode function, 628-631
shading shapes, 72-75
    airbrushing, 76-78
    indistinct horizons, 74,-76
shapes
    fill patterns, 65-72
    filling with _floodfill function, 39, 64-65
    halftoning, 72-75
        airbrushing, 76-78
        indisinct horizons, 74-76
    shading, 72-75
        airbrushing, 76-78
        indisinct horizons, 74-76

sin function, 218
single data series
    bar charts, 153-156
    column charts, 160-161
    line charts, 173-177
    pie charts, 150-154
    scatter diagram charts, 166-169
sprintf function, 100
squares, 52-54
stacked bar charts see bar charts
standard character set text type, 97, 100-101
    color, 103
straight line approximation method for drawing complex curves, 61-62
structures
    axistype, 186-187
    legendtype, 188
    titletype, 185-186
    windowtype, 187-188
style pool for presentation graphics, 182-184
subtitle element (chartenv structure), 185
Sum Color Values to Gray Scale (10H, subservice 1BH) BIOS video service, 261
Sum to Gray Scale (12H, subservice 33H) BIOS video service, 271-272

T

text
    creating character sets, 104-105
        example characters, 117-144
        filled characters, 108-111
        multicolored characters, 113-115
        scaleable fonts, 105-107
        shaded characters, 111-113
        shadowed characters, 116-118
        unfilled characters, 107-109
    font text, 98-101
        color, 103
        displaying, 102
        registering fonts, 102
        selecting registered fonts, 102
    predefined colors, 103
    raster fonts, 98, 103
    standard character set, 97, 100-103
    text cursor, 98-100
        coordinate system, 98-99
        positioning, 98
        retrieving position, 98
    text windows, 144

vector orientation, 102
textcolor element (legendtype structure), 188
three-dimensional drawing
    coordinate system, 230-231
    hidden surface removal, 240-241
    rotating objects, 231- 240
ticdecimals element (axistype structure), 187
ticformat element (axistype structure), 187
ticinterval element (axistype structure), 187
title element (titletype structure), 185
titlecolor element (titletype structure), 185
titletype structure, 185-186
    justify element, 185
    title element, 185
    titlecolor element, 185
TMSRB.FON file, 101
Toggle Blinking or Intensity (10H, subservice 03H) BIOS video service, 256
trackballs, 10-11
two-dimensional drawing
    coordinate system, 217-218
    rotating coordinate pairs, 217-221
    rotating ellipses, 227-231
    rotating polygons, 224-227
    rotating rectangles, 221-225
types of text, 97-98
    font text, 98
        color, 103
        displaying, 102
        registering fonts, 102
        selecting registered fonts, 102
    raster font text, 98
        color, 103
    standard character set, 97, 100-101
        color, 103

U

_unregisterfonts function, 631-633

V

variable-frequency monitors, 9
vector orientation of text, 102
VGA (Video Graphcs Array)
    _VRES16COLOR graphics mode, 8

VGA (Video Graphics Array), 8
Video Enable or Disable (12H, subservice 32H) BIOS video service, 271
Video Screen On or Off (12H, subservice 36H) BIOS video service, 273
video services (ROM BIOS), 245-277
video subsystems
    CGA (Color Graphics Adapter), 6, 7
    composite color monitors, 9
    composite monochrome monitors, 9
    direct drive monochrome monitors, 8
    EGA (Enhanced Graphics Adapter), 7-8
    MCGA (Multi Color Graphics Array), 8
    RGB monitors, 9
    variable-frequency monitors, 9
    VGA (Video Graphics Array), 8
view coordinate system, 31-32, 218-219
    conversion to other coordinate systems, 32-33
    moving graphics cursor, 33-34
    placing origin, 31
    retrieving pixel color, 37
    setting pixel color, 36
viewports, 91-93
    setting dimensions, 32
    window coordinate system, 32
visual pages, 190-192
_VRES16COLOR graphics mode, 8
_VRES2COLOR graphics mode, 8

W

wedge shapes, 79-88
window coordinate system, 32, 218
    conversion to other coordinate systems, 32-33
    moving graphics cursor, 33-34
    retrieving pixel color, 37
    setting pixel color, 36
windows, text, 144
windowtype structure, 187-188
    background element, 187
    border element, 187
    bordercolor element, 188
    borderstyle element, 188
    x1 element, 187
    x2 element, 187
    y1 element, 187
    y2 element, 187
_wrapon function, 99-100, 633-635
Write Character (0AH) BIOS video service, 251-252
Write Character and Attribute (09H) BIOS video service, 251

Write Character String (13H, subservice 00H) BIOS
     video service, 273-274
Write Character String (13H, subservice 01H) BIOS
     video service, 274
Write Character String (13H, subservice 02H) BIOS
     video service, 275
Write Character String (13H, subservice 03H) BIOS
     video service, 275-276
Write Pixel (0CH) BIOS video service, 252-253
Write TTY Character (0EH) BIOS video service,
     253-254

X

x1 element (windowtype structure), 187
x2 element (windowtype structure), 187
xaxis element (chartenv structure), 185

Y

y1 element (windowtype structure), 187
y2 element (windowtype structure), 187
yaxis element (chartenv structure), 185